Model-Based Systems Engineering with OPM and SysML

Dov Dori

Model-Based Systems Engineering with OPM and SysML

Foreword by Edward Crawley

 Springer

Dov Dori
Technion, Israel Institute of Technology
Haifa, Israel

Massachusetts Institute of Technology
Cambridge, MA, USA

Chapter slides and end-of-chapter Q&As can be found at http://esml.iem.technion.ac.il/qanswer/

ISBN 978-1-4939-3294-8   ISBN 978-1-4939-3295-5   (eBook)
DOI 10.1007/978-1-4939-3295-5

Library of Congress Control Number: 2015954175

Springer New York Heidelberg Dordrecht London

Printed on acid-free paper

Springer Science+Business Media LLC New York is part of Springer Science+Business Media (www.springer.com)

Foreword

Architecting and engineering large, complex socio-technical systems, as well as gaining deep understanding of existing natural and man-made systems, have eluded people for many years. Our thinking about systems and their role in improving humans' quality of life has evolved over the last two decades. We now understand better that successful systems do not materialize in a haphazard way. Rather, they must be carefully architected just like edifices, accounting for the needs, wants and requirements of their intended beneficiaries, and alternative architectures—ways in which these desired functions are embodied in form. These early decisions are critical to the system-to-be, as they determine the concept to be followed and consequently the whole direction the system development takes and the nature of the final outcome: how well the system performs in terms of delivering value, i.e., benefit at cost, while maintaining the other requirements of safety, robustness, ease of use, environmental friendliness, and many others.

As I was gaining these insights some 15 years ago, I realized that no matter how convincing your ideas are, and how compelling are the arguments, there is only so much one can do with preaching and hand-waving. It became obvious to me that making progress in the area of architecting and engineering complex systems is contingent upon a solid foundation of language and methodology. It so happened, that at that time, around year 2000, Dov stepped into my office, the office of the Head of the Aero-Astro Department at MIT, with a draft of his first book, titled *Object-Process Methodology—A Holistic Systems Paradigm* (Springer, 2002). Reading this draft in a plane I immediately understood that what I was holding in my hands was exactly what I was looking for.

Object-Process Methodology (OPM) is a systems modeling paradigm that represents the two things inherent in a system: its objects and processes. OPM is fundamentally simple; it builds on a minimal set of concepts: stateful objects—things that exist, and processes—things that happen and transform objects by creating or consuming them or by changing their states. This duality is recognized throughout the community who studies systems, and sometimes goes by labels such as form/function, structure/function, and functional requirements/design parameters. Objects are what a system or product is. Processes are what a system does. Yet, it is remarkable that so few modeling frameworks explicitly recognize this duality. As a result, designers and engineers try to jump from the goals of a system (the requirements or the "program") immediately to the objects. Serious theory in such disparate disciplines as software design, mechanical design and civil architectural design all recognize the value of thinking about processes in parallel with objects. Not only does OPM represent both objects and processes, but it explicitly shows the connections between them.

OPM has another fundamental advantage—it represents the system simultaneously in formal graphics and natural language. The two are completely interchangeable, conveying the exact same information. The advantage in this approach lies in appreciating the human limitation to the understanding of complexity. As systems become more complex, the primary barrier to success is the ability of the human designers and analysts to understand the complexity of the interrelationships. By representing the system in both textual and graphical form, the power of "both sides of the brain"—the visual interpreter and the language interpreter—is engaged. These are two of the strongest processing capabilities that are hard-wired into the human brain. Since each model fact is expressed both graphically and textually, in a subset of natural English, it is readily accessible to non-technical stakeholders, enabling them to take part in the early, critical stages of the system architecting and development, in which the most important decisions are made.

OPM allows a clear representation of the many important features of a system: its topological connections; its decomposition into elements and sub-elements; the interfaces among elements; and the emergence of function from elements. The builder of viewer of the model can view abstractions, or zoom into detail. One can see how specification migrates to implementation. These various views are invaluable when pondering the complexity of a real modern product system.

OPM semantics was originally geared towards systems engineering, as it can model information, hardware, people, and regulation. However, in recent years OPM started to serve also researchers in molecular biology, yielding tangible published new findings related to the mRNA lifecycle. This is a clear indication of the universality of the object and process ontology: As it turns out, one can use this minimal set of concepts to model systems in virtually any domain. Perhaps one exception is quantum physics, where our macro notions of particle (object?) and wave (process?), as well as matter (object?) and energy (process?) get fuzzy as we try to 'inspect' subatomic particles such as electrons. For any system from the molecular level up, all the way to the most complex natural, socio-technical and societal systems, the object-process paradigm works extremely well. OPM models concurrently explicate the function (utility), structure (form) and behavior (dynamics) of systems in a single, coherent model that uses one kind of diagram at any desired number of levels of detail by drilling down into the details of processes hand-in-hand with the objects they transform. The set of these self-similar object-process diagrams are represented not just visually, but also textually, catering to humans' dual channel processing, a key cognitive assumption of how we process information to convert it into actionable knowledge.

Having realized the value of OPM to systems architecting and engineering, I adopted it in my thinking and teaching, and it has become an important cornerstone of courses I have been teaching in systems architecture at MIT and elsewhere. In particular, OPM has become a key element in the teaching of core courses in the Systems Design and Management graduate program at MIT. I have used OPM in the SDM System Architecture course. It has proved an invaluable tool to professional learners in developing models of complex technical systems, such as automobiles, spacecraft and software systems. It allows an explicit representation of the form/function duality, and provides an environment in which various architectural options can be examined. The addition of OPM to my subject has added the degree of rigor of analysis necessary to move the study of technical system architecture towards that of an engineering discipline.

OPM is also used as a representational framework in the new book which I co-authored, *System Architecture: Strategy and Product Development for Complex Systems* (Pearson, 2015), which develops an approach to architecture and demonstrates it with examples ranging from pumps, circuits, and sorting algorithms, to complex systems in networking and hybrid cars. Indeed, the task of architecting and engineering a new system has become more complicated by the increasing number of components involved, the number of disparate disciplines needed to undertake the task, and the growing size of the organizations involved. Despite the common experience that members of many organizations share, they often lack a common product development vocabulary or modeling framework. Such a framework should be based on system science, be able to represent all the important interactions in a system, and be broadly applicable to electrical, informational, mechanical, optical, thermal, and human components.

OPM provides such a framework. Indeed, in 2008, the task force of the International Council on Systems Engineering (INCOSE) has recognized OPM as one of the six leading model-based systems engineering methodologies. Looking at the historical development of engineering disciplines, it is an appropriate time for such a rigorous framework to emerge. Disciplines often move through a progressive maturation. Early in the history of an intellectual discipline, we find observation of nature or practice, which quickly evolves through a period in which things are classified. A breakthrough often occurs when classified observations are abstracted and quantified. These phases characterize much of the work done to date in systems engineering and product development. Mature disciplines, such as mechanics, are well into the era of symbolic manipulation and prediction. Maturing disciplines such as human genomics are in the phase of symbolic representation.

OPM is a parallel development in symbolic representation of systems. Over the past two decades, the understanding of the need for systematic modeling capability has broadened. As OPM was developed in response to this growing recognition, so have other approaches. The most notable of these are UML, which includes 13 kinds of diagrams, geared for software engineering, and its derivative, SysML, which includes nine kinds of diagrams, designed more generally for systems engineering. Both SysML and OPM are listed as leading standards in the Guide to the Systems Engineering Body of Knowledge (SEBoK), an online ongoing project jointly sponsored by the Systems Engineering Research Center (SERC), the International Council on Systems Engineering (INCOSE), and the Institute of Electrical and Electronics Engineers Computer Society (IEEE-CS).

SysML and OPM represent two different approaches to system modeling. In SysML up to nine diagrams are used, which are independently derived, and may not be completely consistent. In OPM one main diagram emerges. The need to integrate several kinds of diagrams may be more *complicated*. I make the distinction between *complexity*—the inherent fact that a system contains many parts interacting in multiple, often inexplicable ways, and *complicatedness*—the way a system model is presented through a certain modeling language and is perceived by a user. While there is not much we can do to reduce systems' inherent complexities, we can and should strive to reduce the complicatedness of the representation to the bare necessities without sacrificing accuracy and details. OPM with its minimal ontology of stateful objects and processes favorably responds to this challenge.

While the emphasis of the book is on OPM, because of the relatively wider spread use of SysML, Dov has included SysML with adequate presentation of its syntax and semantics, as well as synergies with OPM, comparison with OPM in terms of such factors as length of the standard specification, and ways OPM can replace many SysML diagram kinds with a single diagram kind. The coverage of both languages in the same book is unique, as Model-Based System Engineering (MBSE) books to date have mostly used SysML. This dual coverage of OPM and SysML is highly valuable, since the reader gets deeper perspective on MBSE that penetrates beneath the idiosyncrasies of a particular conceptual modeling language.

I recommend using this textbook for an intermediate or advanced course in model-based system engineering, product development, engineering design, and software engineering. It would be ideal for courses that attempt to show how various disciplines come together to form a multi-disciplinary product. With OPM now formally recognized as an ISO specification, it can form the backbone of a corporate or enterprise modeling framework for technical products and large-scale socio-technical systems. Such a representation would be especially valuable in conceptual and preliminary design, when much of the value, cost and risk of a product are established, but when few other modeling frameworks are available for decision support.[1]

Professor Edward Crawley   *Massachusetts Institute of Technology, July 2015*

---

[1]Edward Crawley is the Ford Professor of Engineering and a Professor of Aeronautics and Astronautics at MIT. He is a member of the U.S. National Academy of Engineering and serves as the President of the Skolkovo Institute of Science and Technology in Moscow. Prof. Crawley is the first author of two recent books: "System Architecture: Strategy and Product Development for Complex Systems" and "Rethinking Engineering Education, the CDIO Approach".

Preface

The quest for simplicity in a complex world has occupied thinkers for millennia. How to conceptualize what humans observe around them and what they wish to design in order to improve the quality of people's lives has been one of the major driving forces in advancing civilization. The advent of computers in the middle of the previous century was a great impetus to fostering thoughts about how to conceptually represent things in the real world. The initial accepted train of thought produced procedural programming, which put procedures, routines, functions, etc. at the center of programming. Further contemplations have led to the idea of putting objects, which are more static in nature, as the anchor of programs. The shift to the object oriented (OO) paradigm for programming languages, which occurred in the 1980s and 1990s, was followed by the idea that programming should be preceded by analysis and design of the programs, or, more generally, the systems those programs represent and serve. Naturally, the approach which was taken is also object-oriented.

In the early 1990, a plethora of some three dozen object-oriented analysis and design methods and notations flourished, leading to what was known as the "Methods War". Around that time, in 1991, when I moved from University of Kansas to Technion, Israel Institute of Technology, as I was tasked with teaching software design, I got interested in these topics. It was not long before I realized that just as the procedural approach to software was inadequate, so was the "pure" OO approach, which puts objects as the sole "first class" citizens, with "methods" (or "services") being their second-class subordinate procedures. However, I could not put my finger on what was missing.

My Eureka moment was in 1993, when I and colleagues from University of Washington were trying to model a system for automated transforming of hand-made engineering drawings to CAD models, a topic around which my research focused during that time. Drawing objects as the model's building blocks and connecting them on the white board, it dawned on me that not all the boxes in the model were really objects; some were things that *happen* to objects. When I circled those things, a pattern of a bipartite graph emerged, where the nodes representing objects—the things that exist—were mediated by those circled nodes, which I immediately called processes. This was the first object-process diagram (OPD) ever drawn. I realized then that the pendulum of the previously accepted procedural software to the primarily static OO paradigm moved too drastically. While the shift from procedures to objects as the focus of interest was a right move, it went too far, as it suppressed the systems' procedural aspect, which is essential to faithfully describe how systems change over time.

Forbidding processes, such as cake baking or check cashing, from being conceptual entities in their own right, and allowing their representation only as methods of object classes, results in distorted models, in which a check "owns" the cashing method or the cake owns the baking process. In real life, however, baking is a pattern of transformation of ingredients making up the dough that requires a baker, an oven, and energy to prepare the dough and convert it into a cake. Similarly, a check cannot cash itself; it requires a check writer having an account with sufficient funds, a check casher, and a bank clerk or an ATM. Each of the objects involved in these methods could just as well be the owner of the method. Modeling baking and cashing as stand-alone processes—conceptual things that represent physical or informatical object transformation patterns—open the door for creating models that are much more faithful to the way we conceive reality and convey it to others.

Indeed, recognizing processes as bona fide conceptual modeling building blocks beside, rather than underneath objects, is the prime foundation of Object-Process Methodology (OPM). OPM is founded on a universal minimal ontology, according to which objects exist, while processes transform them. Transformation includes object creation and consumption, as well as change of the state of an object. Therefore, OPM objects are stateful—they can have states. Hence, stateful objects and processes that transform them are the only two concepts in OPM's universal minimal ontology. Two other cornerstones of OPM are its bimodal graphical-textual representation and its built- in refinement-abstraction complexity management mechanisms of in-zooming and unfolding of a single type of diagram—OPD.

When I tried to publish a paper titled "Object-Process Analysis: Maintaining the Balance between System Structure and Behavior" with the buds of these ideas in 1993, it was serially rejected off hand with claims along the line that it had already been proven that what I was suggesting is impossible, like "mixing water with oil." Finally, the *Journal of Logic and Computation* accepted it, perhaps because being mathematics- rather than software-oriented, it was more tolerant toward ideas that went against the then new and glorious OO paradigm.

Meanwhile, in 1997, the "Methods Wars" culminated in the adoption of the Unified Modeling Languages (UML), by the Object Management Group (OMG), making it the de-facto standard for software design. UML 1 had nine types of diagrams. In 2000, when I attended a Technical Meeting of OMG in which UML was considered for progression from version 1 to 2, I proposed considering UML for being extended to handle not just software systems, but systems at large, a proposal that was dismissed off-hand by most attendees, who were software people. However, following a 2001 initiative of the International Council on Systems Engineering (INCOSE), in 2003 OMG issued the UML for Systems Engineering Request for Proposals, and in 2006 OMG adopted SysML (Systems Modeling Language) 1.0 specification, which is based on UML 2. Since then, SysML has become the de-facto standard for systems engineering.

Meanwhile, the first book on OPM, *Object-Process Methodology—a Holistic Systems Paradigm*, (Dori, 2002) was published, and OPM has been successfully applied and papers published in many diverse domains, ranging from the Semantic Web to defense and to molecular biology. In December 2015, after six years of work, ISO adopted and published OPM as ISO 19450—*Automation systems and integration—Object-Process Methodology*.

The realization and recognition that models can and should become the central artifact in system lifecycles has been gaining momentum in recent years, giving rise to model-based systems engineering (MBSE) as an evolving filed in the area of systems engineering. SysML and OPM have been serving as the two MBSE languages, but since SysML was adopted as a standard about eight years before OPM and has been backed by top-notch vendors, its adoption is currently more widespread. However, OPM is rapidly gaining acceptance in academia and its application in diverse industry segments is spreading.

This textbook, designed for both self-learning and as an undergraduate or graduate course, endows its readers with deep understanding of MBSE ideas, principles, and applications through modeling systems using both OPM and SysML. The book is comprised of three parts that encompass 24 chapters. Each chapter ends with a bulleted summary and a set of problems. Solutions to problems may be available in http://esml.iem.technion.ac.il/.

Part I introduces OPM and SysML via step-by-step modeling of a car automatic crash response system. Chapter 1 starts with a description of the system and its initial OPM model. In Chap 2 we enhance the model with text and animated simulation. Chapter 3 introduces links that connect things in the model. In Chap. 4 we introduce and use SysML's first three diagrams. Chapter 5 presents ways for managing the complexity of systems, while the dynamic aspect of the system is modeled in Chaps. 6 and 7. Abstraction and refinement mechanisms as means to manage complexity are the focus of Chap. 8, the last chapter in Part I.

Part II, *Model-Based Systems Engineering Fundamentals*, is a formal, theory-grounded exposure to OPM and SysML that discusses MBSE ontology, conceptual modeling constructs, and applications. Chapter 9 introduces and defines conceptual modeling. Chapter 10 presents the two basic building blocks of OPM—objects and processes, while Chap. 11 is about the textual modality of OPM—OPL. In Chap. 12 we turn to an orderly study of SysML with its four pillars and nine kinds of diagrams. The dynamic, time-dependent aspect of systems is the focus of Chap. 13, followed by studying the structural, time-independent system aspect in Chap. 14. Following Chap. 15, which deals with participation constraints and fork links, in Chap. 16 we introduce the four fundamental structural relations.

In Part III, *Structure and Behavior: Diving In*, we go to the heart of conceptual modeling, elaborating on the four fundamental structural relations and whole system aspects, including complexity management and control. Chapters 17 and 18 discuss aggregation-participation and exhibition-characterization, respectively. Chapter 19 is about states and values, concepts that are needed for generalization-specialization and classification-instantiation, both of which are elaborated on in Chap. 20. Chapter 21 concerns complexity management and the refinement-abstraction mechanisms of OPM, as well as complexity management in SysML. Chapter 22 is about OPM operational semantics and control links—the way control is managed during execution of the system. In Chap. 23 we specify how to model logical operators and probabilities. Finally, Chap. 24 is an overview of ISO 19450—*Automation Systems and Integration—Object-Process Methodology*, adopted by the International organization for Standardization in December 2015.

With respect to OPM, this book can be considered a superset of ISO 19450. While OPM, as specified in this book, is ISO 19450-complaint, the book provides in-depth motivation, rationale, and philosophical foundations for decisions made during the design of ISO 19450. These cannot be elaborated on in a standard, which, by its nature, is expected to be short and decisive, with little justifications. OPM points in the book that are not covered in ISO 19450 can be considered optional, or, in ISO nomenclature, *informative*, as opposed to *normative*—abiding ISO specifications.

This book is a product of six years of work, during which I have made all efforts to make it accurate, consistent, and formal, while also not lose the human touch and the interest of the future reader. It is my sincere hope that the book will serve as a reliable reference to MBSE in general and to OPM and SysML in particular.

Examining the above word cloud of this book (created by a program developed skillfully by Jason Davies),[2] based on close to 140,000 words contained in this book, we can see that the most frequent words are *process*, *object*, and *link*. Indeed, this is a most faithful testimony that OPM focuses on how to *model systems* (two other most frequent words in the cloud) by relating *processes* to *objects* using *links*. *Relation* is there too, along with other notable words, including *diagram*, *attribute*, *structural*, *procedural*, *semantics*, *state*, *control*, *change*, *effect*, *agent*, *time*, *constraint*, and *function*. Of course, *SysML* is there between *process* and *model*, near *OPD* (Object-Process Diagram—OPM's graphical modality) and *OPL* (Object-Process Language—OPM's textual modality). This list gives a good idea of what this book is about.

I wish to thank my three MIT collaborators, Prof. Ed Crawley and Prof. Oli de Weck from Engineering Systems Division and the Aero-Astro Department, and Pat Hale, Director of Systems Design and Management Program. Special thanks to my PhD student, Yaniv Mordecai, who provided insightful comments on many of the chapters in this book. I thank the Technion, Israel Institute of Technology, which provided me with the environment to develop OPM and with the 2013-4 sabbatical to complete this book. Finally, I wish to thank my beloved wife, Prof. Judy Dori, who provided pedagogical guidance and moral support, which made it possible for me to finish the book.

Dov Dori   *Massachusetts Institute of Technology, July 2015*

---

[2]https://www.jasondavies.com/wordcloud/

Table of Contents

Main ISO 19450-compliant OPM Symbols

Things: stateful objects and processes

thing property	value (notation)	thing		
		object	stateful object	process
essence	Informatical (flat)	Recipe	Recipe / outdated / updated	Counting
	Physical (shaded)	Hammer	Hammer / broken / fixed	Mining
affiliation	Systemic (solid)	Balance	Drill / faulty / operational	Producing
	Environmental (dashed)	Record	Recipe / outdated / updated	Exporting

Fundamental structural links

modality	aggregation-participation	exhibition-characterization	generalization-specialization	classification-instantiation
Graphics – Object-Process Diagram (OPD)	Whole / Part	Exhibitor / Attribute	General / Specialization	Class / Instance
Textual – Object-Process Language (OPL)	**Whole** consists of **Part**.	**Exhibitor** exhibits **Attribute**.	**Specialization** is a **General**.	**Instance** is an instance of **Class**.

Tagged structural links

unidirectional tagged link	bidirectional tagged link	Reciprocal tagged link
Sarah —is mother of→ Isaac	Sarah ⇄ is mother of / is son of Isaac	Sarah —family— Isaac
Sarah is mother of Isaac.	**Sarah is mother of Isaac.** **Isaac is son of Sarah.**	**Sarah** and **Isaac** are **family.**

Procedural transforming links

consumption link	result link	effect link	in-out link pair
Consumee → Consuming	Creating → Resultee	Affectee ↕ Affecting	Affectee (input state, output state) → State Changing
Consuming consumes **Consumee.**	**Creating** yields **Resultee.**	**Affecting** affects **Affectee.**	**State Changing** changes **Affectee** from **input state** to **output state.**

Procedural enabling links

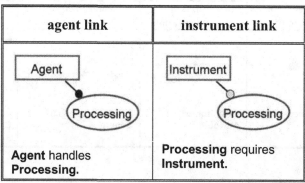

agent link	instrument link
Agent ● Processing	Instrument ○ Processing
Agent handles **Processing.**	**Processing** requires **Instrument.**

Part I

Model-Based Systems Engineering Introduced

This book focuses on conceptual systems modeling with OPM—Object-Process Methodology, and SysML—Systems Modeling Language. SysML is an accepted de-facto standard of the Object Management Group (OMG) since 2006, while OPM has become ISO 19450 publically available specification in 2014. Leaving theoretical background and discussions to Part II and detailed technical specifications to Part III, this first part introduces OPM and SysML via a running case study of a car automatic crash response system that we model step-by-step, exposing modeling principles and practices as we go. Chapter 1 starts right away with a description of the system to be modeled and an initial, gentle OPM model. In Chap. 2 we enhance the model with text and animated simulation. Chapter 3 introduces links that connect things in the model. In Chap. 4 we pause modeling the automatic crash response system with OPM and move to introducing and using SysML's first three diagrams: Use case, block, and state machine diagrams. Resuming modeling the system with OPM, Chap. 5 will expose us to in-zooming—the most powerful refinement mechanism that enables managing the complexity of systems. The dynamic, behavioral, time-dependent aspect of the system is the topic of Chap. 6. In Chap. 7, we are exposed to specifics of controlling the system's behavior. Deepening our knowledge about abstraction and refinement mechanisms as means to manage complexity is the focus of Chap. 8, the last one in Part I.

Chapter 1
Ready to Start Modeling?

...all models are wrong; the practical question is how wrong do they have to be to not be useful.

Box and Draper (1987)

With diagrams the meaning is obvious, because once you understand how the basic elements of the diagrams fit together, the meaning literally stares you in the face.

Steve Cook (1999)

We live in a world of interconnected systems. In fact, as humans, each of us is a highly complex system living in a host of socio-political-technological systems that are no less complex. In order to understand and design complex systems, it is necessary to have a methodology and a language for building models that can express what these systems do, why they do it, how they do it, and what they need in order to do it. While the visual and intuitive nature of diagrams has made them widely used means for building models of systems, natural language text is also an important way of conveying complex ideas. Formal diagrams are a graphic language in that they contain interconnected symbols, expressing meaningful facts and statements about the world. Combining graphics with text reinforces our ability to specify complex ideas in science and engineering.

1.1 The Automatic Crash Response System

We introduce conceptual modeling using OPM, and later SysML, using a running example of specifying the GM OnStar Automatic Crash Response (ACR) system. The specification that we model provided below was taken almost literally from an early version of OnStar Technology's description on the OnStar company website.[1]

> OnStar's in-vehicle safety, security, and information services use Global Positioning System (GPS) satellite and cellular technology to link the vehicle and driver to the OnStar Center. At the OnStar Center, advisors offer real-time, personalized help 24 hours a day, 365 days a year. ...
>
> The accelerometer located within the Sensing and Diagnostic Module (SDM) measures the crash's severity. In the event of a moderate-to-severe frontal or side-impact crash, data is transmitted from the affected sensors to the SDM. The SDM sensor also can identify a rear impact of

---

[1] http://cms.cerritos.edu/auto/basic-its/ost.htm.

© Springer Science+Business Media New York 2016

D. Dori, *Model-Based Systems Engineering with OPM and SysML*, DOI 10.1007/978-1-4939-3295-5_1

sufficient severity. Regardless of whether the air bags deploy, the SDM transmits crash information to the vehicle's OnStar module.

Within seconds of a moderate-to-severe crash, the OnStar module will send a message to the OnStar Call Center (OCC) through a cellular connection, informing the advisor that a crash has occurred. A voice connection between the advisor and the vehicle occupants is established. The advisor can then conference in 911 [emergency] dispatch or a public safety answering point (PSAP), which determines if emergency services are necessary. If there is no response from the occupants, the advisor can provide the emergency dispatcher with the crash information from the SDM that reveals the severity of the crash. The dispatcher can identify what emergency services may be appropriate. Using the Global Positioning System (GPS) satellite, OnStar advisors are able to tell emergency workers the location of the vehicle.

The "big picture" that emerges from this system description is that the ACR system aims to provide an automatic response in case of a severe car crash. In the following sections we methodically model this system using OPM and then SysML.

1.2 The Function-as-a-Seed OPM Principle

In order to start an OPM model of a system, the first step is to determine the *function* of the system. The function is the main process of the system, which is designed to deliver value—benefit at cost—to the system beneficiary. The system beneficiaries are the person or people who get value from using the system. Identifying the system's function is critical, as it expresses the motivation for engineering the system. This function will be the top-level process of our OPM model. Determining the system's function is not just important and recommended, it is also a basic principle, known as the *function-as-a-seed OPM principle*:[2]

The Function-as-a-Seed OPM Principle

Modeling a system starts by defining, naming, and depicting the function of the system, which is also its top-level process.

The term "function-as-a-seed" underscores the centrality of starting off the modeling process in a way that focuses on the *function* of the system; that is, the value that the system provides to its beneficiary. As the next few chapters show, this function is the seed from which the entire model gradually evolves. This guideline may be counterintuitive, since many engineers tend to start with the *form*—the objects, the substance of which the system is comprised—rather than the function, which is the process due to which beneficiaries would use the system in the first place. Function delivers value, while form draws cost that must be paid to achieve that system's function.

Given the centrality of the system's function, it is worth contemplating what this function really is and what it should best be called so everybody involved in the modeling will be on the same page. An appropriate function clarifies and emphasizes the central goal of the system being modeled. Deliberation

---

[2]This is the first of 13 OPM principles, which are listed throughout the book in a frame and also appear at the end of the book for quick reference after Chap. 24 under the heading "OPM Principles at a Glance".

regarding the function often provokes a debate between the system architecture team members at this early stage, but this is highly valuable. Such discussions frequently expose differences and often even misconceptions among the participants regarding the system that they set out to architect, model, and design. Thus, agreement on the system's function and its most appropriate name increases the likelihood of ending up with a useful model.

1.3 Identifying the System's Function

The OnStar system description above makes it clear that the main function of the system—its purpose and the value it delivers—is to automatically provide response in case of a car crash. Therefore, we call this function **Automatic Crash Responding**, and this is the top-level process of the system we are about to start modeling. OPM has just one type of diagram, which is called the object-process diagram (OPD). Any OPD is built using two OPM building blocks: objects and processes.

> *An **object** is a thing that exists or might exist.*

While objects exist, processes happen or occur, and they transform objects by generating, consuming, or affecting them.

> *A **process** is a thing that transforms an object.*

Collectively, objects and processes are called *things*.

> *A **thing** is an object or a process.*

We start by modeling the *system diagram*—the top-level *object-process diagram* (OPD)—in our OPM model. The OPM symbol for a process is an ellipse with the process name recorded within it.

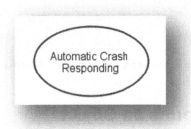

Fig. 1.1 **Automatic Crash Responding** modeled as a process

Figure 1.1 describes the **Automatic Crash Responding** process in OPM notation using OPCAT,[3] an OPM-based modeling software environment such as OPCAT (Dori et al. 2003). It is highly recommended that the reader installs OPCAT and follows the modeling activities presented here.

Based on the definition of a process as a thing that transforms an object, no process is meaningful unless it transforms at least one object. That object is known as the *transformee* of the transforming *process* or the *operand* of the system's function.

1.4 Identifying the System's Beneficiary

A man-made, artificial system is designed to benefit at least some of its *stakeholders*. The stakeholders that benefit are the system's *beneficiaries*. The beneficiary of the **Automatic Crash Responding** process, which is also the transformee in our case, is the driver and any additional passengers who occupy the crashed vehicle. This group of people is the object **Vehicle Occupants Group**. Figure 1.2 shows the OPD of Fig. 1.1 updated with this object. The OPM symbol for object is a rectangle with the object name recorded within it. This is also the standard symbol used in UML—the Unified Modeling Language (OMG UML 2011I, 2011S)—and SysML, where it is referred to as a *block*.

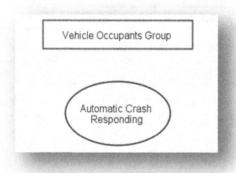

Fig. 1.2 **Vehicle Occupants Group** is added as an object to the **Automatic Crash Responding** process

1.5 A Process Transforms an Object

We have defined an object as a thing that exists or might exist. Our object, the **Vehicle Occupants Group**, does exist, as it did prior to the occurrence of the **Automatic Crash Responding** process. So what

---

[3]The object-process diagrams (OPDs) in this book were drawn using OPCAT, a software environment that enables OPM-based modeling. OPCAT can be downloaded and installed free from http://esml.iem.technion.ac.il/, a website that also contains an OPCAT hands-on tutorial and many articles on OPM. OPCAT tutorial is also found on that site.

transformation does the **Vehicle Occupants Group** undergo? To answer this question, we examine the following definition of transformation.

> ***Transformation*** *is the creation (generation, construction) or consumption (elimination, destruction) of an object or an effect (change of state) of an existing object.*

In our case, the state of the **Vehicle Occupants Group** has clearly changed. In other words, the **Vehicle Occupants Group** has been affected by, and consequently benefited from, the occurrence of the **Automatic Crash Responding** process. To express the fact that the **Automatic Crash Responding** process affects (changes the state of) the **Vehicle Occupants Group** object, we insert a link between the process and the object. The link, shown in Fig. 1.3, is the *effect link*—a bidirectional arrow, ◁—▷—between the affecting (state-changing) process and the affected object; that is, the object whose state has changed as a result of the process occurring.

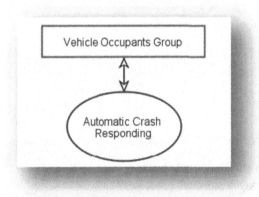

Fig. 1.3 An effect link is added between the **Automatic Crash Responding** process and the **Vehicle Occupants Group** object, indicating that the process affected (changed the state of) the object

Our model currently contains three elements. The first is the **Automatic Crash Responding** process, the second is the object **Vehicle Occupants Group**, and the third is the link between the process and the object.

1.6 Summary

- We have started modeling the Automatic Crash Responding system using OPM.
- OPM has a single diagram type: the object-process diagram (OPD).
- OPM is built of objects, which exist, and of processes, which transform objects.
- Object transformation is object creation, object consumption, or object change.

- We recognize processes—**Automatic Crash Responding** in our example—as stand-alone OPM building blocks that are separate from objects.

- Objects and processes enable concurrent modeling of the system's structure and behavior in the same OPD.

- Transformation is object creation, consumption, or state change.

1.7 **Problems**

An engineering student was asked to sketch a graphical representation of the system of garbage recycling came up with the sketch in Fig. 1.4.

Fig. 1.4 The Recycling System—a graphic representation

1. What things in the sketch represent objects?
2. What things in the sketch represent processes?
3. What elements in the sketch represent relations?
4. Are there concepts in the sketch that do not fall in any of the above categories? If so what are they? What should they be called?

The baggage handling system case study that we start evolving below will serve as the basis for problems at the end of each chapter. You can do the modeling manually, but it is strongly advised that you use an OPM modeling software package such as OPCAT (downloadable from *http://esml.iem.technion.ac.il/*).

> A passenger arriving at an airport deposits her baggage with the airline she is flying with. A baggage handling system manages the transfer of the baggage to the passenger's destination.

5. What is the function of the system? Phrase it as an OPM process name.
6. Draw the function as the main process in a new OPD.
7. Identify the main beneficiary of the system.

8.   Add the beneficiary to the OPD as an object and link it to the process defined as the system's function.

9.   Identify the operand of the system's function.

10. Add the operand to the OPD and link it to the process.

Identify other main objects that the process affects, add them to the OPD, and link them to the process.

Chapter 2
Text and Simulation Enhancements

We went next to the School of Languages. ... The first Project was to shorten Discourse by cutting Polysyllables into one, and leaving out Verbs and Participle, because in Reality all things imaginable are but Nouns. ... However, many of the most Learned and Wise adhere to the new Scheme of expressing themselves by Things.

Jonathan Swift, *Gulliver's Travels* (1726)

Winograd and Flores (1987) noted that "Nothing exists except through language... In saying that some 'thing' exists (or that it has some property) we have brought it into a domain of articulated objects and qualities that exist in language."

Indeed, language greatly enhances our ability to understand systems and communicate our understanding to others. This chapter presents two enhancements to OPM models: textual model representation and animated model simulation.

We introduce the object-process language (OPL) as the textual modality of OPM that complements the graphical representation through OPDs (object-process diagrams). We show the equivalence between this graphical specification and the natural language specification through OPL. The chapter also shows another important means of enhancing model understanding: its animated simulation.

2.1 OPL: A Subset of English

In Fig. 2.1, an effect link has been added between the **Automatic Crash Responding** process and the **Vehicle Occupants Group** object. This link expresses the fact that the process affected the object; that is, changed it in some way. As soon as the effect link is drawn, OPCAT (the OPM modeling software environment we use) automatically generates the first object-process language (OPL) sentence:

Automatic Crash Responding affects **Vehicle Occupants Group**.

This is a clear and unambiguous sentence in plain English that was generated immediately, in response to the modeler linking the two things, and it explains what OPCAT has "understood" from this operation.

Figure 2.1 shows a partial screenshot of OPCAT. The top pane contains the OPD and the bottom contains the OPL sentence generated in response to the modeler's insertion of the effect link.

In OPCAT, the default color of OPL words or phrases (word sequences) that represent objects is green; this is the same color as the corresponding object boxes in the OPD. Likewise, the default color of phrases representing process names in OPL is blue, which is also the color of the corresponding process ellipses.

The graphics-text conversion is a two-way street: just as it was possible to extract the OPL paragraph above from the OPD in Fig. 2.1, that OPD can be reconstructed from its OPL paragraph; that is, the collection of OPL sentences that specify in text what the OPD specifies in graphics. As an exercise, the

© Springer Science+Business Media New York 2016

D. Dori, *Model-Based Systems Engineering with OPM and SysML*, DOI 10.1007/978-1-4939-3295-5_2

graphics-text equivalence principle can be verified by reconstructing Fig. 2.1 versa. It is easier to edit the graphics and get the immediate textual feedback.

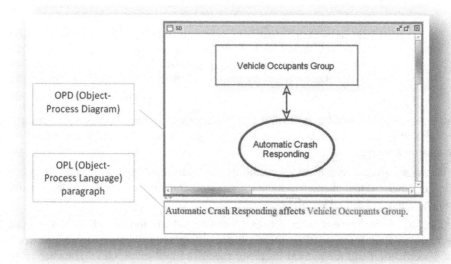

Fig. 2.1 A screenshot of OPCAT showing the OPD on top and the first object-process language (OPL) sentence generated in response to the modeler's insertion of the effect link

The ability to switch back and forth between graphics and text means that OPM system specification writers and modelers are less likely to make costly design errors. Moreover, readers of the textually specified model are more likely to fully comprehend the system and detect mistakes or omissions. The specification reader can fill gaps in his or her understanding of the system that may have formed while examining one modality by looking at the other one. In doing so, the reader reinforces familiarity with the specification and can more easily detect design errors or omissions.

2.2 States and Animated Simulation

States are important entities in a conceptual model. In this section, we introduce states and show how an OPM model can be simulated by animation to play out its dynamics, particularly its state transitions. So far, we have modeled the fact that the object **Vehicle Occupants Group** was affected by the process **Automatic Crash Responding**. To identify the actual nature of this effect, we need to be more specific. To this end, at any point in time during which we inspect a certain object, that object may be in a certain situation, which we refer to as a *state*.

> *A **state** is a situation or position at which an object can be, or a value it can assume, for some positive amount of time.*

Since states are possible situations or values *of an object*, they have no "life" of their own; they have meaning only in the context of the object to which they belong and within which they reside.

2.2.1 The Effect of a Process on an Object

The *effect* that a process has on an object is a *change in the state* of that object. In other words, the process transforms the object from its *input state* (the state before the process occurred) to its *output state* (the state after the process occurred). Therefore, at any given point in time, a stateful object is in *one of its states* or *in transition between two of its states*.

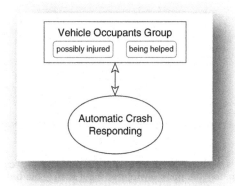

Fig. 2.2 The states of **Vehicle Occupants Group** are added: **possibly injured** is the input state and **being helped** is the output state

In order to be specific about the effect that the **Automatic Crash Responding** process has on the **Vehicle Occupants Group** object, we first need to come up with appropriate names for the states of this object, both before and after the occurrence of the process. Immediately after the crash, the **Vehicle Occupants Group** is **possibly injured**; after **Automatic Crash Responding**, they are **being helped**. These are the corresponding input and output states of the **Vehicle Occupants Group** object with respect to the **Automatic Crash Responding** process.

Figure 2.2 shows the OPD after adding the two states of **Vehicle Occupants Group**, with **possibly injured** being the input state and **being helped**—the output state. The symbol of state is a rounded corner rectangle—rountangle[1] for short—that encloses the state name, which starts with a lower-case letter. The state symbol is drawn inside the rectangle of the object that "owns" the state. This adding of states created the following new OPL sentence:

Vehicle Occupants Group can be **possibly injured** or **being helped**.

---

[1]This term was coined by D. Harel.

OPL sentences in this book are written in **Arial font**. Reserved phrases, such as "can be", are in regular font while all the rest (including commas and periods) are in bold font.

2.2.2 From an Implicit Effect to an Explicit State Change

Having specified the two states of the object **Vehicle Occupants Group**, we can now be more specific about the effect—the state change—that the occurrence of the process **Automatic Crash Responding** has brought about. We do this by replacing in Fig. 2.3 the single bidirectional *effect link* with an *input-output link pair* (also called input-output specified effect link), which is a pair of unidirectional arrows, one from the input state to the process and the other from the process to the output state.

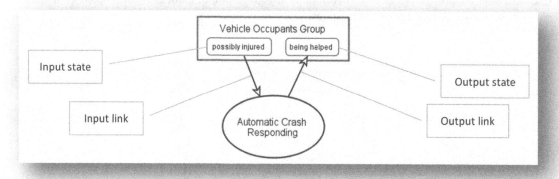

Fig. 2.3 The effect link in Fig. 2.2 is replaced by an input-output link pair that explicates the change of state of the **Vehicle Occupants Group** from the **possibly injured** input state to the **being helped** output state

The arrow from the *input state* to the process is the *input link*, and the arrow from the process to the *output state* is the *output link*. Together, these two links constitute the *input-output link pair*. In response to this editing of the model, the previous OPL sentence, "**Automatic Crash Responding** affects **Vehicle Occupants Group**.", is replaced by the following OPL sentence:

Automatic Crash Responding changes **Vehicle Occupants Group** from **possibly injured** to **being helped**.

By specifying the affecting process and the affected object with its input and output states, this sentence accurately reflects the details of the dynamics of the system.

2.2.3 State Naming

The names of states must reflect the various relevant situations in which their "owning" object can be at any given point in time. For example, **off**, **standby**, and **on** are three possible states of a machine, which would lead to the following OPL sentence:

Machine can be **off**, **standby**, or **on**.

As noted, the convention is that, unlike names of things (objects or processes), which have a capital letter at the start of each word, state names are always written in lower case. More descriptive names, such as **"possibly injured"** or **"being helped"**, as in our case study, should be given. It is important to check that the resulting OPL sentence makes sense.

2.3 Animated Execution of the OPM Model

One of the most attractive and useful features of an OPM model, which enables it to be visualized and tested, is its executability; that is, the ability to simulate a system by executing its model via animation in a properly designed software environment.[2]

Figure 2.4 shows three stages of executing the OPM model in Fig. 2.3. The screenshot on the left-hand side shows the system before the **Automatic Crash Responding** process occurs. At this stage, **Vehicle Occupants Group** is at its input state, **possibly injured**, which is marked by the state being solid (colored brown).

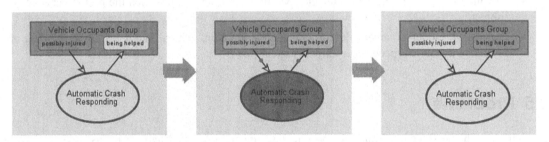

Fig. 2.4 Executing the OPM model shown in the OPD of Fig. 2.3. *Left:* the system before the Automatic Crash Responding process starts. *Center:* the process in action; the object is in transition from its input state to its output state. *Right:* the system after the Automatic Crash Responding process has terminated

The screenshot in the center of Fig. 2.4 shows the process in action, marked as solid (colored blue). During the time that the **Automatic Crash Responding** process is active (that is, when it executes), the object **Vehicle Occupants Group** is in transition from its input state, **possibly injured**, to its output state, **being helped**. This is marked by both states being semi-solid (light brown).

Observing the animation in action reveals that the input state gradually fades out while the output state becomes solid. At the same time, two red dots, shown in the middle of both arrows, travel along the input-output link pair, denoting the "control" of the system; that is, where the system is at each time point. One red dot travels from the input state to the affecting process. At the same time, the second dot travels from the process along the output link to the output state. Finally, the screenshot on the right shows the system after the **Automatic Crash Responding** process had terminated. At this stage, **Vehicle Occupants Group** is at its output state, **being helped**.

The animated execution of the system model has several benefits. Firstly, it is a dynamic visualization aid, which helps both the modeler and the target audience to follow and understand the behavior of the system over time. Secondly, similar to a debugger of a programming language, it facilitates verification of the system's dynamics and spotting of logical design errors in its flow of control. Therefore, it is

---

[2]You may want to try it yourself if you have modeled the system with OPCAT: Click the "Test System" film icon.

highly recommended that the system model be animated frequently as it is being constructed, so that design errors do not accumulate, but are corrected as soon as they are made.

2.4 **Summary**

- OPM has two equivalent representation modalities: the graphic—object-process diagram (OPD) and the textual—object-process language (OPL).
- The OPL sentences and the OPD complement each other, as they appeal to the parallel visual and verbal cognitive processing channels of the human brain.
- A state is a situation at which an object can be.
- An effect link indicates some state change of the linked object by the linked process.
- An input-output link pair indicates the specific state from and to which the process changes the object.
- An OPM model is amenable to animated simulation, which facilitates understanding the system's dynamic aspect and testing its logical flow.

2.5 **Problems**

Continuing with the Baggage Handling System that you modeled in Chap. 1, let us assume that the current model is presented in Fig. 2.5.

1. Match a corresponding OPL sentence for each link in the OPD of the Baggage Management System in Fig. 2.5.
2. Add the states **unloaded** and **loaded** to the object **Baggage**.
3. Replace the effect link between the process in your model and **Baggage** by an input-output link pair.

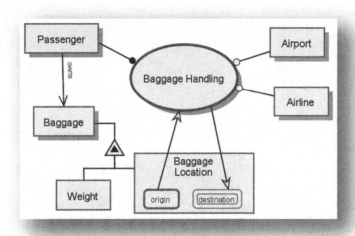

Fig. 2.5 System Diagram—top-level Object-Process Diagram (OPD) of the Baggage Handling System

4. Update the OPL sentence to reflect the change you made.
5. Add to your model and link the remaining objects from the specification above.
6. Using OPCAT, simulate the system by animating it.

Chapter 3
Connecting Things with Links

... The linking words or linking phrases are the set of words used to join concepts to express the relationships between the two concepts. ... Picking the appropriate linking words to clearly express the relationship between two concepts is possibly the most difficult task during the construction of concept maps.

Alberto J. Cañas, cmap.ihmc.us/docs/linkingwords.html (retrieved 2014)

Links are graphical expressions of relations between things. OPM links connect processes with objects or their states, providing meaning to relationships among them. This chapter expands the use of links in our model and explains the semantics of various kinds of links.

3.1 Procedural Links Versus Structural Links

The links we have been using so far—the effect link and the input and output links—are procedural links.

> *A **procedural link** is a link that specifies a dynamic aspect of the system by connecting an object (or one of its states) and a process.*

Procedural links can be *transforming* or *enabling*. Transforming links express transformation—generation, consumption, or state change—of the object by the process to which it is linked. Enabling links express enablement. They connect a process to an *enabler*—an object that enables the occurrence of that process but is not transformed by that process.

Structural links model the structure of the system by expressing long-term relations between things in the model. Structural links include aggregation-participation (whole-part), generalization-specialization, and other long-lasting relations.

> *A **structural link** is a link that specifies a static aspect of the system by connecting an object to another object or a process to another process.*

3.2 Adding Enablers

The top-level OPD that we have been modeling is called the *System Diagram (SD)*. Often called a context diagram, the SD provides a "50,000-foot view" of the system. It allows the modeler and all the stakeholders interested in understanding the system via its OPM model to quickly grasp the *function*—the main process of the system, which in this case is **Automatic Crash Responding**. The SD also shows the *beneficiary.* In our case, **Vehicle Occupants Group** is also the *operand* of the system; it is the main object transformed by the system's function, with its input and output states.

We are not quite done yet; while the function and the operand are important, they do not provide the full picture of the system, even at this most abstract level. Objects that *enable* this function should be presented in addition to the beneficiary. These *enablers* include human and non-human objects, which in OPM are referred to as *agents* and *instruments*, respectively.

3.2.1 Adding an Agent and an Agent Link

Reading through our system description, we note that the advisor is a major human player in our system, so we would like to model her. A human, as part of an OPM system, is an object referred to as an *agent*.

> An **agent** *of a process is a human or a group of humans that interacts with the system*
> *to enable and/or control that process, but is not transformed by it.*

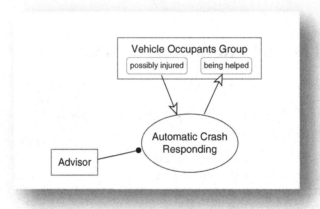

Fig. 3.1 **Advisor** is added as the agent of **Automatic Crash Responding** using the agent link from **Advisor** to **Automatic Crash Responding**. The optional stick figure also indicates that the object is a human

The *agent link*, —•, shown in Fig. 3.1, is a "black lollipop"—a connecting line starting at the object and ending with a black circle at the process end. This symbol denotes that the object linked to the process is a human whose presence is mandatory for the process to happen.

The agent link indicates that there is a "human in the loop", usually indicating that an interface is required between the human—the agent—and the system in order for the agent to interact with it. Fig. 3.1 shows **Advisor** added as an agent to the **Automatic Crash Responding** process. The process cannot start or be sustained without the agent, but the process does not transform the agent: It does not create or consume it, nor does it change the agent's state. Hence, agent is a human *enabler* of the process. The OPL sentence that is generated as a result of adding the agent link is:

Advisor handles **Automatic Crash Responding.**

The OPL reserved word handles denotes the need for an agent to enable the process. While the **Vehicle Occupants Group** object is a group of people, they not an agent. These people are the beneficiary and operand of the system—they do change and are hence transformed by the system's function and benefit from it.

3.2.2 Adding an Instrument and an Instrument Link

While **Advisor** is an agent (a human enabler), our system also has an inanimate enabler—an *instrument*. The instrument that enables the system's function, **Automatic Crash Responding**, is the automatic crash response (ACR) system, which we shall call **ACR System**. The instrument is denoted by an instrument link—a white lollipop, —○. Similar to the agent link, the instrument link is a line that connects the object to the process that requires that instrument. Like the agent, while the instrument is needed for the process to happen, the instrument is not transformed (created, consumed, or affected) by the occurrence of this process.

> *An **instrument** of a process is a non-human that interacts with the system to enable and/or control that process, but is not transformed by it.*

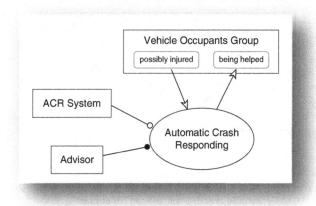

Fig. 3.2 **ACR System** is added as instrument of **Automatic Crash Responding** using the instrument link from **ACR System** to **Vehicle Occupants Group**

Figure 3.2 shows the instrument **ACR System** added using the instrument link from **Advisor** to **Vehicle Occupants Group**. The instrument link is the line ending with a blank circle at the process end, which denotes that the object at the origin of the link is an instrument with respect to this process. An instrument is an inanimate, non-human enabler of the process; in other words, the process cannot start or take place without the existence and availability of the instrument throughout the process duration. Like the agent, the instrument is not transformed as a result of the process occurrence.

The OPL sentence that OPCAT generated as a result of adding the instrument link is:

Automatic Crash Responding requires **ACR System.**

The OPL reserved word requires denotes the need for an instrument to enable the process.

> *An **enabler** is an agent or an instrument.*

3.3 Adding Structural Links

At this stage in the modeling of the system, we have already modeled a portion of the system diagram (SD), which is the top-level OPD. An additional thing (object or process) that we should include in the SD is the **Vehicle**, since this is the object that the driver and passengers occupy—the **Vehicle Occupants Group**—and it is also part of the **ACR system**.

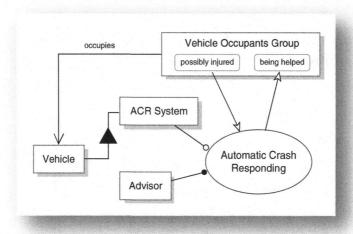

Fig. 3.3 **Vehicle** is added as part of the **ACR System**, and the tagged structural link from **Vehicle Occupants Group** to **Vehicle** is added with the tag "**occupies**"

Figure 3.3 shows our SD with **Vehicle** added and linked to these two objects with two links. These two links are called structural links. The first is aggregation-participation link, from **ACR System** to **Vehicle**. The second link is tagged structural link from **Vehicle Occupants Group** to **Vehicle**. We next discuss each one of these structural links.

Vehicle is connected via an aggregation-participation (whole-part) link as part of the **ACR System**. The aggregation-participation symbol is ▲, a solid equilateral triangle with its tip directed upwards and linked to the whole, and its base linked to the part or parts. This graphical aggregation-participation link is expressed textually the following OPL sentence:

ACR System consists of **Vehicle**.

The OPL reserved phrase consists of denotes the aggregation-participation relation, with the whole (**ACR System** in our case) preceding it and the part (**Vehicle** in our case), or parts, following it.

Vehicle is connected to **Vehicle Occupants Group** via a second type of structural link—the tagged structural link. A tagged structural link is an open arrow that points from one object to another. The tag is a "user-defined" phrase—a phrase that is defined by the modeler and recorded along the link, expressing the nature of the structural relation between the two connected objects (or processes). In our model, the link's tag is **occupies**. It is bold since it is defined by the modeler and is not an OPL reserved phrase. Adding the tagged structural link initiates the generation of the following OPL sentence:

Vehicle Occupants Group occupies Vehicle.

Tags in tagged structural links provide the modeler with the ability to express the semantics of any structural relation between any two objects or any two processes in the system. As the above OPL sentence demonstrates, a tagged structural link gives rise to an OPL sentence in which the name of the object connected to the source of the link's arrow appears first (**Vehicle Occupants Group** in our case), followed by the tag name (**occupies**), followed by the name of the object connected to the destination of the link's arrow (**Vehicle**).

3.4 **Physical Versus Informatical Things**

Things (objects or processes) are classified by their *essence* attribute into two kinds: *physical* things and *informatical* things. All the objects in our model so far have been physical, as denoted in Fig. 3.3 by the shadow behind each object.

The default essence value of a thing can be determined by the system modeler. If the system is an information system, it makes sense to set the default essence value of a thing as informatical, because most of the things in such a system would be informatical. In this case, if a thing is informatical and it is already mentioned in at least one OPL sentence, no additional OPL sentence is required to indicate that this thing is informatical. If, however, the thing is physical, this is denoted in a dedicated OPL sentence. For example, assuming that the system we are modeling was set with informatical essence value, the OPL sentence below was added to denote the fact that the essence of **Vehicle** is physical.

Vehicle is physical.

As for **Automatic Crash Responding**, which is our main process and the system's function, it is possible at this point to say that it is informatical, because it only involves conveying the information that the vehicle has been involved in a crash and that there has been a subsequent call for help for its occupants. The actual helping process, which is physical, is outside the scope of this system. The essence of the **Automatic Crash Responding** process can be changed later to physical if we realize that it involves one or more physical subprocesses.

3.5 **Model Facts and OPL Paragraphs**

As we have seen, each time we introduced a link between two things or changed the essence of a thing from informatical to physical, at least one OPL sentence was added or modified. Thus, as we model, facts start accumulating and be expressed in the model.

> *A **model fact** is a relation between things or states in the model.*

We have been gradually accumulating OPL sentences, which collectively constitute the *OPL paragraph* and together the textual modality. The OPL paragraph describes in plain English precisely what the OPD—the graphical modality—describes visually.

Currently, the OPL paragraph reads as follows.

Vehicle Occupants Group is physical.
Vehicle Occupants Group can be **possibly injured** or **being helped**.
Vehicle Occupants Group occupies **Vehicle**.
Advisor is physical.
Advisor handles **Automatic Crash Responding**.
ACR System is physical.
ACR System consists of **Vehicle**.
Vehicle is physical.
Automatic Crash Responding requires **ACR System**.
Automatic Crash Responding changes **Vehicle Occupants Group** from **possibly injured** to **being helped**.

In order to save space, we take the liberty to omit the sentences expressing the physical essence of things in most of the OPL paragraph examples that follow, since this is obvious from the shading in the OPD.

3.6 **Environmental Versus Systemic Things**

The text that we have started using as the basis of our model is not written in a way that facilitates the modeling process. Details about the system's structure and behavior are scattered throughout the text. We first encounter the crash in the sentence "*The accelerometer ... measures the crash severity.*" Later we read: "*Within seconds of a moderate-to-severe crash ...*"

Combining these specifications with our previous personal knowledge about car crashes, we realize that the specification author meant to express the fact that a **Crashing** process has occurred. This process is not systemic; that is, it is not part of the system. Rather, it is external to the system—it happens in the system's environment: **Crashing** adversely affects **Vehicle** and possibly the **Vehicle Occupants Group**, and the **ACR System** needs to respond to the outcomes of this unfortunate process.

Things that are not part of the system, but interact with it, are referred to as *environmental*. These environmental things are contrasted with *systemic* things—things that are part of the system. Graphically, environmental things are marked by a dashed contour, as opposed to the solid contour of systemic things. In Fig. 3.4, **Crashing** can be identified as an environmental process by its dashed contour and as a physical process by its shading. This is also reflected in the following OPL sentence:

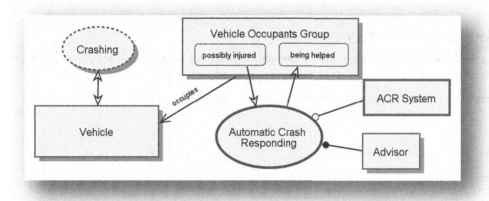

Fig. 3.4 **Crashing** is added as an environmental process that affects **Vehicle**

Crashing is environmental and physical.

Vehicle Occupants Group can also be considered as environmental, because it is not part of the **ACR System** but rather the beneficiary and the operand—the object on which the system operates to transform it. In our case, the transformation is from the **possibly injured** state to the state of **being helped**. Figure 3.4 displays **Vehicle Occupants Group** as a physical object by its shading. This is also reflected in the following OPL sentence:

Vehicle Occupants Group is physical.

The thing's attribute whose values are *systemic* and *environmental* is called *affiliation*.

3.7 Initial and Final States

As soon as **Crashing** occurs, **Vehicle** is affected. Figure 3.4 shows this via the effect link, which is the bidirectional arrow between **Crashing** and **Vehicle**. However, the exact nature of the effect—the state change—is not yet specified in the model. To make the model clearer, we have omitted, for now, the aggregation-participation link from **ACR System** to **Vehicle**. To make the change explicit, the input and output states of **Vehicle** in Fig. 3.5 are specified as **intact** and **crashed**. The corresponding OPL sentence is:

Vehicle can be **intact** or **crashed**.

The input state, **intact**, is the *initial state*; that is, the state at which the object starts its lifecycle after being generated. This is denoted graphically by the thick contour around **intact**. The output state,

crashed, is the *final state*; that is, the state from which the object cannot exit. This is denoted graphically by the double contour around **crashed**. Textually, by the corresponding OPL sentence specifies the two states:

Vehicle is initially **intact** and finally **crashed.**

Using the initial and final state symbols, **possibly injured** and **being helped** are designated in Fig. 3.5 as the initial and final states of **Vehicle Occupants Group**, respectively:

Vehicle Occupants Group is initially **possibly injured** and finally **being helped.**

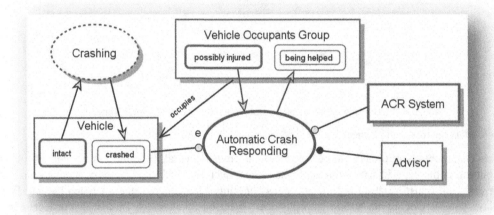

Fig. 3.5 The effect of **Crashing** is made explicit by replacing it with an input-output link pair that specifies the input and output states of **Vehicle**. The event link from the **crashed** state of **Vehicle** triggers **Automatic Crash Responding**

Having specified the states of **Vehicle**, we replace the single effect link between **Crashing** and **Vehicle** by an input-output link pair. The semantics of this change can be best understood by examining the OPL sentences generated before and after this replacement. Originally, the OPL sentence that corresponded to the OPD in Fig. 3.4 read as follows:

Crashing affects **Vehicle.**

After replacing the effect link in Fig. 3.4 by the input-output link pair in Fig. 3.5, the OPL sentence is:

Crashing changes **Vehicle** from **intact** to **crashed.**

The latter sentence is clearly more informative, as it tells us specifically from what input state to what output state the **Crashing** process changed **Vehicle**. However, this additional detail comes at the expense of loading the OPD with two links—the input and output links—instead of the single effect link.

3.8 **Triggering State and Event Link**

As soon as **Vehicle** enters its **crashed** state, the function of the **ACR System—Automatic Crash Responding**—is triggered. To model this, we draw an *instrument event link* from the state **crashed** to the process **Automatic Crash Responding**.

As Fig. 3.5 shows, an instrument event link is a procedural link that is graphically similar to an instrument link with an additional *control modifier*—the letter **e** next to the circle. The semantics of this link is a combination of the semantics of the instrument link with that of triggering an event. In our case, this links denotes the fact that entry of **Vehicle** into its **crashed** state is an event that initiates the process to which it is linked. In other words, the semantics of the event link is that once **Vehicle** enters the **crashed** state (from which the event link originates), the **Automatic Crash Responding** process (to which the event link is directed) is initiated. The instrument component of the link indicates that **Vehicle** is not transformed (neither consumed nor changes its state) by the **Automatic Crash Responding** process it triggers. The OPL sentence generated in response to inserting this event link is:

Crashed Vehicle initiates **Automatic Crash Responding**, which requires **crashed Vehicle**.

This OPL sentence reflects the combined semantics of the event control modifier, which is expressed by the reserved OPL word initiates, with that of the instrument link, which is expressed by the reserved OPL word requires. AS the sentence demonstrates, **Vehicle** at its **crashed** state is simply **crashed Vehicle**.

3.9 **Summary**

- Enablers are required for a process to occur, but are not affected by the occurrence of that process.
- An agent is a human enabler, while an instrument is a non-human enabler.
- Two types of links connect entities with each other: *structural links* and *procedural links*.
  - o Procedural links, which are between a process and an object or one of its states, express the behavior of the system; for example, an effect link.
  - o Structural links express persistent, long-term relations between two connected objects or between two connected processes in the system; for example, an aggregation-participation link.
- Since the structural and the procedural links are expressed in the same diagram, they help integrate the structure and the behavior of the system.
- Things—that is, objects and processes—are classified by their
  - o *Essence* into *physical* things and *informatical* things, and by their
  - o *Affiliation* into *systemic* things and *environmental* things.
- A process is triggered by an event link.

3.10 **Problems**

> When a passenger arrives at the airport with her baggage, she checks it in. The airline loads the baggage on-board the aircraft.

1. Define three states of **Baggage** based on the holder or the location of the baggage from the time the **Passenger** arrives at the **Airport** until **Baggage** is loaded on the **Airplane**.

2. Add three states to the OPD you started to construct in the previous chapter (remember to use lower-case letters).

3. What is the OPL sentence that describes the states of **Baggage**?

4. What is the process that changes **Baggage** from the first state to the second state?

5. Add this process to the OPD along with the input link from the first state to the process and from the process to the second state.

6. What is the OPL sentence that describes the change of **Baggage** states?

7. Repeat problems 4–6 with the process that changes **Baggage** from the second state to the third.

8. Perform animated simulation on your model by triggering each one of the two processes and watch the states change as expected. Provide screenshots of the model at the various states.

> When the aircraft arrives at the destination airport, the baggage is unloaded and returned to the passenger.

9. Based on the text above, repeat problems 7–8 with the process that changes **Baggage** from the third state to the first.

Chapter 4

SysML: Use Case, Block, and State Machine Diagrams

> *SysML supports the specification, analysis, design, verification, and validation of a broad range of complex systems. These systems may include hardware, software, information, processes, personnel, and facilities.*
>
> OMG SysML, v1.3 p.1 (Accessed June 20, 2014)

We leave OPM for a while and turn to start our parallel SysML model. SysML is a multi-view language, where each view uses a different type of diagram. There are nine SysML diagram types in total. In this chapter we are exposed to three diagram types: the use case diagram, the block definition diagram, and the state machine diagram. The use case diagram shows the context of the system and how the system is used to bring value to at least one of its actors. The block definition diagram presents the blocks of the system—major entities of interest. The state machine diagram shows how states of blocks in the system are changed. Comparing OPM and SysML, we already see that the approaches they take are different and complementary. OPM uses a single model that combines the various system aspects, while SysML uses a number of diagram types, each focusing on some particular aspect of the system.

4.1 The SysML Use Case Diagram

We start our model with the *use case diagram*, since this is the view that is used to elicit requirements and to provide initial understanding of the system and its surroundings.

> *A **use case** is a way the system is used, a service it provides to at least one of its users.*

According to the OMG SysML 1.3 (2012) standard, a use case diagram "describes the usage of a system (subject) by its actors (environment) to achieve a goal that is realized by the subject providing a set of services to selected actors" (OMG SysML 1.3, 2012, p.145).

Before drawing use case diagrams, use cases need to be written in text. This text takes on different formats. Depending on need, use cases are written in varying degrees of formality. They can be

- brief—short one-paragraph summary, usually of the main success scenario;
- casual—informal paragraph format, where multiple paragraphs describe various scenarios; and
- fully dressed—the most elaborate level, where all the steps and variations are written in detail, and there are supporting sections, such as preconditions and success guarantees.

Figure 4.1 is a preliminary use case diagram of the Automatic Crash Response (ACR) system.

© Springer Science+Business Media New York 2016
D. Dori, *Model-Based Systems Engineering with OPM and SysML*, DOI 10.1007/978-1-4939-3295-5_4

The name of the use case in our use case model is "**Automatically respond to crash**." As Fig. 4.1 shows, the use case is depicted as an oval with the name inside it. The system users are called actors.

> *An **actor** is an external entity that interacts with the system and can get services from it.*

An **actor** is depicted either as a human stick figure, or as the stereotype «actor»; see Table 4.1. Two actors appear in the use case diagram in Fig. 4.1: **Vehicle Occupants** and **Advisor**. An actor is by definition an external entity. Unlike OPM, SysML does not require that the actor be a person; it can be anything with which the system interacts.

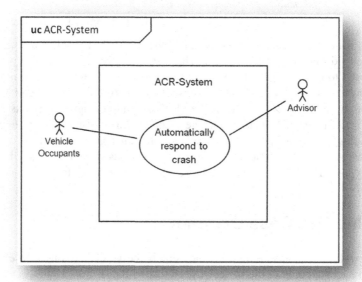

Fig. 4.1 A preliminary SysML use case diagram of the Automatic Crash Response (ACR) system

Vehicle Occupants are undoubtedly an external entity, since they are not part of the system, but rather its users and beneficiaries. The case for the **Advisor** is not that clear-cut, since the **Advisor** can be considered as part of the system, and rather than getting a service from the system, she is the one that provides the service. However, the requirement that an actor gets a service is not mandatory, and as a human, the **Advisor** interacts with the system. In this model, we exclude humans from being considered part of the system; hence **Advisor** is also an actor. Each one of the two actors is linked to the use case via a *communication path*—a line between the actor and the use case.

The system which provides the required function in a use case diagram is called subject.

> *A **subject** in a use case diagram is the system that provides the service.*

A use case subject is depicted as a rectangle with the subject name at the rectangle's top center. As Fig. 4.1 shows, the subject in our use case diagram is called **ACR-System**.

The entire use case diagram is depicted within a diagram frame—a rectangle that is required for any SysML diagram. In its upper leftmost corner, a diagram frame has name tag—a rectangle with a tapered bottom right corner—which contains the heading name. The heading name has the following syntax:

<**diagramKind**> [modelElementType] <modelElementName> [diagramName]

The fields diagramKind, which is bolded, and modelElementName are mandatory. Each diagramKind has a two or three lower case letter abbreviation. As shown in Fig. 4.1, the diagramKind of our use case is **uc**, while the diagramName is ACR-System. The two other tokens, modelElementType and diagramName are optional, and if they appear, they are enclosed within brackets, enabling the diagram reader to tell them apart.

Table 4.1 lists the main elements of a use case diagram, their semantics and symbols.

Table 4.1 The main elements of a use case diagram, their semantics and symbols

Element: Semantics	Symbol
Use Case: A service the system (subject) provides to at least one actor	UseCaseName
Actor: An external entity that interacts with the system and can get services from it	ActorName «actor» ActorName
Subject: The system that provides the service(s)	SubjectName
Communication path: A connection between an actor and a use case	————

Guillemets, also known as the symbols for *rewind* («) and *fast forward* (»), are angle quotes, as the ones surrounding the following word: «guillemets». In SysML, a word within a pair of guillemets denotes a *stereotype*—an extensibility mechanism that enables creating new model elements.

A stereotype is depicted as a rectangular box with the stereotype name, such as "block" within a pair of guillemets, «block», recorded in the top middle of the box, as is the case with «actor» in Table 4.1. The name of the actor, ActorName, is recorded beneath the «actor» stereotype notation.

4.2 **SysML Blocks and the Block Definition Diagram**

A SysML *block* is a modular component which defines a collection of features that describe a part of the system or another element of interest. A SysML block, which roughly corresponds to a UML class, may include both structural and behavioral features, such as properties and operations. A block can include properties to specify its values, parts, and references to other blocks.

> *A SysML **block definition diagram (bdd)** defines features of blocks and relationships between blocks, such as associations, generalizations, and dependencies.*

The block definition diagram captures the definition of blocks in terms of properties and operations, and relationships, such as a system hierarchy or a system classification tree. A related SysML diagram is the *internal block diagram (ibd)*, which captures the internal structure of a block in terms of properties and connectors between properties.

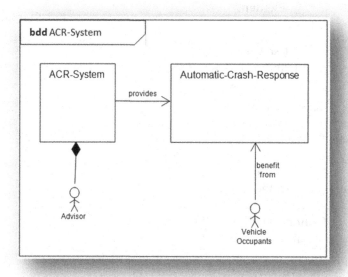

Fig. 4.2 A preliminary block definition diagram of the Automatic Crash Response (ACR) system

Figure 4.2 is a preliminary block definition diagram (bdd) of the Automatic Crash Response (ACR) system. The diagramKind, **bdd**, denotes this. This bdd expresses the two major blocks of the system and the relation between them, as well as the major actors and their relations the blocks.

This two blocks in the bdd are ACR-System and Automatic-Crash-Response. They are linked by the ReferenceAssociation labeled "provides". Advisor is shown as an actor which is part of the ACR-System. This whole-part relation is expressed by the black diamond, the SysML symbol for whole-part relation.

Vehicle Occupants is another actor. It is linked by the ReferenceAssociation labeled "benefit from" to the Automatic-Crash-Response block (Fig. 4.2).

Table 4.2 The main elements of a block definition diagram, their semantics and symbols

Element: Semantics	Symbol
Block A modular component which defines a collection of features to describe a part of the system or another element of interest.	«block» BlockName
Actor: An external entity that interacts with the system and can get services from it	ActorName «actor» **ActorName**
ReferenceAssociation: A link between blocks indicating the nature of their association	► association1 property1 0..1 {ordered} 1..*
PartAssociation: A link between blocks indicating that the block linked to the diamond is the whole	association1 property1 0..1 {ordered} 1..*
Generalization: A link between two block indicating that the block linked to the triangle is the general one	————————▷

4.3 SysML State Machine Diagram

SysML has a diagram type that is dedicated to modeling states of a block and possible transitions among them—the state machine diagram, or stm in short. Following the idea presented initially by Harel (1987, 1988), the SysML State Machine package defines a set of concepts that can model discrete behavior through state transitions. The state machine can represent behavior, expressed as the state history of an object in terms of its transitions and states.

Figure 4.3 is a SysML state machine diagram (stm) of the Vehicle Occupants Group. It is similar to the OPD in Fig. 2.3 in that both contain the same two states for the Vehicle Occupants Group. The stm symbol used to denote a state is a rountangle—the same as in OPM. The main difference between the two is that stm is not of the entire ACR system. Rather, it is only of the Vehicle Occupants Group block. The OPM process **Automatic Crash Responding** is expressed in the stm as a *trigger* by the same name, which causes the *transition* from the **possibly injured** state to the **being helped** state.

The black circle in Fig. 4.3 is the *initial state*. This state is referred to as a *pseudo state* since it is not a real state, just an indication to the diagram reader where to start. It is linked to the initial state, possibly injured, of the block whose state machine is modeled, which in our case is Vehicle Occupants Group. The black circle with the white rim in Fig. 4.3 is the final (pseudo) state—it is pointed to by the (real) final state—being helped. These two symbols enable identification of the initial and final states in a state machine diagram, respectively. As we shall see later, OPM denotes an initial state using a bold line of the state rountangle frame, and a final state—by a double rountangle frame. This eliminates the need for the two kinds of pseudo states that SysML uses.

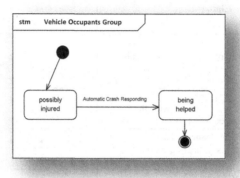

Fig. 4.3 A SysML State Machine diagram (stm) of the ACR system

Table 4.3 The main elements of a state machine diagram, their semantics and symbols

Element (node) name: Semantics	Symbol (Syntax)
State Machine Diagram: A diagram specifying possible states of a block, transitions between them, and conditions for those transitions.	stm OwnedStateMachine1
State: A situation a block can be at during its lifetime. Can be *simple* (atomic, non-decomposable) or *composite*.	State2
Composite State: A state enclosing lower level, possibly atomic (non-composite), states.	CompositeState1 State1 State2
Transition: A connection between two states specifying how states in a state machine change. Labeled by a trigger, which is associated with an event, optional [guard], which is a condition for the trigger, and \activity, which is a possible action done during the transition.	trigger[guard]\activity

Table 4.3 shows the main elements of a state machine diagram, their semantics and symbols. As the table shows, a state can be composite and contain inner, lower-level processes. A transition can be labeled, in addition to a trigger, also by an optional guard in brackets and one or more optional activities that syntactically follow the backslash symbol (\), which are actions done during the transition.

4.4 **Summary**

- SysML has nine types of diagrams that model various aspects of the system
- The use case diagram is often the first to be prepared since it provides the context of the system and how actors interact with it.
- Block is a basic unit, akin to class in UML, used in the block definition diagram and internal block diagram. It serves to define the structure of the system.
- State machine diagram is a SysML diagram that specifies the possible states of relevant blocks in the system and transitions between these states.

4.5 **Problems**

1. Draw a SysML use case diagram of the system described below.

> A passenger arriving at an airport deposits her baggage with the airline she is flying with. A baggage handling system manages the transfer of the baggage to the passenger's destination.

2. Draw a block definition diagram of the system in the system described above.
3. **Baggage Location** has states **passenger, origin airport, aircraft, destination airport, other location**. Model this using a SysML state machine diagram and indicate what causes transitions between states.
4. Compare the three types of diagrams created in the three problems above in terms of their information content.
5. What can be said about the system by looking at each diagram alone?
6. How can the information be integrated to obtain a complete view of the system?

Chapter 5
Refinement Through In-Zooming

The deepest parts of the ocean are totally unknown to us... What goes on in those distant depths? What creatures inhabit, or could inhabit, those regions twelve or fifteen miles beneath the surface of the water? It's almost beyond conjecture.

Jules Verne, 20,000 Leagues under the Sea (1869)

The previous chapters have exposed us to the basic concepts of OPM, yet we have barely scratched the surface of the system we are modeling. In this chapter, we specify more details about the system while revealing some more modeling concepts of OPM and how they can be utilized to represent our system in more detail. In order to examine the text that specifies the system we are modeling, we return our focus to information from the first sentences:

"The accelerometer ... measures the crash severity."

We combine this information with that from a sentence in the sequel:

"Within seconds of a moderate-to-severe crash, the OnStar module will send a message ..."

The text skims over important information that we need to glean indirectly. We have already modeled the fact that the **Vehicle** is (at state) **crashed**. The phrase "*moderate-to-severe crash*" indicates that we need to model the crash severity, as this determines whether a message will be sent. The implicit assumption, which we model here, is that if the crash is light, it is unlikely to have caused an injury, so the system should not be activated. Consequently, it makes sense to have **Crash Severity Measuring** as the next process to model.

5.1 Measuring Crash Severity

We have already determined that **Automatic Crash Responding** is the function of our **ACR System**. This is the main process in the system diagram, SD—the top-level OPD. The **Crash Severity Measuring** process, which we are about to model, is clearly not at the same level of centrality as **Automatic Crash Responding**. Instead, it is a *subprocess* of **Automatic Crash Responding**. Moreover, as we understand the system now, it is going to be one (perhaps the first) of several subprocesses of the **Automatic Crash Responding** function.

We could try modeling **Crash Severity Measuring** in a way similar to **Crashing**. However, this is probably not a good idea, for several reasons. Firstly, **Crashing** is an environmental process. Secondly, modeling **Crash Severity Measuring** at the same level as **Automatic Crash Responding** could be interpreted as meaning that these two processes are at the same level of importance, although they obviously are not. Thirdly, our OPD is already starting to be somewhat crowded, and we would like to keep it simple and readily understandable.

© Springer Science+Business Media New York 2016
D. Dori, *Model-Based Systems Engineering with OPM and SysML*, DOI 10.1007/978-1-4939-3295-5_5

5.2 In-Zooming: Refining a Process in a New OPD

New-diagram in-zooming is an OPM modeling process that creates a new, descendant OPD, in which the details of the in-zoomed process—its subprocesses and objects associated with them—can be specified. In our case, **Automatic Crash Responding** is in-zoomed, making it possible to refine this process by modeling its subprocesses and their interactions with lower-level objects in a new OPD at a level beneath the SD level. Figure 5.1 shows the **Automatic Crash Responding** process after it was in-zoomed and after its first subprocess, **Crash Severity Measuring**, was drawn inside it near the top of the enclosing ellipse of the **Automatic Crash Responding** process. The links that were attached to **Automatic Crash Responding** have migrated to be attached to **Crash Severity Measuring**.

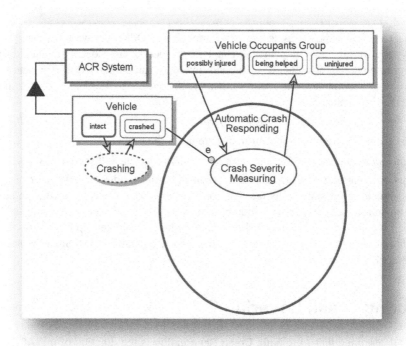

Fig. 5.1 The **Automatic Crash Responding** process is in-zoomed, showing its first subprocess, **Crash Severity Measuring**, nested inside it

5.3 The OPD Tree

The OPD in Fig. 5.1 does not replace the SD that we have been working on. Instead, it is a new OPD that comes in addition to and at a lower level than SD. SD is always the only top-level OPD—it is the *root* of the *OPD tree*. Figure 5.2, which is a screenshot of OPCAT, shows both the top-level OPD, *SD* (in the left window), and the new one, called *SD1—Automatic Crash Responding in-zoomed* (to the right of *SD*). Figure 5.2 also shows at the OPD hierarchy pane on the left hand side the OPD process tree, which currently has just two OPDs: SD and SD1.

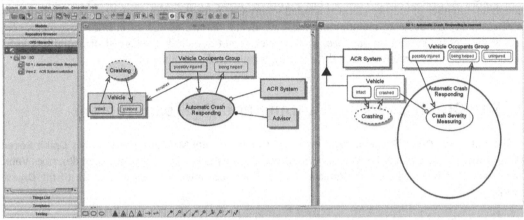

Fig. 5.2 A screenshot of OPCAT, concurrently showing two OPDs: SD (left) and SD1—Automatic Crash Responding in-zoomed (right). The OPD hierarchy tree is presented on the left pane

SD and SD1 are the two OPDs that currently constitute the *OPD set*; that is, the set of OPDs, organized as a process tree, which together specify the system. The OPD set keeps growing as additional OPDs are gradually constructed to increasingly refine the model and make it more concrete. The ability to add a descendant, subordinate OPD whenever the one currently under work reaches its congestion limits makes it possible to avoid over-cluttering any single OPD.

The OPL sentence that links the OPL paragraph of SD to the OPL paragraph of SD1 is:

Automatic Crash Responding from **SD** zooms in **SD1** to **Crash Severity Measuring.**

This kind of sentence indicates the hierarchical relationships between any two OPL paragraphs representing OPDs from adjacent hierarchy levels. In our cases, it indicates that SD1 is a child of SD.

5.4 The Model Fact Representation OPM Principle

The tagged structural link in SD from **Vehicle Occupants Group** to **Vehicle**, which in Fig. 3.3 is labeled with the tag **occupies**, is not repeated in SD1 (Fig. 5.1). This omission is a presentation choice based on the following *model fact representation OPM principle.*

> **The Model Fact Representation OPM Principle**
>
> An OPM model fact needs to appear in at least one OPD in order for it to be represented in the model.

This principle stipulates that it is enough for a model fact to appear only once in any OPD of the OPM model in order for it to be valid for the entire model. This principle does not preclude the possibility of representing any model fact any number of times in as many OPDs as the modeler wishes. However, although any number of entities can be included in any OPD, for the sake of clarity and avoiding clutter, it is often highly desirable to include only those elements that are necessary in order to grasp a certain aspect or view of the system. In our case, we have elected not to include the tagged structural link in SD1, as it does not add to comprehension of the point we want to make in this OPD.

5.5 The Crash Severity Attribute and Its Measurement

The first **Automatic Crash Responding** subprocess, **Crash Severity Measuring**, determines **Crash Severity**. **Crash Severity** is a new object not yet modeled. **Crash Severity** is not just a new object; it describes **Vehicle**. In other words, it is an *attribute* of **Vehicle**. This attribute becomes relevant as a result of the **Crashing** process.

*An **attribute** is an object that characterizes a thing.*

In our case, **Crash Severity** is the attribute that characterizes the object **Vehicle**. Figure 5.3 shows **Crash Severity** linked to **Vehicle** via an *exhibition-characterization* structural relation. The exhibition-characterization symbol is an equilateral black triangle inside a larger white one, like this: ◮. The tip of this triangle is linked to the *exhibitor*, which is the object **Vehicle**, and its base is linked to the object **Crash Severity**, which is an attribute of **Vehicle**.

As an object in its own right, this attribute has four states. More precisely, since states of an attribute are called *values*, **Crash Severity** has four values: **none**, **light**, **moderate**, and **severe**. These are shown in Fig. 5.3 inside **Crash Severity**. The OPL sentence that enumerates these values is as follows:

Crash Severity can be **none**, **light**, **moderate**, or **severe**.

As soon as **Crashing** occurs, the state of **Vehicle** changes from its initial **intact** state to its final **crashed** state. Upon entry of **Vehicle** to its **crashed** state, the state-specified instrument event link from the **crashed** state to **Crash Severity Measuring** initiates this subprocess. **Crash Severity Measuring** is the first (and currently the only) subprocess of the in-zoomed **Automatic Crash Responding** process. **Crash Severity Measuring** changes **Crash Severity** from its initial state, **none**, to exactly one of the three other states.

Figure 5.3 expresses this graphically by way of (1) the input link from the **none** value of **Crash Severity** to the **Crash Severity Measuring** process, and (2) the three alternative output links emanating from the same point on the ellipse of **Crash Severity Measuring** to each one of the three values, **light**, **moderate**, and **severe**, joined by a dashed arc. This dashed arc indicates the XOR (exclusive OR) logical operator among links. In OPCAT it shows up automatically only when the XOR'ed links emerge from a common point, as is the case here, or arrive at a common point (as in Fig. 6.2).

The facts that these three output links originate from the same point and that a dashed arc connects them together symbolize the XOR logical operator between the links: **Crash Severity Measuring** determines that **Crash Severity** can have precisely one of its three possible output values: **light**, **moderate**, or **severe**, but not any two or all three at the same time. Indeed, the OPL sentence that describes this state change is:

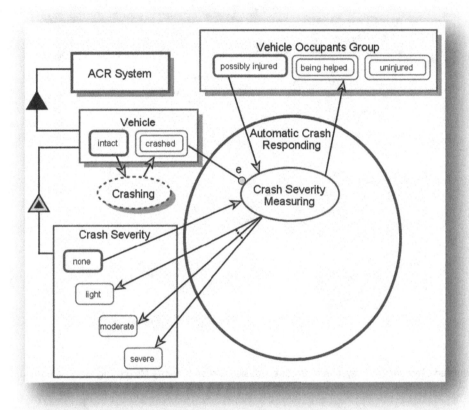

Fig. 5.3 **Crash Severity**, with its four states, is added as an attribute of Vehicle. The state **none** is the initial and input state, and **light, moderate,** and **severe** are the possible output states of the **Crash Severity Measuring** process

Crash Severity Measuring changes **Crash Severity** from **none** to exactly one of **light, moderate,** or **severe.**

5.6 Simulating the System: An Animated Execution Test

At this point, it is worthwhile to start carrying out an animated execution of the system at its current design, in order to test its conceptual operation. Figure 5.4 shows the system after the (environmental) process **Crashing** has changed the state of **Vehicle** from **intact** to **crashed**, which was the event that has initiated the **Automatic Crash Responding** process. Within this process, **Crash Severity Measuring** is about to be finished, changing the attribute **Crash Severity** of **Vehicle** from **none** to one of the **light, moderate,** or **severe** states.

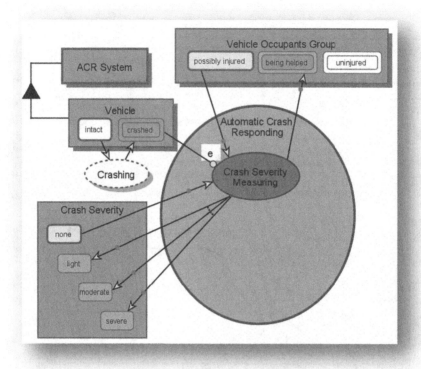

Fig. 5.4 Animated execution of the system at its current design: **Crash Severity Measuring** has just finished, changing **Crash Severity** from **none** to **severe**

5.7 **Summary**

- In-zooming is a refinement mechanism that helps manage system complexity.
- Zooming into a process creates a new OPD with an inflated in-zoomed process.
- Lower-level processes (subprocesses) are nested within this in-zoomed process and they can be linked to lower-level objects inside or outside the in-zoomed process.
- Recursive in-zooming results in an OPD set that has a tree structure, in which lower-level OPDs model increasingly refined details about the system.
- The model fact representation OPM principle stipulates that in order for an OPM model fact to be represented, it needs to appear in at least one OPD in order for it to be represented in the model.
- Using this principle helps decrease diagram clutter, making each diagram simple enough to be grasped without cognitive overload.

5.8 **Problems**

Continuing with the Baggage Handling System, let us assume that the current model is presented in Fig. 2.5.

1. Check if all the enablers—agents and instruments—of the **Baggage Handling** process appear in Fig. 2.5. If there are missing enables, add them.
2. What is the appropriate link type between **Airline** on the one hand and **Aircraft** and **Airline Personnel** on the other? Add the links the model.
3. What is the appropriate link between **Passenger** and **Baggage**? Add it to the model.
4. Which objects are physical? Express this in the model.
5. Which objects are environmental? Express this in the model.
6. Which objects in the model should be stateful? Add the relevant states to each such object.

Chapter 6

The Dynamic Aspect of Systems

The expert may, in the process of explaining some idea or description of a behavior, suddenly reach for pad and draw sketches of what he/she does, and say "it has to look like this" or "I know just by looking at the chart if something is wrong."

Firlej and Helens (1991)

Continuing with modeling our case study, in this chapter we further discuss process issues, such as execution order and how to specify that processes are sequential, concurrent, or alternative. These issues are related to the system's dynamic aspect and to its operational semantics.

6.1 Exiting in Case of Light Severity

Recall that the ACR system specification stipulates:

> Within seconds of a moderate-to-severe crash, the OnStar module will send a message …

Hence, if **Crash Severity** is **light**, we wish to model that the **Automatic Crash Responding** process is exited and the system finished its execution. To do this, in Fig. 6.1, we add to **Vehicle Occupants Group** a third state, **uninjured**, which is also final. Using a condition link (an instrument link with the control modifier c next to its circle end) we connect the state **light** of **Crash Severity** with a new subprocess, **Exiting**, which changes the state of **Vehicle Occupants Group** to **uninjured**. In this case, the execution of the system terminates. The semantics of the condition link is that if the object to which the link is attached exists, or if the state to which the link is attached is the current object state, then the process executes, otherwise the process is skipped. The condition instrument link semantics is weaker than that of the (non-condition) instrument link. The semantics of the latter is that if the linked object does not exist (or is not at the required state), then the execution of the system stops, waiting for the instrument to become existent (or at the required state).

6.2 Message Creating and Sending

We continue with modeling what happens in case **Crash Severity Measuring** has changed **Crash Severity** from **none** to **moderate** or **severe**, based on the following text:

> Within seconds of a moderate to severe crash, the OnStar module will send a message to the OnStar Call Center (OCC) through a cellular connection, informing the advisor that a crash has occurred. Based on the message received, the advisor sends help as needed.

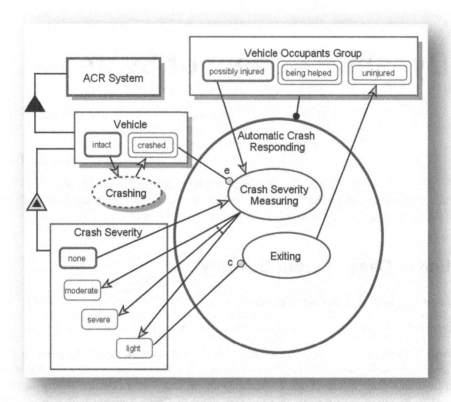

Fig. 6.1 **Crash Severity Measuring** has determined that **Crash Severity** is **light**, so Exiting changes the state of Vehicle Occupants Group to uninjured

According to this description, following **Crash Severity Measuring**, as a result of a crash whose **Crash Severity** is **moderate** or **severe**, a message is created and then sent via the OnStar Call Center to the advisor, who sends help based on the message. Accordingly, as Fig. 6.2 shows, we add three subsequent subprocesses: **Message Creating**, **Message Sending**, and **Help Sending**. The following OPL sentence expresses the XOR relation between the condition links from the **moderate** and **severe** states of **Crash Severity** to **Message Creating**.

Message Creating occurs if **Crash Severity** is exactly one of **moderate** or **severe**.

As we recall, the model fact representation OPM principle states that an OPM element needs to appear in at least one OPD in order for it to be represented. Based on this principle and in order to simplify the OPD, the environmental process **Crashing**, which appeared in Fig. 6.1, has been removed from Fig. 6.2. This enables us to add objects mentioned in the text that are relevant here: the **OnStar Call Center** and the **Cellular System**, which are parts of the **ACR System** (in addition to the **Vehicle**), as well as the **Advisor** and the **Message**.

6.3 Process Execution Order: The Timeline OPM Principle

Figure 6.2 shows that if the **Crash Severity** attribute of **Vehicle** has a value of **moderate** or **severe**, the **Message Creating** process creates **Message** within the scope of the **Automatic Crash Responding** process. **Message Creating** requires both **OnStar Call Center** and **Cellular System** as instruments.

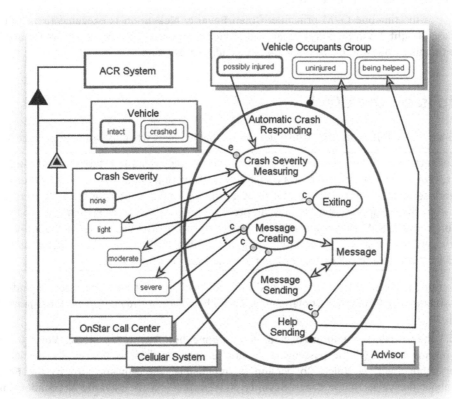

Fig. 6.2 **Message Creating**, **Message Sending** and **Help Sending** are added as three sequential subprocesses along with the objects OnStar Call Center, Cellular System, Message, and Advisor

The five subprocesses in Fig. 6.2 are arranged by their execution order (the timeline perspective) from top to bottom. This is based on the following *timeline OPM principle*.

The Timeline OPM Principle

The timeline within an in-zoomed process is directed by default from the top of the in-zoomed process ellipse to its bottom.

The timeline OPM principle is followed by default, unless there is indication to deviate from the timeline. Indications to deviate from the top-to-bottom timeline within an in-zoomed process include internal events within the scope of the process which can cause loops.

The top-most point of the process ellipse serves as a reference point, so a process whose reference point is higher than its peer starts earlier. If the reference points of two or more processes are at the same height (within some tolerance), these processes start simultaneously.

According to the timeline OPM principle, **Crash Severity Measuring** is executed first, followed by **Exiting** (in case of **light Crash Severity**) or, in case of **moderate Crash Severity** or **severe Crash Severity**, by **Message Creating**, followed by **Message Sending** and **Help Sending**.

6.4 Help Is on the Way!

We go on to model the following text, which describes what happens when the **Advisor** gets the **Message**.

A voice connection between the advisor and the vehicle occupants is established. The advisor then can conference in 911 dispatch or a public safety answering point (PSAP), which determines if emergency services are necessary, and if so, is it ambulance, helicopter, or both. If there is no response from the occupants, the advisor can provide the emergency dispatcher with the crash information from the SDM that reveals the severity of the crash. The dispatcher can identify what emergency services may be appropriate. Using the Global Positioning System (GPS) satellite, OnStar advisors are able to tell emergency workers the location of the vehicle.

This description covers a lot of ground and includes a number of new processes, including **Voice Connection Attempting**, **Public Aid Conferencing**, **Crash Information Providing**, and **Emergency Service Dispatching**.

Figure 6.3 shows **Help Sending** in-zoomed. **Voice Connection Attempting** creates **Voice Connection**, which can be **impossible** (if the passengers do not respond or there is no cellular connection; not modeled) or **established**. If **Voice Connection** is **impossible**, the **Advisor** informs the **Emergency Dispatcher** about the value of the **Crash Severity** and location via the **Severity & Location Informing** process. The **Emergency Dispatcher** is a generalization of **911 Dispatch** and **Public Safety Answering Point**.

If **Voice Connection** is **established**, the conferencing involves **Passenger Inquiring** by the **Advisor** and the **Emergency Dispatcher**. Either **Passenger Inquiring** or **Severity & Location Informing** determines the **Required Emergency Service**, which can be **none**, **ambulance**, **helicopter**, or **ambulance & helicopter**. This decision is used for **Emergency Service Dispatching**, which, if needed, sends the appropriate **Emergency Workers Group**, an environmental object, on its way to help, changing the state of **Vehicle Occupants Group** to **being helped**.

6.5 **Scenarios: Threads of Execution**

Figure 6.4 shows a specific tread of execution of **Help Sending**, which can be traced by following the state of each object. **Voice Connection Attempting** creates **Voice Connection** at state **established**, leading to **Passenger Inquiring**. If this process creates **Required Emergency Service** at state **none**, **Exiting** takes place, otherwise **Emergency Service Dispatching** takes place. Either way, the **Vehicle Occupants Group** transition to the state of **being helped**.

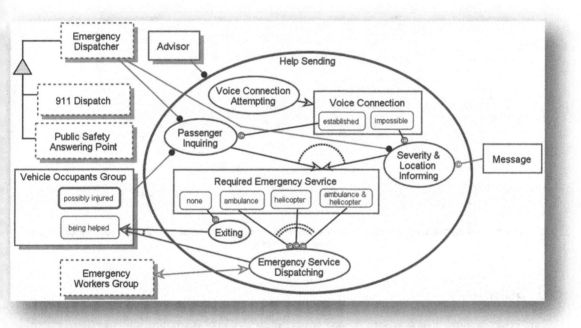

Fig. 6.3 **Help Sending** is in-zoomed, exposing four subprocesses that culminate in the **Vehicle Occupant Group** at the state of **being helped**. (Note: in this and in the next OPD the *c of the condition link* is drawn *inside the circle*)

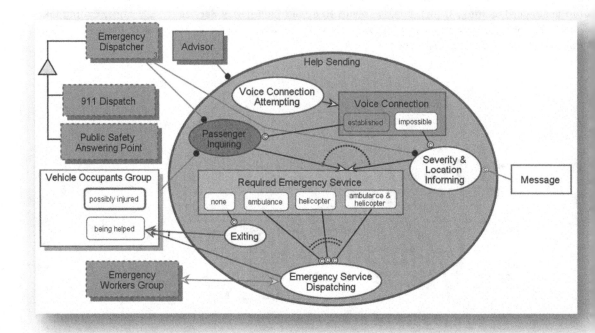

Fig. 6.4 **Help Sending** executed, showing a specific thread of execution in progress. It can be traced by following the state of each object

6.6 **Summary**

- The condition link semantics is that if the object to which the link is attached exists, or if the state to which the link is attached is the current object state, then the process executes, otherwise it is skipped.

- The XOR relation between procedural links indicates that exactly one of the possible interactions denoted by these links materializes.

- XOR is denoted graphically by a common point from which all the XOR'ed links originate or at which they terminate, and a dashed arc through these links whose center is the common links' point.

- The timeline OPM principle stipulates that the timeline within the context of an in-zoomed process is directed by default from the top of the in-zoomed process ellipse to its bottom.

- The subprocess execution order is determined by the height of the top subprocess ellipse points, such that the one at the top starts first.
- If the top ellipse point of two or more subprocesses is at the same height, within a predefined tolerance, they start simultaneously. This is the way to model process synchronization.

6.7 **Problems**

Let us consider the OPD in Fig. 6.5. It the OPD obtained by zooming into the Baggage Handling process in SD in Fig. 2.5, called "SD1 – Baggage Handling in-zoomed".

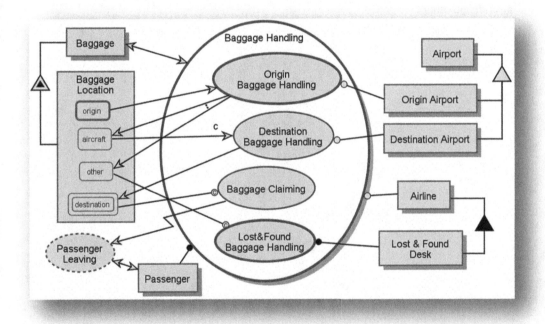

Fig. 6.5 SD1 – Baggage Handling in-zoomed, the OPD obtained by zooming into the Baggage Handling process in SD in Fig. 2.5

> **Baggage Handling** includes (1) origin baggage handling—airline personnel checking-in a passenger's baggage and loading it onto the aircraft at the originating airport, (2) destination baggage handling—unloading it at destination airport, and (3) returning it to the passenger

1. Model all the enablers—agents and instruments—of the **Baggage Handling** process.
2. Identify the three subprocesses specified in the frame above. Which subprocess appears in the OPD but not in the description above?

3. What is the appropriate structural link between **Passenger** and **Baggage** that would be consistent with SD (Fig. 2.5)? Add it to the model.

4. **Baggage Location** is an attribute of **Baggage** whose values (attribute states) are the various possible locations of **Baggage**. What are the four **Baggage Location** values in the model? What is the initial state and what is the final state? How can you tell?

5. Add to **Baggage** a second attribute, called **Baggage Holder**, with three values: **passenger**, **security**, and **airline**.

6. Show how subprocesses of **Baggage Handling** change the value of **Baggage Holder**.

7. How does **Origin Baggage Handling** change the state of **Baggage Location**?

8. What is the semantics of the dashed arc between the arrows from **Origin Baggage Handling** to **aircraft** and **other**?

Chapter 7

Controlling the System's Behavior

> *The picture... corresponds to the concept or memory image associated with the words.*
>
> Schapiro (1996)

Control in the context of conceptual modeling is the ability to determine the flow of processes and how they transform objects under various conditions and circumstances. Several control structures enable us to determine how the system will behave over time. These include Boolean objects for branching and control modifiers—condition and event indicators that are added to procedural links and augment their semantics. In this chapter we discuss and show how control structures are used to model system behavior.

7.1 Branching with Boolean objects

We often need to specify that if some condition holds, do something, otherwise, do something else. In programming languages we use the "if … then … else" or case statements. For example, in our ACR running example, let us focus on the first **Help Sending** subprocess, **Voice Connection Establishing**. The agents of this process are the **Advisor** and the **Vehicle Occupants Group**, while its instruments are the **OnStar Call Center** and the **Cellular System**. Going back to the **Help Sending** text, we read again:

> *A voice connection between the advisor and the vehicle occupants is established. … If there is no response from the occupants, the advisor can provide the emergency dispatcher with the crash information...*

This implies that we need to model whether the **Advisor** received a response from the **Vehicle Occupants Group** or not. What we need is a branching mechanism as in an "if… then" clause. The OPM solution to this need is a *Boolean object*. In most programming languages, a *Boolean variable* is a logical variable which can be represented by a single bit, since it has exactly two values, usually called *True* and *False*. Similar to this concept, an OPM *Boolean object* is an informatical object with two states, which is generated by a process calling for decision making. In other words, a Boolean object is a dual-state decision object that is generated as a result of the process of responding to the need to decide. The Boolean object is created in one of the two states. That state is the one which specifies the decision.

> *A **Boolean object** is a dual-state decision object that is generated as a result of the process of making a decision of choosing between exactly one of the two possible states.*

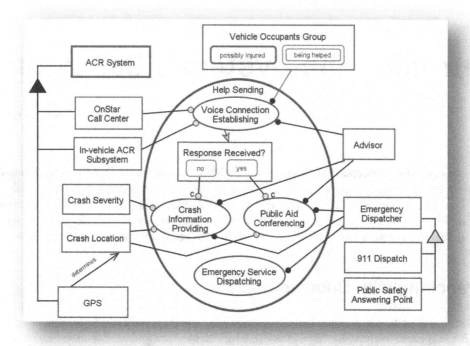

Fig. 7.1 The states of the Boolean object "**Response Received?**" determine the system's behavior

The name of a Boolean object may end with a question mark, in which case its OPL version is put in quotes, as in "**Response Received?**" The question should be phrased such that when combined with the answer using a state-specified instrument link or a condition link the resulting OPL sentence will make sense, although it might not sound very natural.

As Fig. 7.1 shows, the name of our Boolean object is "**Response Received?**" and it has the two states, **yes** and **no**. Each one of these states is linked with a condition link, denoted by the letter c next to the circle of (and in older versions inside) the instrument link. Each condition link is to one of the two alternative processes. Since by the definition of state an object cannot be at the same point in time in more than one state, "**Response Received?**" is either **yes** or **no**, as expressed by the following OPL sentence:

"**Response Received?**" can be **yes** or **no**.

Since both the **no** and the **yes** states are respectively connected to the processes **Crash Information Providing** and **Public Aid Conferencing** with condition (rather than instrument) links, exactly one of these two possible processes can occur: either **Public Aid Conferencing** occurs and **Crash Information Providing** is skipped, or **Crash Information Providing** occurs and **Public Aid Conferencing** is skipped. This is how alternative processes are modeled in OPM. In Fig. 7.1, these two alternative processes are at the same height to emphasize that one or the other happens, but not both. This is good practice that facilitates the diagram comprehension, but the flow of control would be the same even if the alternative process ellipse heights would not be the same.

> *A **Boolean pair** is a pair of inverse names for the states or values of a Boolean object.*

There are several predefined Boolean pairs that can be incorporated into an automated OPM-supporting tool. Examples include the Boolean pairs **true** and **false**, **positive** and **negative**, **black** and **white**, **on** and **off**, **up** and **down**, **black** and **white**, **good** and **bad**, **right** and **left**, **top** and **bottom**, **correct** and **incorrect**, **right** and **wrong**, **right** and **left**, **north** and **south**, **high** and **low**, **big** and **small**, **OK** and **not OK**, **approved** and **denied**, **passed** and **failed**, **greater than or equal to x** and **smaller than x** (which can also be written as **>=x** and **<x**, where x can be any input number), and **greater than x** and **smaller than or equal to x** (which can also be written as **>x** and **<=x**). In addition to these pre-defined Boolean pairs, the user can, of course, use any other Boolean pair simply by specifying the names of the two states of the Boolean object.

There is nothing methodologically special about a Boolean object that differentiates it from any other informatical object, except that is has exactly two states. In the general case, an object can have any number of states (including zero, in which case it is stateless). Having several states is akin to a "*case statement*" in programming languages, as each state, in turn, can be an instrument or a condition for some subsequent process. If a state-specified instrument link originates from the state, the semantics is "wait until the object is at the specified state." If a condition link originates from the state, the semantics is "do the process if the object is at the specified state, else skip this process."

7.2 Condition Link Versus Instrument Link

Two links originate from the "**Response Received?**" Boolean object. One is from the **yes** state of this Boolean object to the **Public Aid Conferencing** process, while the other—from the **no** state of this object to the **Crash Information Providing** process. These two links are condition links.

As Fig. 7.1 shows, a condition link is syntactically (graphically) similar to an event link, except that the control modifier (the letter inside the blank circle) is "**c**" (for condition) instead of the letter "**e**", which is the control modifier of the event link.

Semantically, the condition link is akin to an "if…then" command: If the object is at the state from which the condition link originates, then execution of the target process, i.e., the process to which the link's circle is attached, is attempted. If the object is not in the state linked to the condition link, or if not all the preconditions for the occurrence of this process are fulfilled, the process is simply skipped.

The preconditions for a process occurrence include existence of all the process' consumees (objects that the process needs to consume), affectees (objects whose state the process changes), which must all be in their input state, and enablers (agents and instruments).

This semantics is partly expressed by the two OPL sentences corresponding to the two condition links:

Public Aid Conferencing occurs if "**Response Received?**" is **yes**.

and

Crash Information Providing occurs if "**Response Received?**" is **no**.

Like an instrument link, a condition link can also originate from a stateless object (an object without states) rather than from an object's state. In this case, if the object exists (either from the beginning of the system execution or because it was created at some point during the system execution), then execution of the target process is attempted, and if not—the process is skipped.

Comparing the condition link to the instrument link, we see that the semantics of a condition link is weaker than an instrument link. This is so because in the case of a condition link, the process being triggered is skipped if not all the preconditions for the occurrence (execution) of that process are fulfilled. Conversely, in the case of an instrument link, the execution of the system halts and waits until all the conditions for the target process occurrence are fulfilled. In a programming language terms, the condition link is analogous to "*if...then*", whereas the instrument link is analogous to "*wait until...*" Indeed, the OPL reserved phrase of the condition link is "**occurs if**", while for the instrument link it is "**required**".

7.3 **Generalization-Specialization**

Let us now consider the text that follows:

*... The advisor then can conference in **911 dispatch** or a **public safety answering point** (PSAP)... If there is no response from the occupants, the advisor can provide the **emergency dispatcher** with the crash information.*

Three help entities are mentioned here: **911 Dispatch**, **Public Safety Answering Point**, and **Emergency Dispatcher**. From the text it is evident that the entity getting the crash information, **Emergency Dispatcher**, is a *generalization* of both **911 Dispatch** and **Public Safety Answering Point**. Conversely, **911 Dispatch** and **Public Safety Answering Point** are both *specializations* of **Emergency Dispatcher**.

Generalization-specialization is a powerful structural relation, which provides for abstracting any number of objects or process classes into superclasses. Syntactically, the generalization-specialization relation is a white triangle whose tip is linked to the generalizing link and whose base—to the specializing ones. In Fig. 7.1, this link is shown connecting the general **Emergency Dispatcher** to the two specializations, **911 Dispatch** and **Public Safety Answering Point**. The OPL phrase expressing this relation is "**is a**" (or "**is an**"). The following OPL sentences express this:

911 Dispatch is an **Emergency Dispatcher**.
Public Safety Answering Point is an **Emergency Dispatcher**.

More succinctly, these two sentences can be expressed as one:

911 Dispatch and **Public Safety Answering Point** are **Emergency Dispatchers**.

Semantically, the generalization-specialization link induces *inheritance* of features, states, and links from the generalizing superclass—the general to its subclasses—the specializations. For example, the single agent link from **Emergency Dispatcher** to **Emergency Service Dispatching** in Fig. 7.1 is inherited to both **911 Dispatch** and **Public Safety Answering Point**. This is an example of the power of generalization and the inheritance it induces: instead of drawing six agent links from **911 Dispatch** and **Public Safety Answering Point** to each one of the three bottom subprocesses in Fig. 7.1, only three are drawn, but they are interpreted as six.

7.4 Zooming into Crash Severity Measuring

We left some of the system specification early in the text, so this part is not yet modeled. Let us back up and complete the model based on what we read:

> *The ... ACR system uses front and side sensors as well as the sensing capabilities of the Sensing and Diagnostic Module (SDM) itself. The accelerometer located within the SDM measures the crash severity.*

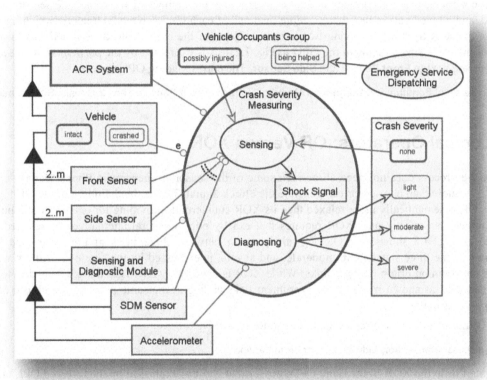

Fig. 7.2 Zooming into **Crash Severity Measuring**

The focus here is on using sensors to measure the crash severity with objects that we have not yet included in our model. We already have modeled the process **Crash Severity Measuring** as the first subprocess of **Automatic Crash Responding** (see Fig. 6.3) and the **Sensing and Diagnostic Module** as the instrument of this process. Therefore, to add details, such as the various sensors and their sensing processes, what we need to do now is zoom into **Crash Severity Measuring**.

Figure 7.2 is an OPD in which **Crash Severity Measuring** is in-zoomed, showing that it consists of two subprocesses: **Sensing** and **Diagnosing**, which are performed sequentially in the top-to-bottom order of their appearance in the in-zoomed process: First **Sensing**, then **Diagnosing**. Not surprisingly, the **Sensing and Diagnostic Module** is the instrument for both these subprocesses. Therefore, the instrument link from this object touches the outer **Crash Severity Measuring** process, acting like parentheses in algebra to denote that it applies to all the subprocesses within it.

7.5 Participation Constraints

The instruments of **Sensing** are also front and side sensors, as well as a sensor inside the **Sensing and Diagnostic Module**, which we model as **SDM Sensor**. Since the number of front and side sensors in not specified, and all we know is that there is more than one of each kind, we model **Vehicle** (which, in turn, is part of the **ACR System**) as having two to many objects of the class **Front Sensor** and two to many objects of the class **Side Sensor**. In the OPD in Fig. 7.2, this is expressed by the *participation constraint* **2..m** appearing next to **Front Sensor** and **Side Sensor**. The corresponding OPL sentence is:

Vehicle consists of **Sensing and Diagnostic Module, 2** to many **Front Sensors,** and **2** to many **Side Sensors.**

7.6 Logical Operators: OR Versus XOR

The **Sensing** process does not need all or even some of the sensors to generate a **Shock Signal**—one is enough. Yet, more than one sensor can generate the **Shock Signal**. This is the definition of the OR logical operator. OR is semantically more relaxed than its XOR counterpart, providing for one or more inputs or outputs rather than exactly one. XOR requires that exactly one of several alternatives be selected. For example, as Fig. 7.2 shows, a XOR logical operation between three links of the same type from **Diagnosing** to the three states **light, moderate**, and **severe**, is expressed by the single dashed arc whose center is the common origin of these links. While XOR is denoted by one dashed arc, OR is denoted by two dashed arcs, as shown by the three instrument links ending at the same point on the ellipse of the **Sensing** process in Fig. 7.2.

The OPL sentence that expresses the OR operator is simply:

Sensing requires **SDM Sensor, Side Sensor,** or **Front Sensor.**

Comparing this to the XOR in the same OPD, we see that XOR is expressed by the reserved OPL phrase "exactly one of", as in the following OPL sentence.

Diagnosing changes **Crash Severity** to exactly one of **light, moderate,** or **severe.**

7.7 Crash Severity Measuring Refined

Reading the specification more carefully, we notice that we did not model the following sentence:

The accelerometer located within the SDM measures the crash severity.

Instead, in Fig. 7.2 we modeled the **Accelerometer** as the instrument for the **Diagnosing** subprocess. From its name, we deduce that the function of the **Accelerometer** is the measure acceleration, so although this is not explicitly specified, in Fig. 7.3 we add the process **Acceleration Measuring**, with **Accelerometer** as its instrument and **Acceleration Measuring** as its *resultee*—the object that results from this process.

7.8 Scope of Things: Signal as a Temporary Object

Inspecting the content of the in-zoomed **Crash Severity Measuring** in Fig. 7.3, we realize that in addition to the two processes it also contains two objects, **Shock Signal** and **Acceleration Signal**. Indeed, this is also reflected in the following three corresponding OPL sentences. The first one is:

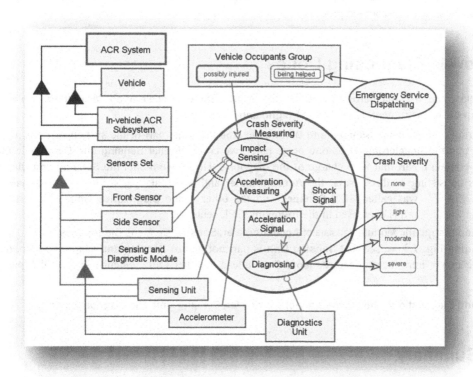

Fig. 7.3 **Crash Severity Measuring** refined

Crash Severity Measuring zooms into **Impact Sensing, Acceleration Measuring,** and **Diagnosing** in that sequence, as well as **Acceleration Signal** and **Shock Signal.**

This sentence lists the three subprocesses that get exposed in the in-zoomed **Crash Severity Measuring**: **Impact Sensing, Acceleration Measuring,** and **Diagnosing**. The reserved phrase "in that sequence" indicates that the top-to-bottom order in which the subprocesses are listed is their execution order. This list of processes is followed by the reserved OPL phrase "as well as", followed by the list of two contained objects: **Shock Signal** and **Acceleration Signal**. The reserved OPL phrase "as well as" separates between the list of processes and the list of objects in an in-zoomed process. The subprocesses are parts of the in-zoomed process while the objects are attributes of that in-zoomed process. For an in-zoomed object, the order would be reversed: The list of objects would come first, followed by "as well as", followed by the list of processes. In this case, the internal objects are parts of the in-zoomed object, while the internal processes are operations of that in-zoomed object.

The two informatical objects **Shock Signal** and **Acceleration Signal** are created inside the **Crash Severity Measuring** process by two of its subprocesses. They are then immediately consumed by the third subprocess, **Diagnosing**, and disappear. In general, objects inside an in-zoomed process are temporary: they exist and are recognized solely within the scope of that process. This would remain true even if we use two instrument links instead of the two consumption links. If we wish to preserve these objects, they must reside outside the in-zoomed process.

7.9 How Is Diagnosing Done?

As we retargeted the **Accelerometer** to be the instrument of **Acceleration Measuring**, we stripped **Diagnosing** off its instrument. How then is **Diagnosing** carried out?

Pondering into the name **Sensing and Diagnostic Module** as the part of the system that has a sensing capability and the **Accelerometer** as one of its parts, we conclude that **Sensing and Diagnostic Module** must also contain a part that is in charge of the diagnosis. Hence we model the **Sensing and Diagnostic Module** as consisting of three parts: the **Accelerometer** and two other parts. One is the **Sensing Unit** (which in Fig. 7.2 was called **SDM Sensor**), and the other is the **Diagnostics Unit**. This structure is modeled in Fig. 7.3 and is expressed in the following OPL sentence:

Sensing and Diagnostic Module consists of **Accelerometer, Sensing Unit,** and **Diagnostics Unit.**

Examining Fig. 7.3 we see that **Sensing Unit** is part not just of **Sensing and Diagnostic Module**, but also of the newly introduced object **Sensors Set**. Indeed, another OPL sentence in our OPL paragraph reads:

Sensing and Diagnostic Module consists of **Accelerometer, Sensing Unit,** and **Diagnostics Unit.**

7.10 Summary

- A Boolean object has two states and is used for modeling flow of control.
- A condition link has a control modifier c added to a procedural link, augmenting its semantics with skip meaning.
- Generalization-specialization is a fundamental structural relation that induces inheritance of features (attributes and operations), links, and states from the general thing to the specialized thing.
- Participation constrains enable specifying how many objects of the same class participate in a relation.

- OR is a relaxed version of the XOR logical operator that allows any subset of participating links to be active at once, rather than exactly one of them, as XOR does.
- Objects within an in-zoomed process are recognized only in the scope of that process. If they are used in places outside that scope they must be placed outside the in-zoomed process.

7.11 **Problems**

Figure 7.4 is SD1.1—Origin Baggage Handling in-zoomed. This is the OPD obtained by zooming into the **Origin Baggage Handling** process in SD1 (Fig. 6.5).

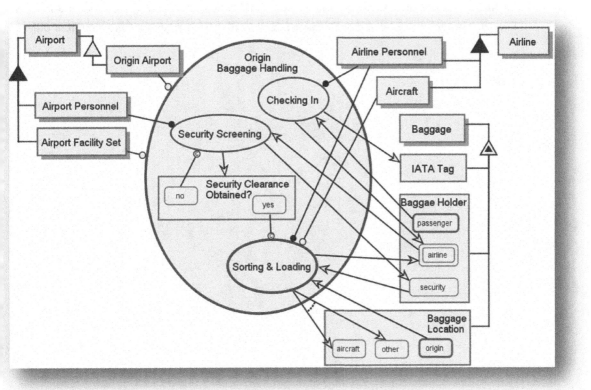

Fig. 7.4 SD1.1—Origin Baggage Handling in-zoomed

1. **Checking In** creates (yields) an object—what is it?
2. **Checking In** also affects another object—what is it? What are the input and output states of **Checking In**?
3. Who is the agent for **Security Screening**?
4. What object does **Security Screening** create?
5. What type of object is it?
6. Explain how this object controls branching.
7. What subprocess affects **Baggage Location**?
8. Can you find a loop in the OPD? Describe it.
9. How is it possible that in Fig. 6.5 the process **Origin Baggage Handling** changed **Baggage Location** from **origin** to either **aircraft** or **other**, while here, in Fig. 7.4, the process **Sorting & Loading** changes the same object, **Baggage Location**, also from **origin** to either **aircraft** or **other**?

Chapter 8

Abstracting and Refining

Make everything as simple as possible, but not simpler.
Albert Einstein

So far we always increased the refinement (detail) level of our model and we did it via zooming into processes. There are cases where we need to decrease the refinement level, or, in other words, abstract the model. This can happen when we realize that there are too many details already squeezed into a single diagram, making it too crowded and hence less comprehensible. We do not want to delete details of the model, as they are important for complete system specification. Yet we want then taken out of a specific crowded diagram. We do this by creating a new OPD at an intermediate detail level by zooming out of the too detailed OPD and creating one at a higher level of abstraction. In this chapter we focus on this abstracting process and then discuss and improve a structural view of the system.

8.1 In-Zooming: Refining a Process in a New OPD

Reading carefully the sentence:

> *Regardless of whether the air bags deploy, the SDM [Sensing and Diagnostic Module] transmits crash information to the vehicle's OnStar module.*

It looks like airbags are not really essential in our model. However, examining the sentence further, we notice that our model is missing a subprocess of transmitting the crash information from the **Sensing and Diagnostic Module** to the **OnStar Module**, which apparently is another part of the **ACR System** located inside the **Vehicle** that we have not yet modeled.

The natural place to add the **OnStar Module** object and the **Crash Info Transmitting** process is in the OPD in Fig. 6.2, which, for the sake of convenience, is shown here again as Fig. 8.1. As we see, this OPD is already crowded, so adding it **OnStar Module** as an object and **Crash Info Transmitting** as a fifth subprocess inside **Automatic Crash Responding** would further complicate it, making it even less comprehensible. An important objective in OPM modeling is to keep each OPD sufficiently clear and readable in order to avoid overwhelming the diagram reader. Thus, we need to figure out a way to add the new things without overcomplicating this or any other OPD.

Examining the four subprocesses in Fig. 8.1 we notice that the two middle ones, **Message Creating** and **Message Sending**, are of similar nature to that of **Crash Info Transmitting**, the new subprocess we wish to introduce. The solution will therefore be to merge **Message Creating** and **Message Sending** into a new subprocess which we will call **Message Handling**. Then, we will zoom into this new process in a new, separate OPD, exposing three subprocesses: **Message Creating**, **Message Sending**, and **Crash Info Transmitting**. The merging of **Message Creating** and **Message Sending** results in process *out-zooming*, in which two or more processes are abstracted them into a higher-level process.

© Springer Science+Business Media New York 2016
D. Dori, *Model-Based Systems Engineering with OPM and SysML*, DOI 10.1007/978-1-4939-3295-5_8

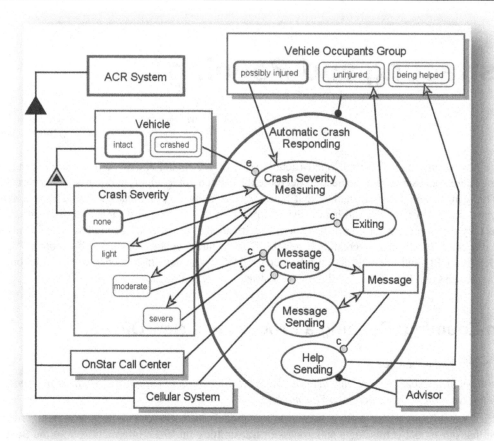

Fig. 8.1 **Message Creating** and **Message Sending** are about to be out-zoomed and replaced by **Message Handling**

Doing so has another advantage: in Fig. 8.2 we define an aggregate object, called **In-vehicle ACR Subsystem** as a part of **Vehicle**. Having done this, we can now model only **In-vehicle ACR Subsystem** as part of **ACR System** rather than modeling the entire **Vehicle** as part of **ACR System**. This new **In-vehicle ACR Subsystem** object consists of **OnStar Module** and all the other objects inside **Vehicle** that are part of the **ACR System**. This modification further simplifies the OPD. Figure 8.2 indeed looks simpler than its previous version in Fig. 8.1.

This simplified version enables us to explicate the relation between **Advisor** and **OnStar Call Center** without overcomplicating it. We add a tagged structural link with the tag **operates from**, yielding the following OPL sentence:

Advisor operates from OnStar Call Center.

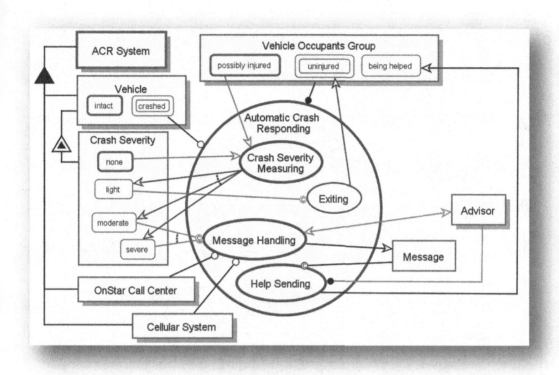

Fig. 8.2 Abstracting **Message Creating** and **Message Sending** from Fig. 8.1 into **Message Handling**. Link colors facilitate OPD comprehension and highlight the c of instrument condition links inside the circle

8.2 **Message Handling In-Zoomed**

Figure 8.3 presents the OPD in which **Message Handling** is zoomed into. We rename **Message Creating** to be **Crash Info Creating**. As the two XOR'ed event links from the **moderate** and **severe** states of **Crash Severity**, this process is triggered either by a moderate or a severe crash.

Only two of the four values of are modeled in Fig. 8.3: **moderate** and **severe**. To remind the diagram reader that there are additional values that are not shown here, the "at least one other state" symbol—a small state symbol with ellipsis (three dots)—is added at the bottom of **Crash Severity**. The corresponding OPL sentence is:

Crash Severity can be **moderate, severe,** or at least one other state.

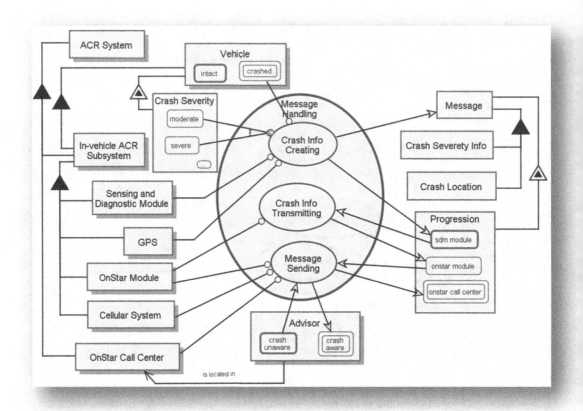

Fig. 8.3 Zooming into **Message Handling**

When a process like **Message Handling** is in-zoomed, there are initially no internal subprocesses, so all the procedural links that start from or end at the in-zoomed process are placed along that process ellipse contour. As the modeler specifies the internal subprocesses, each one of these links must be migrated (in GUI terms, its process end needs to be dragged) to the appropriate subprocess. Gradually, all the links surrounding the parent, in-zoomed process trickle inwards until none is linked to the parent process, as shown in Fig. 8.3. This should be done unless the link applies to all the subprocesses inside the in-zoomed process, in which case it should be left there. A link touching the parent process is supposed to be linked to each one of the subprocesses inside that process. An example appears in Fig. 8.2, where **crashed Vehicle** is instrument to all the four subprocesses inside **Automatic Crash Responding**.

The **Message Creating** process creates the informatical object **Message**, which consists of two parts: **Crash Severity Info** and **Crash Location**. **Crash Severity Info** is created by the **Sensing and Diagnostic Module**, while **Crash Location**—by the **GPS**. These two objects are therefore modeled as instruments of **Crash Info Creating**. These details of which module creates what part are not modeled at this level; they would be shown in the next level down, when **Message Creating** is in-zoomed.

8.3 Structural View of the ACR System

As Fig. 8.5 shows, the structure of the **ACR System** has undergone quite a few changes. I would be beneficial to examine the entire structure alone without any dynamic aspects of processes and state transitions. OPCAT provides such an automatic facility. Figure 8.4 shows the automatically-generated *structural view* of the **ACR System**, after manual rearrangements for improved readability. A four-level hierarchy is exposed, which is also expressed in the following OPL sentences, where the indentation helps realize the hierarchy.

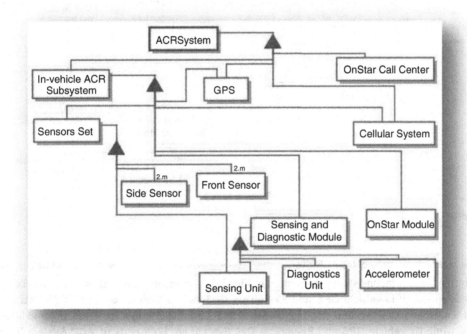

ACR System consists of **OnStar Call Center, Cellular System, GPS,** and **In-vehicle ACR Subsystem**.
In-vehicle ACR Subsystem consists of **Sensing and Diagnostic Module, Cellular System, GPS, OnStar Module,** and **Sensors Set**.
Sensing and Diagnostic Module consists of **Accelerometer, Sensing Unit,** and **Diagnostics Unit**.
Sensors Set consists of **2** to many **Front Sensors, 2** to many **Side Sensors,** and **Sensing Unit**.

Fig. 8.4 The automatically-generated structural hierarchy of the **ACR** System

Examining the OPD and the corresponding OPL, two objects stick out as ones in need of remodeling: **GPS** and **Cellular System**. The reason is that each one of these objects is part of both **ACR Subsystem** and **In-vehicle ACR Subsystem**. However, **In-vehicle ACR Subsystem** is also part of **ACR System**. While this is not a contradiction, it is an inconsistency, because **GPS** and **Cellular System** are both direct and indirect parts of **ACR System**. As we know, neither **GPS** nor **Cellular System** in their entirety are parts of the **In-vehicle ACR Subsystem**; each has components both inside and outside the vehicle.

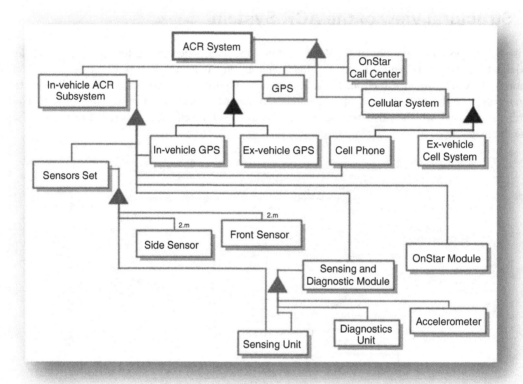

Fig. 8.5 The structural hierarchy of the **ACR** System after resolving the inconsistencies with GPS and Cellular System

The solution for this inconsistency, presented in Fig. 8.5, is to break each of these two objects into two parts: **GPS** is split into **In-vehicle GPS** and **Ex-vehicle GPS**, while **Cellular System** is divided into **Cell Phone** and **Ex-vehicle Cell System**. Both **In-vehicle GPS** and **Cell Phone** are parts of **In-vehicle ACR Subsystem**, while **Ex-vehicle GPS** and **Ex-vehicle Cell System** are both parts of **ACR System** but not of the **In-vehicle ACR Subsystem**.

8.4 **Summary**

- While the objective of OPM-based modeling is to go top-down and refine model facts as we go, to avoid diagram clutter it is sometimes required to abstract two or more processes in the crowded OPD and create a new OPD at an interim level.

- Abstraction can be achieved by process out-zooming: Creating an abstract process, which, when in-zoomed, will include the out-zoomed subprocesses (and possibly others).

- Right after a process is in-zoomed, all the procedural links are still attached to it.

- As subprocesses are added, procedural link edges should be dragged from the in-zoomed process ellipse to the appropriate subprocesses.
- Only links that apply to all the subprocesses inside the in-zoomed process should remain attached to the in-zoomed process.
- A structural view is achieved by removing all the processes and the procedural links from the model.
- The structural view enables focusing on the system structure and examining possible structural improvements.

8.5 **Problems**

During **Sorting & Loading**, the **Airline Personnel** carries out **Baggage Sorting**, changing the **Baggage Holder** from **security** to **airline**. This **Baggage Sorting** process can result in correct or incorrect sorting. If sorting is correct, Loading of the **Baggage** to the correct **Aircraft** takes place, so the **Baggage Location** changes from **origin** to **aircraft**. Otherwise, loading of incorrectly sorted baggage changes its **Baggage Location** from **origin** to **other**.

In the OPD SD 1.1.1 in Fig. 8.6, **Sorting & Loading** from Fig. 7.4 is in-zoomed. Referring to Fig. 8.6 and Fig 7.4, answer the following questions.

1. What is "**Soring Is Correct?**" what is it used for?
2. **Correct Sort Loading** is above **Incorrect Sort Loading**. Does this mean that the former process will always be performed prior to the latter? Explain.
3. Can both Correct Sort Loading and Incorrect Sort Loading happen in the same execution of Sorting & Loading? Explain.
4. Is it possible that when Baggage Location is other, the Baggage Holder is security?
5. Under what condition does the process **Sorting & Loading** takes place? Explain.
6. Why does only **Origin Airport** and not **Destination Airport** appear is the OPD?
7. In Fig. 7.4, there is a XOR relation to states **aircraft** and **other** of **Baggage Location**. When **Sorting & Loading** is in-zoomed in Fig. 8.6, this XOR relation does not show up. Is this OK? Explain.
8. Why is the XOR relation to states **aircraft** and **other** of **Baggage Location** needed in Fig. 7.4?
9. What two instrument links end at the **Sorting & Loading**? Explain the meaning of this, and why **Aircraft** is only linked with **Correct Sort Loading**?

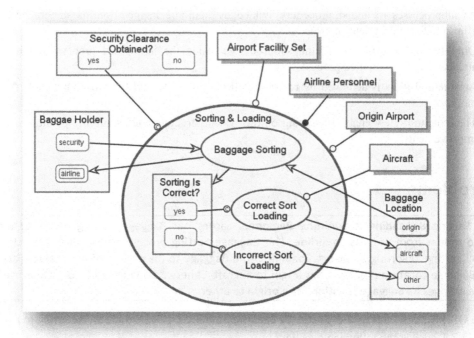

Fig. 8.6 SD1.1.1—Sorting & Loading in-zoomed

If the baggage is not located in the destination airport (**Baggage Location** is **other**), **Lost&Found Handling** occurs. The **Lost & Found Desk** uses the **SITA World Tracer** and the **IATA Tag** to locate the baggage. If it is located, **Corrective Handling** takes place, otherwise the passenger is reimbursed.

In the OPD SD1.2 in Fig. 8.7, **Lost&Found Baggage Handling** is in-zoomed. Referring to Fig. 8.7, answer the following questions.

10. What are the attributes of **Baggage**?
11. Under what condition does **Baggage Locating** happen?
12. What are the instruments of **Baggage Locating**?
13. What kind of thing is **Baggage Located**?
14. Can Reimbursing and Corrective Handling both happen at the same execution of Lost&Found Baggage Handling? Explain.
15. What states of what attributes of **Baggage** does **Corrective Handling** change? From what state to what state?

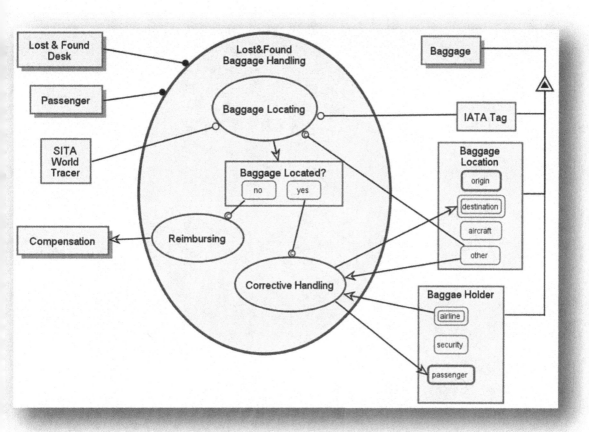

Fig. 8.7 SD1.2—Lost&Found Baggage Handling in-zoomed—the OPD obtained by zooming into the Lost&Found Baggage Handling process in SD in Fig. 6.5

Part II

Foundations of OPM

and SysML

Part I was an informal introduction to OPM and SysML, in which we used a detailed case study of the Automatic Crash Response system. We have discussed aspects of OPM and various SysML diagram kinds. Part II provides a more formal and theory-grounded exposure of OPM and SysML. It covers in an orderly fashion the ontology, conceptual modeling constructs, and applications. Chapter 9 introduces and defines what conceptual modeling is and what is its purpose and context. Chapter 10 presents the two basic building blocks of OPM—objects and processes. In a similar fashion to the way Part I is structured, Chap. 11 is about the textual modality of OPM—OPL. In Chap. 12 we turn to an orderly study of SysML with its four pillars and nine kinds of diagrams. The dynamic, time-dependent aspect of systems is the focus of Chap. 13. This is naturally followed by studying the structural, time-independent system aspect in Chap. 14. Following Chap. 15, which deals with participation constraints and fork links, in Chap. 16 we introduce the four fundamental structural relations. This concludes Part II. In Part III, titled *Structure and Behavior—Diving In*, we turn to elaborate on each of the four fundamental structural relations separately and continue with whole system aspects, including complexity management and control.

Chapter 9

Conceptual Modeling: Purpose and Context

> *A conceptual model is a formal model, in which every entity being modeled in the real world has a transparent and one-to-one correspondence to an object in the model.*
>
> Simmons (1994)

Before going into formal presentations of OPM and SysML as conceptual system modeling languages and OPM as a systems engineering methodology, we discuss the theoretical aspects underlying the framework of systems, systems architecture, and systems engineering, within which conceptual modeling is a valuable intellectual activity.

9.1 Systems, Modeling, and Systems Engineering

Systems are all around us. Natural systems have been around for eons, and biological organisms have evolved into extremely complex systems. Artificial, human-made systems, products, and services are also becoming increasingly complex. Systems of infrastructural nature, such as air traffic control, the Internet, and electronic economy, are orders of magnitude more complex than products individuals normally use. The combination of miniaturization and computational power has been so pervasive that even common household products exhibit intelligent features embedded within increasingly minuscule, commodity-like hardware, giving rise to the emerging Internet of Things—a conglomerate of weakly interconnected devices of all kinds, creating a loosely coupled mega system-of-systems.

9.1.1 Science and Engineering: Commonalities and Differences

The main difference between *science* and *engineering* is that scientists aim to explore and understand observable physical, informatical (cybernetic) and human phenomena, while engineers, who are informed by scientific discoveries, architect, design, develop, maintain and evolve artificial systems for the benefit of humans. Sometimes, engineers are required to perform reverse engineering—the exploration of an existing system whose function, structure, behavior, or working principles are not available and unknown.

Considering this exploratory character of reverse engineering, *science* can be thought of as *reverse engineering of nature*. When a system is being designed (by engineers) or investigated (by scientists), details about it accumulate quickly. The collected facts, be they real, assumed, contemplated or conjectured, become so voluminous that they are hard to master without an orderly way of making sense of what is being revealed. Managing these facts is mandatory in order for them to make sense as a whole. In view of the rapid development of systems' complexities, the need for an intuitive yet formal way of documenting designs of new systems or collected information about existing ones becomes ever more

© Springer Science+Business Media New York 2016
D. Dori, *Model-Based Systems Engineering with OPM and SysML*, DOI 10.1007/978-1-4939-3295-5_9

apparent. This, in turn, requires a solid infrastructure for recording, storing, organizing, querying, and presenting the knowledge being accumulated and the creative ideas that build on this knowledge.

9.1.2 Conceptual Modeling and Model-Based Systems Engineering

The process of representing system-related knowledge in both science and engineering is conventionally referred to as *conceptual modeling*, and the outcome of this activity is a *conceptual model*. Subsequent, higher order cognitive activities, including understanding, analyzing, designing, presenting, and communicating the analysis findings and design ideas, can be based on the evolving conceptual model.

The vision of the Massachusetts Institute of Technology Engineering Systems Division (MIT ESD, 2015) is that "the fundamental principles and properties of engineering systems are well-understood, so that these systems can be **modeled**, **designed**, and **managed** effectively."

Conceptual modeling, which often precedes or done alongside mathematical and physical modeling, is the primary activity required for engineering systems to be understood, designed, and managed. Modeling is the process underlying **model-based systems engineering** (MBSE), the focus of this book. MBSE is not just about modeling, as some people mistakenly perceive; it is systems engineering (SE) that is based on formal modeling of various kinds—conceptual, mathematical, and physical). The conceptual model is the comprehensive underlying blueprint—the reference artifact that constitutes the source of authority of the various system aspects—requirements, performance, functionality, structure, dynamics, and many other physical and informatical (cybernetic) aspects. Thus, MBSE requires a rigorous conceptual modeling methodology that encompasses a universal ontology, a language, a set of principles and guideline, and a supportive modeling software environment.

Understanding physical, biological, artificial, and social systems requires a well-founded, formal, yet intuitive methodology and language that is capable of modeling the complexities inherent in these systems in a coherent, straightforward manner. The same modeling paradigm, the heart of the methodology, should serve for both designing new systems (engineering) and for studying (science) and improving existing ones. It should apply to artificial as well as natural systems and represent both equally faithfully. A common, unified conceptual modeling framework for both artificial and natural systems is most important, because complex engineered systems and physical phenomena often mutually affect each other. For example, in order to model a system such as an aircraft, a satellite, a ballistic missile defense system, or a medical device, one must understand the relevant mechanical, electrical, chemical, biological, and physical principles that govern both the system and the environment in which it operates and with which it interacts.

9.2 A Foundational Systems Engineering OPM Ontology

> **Ontology** *is a set of concepts and their relations in some domain of discourse.*

The size of the ontology is the number of concepts and relation in the ontology. Systems science and engineering are in need of a well-defined foundational, universal, general, necessary and sufficient ontology that would underpin concepts and terms it uses in order for them to be precise and unambiguous. The following *minimal ontology* principle provides a good starting point for our discussion.

> **The minimal ontology principle**
>
> If a system can be specified at the same level of accuracy and detail by two languages of different ontology sizes, then the language with the smaller size is preferable to the one with the larger size, provided that the specification comprehensibility of the former is at least comparable with that of the latter.

Not only does this principle make perfect sense; it is also in line with the long accepted Ockham's Razor (Ockham, 1495)—a principle attributed to 14th Century logician and Franciscan friar William of Ockham, England, which states that *"**Entities should not be multiplied unnecessarily**"* (in Latin: *"Pluralitas non est ponenda sine necessitate"*). Often called the principle of parsimony, three more useful variation on Ockham's Razor follow.

- *"When you have two competing theories that make exactly the same predictions, the simpler one is the better."*

- *"One should not increase, beyond what is necessary, the number of entities required to explain anything"* (Helighen 1997).

- *"One should always choose the simplest explanation of a phenomenon, the one that requires the fewest leaps of logic."*

The reason for adding to the minimal ontology principle the condition *"... provided that the specification comprehensibility of the former is at least comparable with that of the latter"* is that taken to extreme, one can argue that the binary code of 0 and 1 is the shortest, so it is the best. This is true for computers, for which real human comprehension is (still?) meaningless anyway. For humans, from a semantic viewpoint, a binary specification of any non-trivial system (e.g., a computer program in machine code, to make the case clearer) is completely undecipherable without disproportionate effort. Therefore we require that both ontologies enable specification (or modeling) of systems with about the same level of comprehensibility, or better yet, that the specification that uses the smaller ontology is more comprehensible. If the ontology is defined carefully and is grounded on deep philosophical foundations, there is not necessarily a tradeoff between the size of the ontology and the specification length or comprehensibility of the system modeled based on that ontology.

Ockham's Razor inspired also the minimum description length (MDL) principle (Rissanen 1978), a method for inductive inference that provides a generic solution to the model selection problem, i.e., how does one decide among competing explanations of data given limited observations. MDL is based on the insight that any regularity in a given set of data can be used to compress the data by describing it with fewer symbols than the number of symbols needed to describe the original data. In a similar vein, we formulate the following *minimal conceptual modeling language OPM principle*.

> **The Minimal Conceptual Modeling Language OPM Principle**
>
> A symbol system—a language—that can conceptually model a given system using ontology with fewer diagram kinds and fewer symbols and relations among them is preferable to a larger language with more diagram kinds and more symbols and relations among them.

Using the smaller ontology puts less cognitive load on the human modeler, making the conceptual model more comprehensible and communicable to all the stakeholders without compromising the fidelity and detail level of the model. We can rephrase the above principle almost inversely: A language with fewer symbols and fewer diagram kinds that is based on a universal ontology can describe any system with better comprehensibility than a language with more symbols and more diagram kinds.

Alleviating the human cognitive load is highly desirable, because the modeler must cope with the inherent, irreducible complexities of man-made systems to be built (systems engineering) or natural systems to be investigated (science), so reducing the unnecessary complexity (often called complicatedness) by providing a simpler language is of tremendous value.

9.2.1 Objects Exist, Processes Happen? Some Thought-Provoking Q&As

If we accept the minimal ontology principle, then we need to find the ***minimal universal ontology***—the ontology that is necessary and sufficient to model the universe and systems in it. We start by first asserting that anything in the universe either exists or happens. We proceed with a series of questions and answers designed to lead us to insights about a possible minimal universal ontology.

Q1: Assuming that everything in the universe is a thing, what can things in the universe "do"?

A1: *Things can **exist** or **happen**. Any thing can either exist or happen. Nothing can be said to neither exist nor happen, in fact or potentially, and physically or informatically.*

Q2: What would be a general name for all the things in the universe that ***exist*** or might exist physically or conceptually?

A2: ***Objects*** *exist or might exist.*

Q3: What are the things in the universe that ***happen*** or might exist physically or conceptually?

A3: ***Processes*** *happen or might happen.*

Processes cannot just happen in vacuum, without "doing" something, which leads to the next question.

Q4: What are the things to which processes happen?

A4: ***Processes*** *happen or might happen to **objects**.*

Q5: What do processes do to objects?

A5: *Processes **transform** objects.*

Q6: What does it mean for a process to ***transform*** an object?

A6: ***Transforming*** *an **object** by a **process** means one of the following three options:*

1. ***creating*** *(generating) an object,*
2. ***destroying*** *(consuming) an object, or*
3. ***affecting*** *(changing) an object.*

Q7: What does it mean for a **process** to *affect* an **object**?

A7: *A process affects an object by **changing** its state.*

*Hence, objects must be **stateful**, i.e., they must have states.*

Q8: In what way are things semantically associated? Is this the only way?

A8: *Things are semantically associated through **relations**. Relations are the only way we can think about the way things relate or refer to or are associated with each other.*

Q9: Is there a difference between how objects and processes are related?

A9: *Objects are associated to objects (and processes to processes) via **structural** (static) relations, while objects and processes are associated via time-dependent **procedural** (dynamic) relations.*

Q10: what are the two universal aspects, i.e., the two aspects from which things in the universe can be viewed, considered, and described?

A10: *The two universal aspects are (1)* **structure**—*the way* **objects** *relate to each other and processes relate to each other—and (2)* **behavior**—*the way* **processes** *transform objects over time.*

9.2.2 The Object-Process Theorem

The answers to the questions above can be thought of as *universal axioms*, because while they make sense, they are difficult to prove. If we accept these axioms, the conclusion is that things—stateful objects and processes—and relations among them are the only three elements needed to describe the universe! We can use the universal axioms to prove the following *Object-Process Theorem*.

The Object-Process Theorem

Stateful objects, processes, and relations among them constitute a minimal universal ontology.

Proof:
The proof is based on (1) necessity and (2) sufficiency of stateful objects, processes, and relations among them as the only three kinds of elements needed to constitute a minimal universal ontology. Accordingly, the proof is divided in two parts: necessity and sufficiency.

Part 1—necessity: Stateful objects and **processes** are necessary to specify the two universal aspects, structure and behavior: Specifying the **structural**, *static* system aspect requires **stateful objects** and **relations** among them. Specifying the **procedural**, *dynamic* system aspect requires **processes** and **relations** between them and the objects they transform.

Part 2—sufficiency: Things can either exist (we call these things stateful objects) or happen (we call them processes) and nothing else. Things can be associated with each other only through relations. Therefore, **things** (objects and processes) and **relations** among them are the only elements needed to specify facts or ideas. **Q.E.D.**

9.2.3 The Object-Process Corollary

The Object-Process Theorem gives rise to the following ***Object-Process Corollary***.

The Object-Process Corollary

Using stateful objects, processes, and relations among them, one can conceptually model any system in any domain.

Since according to the Object-Process Theorem stateful objects, processes, and relations among them constitute a minimal universal ontology, and the universe is the union of all the domains it comprises, this assertion makes sense. One possible exception to this is the subatomic particle quantum domain, where our macro-world distinction between objects and processes becomes blurry. For example, electrons and photons are described as both particles (objects) and waves (processes). As soon as we step into the atomic and molecular level, e.g., molecular biology (Somekh et al. 2014), the Object-Process Corollary becomes valid, and OPM becomes a viable and attractive modeling paradigm.

This first version of the Object-Process Corollary says nothing about the level of complexity of the systems that are amenable to being modeled with stateful objects, processes, and relations among them.

9.2.4 The Object-Process Assertion: The Basis for OPM

Combining the Object-Process Corollary with the Model Complexity Assertion, we get the following *Object-Process Assertion.*

The Object-Process Assertion

Using stateful objects, processes, and relations among them, along with refinement mechanisms of in-zooming and unfolding, one can conceptually model systems in any domain and at any level of complexity.

Combining the Object-Process Theorem, according to which stateful objects, processes, and relations among them constitute a minimal universal ontology, with the minimal ontology principle, the optimal conceptual modeling language must have just two types of concepts—*stateful objects* and *processes, collectively called **things**—along with **relations** among them. Collectively, **things** and **relations** are the only two OPM's **elements**.

Things in the same system must be related, either directly or indirectly. Graphically, these relation are expressed by *links*. Things and links are collectively called elements, and so *element* is the top-level OPM concept.

---

*An OPM **element** is a thing or a link.*

9.2.5 Why Not Just One Kind of Thing? A Graph with Nodes and Links?

One may argue that an even more minimalistic representation than three kinds of elements—objects, processes, and relations among them—could be just two: things and relations among them. Indeed, quite a number of knowledge representation frameworks have come up with this idea of representing knowledge via a graph with nodes of just one kind and links connecting them. Some of these frameworks, which vary in their level of formality, are surveyed in Dori (2004). These include the concept maps (Arnheim 1969), entity-relationship diagram (Chen 1976), semantic networks (Lehman 1999), conceptual graphs (Chein and Mugnier 1992), and systemigrams (Blair et al. 2007). Looking at examples of graphs expressed in these approaches, one quickly reveals that since there is only one kind of node, there is no distinction between an object and a process, so the ability to distinguish between structure and behavior—the two distinct facets that must be represented in any model—is severely crippled, or even nonexistent. At the small price of increasing the number of elements in the ontology from two to three, we gain a tremendous capability of concurrently modeling both the structure and the behavior of a system.

Indeed, objects are the things that *exist*. Relations among them constitute the *structure* of the system. This is the static, structural aspect of the system. To understand the system's dynamic, procedural aspect, to know what *happens* to objects in the system and how it operates to provide value, a second, complementary type of thing is needed—a *process*. We know of the existence of an object if we can name it and refer to its unconditional, relatively stable existence, but without processes we can neither tell how this object is created or destroyed, nor how its states change over its lifetime.

A *stateless object* is an object that has no states. A *stateful object* is an object that has one or more states. These states are *stable* in the sense that it takes a process to switch an object from one of its states to another, and as long as no process acts on the object, the object remains in the same state.

Figure 9.1 presents the main symbols of OPM. The symbols for object, state, and process are respectively shown as the first (left-most) group of symbols. The rest of the symbols are links: *structural links* are shown in the middle group and *procedural links*—in the right-most group. Their names and semantics have been mentioned in Part I, and will be further elaborated as we proceed.

Objects and processes, collectively referred to as OPM *things*, are the two types of OPM's universal building blocks. OPM views objects and processes as being on equal footing, so processes are not necessarily subordinate to or owned by objects. Symmetrically, objects are not necessarily inferior to processes, nor are processes necessarily owned by objects.

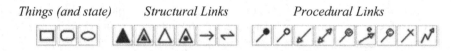

Things (and state)   Structural Links   Procedural Links

Fig. 9.1 The three groups of OPM element symbols

State is depicted in Fig. 9.1 between object and process. Discussed in more detail later on, state is a situation in which an object can be at some point during its lifetime.

9.2.6 The Thing Importance OPM Principle

In OO, objects "own" processes, which in the OO jargon are called operations, or services, or methods. OPM takes a different stand: Major system-level processes can be as important as, or even more important than objects in the system model. In particular, we already noted that the top-level process of a system (or subsystem) is its *function*, the top-level value-providing and purpose-serving process, for the performance of which the system is built and used. Hence, a process must be amenable to being modeled independently of any particular set of objects involved in its occurrence. Therefore, OPM views both *objects* and *processes* as *first-class citizens*. They stand on equal footing; neither has supremacy over the other. Rather, their importance is related the model hierarchy as expressed in the following *thing importance OPM Principle*.

> **The Thing Importance OPM Principle**
>
> The importance of a thing T in an OPM model is directly related to the highest OPD in the OPD hierarchy where T appears.

For example, the object **ACR System** and the process **Automatic Crash Responding** in Fig. 1.2 are of the same relative importance, as they show up for the first time in SD, the System Diagram, which is the top-level OPD. Indeed, the object **ACR System** is required for the process **Automatic Crash Responding** to take place, so one cannot argue for the supremacy of the object **ACR System** over the process **Automatic Crash Responding** or vice versa.

Being able to tell objects and processes apart and use them properly in a model is key to modeling in OPM. To define these fundamental concepts and to communicate their semantics, we next discuss the concepts of *existence* and *transformation*.

9.3 **Object, State, Transformation, and Process Defined**

Since objects OPM can be physical or informatical (cybernetic), we define object as something that captures these two facets without committing to either one, while including the element of "existence throughout time."

> *An **object** is a thing that exists or can exist physically or informatically.*

The object's existence can be physical or informatical. It can be as simple as a block of ice, a word in a book or a record in a file, or as complex as an organization, the Internet, a human brain, or a galaxy.

> *A **state** is a possible situation or position at which an object can be for some positive amount of time.*

This definition implies that a state has a meaning only within and in the context of an object. A state has no meaning out of the contexts of its owning object. For example, states of the object **Organization** can be **private** or **public**, and states of the object **Record** can be **locked** or **unlocked**. The states **private** and **locked** have no meaning outside the context of their respective owning objects.

> ***Transformation** is (1) creation (generation, construction), (2) consumption (elimination, destruction), or (3) effect—change in the state of an object.*

Transformation takes a positive amount of time.

> *A **process** is a thing that transforms an object.*

By this definition, a process must be associated with at least one object: the one which that process transforms. For example, **Freezing** is a process that changes the state of **Water** form **liquid** to **ice**. This is the basis for the *object transformation by process OPM principle*.

> **The Object Transformation by Process OPM principle**
>
> In a complete OPM model, each process must be connected to at least one object that the process transforms or one state of the object that the process transforms.

A non-trivial synchronous process (i.e., a process whose subprocesses have a defined order of execution) comprises a hierarchical network of subprocesses. At every level of the process hierarchy there is a time-induced partial order on the processes, i.e., some processes must end before others start, while others can occur in parallel to other processes or as their alternatives.

9.4 **System and Related Concepts**

Deferring the formal definition of system for just a little, this is a good place to add a couple of questions to our line of questions from Sect. 9.2.1:

Q11: What are the two main aspects all systems share?

A11: *Being part of the universe, all systems can be viewed from the two major aspects:* **structure** *and* **behavior***.*

Structure *is the static aspect; it relates to the question* **what** *is the system made of? From the structural aspect, a* **System** *is a finite* **set of components** *and their time-invariant interconnections.*

Behavior *is the dynamic aspect; it relates to the question* **how** *does the system change over time?*

Q12: What is the additional major aspect that pertains primarily to premeditated man-made systems?

A12: **Function**—*the utilitarian, subjective aspect:* **Why** *is the system built? For* **whom***?* **Who** *are the beneficiaries who gain from operating it?* **What value** *do these beneficiaries get from the system's operation*?

To some extent, biological organisms can be argued to be systems which provide functions that benefit themselves or other systems, but such (often mutual, e.g., symbiotic) benefits are a result of evolutionary processes rather than a premeditated intention, which is characteristics of humans as "tool building" organisms. Indeed, as the Smithsonian Institute (2015) experts indicated:

Spanning the past 2.6 million years ... stone tools provide evidence about the technologies, dexterity, particular kinds of mental skills, and innovations that were within the grasp of early human toolmakers...

Function is a key concept in man-made systems; it is a process which provides (functional) *value* to a *beneficiary.* The beneficiary is a person or a group of people, and the value is their *benefit at cost*—the difference between the system's perceived benefit and the system's cost. Based on this definition of function, we define system as follows.

> *A* **system** *is a function-providing object.*

This succinct definition is quite unorthodox. It is worth comparing this definition to the definition of system in ISO/IEC 15288 standard. According to ISO/IEC 15288, *system* is a *combination of interacting elements organized to achieve one or more stated purposes.* The standard definition is compatible with ours, since it contains the element of purpose, which is akin to function—providing value to some beneficiary. Our definition of a system is more general in that it does not require that the system be combined of interacting elements. While that description is generally true, it does not convey the essence of a system. In complex systems, and even more so in systems-of-systems, such as the international air-traffic control system, whose emergent function is to regulate the air transportation worldwide, there are numerous interacting physical and informatical parts, including airplanes, airports, communication networks, and air carriers.

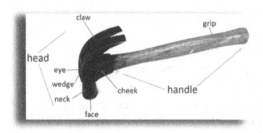

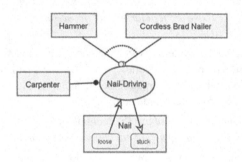

Nail **can be** loose **or** stuck.
Carpenter **handles** Nail-Driving.
Nail-Driving **requires either** Cordless Brad Nailer **or** Hammer.
Nail-Driving **changes** Nail **from** loose **to** stuck.

Fig. 9.2 Two concepts for a nail-driving system: Top-left: hammer; Top-right: DEWALT 18-Volt 18-Gauge 2 in. Cordless Brad Nailer; Botto-left: OPD of the Nail-Driving System; Bottom-right: The corresponding OPL[1]

In a simple system, such as a nail-driving system—the hammer shown at the top-left of Fig. 9.2, being a combination of two interacting elements—head and handle—the number of interacting parts is not the predominant feature. What is important is that the hammer is a system that provides the function of nail driving. Looking closely at this hammer, one can distinguish lower-level functional elements, such as claw to extract nails, but they are not really separate parts, further emphasizing the functional aspects of this system. The same function of nail driving can be accomplished by a much sophisticated system, such as the one presented on the top-right of Fig. 9.2. Although this is a much more complex system, it provides basically the same nail-driving function (and is indeed called "nailer").

The OPM model (the OPD and the corresponding OPL) at the bottom of Fig. 9.2 emphasize the common function of these two systems. The difference between the two systems is in several performance metrics that can be deduced from the following description, provided in the Web site of this product: "*The DEWALT DC608K—18 Gauge 2 in. Cordless Brad Nailer delivers consistent nail*

---

[1]From this point on, the OPDs are not shaded, as they are accompanied by their corresponding OPL paragraphs. The colors of the various OPL phrases in the OPL here are as they appear in OPCAT. In subsequent OPLs, reserved OPL phrases are in non-bold Arial font, and non-reserved phrases—in **Bold Arial**.

penetration into both soft and hard joints. The sequential operating mode allows for precision placement and the bump operating mode provides the user with production speed. The straight magazine, accepts 18 gauge nails ranging in lengths from 5/8 in. to 2 in. Its 12-position dial allows the user to move between applications without having to re-acquire exact depth setting." As we see, the function of this system is described as delivering "nail penetration", same as a hammer, albeit possibly with better speed, power, and accuracy. Thus, according to our definition of system, both hammer and the Cordless Brad Nailer are nail driving systems.

> A **subsystem**, *also known as a* **component**, *or a* **module**, *is a part of the system, which, in itself, does not provide the function that system provides.*

The system is comprised of subsystems or modules or components—all being objects—which only when put together deliver the (emergent) function, making it a system. This is a good place to define a system-of-systems (SoS), which in the sense explained below, can be thought of as the "opposite" of a subsystem.

> A **system-of-systems**, *(SoS) is a system whose set of subsystems contains at least two systems.*

This definition of SoS implies that a SoS is comprised of at least two components, each of which is a system in its own right, and therefore, by definition, has its own function. In other words, if we take a SoS apart, we will end up with at least two functioning entities. Since a SoS is also a system, it has an emergent function of its own in addition to the functions of its constituent systems. For example, the global air traffic control system is a SoS whose function is air traffic controlling. It is comprised of many systems, such as airports, national aviation authorities, national and international airspaces, the International Air Transport Association (IATA, the trade association for the world's airlines, representing some 250 airlines or 84% of total air traffic; IATA 2015), international air traffic communication protocol, emergency regulations, aircraft carriers, aircrafts, pilots, crews, passengers, and much more. Many of the comprising systems, such as airport and air carrier, are SoSs in their own right. Conversely, while a highly complex system, aircraft, for example, is not a SoS, because operating on its own, none of its components, such as wing or fuel tank or fuselage, can provide any substantial function. In the rest of the book, most of the claims about a system are applicable also to subsystems and SoSs.

9.4.1 Default System Naming

In spoken language, simple systems, such as a hammer, are often called tools, more complex systems, such as an electric current meter, are instruments, and yet more complex ones are "systems," but they all provide some function—their stated goal—and the difference between them is their level of complexity. A default system name is the name of the function this system provides followed by the word "system." For example, the system called printer, whose function is printing, can be called "printing system." A hospital is a health level improving system, a chair is a sitting system, a home is a residing system, a bathtub is a bathing system, and an airplane is a flying system. Indeed, searching the Web for images of a "bathing system" and a "sitting system", one gets an incredible variety, some of which are presented in Fig. 9.3, of what people refer to as bathing (top) and sitting (bottom) systems. The common function of the former is their ability to cleanse or sooth people, and the latter—to seat people with some level of comfort.

Fig. 9.3 Search results of images of "bathing system" (top) and "sitting system" (bottom)

Figure 9.4 is an OPM model of the **Nail-Driving** function and the **Nail-Driving System**—the instrument for achieving this function. The method used with each kind of **Nail-Driving System** can be captured in the diagram as a specialization of **Nail-Driving**. **Hammer** and **Cordless Brad Nailer** are two such specializations; they are incarnations of two different *concepts* for achieving the system's function: The **Hammer**, which is basic, and the **Cordless Brad Nailer**, which is more complex (and consequently more expensive).

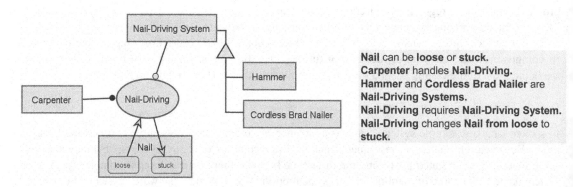

Nail can be **loose** or **stuck**.
Carpenter handles **Nail-Driving**.
Hammer and **Cordless Brad Nailer** are **Nail-Driving Systems**.
Nail-Driving requires **Nail-Driving System**.
Nail-Driving changes **Nail from loose** to **stuck**.

Fig. 9.4 OPM model of the Nail-Driving function and Nail-Driving System with its Hammer and Cordless Brad Nailer specializations

9.4.2 Involved Humans: Stakeholder, Beneficiary, Customer, User, Supplier

System *stakeholders* are entities that are concerned with the system.

> *A **stakeholder** is an individual, an organization, or a group of people that has an interest in, or might be affected by, a system.*

Below we define the main stakeholder types. One or more of the system stakeholders is the *beneficiary*—the stakeholder that extracts value and benefits from the system.

> *A **beneficiary** is a stakeholder who extracts value and benefits from the system.*

Customers (either real or potential) are key stakeholders.

> *A **customer** is the stakeholder who orders the system and sponsors its development, implementation, deployment, and support, or purchases a product that is part of the system.*

The first kind of customer in the definition above is usually an organization who needs a specially-designed system and orders it from the supplier (defined below). The second kind is usually an individual who purchases a consumer good that was designed and manufactured by a supplier based on the anticipation that people will be willing to pay for it because the customer foresees the value that this system (in this case product, defined below) would deliver. Either way, without customers it is hard to imagine why a system would be developed in the first place.

> *A **user** is a stakeholder who operates the system or directly interacts with it.*

For relatively simple systems, such as household products, the customer and the user are the same. For example, a car owner who drives it is the customer, user, and beneficiary, while other passengers are only beneficiaries. Beneficiaries of a national missile defense system are the country's citizens, although they are neither the users nor the customers. The supplier is another key stakeholder.

> *A **supplier** is a stakeholder who oversees the development, support, and maintenance of the system or product.*

Other stakeholders might include regulators, the judicial system, the public, and entities that might be affected by the system.

9.4.3 System Source: Natural or Artificial

Systems originate from a *source*, which can be natural or artificial (human-made). The source determines the mechanism through which the system has become functional. In natural systems, this is a result of the actions governed by the laws of physics. In biological systems, a subset of natural systems, principles of evolution play an additional critical role.

As this book focuses on engineering of artificial systems, from this point on, unless otherwise specified, the term *system* will refer to an *artificial* system. The mechanism through which a system is created and becomes functional involves some level of intellectual and physical human endeavor, be it as primitive and as rudimentary as it might be. When this endeavor becomes considerable and passes some threshold of complexity while showing signs of planning and coordination, we call it engineering, and more recently, *systems engineering*. Non-trivial systems, which are the focus of interest of systems engineering, comprise a significant amount of *processes* acting to transform a large number of interconnected *objects* (the system's components) in a way that enables the attainment of the system's *function*.

> A **socio-technical system**, *also known as* **engineering system**, *is a system that integrates technology, people, and services, combining perspectives from engineering, management, and social sciences.*

Products are designed and manufactured by a commercial entity and sold to another entity for profit.

> A **product** *is a commercially-viable system.*

Since a system is an object, a product is a commercially-viable *object*. Analogously, a service is a *process* that is sold by a commercial entity for profit.

> A **service** *is a commercially-viable process.*

Here we refer to a business service. In the world of software, a service is similar to a method, or an operation. More specifically, in Service-Oriented Architecture, the concept of service includes any interface provided by a component in the system to other components, and by a system to other systems.

9.4.4 Function, Structure, and Behavior Definitions Refined

Having defined beneficiary, we can now refine our definition of function.

> A **function** *of an artificial system is its top-level value-providing process, as perceived by the beneficiary.*

For example, the function of a hammer is nail driving, the function of a printer is printing, the function of chair is sitting, key and lock—locking and unlocking, window—ventilating and lighting, refrigerator—food shelf life prolonging, fire alarm—fire break alerting. More complex systems have higher-level, more abstract functions. Thus, the function of the system called hospital is patients' *health level improving*. Each patient is a beneficiary of this system, the customer may be a government or a private entity, and the medical staff constitutes the group of users. As another example, the function of a missile defense system is defending a country from a missile attack. The customer of the system is that country's government, the user is its military, and the beneficiary is the people living in that country.

At lower levels of subsystem or component, a subsystem's function can also benefit the system's higher-level function or other systems or subsystems. For example, Dictionary.com provides the following nouns for rudder:

1. Nautical: a vertical blade at the stern of a vessel that can be turned horizontally to change the vessel's direction when in motion.
2. Aeronautics: a movable control surface attached to a vertical stabilizer, located at the rear of an airplane and used, along with the ailerons, to turn the airplane.

In both the nautical and the aeronautics cases, rudder is a subsystem of a vehicle—a vessel and an airplane, respectively, with the function of changing course or turning or navigating the vehicle. This function of the rudder is part of the function of the vehicle, which is people and goods moving, and which requires also propulsion, supplied by the vehicle's propulsion subsystem.

Structure is the static, time-independent aspect of the system:

> ***Structure*** *of a system is its form—the assembly of its physical and informatical components along with the long-lasting relations among them.*

Behavior is the varying, time-dependent aspect of the system:

> ***Behavior*** *of a system is it dynamics—the way the system changes over time by transforming systemic (internal) and/or environmental (external) objects.*

9.4.5 The Need for Concurrent Structure-Behavior Modeling

During analysis and design, facts and ideas about objects in the system and its environment, and processes that transform them are gathered and recorded. For almost each process that is discovered or contemplated, the first questions asked refer to the objects involved in this process. Similarly, for each object identified in the system, a key question is what processes this object participates in. As soon as a new object is introduced into the system, the process that transforms it or is enabled by it begs to be modeled as well.

There is thus intimate cohesion of the two key system facets: structure (objects and relations among them) and behavior (processes and their relations to objects). Due to this structure-behavior complementarity, system analysts and architects intuitively and justifiably tend to model the structure and the behavior of the system *concurrently*.

With its single, unifying object-process model, OPM caters to this structure-behavior concurrent modeling requirement. It enables modeling these two major system aspects at the same time within the same model without the need to constantly switch between different diagram types.

For an investigated (as opposed to an architected) system, the researcher tries to make sense of gathered observations and to understand their cause and effect relations. In a sense, an attempt is made to reverse-engineer the system under study, which is the task of scientists. In both the architected and the investigated system cases, the system's structure and behavior go hand in hand, and it is very difficult to understand one without the other, so presenting both in the same single diagram makes sense.

9.4.6 System Architecture

With the understanding of what structure and behavior are, we can define a system's architecture.

> ***Architecture*** *of a system is the combination of the system's structure and behavior which enables it to perform its function.*

It might be interesting to compare our definition of architecture to the one used by the U.S. DoD Architecture Framework (DoDAF 2007), which is based on IEEE STD 610.12:

Architecture: *the structure of components, their relationships, and the principles and guidelines governing their design and evolution over time.*

TOGAF (2011) provides a similar definition in response to the question "What is an Architecture?"

*An **Architecture** is the fundamental organization of something, embodied in its components, their relationships to each other and the environment, and the principles governing its design and evolution.*

The common element in both definitions and our definition of architecture is the system's structure. However, the DoDAF and TOGAF definitions lack the integration of the structure with the behavior to provide the function. On the other hand, the DoDAF definition includes "the principles and guidelines governing the design and evolution of the system's component over time". However, these do not seem to be part of the system's architecture. Rather, principles and guidelines govern the architecting *process*, which culminates in the system's architecture. Interestingly, DoDAF Architecture Framework Version 2.02, Change 1 (DoDAF 2015), the version of January 2015 does not contain any clear definition of architecture (and neither does the 2009 edition)!

9.4.7 System Environment and Thing's Affiliation

In recent years, the term *environment* has increasingly taken on the meaning of the ecosystem of planet earth in which we all live and which is continuously compromised as a result of cumulative effects of large-scale man-made systems (such as power plants) and a large number of smaller scale man-made system (such as automobiles and aircrafts). Our definition of the system's environment is indeed compatible with this realization, as it provides for the possibility that the environment can change as a result of the system's function.

> *The system's **environment** is a collection of things that are outside the system but interact with it.*

The interaction of the system with its environment causes the system, and possibly its environment, to change. To ensure sustainability, systems engineers must make sure to prevent or undo this adverse change, especially as it pertains to possibly irreversible detrimental effects of current and contemplated systems on global warming and natural resource depletion. This is not just a moral or ethical obligation—it is a matter of securing sustainable life on earth of all organisms, including people, beyond the next couple of decades...

A thing which is part of the system is *systemic*, while a thing which is part of the system's environment is *environmental*. The OPM thing's attribute whose values are systemic and environmental is *affiliation*. Making the distinction between systemic and environmental things is very important in modeling, as it indicates what are the things that the architect can have control of and what should be considered as given. For example, in designing a gas station, is the car systemic or environmental? Obviously, cars and their drivers are going to interact with the gas station, but the gas station architect does not have a control over the sizes of the cars and the locations of their gas tank openings—these are given and must be accounted for. Therefore, car is environmental to gas station.

9.4.8 Function Versus Behavior

The above definitions lead to the conclusion that the function of a system is its top-level process. Moreover, the architecture of the system, namely its structure-behavior combination, is what enables the system to execute its top-level process, thereby to perform its function and deliver value to its beneficiary.

The value of the function to the beneficiary is often implicit; it is expressed in process terms, which emphasize *what* happens, rather than the *purpose* for which the top-level process happens. This implicit function statement can explain why the function of a system is often confused with the behavior or dynamics of the system. However, it is critical to clearly and unambiguously distinguish between the two, namely between function and behavior. Behavior is how the system changes along the time dimension. Function is what value the system delivers to its beneficiary through its operation. Hence, behavior is objective—it is the way the system changes, regardless of who describes the change, while function is subjective—it is the value gained from the beneficiary's perspective. This distinction between function and behavior is of utmost importance since in many cases a system's function can be achieved by different architectures, i.e., different combinations of processes (system behavior) and objects (system structure).

Consider, for example, a system for enabling humans to cross a river with their vehicles. Two obvious architectures are ferry and bridge. While the two systems' function and top-level process—river crossing—are identical, they differ dramatically in their structure and behavior. Failure to recognize this difference between function and behavior may lead to a premature choice of a sub-optimal architecture. In the example above, this may amount to making a decision to build a bridge without considering the ferry option altogether.

9.5 **Language and Modeling**

We now turn to definitions that concern language and modeling.

> *A **language** is a means of communication among humans, and possibly also machines, to express concepts, ideas, processes, and methods.*

A language comprises two components: syntax and semantics.

> ***Syntax** is the language's set of symbols and rules that specify how the symbols can be combined to yield syntactically-legal constructs.*

Not any syntactically-legal construct in the language is meaningful.

> ***Semantics** is the meaning that a subset of the language's syntactically-legal constructs conveys.*

9.5.1 Model and Modeling

Languages not only enable humans and machines to communicate; they are also means to building models.

> *A **model** is an abstraction of some portion of conceived reality (the system "as-is") or of a contemplated system (the system "to-be") expressed in some language.*

For example, a sufficiently detailed textual description of a machine part in free English text can be considered a model of that part. However, this model is not formal as it is expressed in English, a natural, non-formal language. Hence, at least with current technology, it cannot be automatically constructed or analyzed, requiring a human in the loop.

> *A **modeling language** is a language for constructing models in some domain.*
>
> *A **formal modeling language** is a modeling language that has a mathematically-grounded syntax definition, enabling its automated analysis, checking, and synthesis.*

For example, machine drawings of mechanical parts utilize a formal modeling language, drafting, in which symbols convey formal syntax with agreed-upon semantics that mechanical engineers understand and share. Thus, a dash-dotted line expressed an axis of symmetry, a dimension set with arrows, guides and a text box expresses a part's dimension, etc.

A formal modeling language is expressed using one or two *modalities*, i.e., modes of expression. Two prominent modalities for expressing models are *graphics* and *text*. OPM is unique in that it is the only known modeling language which uses these two modalities interchangeably and in tandem.

> ***Modeling*** *is the process of creating a model in some domain using a modeling language that is appropriate for that domain.*

Modeling is a foundational engineering activity. The resulting model is a centerpiece infrastructural entity that supports the evolution of the system throughout its lifecycle in a "model-based" or "model-driven" context.

9.5.2 Informal Versus Formal Models

People are used to freely drawing informal models of systems. The ad-hoc symbols in such models are inconsistent and cannot scale up, allowing for expressing only simple system ideas. An example of such an informal model is provided in Fig. 9.5. As the legend tells us, hatching of the boxes differentiates between lifecycle processes and the "product hierarchy". This ad-hoc model leaves many questions unanswered. For example, what is the semantics of the implied hierarchy? Is it aggregation? Specialization? Why does a system contain lifecycle processes alongside products? Why does one product consist of five subsystems and the other of none? Interestingly, this model appears in an international standard (ISO/IEC 26702 IEEE Std. 1220-2005), which, of all documents, should maintain the highest level of formality possible. Clearly, this model lacks formality and presenting it as part of an international standard can be more misleading than leaving it out.

> *A **formal model** is a model expressed in a formal modeling language.*

Continuing our machine drawing example, a part drawing is a formal three-dimensional model of that part. A CAD/CAM system which is designed to "understand" this language can automatically generate an actual part from this model. As another example, Newton's second law, $F = m \times a$, is a formal model of the relation between a rigid body's force, mass, and acceleration, expressed as a mathematical equation. Interestingly, however, the rigid body, with which this model is concerned, with mass and acceleration being its attributes, is nowhere to be found in this model. Rather, it is implicit that this is the subject of this model. This still conforms to our definition of a model as an abstraction of some portion of conceived reality.

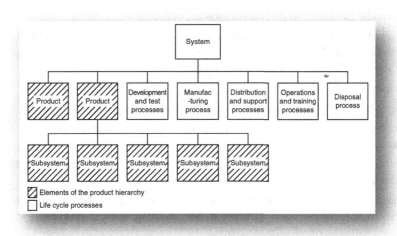

Fig. 9.5 An example of an informal model—Basic building blocks of a system (ISO/IEC 26702 IEEE Std. 1220-2005)

> *A **conceptual model** is a formal model of a system which expresses its architecture by depicting its structure and behavior to a level of detail that is sufficient for its subsequent detailed design and eventual materialization.*

The part of OPM that specifies how to construct Object-Process Diagrams (OPDs) along with their textual representations in OPL is an example of a conceptual modeling language. SysML is another example.

> *A **conceptual modeling language** is a formal modeling language for constructing conceptual models of systems.*

9.5.3 Complexity Management

In later chapters, we discuss in detail how OPM handles complexity management. Briefly, each thing (object or process) can undergo two refinement mechanisms: in-zooming and unfolding. In-zooming of processes specifies the subprocesses of a process and their temporal ordering. In-zooming of objects specifies the parts of an object and (roughly, to the extent relevant and possible) also their spatial ordering (currently only schematically and in two dimensions). Unfolding of things (objects or processes) exposes their parts, features (attributes or operations), specializations, or instances. Both refining processes—in-zooming and unfolding—can be done in the same OPD or in a new OPD. New OPD refining (in-zooming or unfolding) creates a new OPD in which the refined thing is elaborated to express more details.

9.6 **Summary**

- Science can be thought of as reverse engineering of nature.
- The Minimal Ontology principle states that if a system can be specified at the same level of accuracy and detail by two languages of different ontology sizes, then the language with the smaller size is preferred over the one with the larger size.
- Objects exist, processes happen.
- Ontology is a set of concepts and their relations in some domain of discourse.
- A minimal universal ontology is the ontology that is necessary and sufficient to model the universe and systems in it.
- The Object-Process Theorem: Stateful objects, processes, and relations among them constitute a minimal universal ontology.
- The Object-Process Assertion: Using stateful objects, processes, and relations among them, along with refinement mechanisms of in-zooming and unfolding, one can conceptually model systems in any domain and at any level of complexity.
- The thing importance OPM principle: The importance of a thing T in an OPM model is directly related to the highest OPD in the OPD hierarchy where T appears.
- An object is a thing that exists or can exist physically or informatically.
- A state is a possible situation or position at which an object can be for some positive amount of time.
- Transformation of an object is (1) creation (generation, construction), (2) consumption (elimination, destruction), or (3) effect—change in the state of that object.
- A process is a thing that transforms an object.
- The object transformation by process OPM principle: In a complete OPM model, each process must be connected to at least one object that the process transforms or one state of the object that the process transforms.
- A system is a function-providing object.
- A stakeholder is an individual, an organization, or a group of people that has an interest in, or might be affected by, a system being contemplated, developed, or deployed.
- A beneficiary is a stakeholder who extracts value and benefits from the system.
- A customer is the stakeholder who orders the system and sponsors its development, implementation, deployment, and support.

- A user is a stakeholder who operates the system or directly interacts with it.
- A supplier is a stakeholder who oversees the development, support, and maintenance of the system or product.
- A function of an artificial system is its top-level value-providing process, as perceived by the beneficiary.
- Structure of a system is its form—the assembly of its physical and informatical components along with the long-lasting relations among them.
- Behavior of a system is it dynamics—the way the system changes over time by transforming systemic (internal) and/or environmental (external) objects.
- Architecture of a system is the combination of the system's structure and behavior which enables it to perform its function.
- The system's environment is a collection of objects that are outside the system but interact with it, causing the system and possibly its environment to change.
- The function-behavior distinction: Behavior is how the system changes along the time dimension, while function is what value the system delivers to its beneficiary through its operation.
- A language is a means of communication among humans, and possibly also machines, to express concepts, ideas, processes, and methods.
- Syntax is the language's set of symbols and rules that specify how the symbols can be combined to yield syntactically-legal constructs.
- Semantics is the meaning that a subset of the language's syntactically-legal constructs conveys.
- A model is an abstraction of some portion of conceived reality or of a contemplated system expressed in some language.
- A modeling language is a language for constructing models in some domain.
- A formal modeling language is a modeling language that has a mathematically-grounded syntax definition, enabling its automated analysis, checking, and synthesis.
- A formal model is a model expressed in a formal modeling language.
- A conceptual model is a formal model of a system which expresses its architecture by depicting its structure and behavior to a level of detail that is sufficient for its subsequent detailed design and eventual materialization.
- A conceptual modeling language is a formal modeling language for constructing conceptual models of systems.

9.7 Problems

1. Referring to the OPD in Fig. 7.4, find:
   - A process which is more important than an object,

- an object which is more important than a process,
- an object and a process of equal importance,
- two objects of equal importance, and
- two objects of equal importance.

2. Explain why removing stateful objects, processes, or relations among them from the minimal universal ontology makes it unusable.

3. Model a small OPD which is syntactically correct but semantically not.

4. Explain the connection between the object transformation by process OPM principle and the definition of process.

5. Define two architectures for each one of the systems that deliver the following
   a. River crossing
   b. Time-of-day showing
   c. Food shelf-life prolonging
   d. Humans transporting
   e. Movie viewing

Chapter 10

Things: Objects and Processes

*Each convex mirror shall have ... marked at the lower edge of the mirror's reflective surface... the words "**Objects in Mirror Are Closer than They Appear.**"*

U.S, PART 571 Federal Motor Vehicle Safety Standards, Sec. 571.111 S5.4.2 (2004)

Immanuel Kant said that *"Objects are our way of knowing."* While this is obviously true, it is not the whole truth, but only about half of it. Objects are our way of knowing what *exists*, or in other words, the *structure* of systems. To know what *happens*, to understand systems' behavior, a second, complementary type of things is needed—processes. We know of the existence of an object if we can name it and refer to its unconditional, relatively stable existence, but without processes we cannot tell how this object is transformed—how it is created, how its states change over time, and how it disappears. These two fundamental concepts—objects and processes, generalized as things—are the focus of this chapter.

10.1 The Object-Oriented Versus The Object-Process Approach

As we saw in Sect. 9.2.5, objects and processes are the two types of OPM's universal building blocks, and processes are modeled as "first class citizens" that are not subordinate to objects. This object-process orientation is a principal departure from the object-oriented (OO) software paradigm, which places objects as the only major players. Objects "own" processes, which in the OO nomenclature are often called "operations" or "services" or "methods".

Major system-level processes can be as important as, or even more important than objects in the system model. Hence, processes must be amenable to being modeled independently of a particular object class. This is in line with the thing importance OPM principle, introduced in the previous chapter, which states that the importance of a thing *T* in an OPM model is directly related to the highest OPD in the OPD hierarchy where *T* appears. This object-process status equality paradigm enables OPM to conceptually model real-world systems in graphics and text.

Being able to tell objects and processes apart and use them properly in a model is a key to mastering OPM. To define these fundamental concepts and to communicate their semantics, we shall first discuss "existence" and "change," laying the foundation for defining objects and processes and distinguishing between them. We will then introduce the "essence of things" and examine the difference between "physical" and "informatical" things. The word *informatical*, or *cybernetic*, refers to a generalization of being related to data, information, knowledge, expertise, or ingenuity without any reference to their physical manifestation.

© Springer Science+Business Media New York 2016
D. Dori, *Model-Based Systems Engineering with OPM and SysML*, DOI 10.1007/978-1-4939-3295-5_10

10.2 **Existence, Things, and Transformations**

Webster's New Dictionary (1997) defines *existence* as the noun derived from exist, which is *be, have being, continue to be*. To exist means to stand out, to show itself, and have an identifiable, distinct uniqueness within the physical or mental realm. A thing that exists in physical reality has "tangible being" at a particular place and time. Because it stands out and shows itself, we can point to it and say: "Now, there it is."

To stand out means to present a stable form against a background of something else that exists. The notion of "background" is essential, for if there were nothing else that existed, there could not be the contrast of one thing standing out and distinguishing itself from a background of things that exist along with it. The stable form that the existing thing must exhibit is "substantially unchanging" long enough (relative to the typical rate of change of the background) for it to be recognized as "standing out." That which we cannot identify, nor have its identity be inferred in some way, can have no existence for us. In other words, "to stand out" requires a continuous identifiability over an appropriate duration of time, either physically or informatically.

Considering existence along the *time* dimension, there are two modes of "standing out," or existence of things. In the first mode, the "standing out" takes place during a positive, relatively substantial time period. This "standing out" needs to be observable in a form that is basically unchanging, stable, or persistent. We call that which stands out in this mode *object*. Webster's Dictionary (1997) defines an object as *a material thing; that to which feeling or action is directed; end or aim; word dependent on a verb or preposition*. The verb on which the object "depends" is the syntactic manifestation of process. Indeed Dictionary.com defines verb as "The key word in most sentences, the word that reveals what is happening." The pattern in our minds of "what is happening" is the process.

10.2.1 Object Refined

An earlier version of Webster's Dictionary (1984) provides a different set of two relevant definitions for object:

- *Anything that is visible or tangible and is stable in form.*
- *Anything that may be apprehended intellectually.*

These two definitions respectively correspond to our notions of *physical* and *informatical* (or *cybernetic*) objects. The first definition is the one we normally think of when using the term object in daily usage. The second definition pertains to the informatical, conceptual, cybernetic, logical, intangible facet of objects. Informatical objects are different from their physical counterparts in that they have no physical existence, so they are not subject to the laws of physics. However, the carrier of an informatical object is a physical object; the *existence* of informatical objects depend on their being symbolically recorded, inscribed, impressed, or engraved on some physical medium: a stone, papyrus, paper, an electromagnetic medium, or a group of neurons in a brain. This is where the physical and informatical aspects of an informatical object are tangential, giving rise to concepts such as noise and the correspondence between statistical mechanics and information theory through entropy (Shannon and Weaver 1949).

Since OPM objects are physical or informatical, we define object as something that captures these two facets without committing to either one, while including the element of "existence throughout time."

> *An **object** is a thing that exists or has the potential of physical or informatical existence.*

This definition is quite remote from the classical definitions of object in the OO literature, which can be phrased as "*An object is an abstraction of attributes and operations that is meaningful to the system.*" For example, in the eBook Object-Oriented Programming Basics with Java, an object is defined as "*an encapsulated completely-specified data aggregate containing attributes and behavior.*"

10.2.2 Objects and Human Memories

Qualifying the human brain as a tangible medium that can store intangible things may perhaps seem to some readers cynical or inappropriate. It therefore deserves special discussion and justification. The central nervous system, of which the brain is the major part, is the information system in humans and other organisms. It controls and regulates the entire organism. The human recollection or the mental record of a thing is still a mostly mysterious way that a thing is inscribed in one's mind, but progress in understanding brain structure and function is being constantly made (e.g., Kostovic and Rakic 1990).

Among many other, more elated capabilities of intelligence and emotions, the magnificent capability of the human brain to remember things qualifies it as a superb recording medium. A human brain stores vast amounts of data, information, and knowledge of various forms that are the essential basis for intelligence, including inference, prediction, decision-making and behavior. Human memories are not just a series of objects representing facts, images, faces, names, shapes, figures, forms, and symbols. They also include structural and behavioral relationships that exist among these objects, and the rules that govern them. Anything that is recorded in the human brain is an informatical object. This informatical object may be the record of some (tangible and/or intangible) set of objects and the processes that the objects in the set undergo.

10.3 **Object Identity**

The identity of objects is important, yet elusive. Physical objects must be treated differently than informatical objects. Since a physical object is made of matter (or energy, which, following Einstein's teachings can be converted to matter and vice versa), two instances of a physical object are identical if and only if they occupy the same space at the same time. This is possible if and only if the two are actually the same object, implying that no two distinctly identifiable instances of a physical object are the same. Thus, two new identical cars of Model X that just emerged from the assembly line are different instances of the same object class.

10.3.1 The Identity of Informatical Objects

The situation with object identity is different when informatical objects are concerned, since here the essential object feature is the idea, concept, pattern, or symbol it represents, rather than physical matter documenting it. From the physical medium point of view, each informatical object instance, such as a copy of the same book, is distinct, just like the two cars emerging from an assembly line. However, from the informatical point of view, all the physical copies of some informatical object are the same. Two copies of the same book are identical insofar as their informatical content (semantics) is considered. They are printed on separate pages and bound as two distinct physical object instances. Even if one copy is a paper copy and the other is electronic, from the informatical viewpoint they are still the same.

From the informatical viewpoint, two identical (paper or computer) files containing blueprints and manufacturing instructions for a Model X car are, the same object, because the informatical content they convey is identical. Physically, the pieces of media, on which this physical object is recorded, are different, since they are physical matter that obeys the laws of nature. Likewise, two copies of the same file are physically different, as they occupy different address spaces in the computer's primary or secondary memory. However, when viewed as informatical objects, they are identical.

10.3.2 Process as a Transformation Metaphor

We noted that there are two modes of standing out. The first is in space, the second—in time. In the time mode of "standing out", the standing out is still of an object, but this time it occurs "in a changing way" against a background, which is substantially stable. Because the object that stands out is undergoing transformation, it may have different names before and after the transformation. It is convenient to think of the thing that has brought about a transformation as some carrier that is "responsible" for this transformation.

When we are inclined to think in this way, what we really are thinking about is the patterned changing, the series of transformations that one object or more undergo. For the convenience of language or thinking, we associate this patterned changing with the "carrier," to which we mentally assign the "responsibility." We define *transformation* as a generalization of change, generation and destruction of an object.

> **Transformation** *is generation (construction, creation) or consumption (destruction, elimination) or change (effect, state transition), of an object.*

10.3.3 Process Definition Refined

According to Webster's dictionary (1997), a process is "a state of going on, series of actions and changes, method of operation, action of law, outgrowth." The American Heritage Dictionary (1996) defines process as "a series of actions, changes, or functions, bringing about a result." In Dictionary.com, verb, which is roughly the syntactic analogue of process, is defined as "The key word in most sentences, the word that reveals what is happening."

We call the carrier that causes transformation *process*, and we say that the process is "that which brought about the transformation" of an object. However, that carrier is just a metaphor, as we cannot "hold" or touch a process, although that process may be entirely physical, as it involves transformation of one or more physical objects. The only thing(s) we may be able to touch, see, or sense in any other way, is the object being transformed. We can measure one or more of the object's *attribute values* at certain points in time, or as the process is transforming that object. For example, we can measure the values (in degrees Celsius) of the temperature attribute of an iron bar object as it undergoes the process of heating, or we can touch it and feel it getting hotter relative to some past time point, but we cannot touch the heating process.

At any given point in time before, during, or after the occurrence of the process, the observed object can potentially be different from what it was in a previous point in time. Using our human memory, we get the sense of a process by comparing the present form of the object being transformed to its past form. Hence, *a process exists only as a concept, a mental construct in humans' minds*. We give names to processes to refer to changing patterns of objects. Focusing on transformation, we adopt the following definition.

Earlier we said that objects exist and processes happen. Here we just said that a process exists, but only as a mental construct. In this regard, we could think of processes as (mental) objects too, and devise a modeling paradigm that is based only on objects as "first class citizens", arguably having an even more compact universal ontology than OPM. Indeed, this is the object-oriented approach. However, as we show throughout the book, the value of adding process as a concept in the universal ontology that is separate from object far exceeds the price of adding another concept to this ontology.

> *A **process** is a mental construct representing a pattern of object transformation.*

This definition of process acting on an object immediately implies that no process has meaning unless it is associated with at least one object—that which the process transforms. The transformation of the object(s) is the necessary and inevitable result of the process execution. This is the first instance in which the symmetry between objects and processes breaks. While we defined and could refer to an object without necessarily using the term "process," the ability to define and think of a process, including its transformation, depends on the existence of at least one object being transformed by that process.

Referring to the syntactic meaning of object, Dictionary.com provides the following definition:

Grammar. (in many languages, as English) a noun, noun phrase, or noun substitute representing by its syntactical position either the goal of the action of a verb or the goal of a preposition in a prepositional phrase, as ball in John hit the ball...

Here, like in our definition, a linkage is made between the object and the verb, which is the process. In *John hit the ball*, hitting is the process and ball is the object. This example shows that it is often the case that the *syntactic* term object—that to which action is directed—coincides with the *semantic* term object. However, semantically, John is also an object (an instance of the object person), while syntactically it is a subject. The syntactic term *verb* is often analogous to the semantic term *process*. We elaborate on this in Sect. 10.6 when we discuss the process test.

10.3.4 Transformee Defined

When we say that the process brought about the *generation* of an object, we mean that the object, which had not existed prior to the occurrence of the process, now exists—it is identifiable against its background. Analogously, when we say that the process brought about the *elimination* of an object, we mean that the object, which once stood out, cannot be identified so it no longer exists. These radical changes of generation and elimination are extreme versions of transformation. A less radical transformation is change of the objects' states. The object which a process transforms is called *transformee*.

> ***Transformee*** *of process P is an object that P transforms.*

We use the suffix "ee", as in employee, here and in several other cases defined soon, to create a new word that denotes an object which a process (verb) X acts on. Here, X = Transform. We will soon encounter also Consumee, Resultee, and Affectee.

In a theoretic, frozen, static universe at absolute zero, no processes exist and no transformation occurs. Without processes, all we can describe are static, persistent structural relations among objects. In realistic earthly settings, processes and objects are of comparable importance as building blocks in the description and understanding of natural systems and the universe as a whole (which is the mission of science), and of designing artificial systems (which is the mission of engineering).

10.3.5 Cause and Effect

One insight from investigating the time relationship is *cause and effect*. Certain objects, when brought into the right spatial and temporal relationship (e.g., being at the "same" place at the "same" time), enable a process to take place, causing at least one object to be transformed: When the process is over, at least one of the objects involved (as input, output, or both) is transformed (consumed, generated, or changed). The "cause" in the "cause and effect" idiom is a triggering event that takes place in the concurrent or otherwise time-orchestrated presence of the collection of objects, some of which might need to be in a certain state. The "effect" in this "cause and effect" idiom is the transformation that one or more of these objects undergo.

For example, running of an internal combustion engine is contingent upon the presence of the objects air and gasoline vapor mixture inside the object cylinder at the right pressure and temperature (attributes of mixture). The triggering event is the point in time when a spark (created by a previous timed process) ignites the mixture. As a result of this process, the gasoline mixture is consumed and the piston's kinetic energy value increases. In feedback, cause and effect are circular: The effect at a given time is the cause for a change later.

10.4 Syntax Versus Semantics

To make it possible to refer to things (objects and processes) and distinguish among them, natural languages developed by humans to enable communication, assign names to the things. The name of a thing constitutes a primary identifying symbol of that thing, making it amenable to reference and human communication. These thing names are known as *nouns*. However, being part of speech, noun is a syntactic term, while objects and processes are semantic terms. We elaborate on this issue next.

10.4.1 Are Objects and Processes the Semantic Analogues of Nouns and Verbs?

In natural languages, almost invariably, objects are syntactically represented as nouns. Processes are syntactically often represented as verbs, but they can be nouns too. For example, brick is syntactically a noun and semantically an object, while constructing is a verb and a process. However, construction in the context of "the construction process" is also a noun, although semantically it is the same as "the constructing process." To make the point, we note that the phrase *the construction process* is plausible, while *the brick process* is not. Likewise, the phrase *the brick object* is plausible, while *the construction object* (where *object* is not referred to as a synonym for *goal*) is much less plausible. Even more confusing is the object building (noun), which is the outcome of the building (constructing) process. It is spelled and uttered the same as the process of building (verb). It is only from their context inside a sentence that these two semantically different words are distinguishable.

A common software design strategy is the noun/adjective/verb object oriented design strategy (MacIntyre 2010). In his blog, MacIntyre wrote:

… Then I learned C++, object oriented programming, and was introduced to the holy grail of object oriented design advice, which went something like this: Take your requirements and circle all the nouns, those are your classes. Then underline all the adjectives, those are your properties. Then highlight all your verbs, those are your methods.

This Noun/Adjective/Verb design strategy seemed like the most ingenious piece of programming wisdom ever spoken … but it's led us down a misguided path. It's the verb that's misunderstood. **The verb should be another class, not a method**. It should be a process class. As a programming concept, a process is just as much a 'thing' as any real world object. The verb should be a class, which accepts the noun as an input to be processed.

Interestingly, MacIntyre intuitively arrived at the conclusion that the verb is "*another class*" (emphasis in source). He realized that a process is not less important than an object, and therefore should not be a method owned by an object but a "process class" in its own right.

The examples discussed above demonstrate that the tempting assertion that object and process are the semantic analogues of the syntactic concepts noun and verb is at best crude and inaccurate. Hence, rather than relying on the syntactic notions of parts of speech, we need to establish a semantic, content-based way to analyze words in a sentence that would enable us to tell objects from processes. This will enable us to overcome the pitfalls and idiosyncrasies of natural languages.

10.4.2 Syntactic Versus Semantic Sentence Analysis

The difficulty we often experience in making the necessary and sufficient distinction between objects and processes is rooted in our education: As students in high school, we have been trained to think and analyze sentences in syntactic, parts of speech terms—nouns, verbs, adjectives and adverbs—rather than in semantic, deeper sense-making terms—objects, processes, attributes, and operations. This is probably true for any natural language we study and use, be it our mother tongue or a foreign language.

The same idea can very often be expressed by more than one sentence, giving rise to different assignments of parts of speech. *Semantic sentence analysis* is the dissection of a sentence by its semantics rather than its syntax. Only through semantic sentence analysis can we overcome superficial differences in expression and get down to the intent of the writer or speaker of some text. Nevertheless, the idea of semantic sentence analysis, in which we seek the deep meaning of a sentence beneath its appearance, is probably a relatively less accepted idea.

To apply OPM in a useful manner, one should be able to analyze sentences semantically. This primarily entails telling the difference between an object and a process. How to do this systematically is the topic of the next sections. First we define three sets of objects with respect to their participation and role in a process.

10.4.3 The Preprocess Object Set

For a process to start, it needs to be triggered. This triggering can be external, by an object becoming existent or available or by an object entering a certain state, or internal, by an event marking the end of a preceding process in the context of a higher-level, in-zoomed process. Once triggered, the process "tries" to operate (occur, happen, or execute). To this end, it needs to check for the existence of a set of objects—the preprocess object set—which would allow it to be performed.

> *The **preprocess object set** of a process P, Pre(P), is the set of objects required to exist, possibly in certain states, in order for P to start executing once it was triggered.*

The triggering object itself is not part of the preprocess object set. Existence of the preprocess object set, is the *process precondition*—the condition for the occurrence of the process. Being a process, the noun representing it does not exist, but rather occurs, happens, operates, executes, transforms, changes, or alters at least one other noun, which would be an object.

Let us consider two process examples: **Flight** and **Manufacturing**, shown in Fig. 10.1. In the **Flight** example (the OPD on the left), **Airplane**, **Pilot**, and **Runway** are objects in the preprocess object set, since **Flight** cannot occur without them. In set notation: *Pre*(**Flight**) = {**Airplane**, **Pilot**, **Runway**}.

For **Manufacturing** (the OPD on the right), the preprocess object set consists of **Raw Material**, **Operator**, **Machine** and **Model**: *Pre*(**Manufacturing**) = {**Raw Material**, **Operator**, **Machine**, **Model**}. **Product** is not in this set since it does not exist yet and is not needed for the process to start happening.

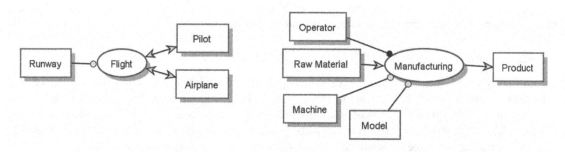

Flight requires **Runway**.
Flight affects **Pilot** and **Airplane**.

Operator handles **Manufacturing**.
Manufacturing requires **Machine** and **Model**.
Manufacturing consumes **Raw Material**.
Manufacturing yields **Product**.

Fig. 10.1 Preprocess and postprocess object set examples

There may be requirements on the states of some of the objects in the preprocess object set. For example, as the OPD on the left in Fig. 10.2 shows, in order for **Flight** to take off, it is required that **Runway** be (at the state) **open**. In set notation: *Pre*(**Flight**) = {**Airplane**, **Pilot**, **open Runway**}. In other words, this is expressed in the corresponding OPL sentence:

Flight requires **open Runway**.

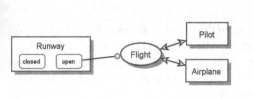

Machine can be operational or broken.
Model can be updated or outdated.

Flight requires open Runway.
Flight affects Pilot and Airplane.

Operator handles Manufacturing.
Manufacturing requires operational Machine and updated Model.
Manufacturing consumes Raw Material.
Manufacturing yields pre-tested Product.

Fig. 10.2 Example of a state-specified object, **open Runway**, in the preprocess object set of **Flight**

Similarly, as the OPD on the right in Fig. 10.2 shows, in order for **Manufacturing** to take place, it is required that **Machine** be **operational** and **Model** be **updated**. In this case, the result will be **pre-tested Product**. In set notation: Pre(**Manufacturing**) = {**Operator, Raw Material, operational Machine, updated Model**}. This is expressed in the three corresponding OPL sentences:

Operator handles Manufacturing.
Manufacturing requires operational Machine and updated Model.
Manufacturing consumes Raw Material.

10.4.4 The Postprocess Object Set

The postprocess object set is defined analogously to the preprocess object set as follows.

> *The **postprocess object set** of process P, Post(P), is the set of one or more objects that exist, possibly in certain states, after P finished executing.*

Existence of all the objects in the postprocess object set, some possibly in specified states, is the *postcondition* of that process.

The preprocess object set and the postprocess object set are not necessarily disjoint; they may be at least partially overlapping. In the **Flight** example in Fig. 10.1, all three objects in the preprocess object set, **Airplane, Pilot**, and **Runway**, are also in the postprocess object set: $Post$ (**Flight**) = {**Airplane, Pilot, Runway**}. We should note, however, that only **Airplane** and **Pilot** are transformed: their **Location** attribute change from **origin** to **destination**. In Fig. 10.2 this is not modeled explicitly, only implicitly, specifying that **Airplane** and **Pilot** each undergoes some state change.

In the **Manufacturing** example in Fig. 10.1, **Raw Material, Operator, Machine** and **Model** are in the preprocess object set, while **Operator, Machine, Model**, and **Product** are in the postprocess object set: $Post$

(**Manufacturing**) = {**Operator, Machine, Model, Product**}. **Raw Material** is transformed by being consumed, while **Product** is transformed by being created.

If a process affects and object then the input state—the state of the affected object prior to the process occurrence—is different than the output state—the state of the affected object following the process occurrence. In this case, while the same object is in both the preprocess object set and in the postprocess object set, it is in different states. This is demonstrated in Fig. 10.3, where **pre-tested Product** is in the preprocess object set, while **tested Product** is in the postprocess object set.

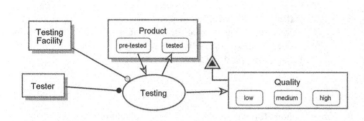

Product is physical.
Product can be **pre-tested** or **tested**.
Product exhibits **Quality**.
Quality can be **low, medium,** or **high**.
Tester is physical.
Tester handles **Testing**.
Testing Facility is physical.
Testing requires **Testing Facility**.
Testing changes **Product** from **pre-tested** to **tested**.
Testing yields **Quality**.

Fig. 10.3 **pre-tested Product** is in the preprocess object set, while **tested Product** is in the postprocess object set

10.4.5 The Involved Object Set

The involved object set is defined as follows.

> *The **involved object set** of process P, Inv(P), is the union of P's preprocess object set and postprocess object set.*

In set notation: $Inv(P) = Pre(P) \cup Post(P)$.

In the examples in Fig. 10.1, *Inv* (**Flight**) = {**Runway, Pilot, Airplane**}, and *Inv* (**Manufacturing**) = {**Operator, Machine, Model, Raw Material, Product**}.

10.5 The Procedural Link Uniqueness OPM Principle

By the definition of process, a process transforms at least one object, so in a complete OPM model a process must be linked to at least one object, or any one of its states, via a transforming link, either directly or indirectly. A process and an object can be connected only via a procedural link, with the exception of exhibition-characterization, which is a structural link. Any procedural link, with the exception of invocation and exception links, connects a process with an object.

An object has some role with respect to a process. It can be an agent, an instrument, or a transformee. Therefore, an object, or a state of an object, and a process cannot be connected by more than one procedural link. This is the rationale behind the following *procedural link uniqueness OPM principle*.

The Procedural Link Uniqueness OPM Principle

At any level of detail, an object and a process can be connected with at most one procedural link, which uniquely determines the role of the object with respect to the process.

The reason for qualifying this principle to a given level of abstraction is that at different abstraction levels an object might be modeled differently. The role of an object can change with the level of detail. The procedural link uniqueness guides the modeler to retain the most semantically meaningful model fact at any given detail level.

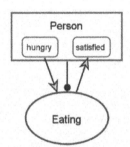

Person can be **hungry** or **satisfied**.
Person handles **Eating**.
Eating affects **Person**.
Eating changes **Person** from **hungry** to **satisfied**.

Eating affects **Person**.

Fig. 10.4 The procedural link uniqueness OPM principle demonstrated Left: Expressing **Person** as both agent and affectee of **Eating** is made possible via state expression. Right: When the states are suppressed, only the effect link remians

For example, in the OPD on the left of Fig. 10.4, when a **Person** is engaged in **Eating**, **Person** is both the agent, since **Person** handles **Eating**, and the affectee of this process, since **Eating** changes **Person** from **hungry** to **satisfied**. This is possible because the states **hungry** and **satisfied** of **Person** are expressed. When the states are suppressed (on the right), we cannot have both agent and effect links between **Person** and **Eating**, so we must make a choice. As we define formally and explain in more detail in Sect. 21.13, the choice of the link is based on the precedence of the procedural links. Since a transforming (in our case effect) link is semantically stronger than an enabling link (in our case agent), the effect link prevails. We can still use both links if we zoom into **Eating**, exposing its three subprocesses: **Food Picking**, **Food Swallowing**, and **Food Digesting**. Only the latter subprocess affects the **Person**, so now **Person** can be linked with an agent link to **Food Picking** and **Food Swallowing**, and with an effect link to **Food Digesting**. When zooming out of **Eating** and suppressing the states of **Person**, **Person** and **Eating** will again be linked by the effect link, since overall the state of **Person** changed, in line with the link precedence.

As another example, **Truck** is obviously an instrument for **Transporting**. **Transporting** zooms into **Loading**, **Moving**, and **Unloading**. **Loading** changes **Truck** from **unloaded** to **loaded**, so **Truck** it is obviously affected. However, after **Moving** is over, **Unloading** changes **Truck** back from **loaded** to **unloaded**, so as a whole, inspecting **Truck** from the **Transporting** level, **Truck** is unaffected and hence can be modeled as an instrument of **Transporting** rather than its affectee.

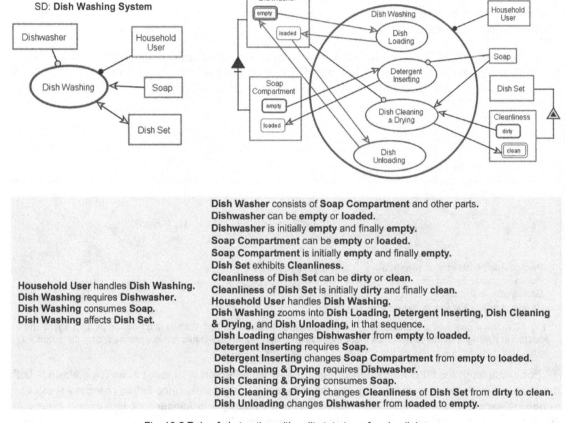

SD: **Dish Washing System**

SD1: **Dish Washing** in-zoomed

Dish Washer consists of **Soap Compartment** and other parts.
Dishwasher can be **empty** or **loaded**.
Dishwasher is initially **empty** and finally **empty**.
Soap Compartment can be **empty** or **loaded**.
Soap Compartment is initially **empty** and finally **empty**.
Dish Set exhibits **Cleanliness**.
Cleanliness of **Dish Set** can be **dirty** or **clean**.
Cleanliness of **Dish Set** is initially **dirty** and finally **clean**.
Household User handles **Dish Washing**.
Dish Washing zooms into **Dish Loading, Detergent Inserting, Dish Cleaning & Drying**, and **Dish Unloading**, in that sequence.
Dish Loading changes **Dishwasher** from **empty** to **loaded**.
Detergent Inserting requires **Soap**.
Detergent Inserting changes **Soap Compartment** from **empty** to **loaded**.
Dish Cleaning & Drying requires **Dishwasher**.
Dish Cleaning & Drying consumes **Soap**.
Dish Cleaning & Drying changes **Cleanliness** of **Dish Set** from **dirty** to **clean**.
Dish Unloading changes **Dishwasher** from **loaded** to **empty**.

Household User handles **Dish Washing**.
Dish Washing requires **Dishwasher**.
Dish Washing consumes **Soap**.
Dish Washing affects **Dish Set**.

Fig. 10.5 Role of abstraction with split state transforming links

An object may have the role of an instrument in an abstract OPD and a transformee in another descendent, more detailed and concrete OPD. At the abstract OPD, the process does not appear to affect the object, because the object's initial state is the same as its final state. Therefore, at the abstract OPD the object is an instrument, as indicated by an instrument link. However, at a descendent, more concrete OPD, that same process does appear to change the state of that object from the initial state and then back to the initial state.

As a final example, in Fig. 10.5, the left OPD (SD: **Dish Washing System**), a **Dishwasher** object is an instrument for the **Dish Washing** process, since no change in state of the **Dishwasher** is visible at that extent of abstraction. In the descendent OPD (SD1: **Dish Washing** in-zoomed), **Dish Washing** zooms into **Loading** (of a **dirty Dish Set**), **Cleaning** (which changes **Dish Set** from **dirty** to **clean**), and **Unloading** (of a **clean Dish Set**). **Loading** changes the state of **Dishwasher** from **empty** to **loaded**, while **Unloading** changes it back from **loaded** to **empty**, so **empty** is both the initial and final state. While the **Dishwasher** is an instrument in SD, the System Diagram, at the descendent, more detailed OPD, the **Dishwasher** is an affectee—it becomes **loaded** and then **empty** again. The only effect visible in the System Diagram is the effect on **Dish Set**.

10.6 **The Process Test**

As argued, while a basic tenet of OPM is the distinction between objects and processes, it is sometimes difficult to tell an object from a process, especially if both are nouns. The object-process distinction problem is stated simply as follows:

> Given a noun, how can we tell if it is an object or a process?

The *process test*, specified in this section, is a formal procedure for solving the object-process distinction problem. It enables identifying nouns that are processes rather than objects, a prerequisite for successful system analysis and design.

By default, a noun is an object. To be a process, the noun must meet each one of the following three *process test criteria*: (1) *Object transformation*, (2) *time association*, and (3) *verb association*.

Finally, if the outcome is still not clear, using common sense is of course the best option.

10.6.1 The Object Transformation Criterion

The *object transformation* process test criterion stipulates that a process must transform (consume, create, or change the state of) at least one of the objects in the involved object set.

> The **object transformation criterion** *is satisfied if the noun in question transforms at least one of the objects in the involved object set.*

The membership of the transformee B of P is determined as follows.

- If P consumes B then $B \in Pre(P)$: B is only in the preprocess object set of P.
- If P yields (creates) B, then $B \in Post(P)$: B is only in the postprocess object set of P.
- If P affects (changes the state of) B, then $B \in Inv(P)$: B is in the involved object set, i.e., in both the preprocess object set and the postprocess object set.

Enablers (agents or instruments) are also members of $Inv(P)$ as their presence is required throughout the entire duration of the process occurrence.

Continuing the previous examples, the **Flight** process transforms **Airplane** (by changing its **Location** attribute from **origin** to **destination**). Hence, **Airplane** $\in Inv$ (**Flight**). **Manufacturing** transforms two objects: it consumes **Raw Material** and creates **Product**, hence **Raw Material** $\in Pre$ (**Manufacturing**) while **Product** $\in Post$ (**Manufacturing**). Finally, **Machine** $\in Inv$ (**Manufacturing**) since **Machine** is an instrument for **Manufacturing**.

10.6.2 The Time Association Criterion

The *association with time* process test criterion requires that the noun in question represent some happening, occurrence, action, procedure, routine, execution, operation, or activity that takes a positive amount of time along the timeline.

> The ***time association criterion*** *is satisfied if the noun in question can be thought of as happening through time.*

Continuing our example, both **Flight** and **Manufacturing** start at a certain point in time and take a certain amount of time. Both time and duration are very relevant features of these two nouns in question.

10.6.3 The Verb Association Criterion

The *association with verb* process criterion requires that a process be associated with a verb.

> The ***verb association criterion*** *is satisfied if the noun in question can be derived from, or has a common root with a verb or has a synonym which is a verb.*

Flying is the verb associated with **Flight**. The sentence "The airplane flies" is a short way of expressing the fact that the **Airplane** is engaged in the process of **Flight**. Similarly, to manufacture (produce, yield, make, create, generate) is the verb associated with **Manufacturing**. The sentence "The operator manufactures the product from raw material using a machine and a model." is the natural language short way of the OPL paragraph on the right in Fig. 10.1.

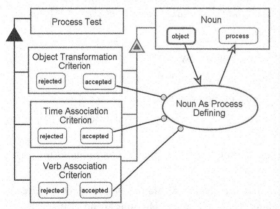

Noun can be **process** or **object**.
Noun exhibits **Object Transformation Criterion, Time Association Criterion**, and **Verb Association Criterion**. The state **object** is initial.
Process Test consists of **Object Transformation Criterion, Time Association Criterion**, and **Verb Association Criterion**.
Object Transformation Criterion of **Noun** can be **rejected** or **accepted**.
Time Association Criterion of **Noun** can be **rejected** or **accepted**.
Verb Association Criterion of **Noun** can be **rejected** or **accepted**.
Noun As Process Defining requires **accepted Verb Association Criterion** of **Noun, accepted Time Association Criterion** of **Noun**, and **accepted Object Transformation Criterion** of **Noun**.
Noun As Process Defining changes **Noun** from **object** to **process**.

Fig. 10.6 An OPM model of the **Process Test** system

Here we rely on verb—a syntactic construct, but is not mandatory that the verb be syntactically from the same root as the process name; it can be a synonym as long as the semantics is the same. For example, **Marrying** is a process, which is associated with the verb to marry. To wed is also a legal verb, albeit less frequently used. Alternatively, we could use **Wedding** to fit it to the verb wed. Many objects, such as

Apple and **Airplane**, are not associated with any verb, so they do not fulfill this process criterion. It is easy to verify that both **Apple** and **Airplane** do not meet the other process test criteria either. Boundary cases of things exist, as discussed in Sect. 10.10 with examples.

10.6.4 An OPM Model of the Process Test System

Figure 10.6 is an OPM model of the process test system.

The **Noun** in question is initially defined as **object**. **Process Test** is shown to be comprised of its three criteria, **Object Transformation Criterion**, **Time Association Criterion**, and **Verb Association Criterion**, each of which can be at a state **accepted** or **rejected**. The three instrument links from the three **accepted** states of these three criteria indicate that only when all the three criteria are accepted, the **Noun As Process Defining** process is enabled, changing **Noun** from **object** to **process**. The self-explanatory OPL paragraph of this system is also recorded in Fig. 10.6.

10.7 **Naming OPM Elements**

Selecting appropriate names for OPM objects, processes, and states is very important, because names affect how easily and how well our model is communicated to, and understood by, the target audience. Naming conventions for processes and objects help humans to tell them apart. Moreover, since these modeler-defined names are also embedded in the automatically-generated OPL sentences, these sentences will make sense only to the extent that the entities names in them are meaningful and result in correctly phrased OPL sentences. For example, in the OPL paragraph above, suppose we called this process simply **Process Testing**. This would result in the following OPL sentences:

> **Process Testing** requires **accepted Verb Association Criterion** of **Noun, accepted Time Association Criterion** of **Noun, and accepted Object Transformation Criterion** of **Noun.**
> **Process Testing** changes **Noun** from **object** to **process.**

After changing the process name, the following, more accurate OPL sentences are produced.

Noun As Process Defining requires **accepted Verb Association Criterion** of **Noun, accepted Time Association Criterion** of **Noun, and accepted Object Transformation Criterion** of **Noun.**
Noun As Process Defining changes **Noun** from **object** to **process.**

10.7.1 Capitalization, Bolding, Phrase, and Thing Naming

The *capitalization OPM convention* is that the first letter in each word in the name of a thing (object or process) is capitalized, while states are lower-case (non-capitalized). Thus, **possibly injured Vehicle Occupants Group** denotes the object **Vehicle Occupants Group** at its **possibly injured** state.

Box contains Pencil.   **Box contains 6 Pencils.**

Fig. 10.7 An OPM model of a box with one (left) and six (right) pencils

Tags of tagged structural relations are also non-capitalized either, as in the OPL sentence "**Box contains Pencil.**" which is the textual modality of the OPD on the left of Fig. 10.7. The tag contains along the arrow from **Box** to **Pencil** is lower-case.

> *A **phrase** is a collection of one or more words that do not constitute a sentence.*

Object naming is simple—it is a capitalized noun. Object names can be phrases with more than one word, as in **Apple Cake** or **Insurance Claim**.

10.7.2 The Singular Name OPM Principle

An important OPM principle that must be adhered to while naming an object or a process is the *singular name OPM principle*:

> **The Singular Name OPM Principle**
>
> A name of an OPM thing must be singular. Plural has to be converted to singular by adding the word "Set" for inanimate things or "Group" for humans.

There are two reasons for defining this principle. First, an automated tool takes care of converting singular to plural as needed. For example, in the OPD in the right of Fig. 10.7, when the participation constraint (defined later) "**6**" is added, the OPL sentence now reads **Box contains 6 Pencils**. Second, we want to be able to specify parts or attributes or specializations of a thing in its singular form.

So what should we do if we wish to model more than one instance? We convert the plural object in the OPM model to singular by adding the word "Set" for inanimate things or "Group" for humans. Thus, the object "Ingredients" (say, of a cake) becomes "**Ingredient Set**", the process :"Modifications" becomes "**Modification Set**", and "Customers" becomes "**Customer Group**".

10.7.3 Process Naming

Unless it makes no sense in English, the OPM process naming convention is to name a process by making its last word a gerund, i.e., the root of the verb followed by the "**ing**" suffix, as in **Igniting**. We call this the *gerund process naming mode*. If there are several choices, such as in **Construction** vs. **Constructing**, the latter is preferable, unless domain experts indicate that the non-gerund form is the one that is commonly used and understood in the domain.

This naming convention clarifies the dynamic nature of the process as a dynamic thing, a thing that *happens* along the time dimension rather than a static thing that *exists* without change. To enhance clarity and make the function of the process explicit, the gerund may be preceded by the primary object that the process transforms, as in **Engine Igniting**. The object name that can precede the gerund qualifies the process, making it a specialization of the original process. For example, **Wall Painting** and **Car Painting** are two different (yet similar) processes that specialize **Painting**. Both transform the object being painted by changing the color attribute value of the affectee (operand)—the object being painted. However, since the objects being painted are different, the instruments and techniques of each kind of painting differ.

The process name in the running example in Part I of this book, **Automatic Crash Responding**, could be simply **Responding**, but that might seem too general, since it does not specify what the response is for. Even **Crash Responding** alone is not quite sufficient, as it could be done without an automated system. We also avoid calling this process **Response**, as this name does not follow the gerund process naming mode and can be justifiably conceived as an object—the outcome of the responding process.

The recommended gerund process naming mode comes in several versions of increasing length and information content:

1. The *transforming* (verb) version: the process name (syntactically the gerund form of the verb, namely *verb* + *ing*), as in **Making** or **Responding**.
2. The *object transforming* version: a concatenation of an OPM object (syntactically a noun) with the process name (syntactically the verb's gerund), as in **Cake Making** or **Crash Responding**. This is the recommended naming mode in most cases.
3. The *qualified transforming* version: a concatenation of an attribute value (syntactically an adjective) with the process name, as in **Quick Making** or **Automated Responding**.
4. The *qualified object transforming* version: a concatenation of an attribute value with an object and the gerund. The attribute value can qualify the process, as in **Quick Cake Making** or **Automatic Crash Responding**, or it can qualify the object, as in **Sweet Cake Making** or **Fatal Crash Responding**.

A second process naming option, often used by modelers, is the *imperative process naming mode*, as in "respond" or more specifically, "respond to crash", or "automatically respond to crash". OPM discourages this mode, because it is less compact and less elegant, and the OPL sentences created using this mode in the current OPM 19450 are awkward. Modeling languages usually do not prescribe such naming conventions. Modelers are therefore unaware of nuances such as the difference between the gerund and imperative process name modes. The Functional Analysis approach advocates naming functions imperatively: "Start Engine". "Launch Missile", "Turn Left", but this does not seem to be a premeditated and mandatory way, just a short and sometimes convenient way of expression. Consequently, many modelers use both the gerund and the imperative process name modes interchangeably or in a mixed way, making the model less coherent and unnecessarily more cognitively demanding.

10.8 **Thing Defined**

We have seen that objects and processes are two types of tightly coupled and complementary *things*. Objects cannot be transformed (generated, affected or eliminated) without processes, while processes have no meaning without the objects they transform, and often also the objects that enable their occurrence. The extent of this coupling is so intense that if we wish to be able to analyze and design systems in any domain as intuitively and naturally as possible, we must consider objects and processes concurrently. Objects *exist* as relatively persistent, static things, while processes *occur* as transient, dynamic things.

The extent to which objects and processes are interwoven is even lager; we must be able to specify what state an object was at before the process affected it, which objects were consumed, and which were generated. At the same time, we need to be able to show how parts, features and specializations (discussed later) of these objects play role in subprocesses of the higher-level process.

As we shall see, objects and processes have much in common in terms of being specified through structural relations such as aggregation, generalization, and characterization. The need to talk about these two concepts in a generalized way, without repeating "object or process" over and over again, necessitates the advent of a yet more abstract term. We call this simply a "thing."

> ***Thing*** *is a generalization of object and process.*

The concept of "thing" enables us to think and express ourselves in terms of this abstraction and refer to it without the need to reiterate the words "object or process". Based on the ontology of Bunge (1987, 1989), Wand and Weber (1989, 1993) have used the term *thing* as a synonym to what we refer to as object. Their first premise is that *the world is made of things that have properties.* According to this definition, *thing* seems to be synonymous with *object*. However, during the last two decades, the term *object* has become deeply rooted, at least in the software engineering community. In SysML and UML, object has been replaced by the terms *block* and *class*, respectively. Interestingly, the emergence of the term "Internet of Things" (IoT; Weber and Weber 2010) is in line with the notion of thing as a generalization of object and process since IoT is about processes taking place among physical interconnected objects.

10.9 Properties of OPM Things

A property is an attribute at the metamodel level. Property can be thought of as a meta-attribute—an attribute of an element in a metamodel of OPM.

> ***Property*** *is an attribute of an OPM model element.*

Unlike "regular" attribute, whose values can change during the execution of an OPM model, a property value of any element in an OPM model is fixed. We will see an example at the end of this section. All OPM things have the following three properties:

- **Perseverance**, which pertains to the thing's persistence and denotes whether the thing is **static** (persistent), i.e. an **Object**, or **dynamic** (transient), i.e. a **Process**. Boundary examples of static, persistent processes and dynamic, transient objects exist, as discussed later in this chapter. Based on the value of **Perseverance**, this property of **Thing** discriminates between an **Object** and a **Process**. At the model level we call such attributes discriminating attributes, as discussed in a later chapter.
- **Essence**, which pertains to the thing's nature and denotes whether the thing is **physical** or **informatical**.
- **Affiliation**, which pertains to the thing's scope and denotes whether the thing is **systemic**, i.e., part of the system, or **environmental**, i.e., part of the system's environment.

Graphically, as shown in Fig. 10.8, shading effects denote physical OPM things and dashed lines denote environmental OPM things. All eight **Perseverance-Essence-Affiliation** property combinations of an OPM thing shown in Fig. 10.8 may occur. The lower portion of Fig. 10.8 expresses, from left to right and top to bottom, the OPL sentences corresponding to the graphical elements.

We noted that a property value of any element in an OPM model is fixed. Indeed looking at the example of **Perseverance**, a property of an OPM **Thing**, if the value of a certain **Thing** in an OPM model is set as **static** (i.e., the **Thing** is an **Object**), then this value is fixed and the **Object** cannot become a **Process**.

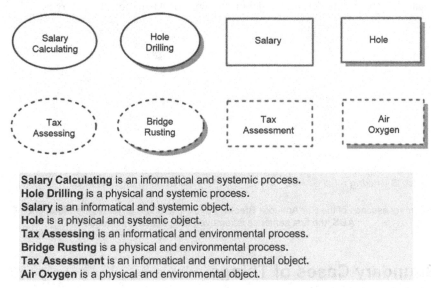

Salary Calculating is an informatical and systemic process.
Hole Drilling is a physical and systemic process.
Salary is an informatical and systemic object.
Hole is a physical and systemic object.
Tax Assessing is an informatical and environmental process.
Bridge Rusting is a physical and environmental process.
Tax Assessment is an informatical and environmental object.
Air Oxygen is a physical and environmental object.

Fig. 10.8 OPM thing generic attribute combinations exemplified

10.9.1 Default Values of Thing Generic Properties

The **Affiliation** property of thing is by default **systemic**. With respect to **Essence**, we note that the majority of things in non-trivial systems tends to have the same property value: either most of the things in the system are **physical** or most of them are **informatical**. For example, Data processing systems are informatical, although they have physical components. Transportation systems, such as a railway system or an aviation system, are physical, although they have informatical components.

> *A system's **primary essence** is the Essence value of the majority of the things in the system.*

The default essence value of a thing is the primary essence of the system. The motivation, based on experience, for defining the primary essence is to save the modeler the need to mark the vast majority of the things in the system as either informatical or physical. A supporting tool should therefore provide an option for the modeler to specify a system's primary essence as a means to reduce the amount of things for which the modeler has to specify their essence.

The OPL paragraph corresponding to an OPD should not include an OPL sentence to indicate the Essence or Affiliation value of a thing if it is the default, unless the thing is isolated—it has not yet been connected to any other thing during the course of the modeling process. The reason for this is the need to avoid violating the graphics-text OPM principle. Suppose the default essence of the OPDs in Fig. 10.9 is physical. Upon drawing the physical object **Car** and prior to linking it to anything, the OPL sentence "Car is physical" shall appear, as shown in the OPD on the left, otherwise there would be a thing (**Car**) depicted in the OPD that has no mention in the OPL, violating the graphics-text OPM principle. However, as soon as the isolated thing becomes linked to another thing, as shown in the OPD on the right, the OPL sentence dedicated to specifying the thing's default Essence or Affiliation shall be removed.

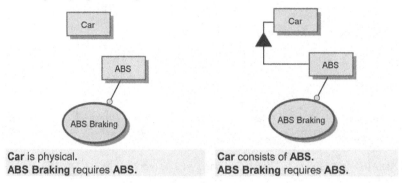

Fig. 10.9 The primary essence of the Car Anti-lock Breaking System (ABS) is physical, therefore, once **Car** is linked to **ABS**, the first sentence is removed from the OPL sentence

10.10 **Boundary Cases of Things**

While objects are persistent and processes are transient, boundary case of state-preserving (persistent) processes and transient objects, exist. These are discussed in this section.

10.10.1 State-Preserving Processes

We have defined a process as a thing that transforms an object. There are cases in which the *absence* of a process, rather than its occurrence, causes a change in the state of the object. One example is supporting: Any object on Planet Earth (or on any other planet for that matter) is maintained in its vertical position by a **Supporting** process that prevents it from freely falling. There is a whole family of such *state-preserving processes* that have a static connotation as they act to maintain the state of an object rather than change it.

> *A **state-preserving process** is a process that acts to maintain a steady state or status quo of an object rather than to change it.*

The process of **existing** is the most prominent example, describing a situation of an object being "out there" without specifying any change in that object. For biological objects, existing entails maintenance of the necessary life processes, so they are definitely not static. Non-biological systems such as the solar system or the global air traffic control system also exist while constantly changing.

Members of this *state-preserving process* family include such processes as **Supporting, Holding, Maintaining, Keeping, Staying, Waiting, Prolonging, Delaying, Occupying, Persisting, Including, Containing, Continuing, Enclosing, Fastening, Connecting, Postponing, Dragging, Storing, Owning, Restraining, Drawing, Attracting**, and **Remaining**. Rather than induce any real change, the semantics of these verbs is leaving the current state of the object as is, in its status quo, for some more time.

Each one of these processes can be considered as a *change-preventing process*—a process that works against some "force" which would otherwise change the operand—the object being operated on. For example, **Supporting** of a **Laptop** can be rephrased as **Fall Preventing**, **Keeping** of a **Coin** can be rephrased as its **Loss Preventing**, and **Holding** of a **Hostage** can be rephrased as **Escape Preventing** of that **Hostage**. Due to their nature as state-preserving, these "pseudo-processes" might rather be modeled using tagged structural relations between two objects. We discuss this in the context of structural relations.

10.10.2 How to Model State-Preserving Processes with Tagged Structural Links

Many of the state-preserving verbs can be considered as working against some "force," which would otherwise change some object. For example, a **Pedestal** supporting a **Statue** works against gravity, so we can think of **Supporting** as a "fall preventing" process, without which the state of the **Statue** would change from **stabilized** to **fallen**. The **Supporting** process starts as soon as the **Statue** is positioned and keeps going until something in the system changes, e.g., the **Pedestal** undergoes a process of **Breaking**, changing its state from **intact** to **broken**. As a more modern example, an **Autopilot** is a system that is designed to maintain and stabilize an **Aircraft** in its course, working against lift, drag, gravity, and the centrifugal force. Once the state-maintaining process ends, the state will change, so you need to capture this process as a recurring one—whether through self-invocation, presented in Sect. 22.4.6 or controlled response to an external trigger.

The static nature of state-preserving processes is contradictory to the definition of process, which requires that it *transforms* some object. In such cases, it is often possible, and even desirable, to model the relation between the two pertinent objects using a tagged structural link instead of a process. This approach to modeling persistent processes is exemplified in Fig. 10.10, which shows **Supporting** as a state-preserving process. On the left hand side is the dynamic version of the model, in which **Supporting** is an explicit process, presented with its corresponding OPL paragraph. On the right is the static model version, in which the tagged structural relation **supports** expresses the time-invariant relation between **Foundation** and **House**, giving rise to a corresponding more compact and more expressive one-sentence OPL paragraph: **Foundation supports House**.

10.10.3 Transient Objects and Their Invocation Link Substitute

Transient objects are the analogous counterparts of persistent processes. A *transient object* is a short-lived physical or informatical object. Examples of transient objects are unstable materials, such as an interim short-lived compound in a chemical reaction or an atom in an excited state that spontaneously decays to the ground state by emission of X-rays and fluorescent radiation. Another example of a transient object is a packet in a telecommunication network. Such a packet can reside for a short while at some router on its way and leave no trace once the target node has received it.

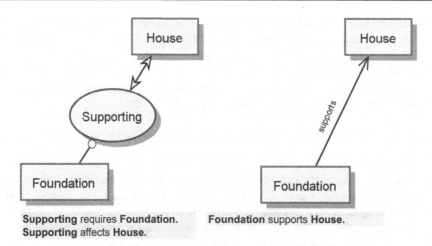

Fig. 10.10 Supporting as a state-preserving process

In an OPM model, a transient object that is created by a process and immediately consumed by the next process can be skipped by using the *invocation link*, a lightning-shaped procedural link that directly connects the two processes. Figure 10.11 demonstrates the notions of transient object and invocation link. On the left hand side is a model in which **Spark** is an explicit object created by **Igniting**. The presence of **Spark** is an event that initiates (triggers) **Exploding**, as denoted by the letter **e** next to the arrowhead pointing to **Exploding**. **Exploding** immediately consumes **Spark**, so **Spark** is transient and short-lived. On the right hand side is an alternative, more compact model, in which the transient **Spark** is suppressed by the invocation link. The semantics of the invocation link is that the end of **Igniting** is the event that triggers **Exploding**. The OPL paragraph in this case is also more compact.

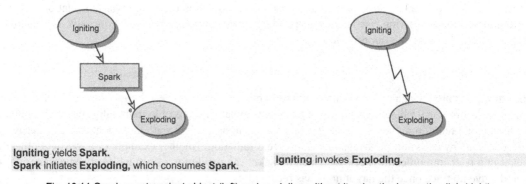

Fig. 10.11 Spark as a transient object (left) and modeling without it using the invocation link (right)

Looking back at Fig. 10.10 and comparing it to Fig. 10.11, we can see the pattern: The use of the invocation link as a shorter version of modeling generation and immediate consumption of a transient object is analogous to the use of the tagged structural link as a shorter version of modeling a persistent process. Another example is **Signaling** and the transient object **Signal**.

10.11 **Operator, Operand, and Transform**

Before concluding this chapter on the dynamics of systems, it may be interesting to compare the OPM ontology to the definitions of Ashby (2001) regarding operand, operator and transform:

Consider the simple example in which, under the influence of sunshine, pale skin changes to dark skin. Something, "the pale skin", is acted on by a factor, "the sunshine", and is changed to dark skin. That which is acted on, the pale skin, will be called the OPERAND, the [causing] factor will be called the OPERATOR, and that what the operand has changed to, will be called the TRANSFORM.

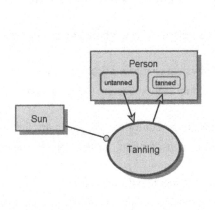
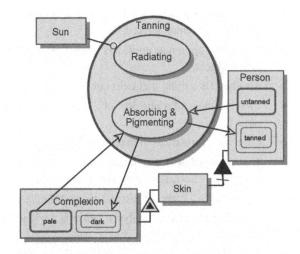

Person consists of **Skin** and at least one other part.
Skin exhibits **Complexion**.

Person can be **untanned** or **tanned**.
Person is initially **untanned** and finally **tanned**.
Radiating requires **Sun**.
Tanning changes **Person** from **untanned** to **tanned**.

Complexion of **Skin** can be **pale** or **dark**.
Complexion of **Skin** is initially **pale** and finally **dark**.
Tanning zooms into **Radiating** and **Absorbing &
Pigmenting**, in that sequence.
Radiating requires **Sun**.
Absorbing & Pigmenting changes **Person** from **untanned** to
tanned and **Complexion** of **Skin** from **pale** to **dark**.

Fig. 10.12 Tanning top level (left) and an in-zoomed view (right)

In the OPM ontology, **Skin** is an object, while **dark** and **pale** are states of an attribute of the object **Skin** called **Complexion**. **Skin** is one of the parts of **Person**. **Tanning** is a process, and **Sun** is an instrument that enables the **Tanning** process, the effect of which is to change the **Complexion** of the **Skin** from **pale** to **dark**. This terminology and the OPM model in Fig. 10.12 seem more intuitive and appropriate for non-mathematical systems than the operand, operator and transform ontology. The "sunshine factor" is a bit problematic to describe. It is not clear whether it refers to the shining process of the sun or to the object that aggregates the photons of energy radiated by the sun, which the skin absorbs.

In OPM, we would model **Radiating** as a first subprocess of **Tanning**. **Radiating requires** (i.e., is enabled by the instrument) **Sun**. **Radiating**, in turn, produces the object **Solar Energy**, which is absorbed by the **Skin** via the second subprocess, **Absorbing & Pigmenting**, the one that changes the **Complexion** of **Skin** from **pale** to **dark**. In summary, the operator is the process (**Tanning**). The operand is the affectee in its state before the process occurred (**Skin** in its **pale Complexion** state), while the transform is its state after the process occurred (**Skin** in its **dark Complexion** state).

10.12 **Summary**

- A *property* is a metamodel attribute of an OPM element. A property value of each element in an OPM model remains fixed.

- The OPM approach considers processes as "first class citizens" alongside objects rather than below object.

- An *object* is a thing that exists or has the potential of physical or informatical existence.

- Two instances of a physical object are identical if and only if they occupy the same space at the same time.

- From an informatical viewpoint, all the physical copies of some informatical object are the same.

- *Transformation* is generation (construction, creation) or consumption (destruction, elimination) or change (effect, state transition), of an object.

- A *process* is a mental construct representing a pattern of object transformation.

- In "cause and effect" analysis, *cause* is a triggering event that attempts to cause a process to start executing.

- The *effect* in "cause and effect" analysis is the transformation that one or more of the objects linked to the executing process undergo.

- Parts of speech (noun, verb, adjective, adverb …) are *syntactic* constructs, while OPM things (object and process) are *semantic* constructs.

- The *preprocess object set* of a process P, $Pre(P)$, is the set of objects required to exist, possibly in certain states, in order for P to start executing once it was triggered.

- The *postprocess object set* of process P, $Post(P)$, is the set of one or more objects that exist, possibly in certain states, after P finished executing.

- The *involved object set* of process P, $Inv(P)$, is the union of P's preprocess object set and postprocess object set: $Inv(P) = Pre(P) \cup Post(P)$.

- The *object-process distinction problem* is the problem of telling whether a given a noun is an object or a process.

- The *process test* is a formal procedure for solving the object-process distinction problem.

- The process test assumes that by default, a noun is an object, so to be a process it must meet three criteria: (1) *object transformation*, (2) *time association*, and (3) *verb association*.

- o   The *object transformation criterion* is satisfied if the noun in question transforms at least one of the objects in the involved object set.

- o   The *time association criterion* is satisfied if the noun in question can be thought of as happening through time.

- o   The *verb association criterion* is satisfied if the noun in question can be derived from, or has a common root with a verb or has a synonym which is a verb.

- The *capitalization OPM convention* is that the first letter in each word of the name of a thing is capitalized, while states are lower-case.

- The *singular name OPM principle* specifies that a name of an OPM thing must be singular.

- The *OPM process naming convention* is to name a process by making its last word a gerund whenever this is possible and is acceptable and makes sense in the domain nomenclature.

- *Thing* is a generalization of object and process.

- A *state-preserving process* is a process that maintains a steady state of status quo, and can be suppressed by replacing it with a tagged structural relation.

- A *transient object* is a short-lived object, and can be suppressed by replacing it with an invocation link.

10.13 **Problems**

1. Give an example of a scientific discovery and explain how it can be thought of as reverse engineering of nature.
2. Why is it impossible to touch a process even if it is physical?
3. Why is a process in an OPD that has no transforming link attached to it meaningless?
4. Who are the "players" in cause and effect analysis? What is the role of each one of them?
5. Give an example of two sentences that express the same fact but have different parts of speech.
6. What are the objects and processes in the first sentence above? And in the second?
7. Construct an OPM model of the system described in the previous question.
8. In the OPM model of the process test system in Fig. 10.6, what are the members in the preprocess object set, in the postprocess object set, and in the involved object set?
9. Select two things from the OPD in Fig. 10.3 and apply the process test on each one of them.
10. What is the preferred way of modeling persistent processes?
11. What is a possible shortcut for modeling transient objects?
12. Model the following specification: Running of an internal combustion engine is contingent upon the presence of the objects air and gasoline vapor mixture inside the object cylinder at the right pressure and temperature (attributes of mixture). The triggering event is the point in time when a spark (created by a previous timed process) ignites the mixture. As a result of this process, the gasoline mixture is consumed and the piston's kinetic energy value increases.

Chapter 11

Object-Process Language: The Text

> *Among general-purpose modeling languages dominate the graphical ones such as UML; textual modeling languages are not as popular though they have a big potential.*

Mazanec and Macek (2012)

OPM is bimodal: it employs both the visual (graphical) modality—OPD, and the verbal (textual) modality—OPL. The textual OPL representation of the OPM model has both human-oriented and machine-oriented goals. This chapter is devoted to presenting OPL and discussing its merits.

11.1 OPL: The Textual Modality

To enhance OPM's expressive power, we associate with each OPD a collection of sentences in Object-Process Language (OPL) as a textual, natural interpretation of the OPD's graphic representation.

> **Object-Process Language (OPL)** *is a subset of English that expresses textually the OPM model that the OPD set expresses graphically.*

OPL is the textual counterpart of the graphic OPM system specification. It is extracted from the diagrammatic description in the OPD set. Using a tool such as OPCAT, OPL is an automatically generated textual description of the system in a subset of natural English. Devoid of the idiosyncrasies and excessive cryptic details that characterize programming languages, OPL sentences are understandable to people without technical or programming experience.

> A **model fact** *is a relation between two or more things in an OPM model.*

Each model fact is expressed in the OPM model in two modalities: in the graphic modality in one or more OPDs, and in the textual modality in an OPM sentence for each graphical expression of that model fact.

Each OPD element (thing or link) has a graphic symbol. An *OPD construct* is a syntactically valid combination of OPM graphic symbols, which expresses a *model fact*. That model fact is equivalently expressed by a sentence or part of a sentence in *Object-Process Language (OPL)* text. This is summarized in the following set of definitions.

> An **OPD element** *is the graphical expression of a thing or a link.*
>
> An **OPD construct** *is a collection of connected OPD elements.*

A model fact is expressed graphically by an OPD construct and textually by an equivalent OPL sentence or sentence part.

© Springer Science+Business Media New York 2016
D. Dori, *Model-Based Systems Engineering with OPM and SysML*, DOI 10.1007/978-1-4939-3295-5_11

11.2 **The Dual Purpose of OPL**

OPL serves two goals, oriented to two directions: humans and machines.

11.2.1 The Human-Oriented OPL Goal

The human-oriented OPL goal is to convert the set of OPDs comprising the OPM model into a natural language text that can be used to express and communicate analysis and design results among the various stakeholders involved in the system under construction. Users include domain experts and their executives on the customer side of the system under development, as well as architects and modelers on the supplier side of the same system.

OPL enables involving the customer-side stakeholders, who are often non-technical, in the requirements elicitation and initial conceptual modeling of the system under development. Engaging these stakeholders as active participants helps streamline requirements, obtain stakeholders buy-in, and detect errors soon after their inadvertent introduction.

Usually, these stakeholders do not have a command of programming languages, and it is not realistic to expect them to read diagrams in a conceptual modeling language, let alone program code. Being used to reading text (or viewing high-level slide presentations) rather than relating to diagrams, they (or their engineers or lawyers) are likely to prefer reading text over examining and interpreting OPDs. For them, OPL serves the purpose of verification and validation of the requirements, which are usually provided initially in text and then modeled in OPM. This requirement model helps identify gaps and inconsistencies so requirements can be improved and be acceptable to both sides—the customer and the contractor or developer.

For the system architects and modelers on the supplier side, the bimodal representation of the OPM model is instrumental in getting immediate feedback on each graphic editing operation, enabling them to spot modeling errors as soon as they are made, before they propagate and start to cause damage whose magnitude increases exponentially with the error detection latency. Moreover, novice OPM users can experience steep learning curve by quickly gaining familiarity with the semantics of the OPM graphic modality by inspecting the text and corresponding graphic in tandem.

Since textual documents are still the prominent way for communicating requirements and specifications of systems among parties, a formal textual modality that is generated "for free" and always matches the graphical specification is of great value. There are various other ways beside text to define and specify requirements including storyboards and mockups, which are gaining popularity in the software industry where people have decreasing patience neither for tiring text documents nor for complex conceptual models. The formal OPM model can serve as a basis for generating such popular means. Indeed, work in this direction has started by creating an animated cartoon from the simulated animation of OPM models in OPCAT (Bolshchikov et al. 2015).

11.2.2 The Machine-Oriented OPL Goal

The machine-oriented OPL goal has to do with its formality. OPL provides a firm basis for automatically generating the designed application—the infrastructure needed to continue the application development.

OPL is defined formally using a context-free grammar, so the OPL text file can serve as a basis for generating application artifacts that include executable code and database schema. This approach enables round-trip engineering, in which changes in the analysis, design and specification are almost automatically reflected in the final application. These traits make the combination of the graphic-oriented OPD and its equivalent text-based OPL counterpart an ideal infrastructure for systems specification.

11.3 The Graphics-Text Equivalence OPM Principle

The default OPL is English, but any natural language can serve as a basis for OPL. Since the OPD is based on graphics and iconic symbols, it can serve as a common platform for translation among OPLs in various natural languages.

> *An **OPL paragraph** of an OPD is a collection of OPL sentences that express textually the same model facts that this OPD expresses graphically.*

At each point in time during the modeling (when there are no unlinked things in the model), one can precisely reconstruct the OPD from its OPL paragraph and vice versa. This is expressed in the following *graphics-text equivalence OPM principle.*

> **The Graphics-Text Equivalence OPM Principle**
>
> Any model fact expressed graphically in an OPD is also expressed textually in the corresponding OPL paragraph.

The OPD set is complete graphical representation of the OPM model. It is the set of (hierarchically organized) OPDs that together specify all the model facts in the OPM model.

> *An **OPL specification** (OPL Spec) of an OPM model is the collection of all the unique OPL sentences that express textually all the model facts that the OPD set expresses graphically.*

11.4 Metamodel of OPM Model Structure

While a comprehensive metamodel of OPM appears in an annex of ISO 19450 (see Chap. 24), in Fig. 11.1 we provide a high-level model of the structure of an OPM model that puts the above definitions in context. A model of a model is a metamodel. Therefore, this OPM model is a metamodel. Using OPM to specify the structure of an OPM model of a system, it depicts the conceptual aspects of OPM as parallel hierarchies of the graphic and textual OPM modalities and their correspondence to produce equivalent model expressions. This OPD is the system diagram (SD, or SD0)—the top-level diagram (level zero) of the entire OPM metamodel.

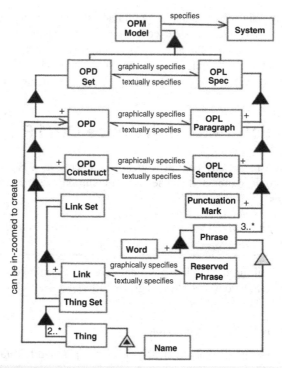

OPM Model specifies System.
OPM Model consists of OPD Set and OPL Spec.
OPL Spec consists of at least one OPL Paragraph.
OPD Set consists of at least one OPD.
OPD Set graphically specifies OPL Spec.
OPL Spec textually specifies OPD Set.
OPD consists of at least one OPD Construct.
OPL Paragraph consists of at least one OPL Sentence.
OPD graphically specifies OPL Paragraph.
OPL Paragraph textually specifies OPD.
OPD Construct graphically specifies OPL Sentence.
OPL Sentence textually specifies OPD Construct.
OPD Construct consists of Thing Set and Link Set.
Thing Set consists of 2 to many Things.
Link Set consists of at least one Link.
Thing exhibits Name.
OPL Sentence consists of 3 to many Phrases and at least one Punctuation Mark.
Phrase consists of at least one Word.
OPL Reserved Phrase and Name of Thing are Phrases.
Link graphically specifies Reserved Phrase.
Reserved Phrase textually specifies Link.
Thing can be in-zoomed to create OPD

Fig. 11.1 Metamodel (OPM model) of an OPM model structure

The two objects at the top of the OPD in Fig. 11.1 are **OPM Model** and **System**, connected with a unidirectional tagged structural link from the former to the latter, yielding the OPL sentence **OPM Model specifies System**. Further, **OPM Model** consists of **OPD Set** and **OPL Spec**. These are the two complementary modalities—the graphical and the textual. From this point on, the OPD shows two parallel hierarchies—the graphical and the textual—where going down entails increased level of detail.

The graphical hierarchy is **OPD Set**, **OPD**, **OPD Construct**, and (at the same level) **Link Set** and **Thing Set**. The textual hierarchy that is parallel to the graphical **OPD Set** and **OPD** is **OPL Paragraph** and **OPL Sentence**. An **OPD** and its corresponding **OPL Paragraph** are collections of model facts that a modeler places into the same diagram—the same model context. At the next refinement level in this hierarchy, an **OPD Construct** is the graphical counterpart of its corresponding textual **OPL Sentence**, and again, both express the same model fact. Then, **Link**, which is a graphic element, is paralleled by **Reserved OPL Phrase**, since the latter textually specifies the former, as in the reserved OPL phrase consists of, which is the textual counterpart of the aggregation-participation symbol, ▲, and in affects, which is the textual counterpart of the effect link, ↙ .

11.5 Reserved and Non-Reserved OPL Phrases

While OPL is a subset of English, it is formal. The formal syntax for OPL is expressed by a context-free grammar in Extended Backus-Naur Form (EBNF) in Annex A of ISO 19450 Publically Available Specification (see section 24.4.1). The EBNF OPL specification comprises about 400 production rules occupying 12 pages. Using EBNF, a set of production rules unambiguously defines how OPL sentences are to be constructed and parsed. Figure 11.2 presents three production rules as examples of expressing the OPL syntax in EBNF. Each production rule has a right hand side and a left hand side, separated by the = sign. The first production rule specifies that an OPL paragraph comprises one or more OPL sentences, separated by a "new line" symbol. The second production rule specifies that an OPL sentences comprises an OPL formal sentence followed by a full stop (".") symbol. The third production rule specifies that an OPL formal sentence can be of one of four types: a thing description sentence, a procedural sentence, a structural sentence, or a context management sentence.

In programming languages, the analogues of words are tokens—the atomic units resulting from lexical analysis. In most programming languages, spaces separates tokens apart. Tokens are input to the next process, parsing. OPL sentences are obviously far more readable than a script of any computer programming language. These sentences are carefully designed using a subset of English to convey a clear and straightforward meaning through well-phrased and humanly understandable constructs. Yet, using the OPL EBNF-based formal syntax definition, OPL sentences can undergo parsing just like commands or lines in a programming language. As in programming languages, parsing an OPL sentence yields phrases.

A *phrase* is a combination of one or more words, separated by spaces, which constitutes a logical entity, but not a complete sentence. OPL phrases can be reserved and non-reserved. Any OPL sentence consists of non-reserved OPL phrases—domain- or system-specific words or word combinations—which the system architect or modeler uses, and reserved OPL phrases, which link the non-reserved phrases and provide for creating a sentence in a natural language.

A.4　OPL Syntax

A.4.1　OPL document structure

(* Region OPL document *)

```
OPL paragraph – OPL sentence, { new line, OPL sentence};
OPL sentence = OPL formal sentence, ".";
OPL formal sentence = thing description sentence
                    | procedural sentence
                    | structural sentence
                    | context management sentence;
```

Fig. 11.2 Three exemplary production rules expressing the OPL syntax in EBNF

> *An **OPL phrase** is a sequence of one or more words in an OPL sentence.*
>
> *A **non-reserved OPL phrase** is a modeler-defined OPL phrase that expresses a system- or domain-specific OPM model entity or relation name.*

Non-reserved OPL phrases are names of OPM objects, processes, and states that the modeler assigns while creating the OPDs that comprise the OPM model. Non-reserved OPL phrases also include less frequently used ones, such as (user defined) tagged structural relations and participation constraints.

> *A **reserved OPL phrase** is an OPL phrase built into the OPL EBNF syntax definition that connects two or more non-reserved OPL phrases.*

Reserved OPL phrases are parts of the sentence syntax that express relations or connections between non-reserved OPL phrases, or constrains on them. Examples of reserved OPL phrases are "requires", "yields", "consumes" "and", "or", "affects", "exactly one of", "at least one", and "consists of". These definitions of reserved and non-reserved phrases stipulate that the former are the mortar that "glues" and holds together in a meaningful way the model building blocks—the non-reserved phrases that express system-specific terms.

The following *bolding OPL convention* helps distinguish between the two kinds of OPL phrases.

> The Bolding OPL Convention
>
> **Non-reserved OPL phrases** appear in **Arial bold** font, while reserved OPL phrases appear in Arial non-bold font. Punctuation marks are bolded.

For example, the OPL phrase "**Automatic Crash Responding**" in the OPL sentence "**Automatic Crash Responding** affects **Vehicle Occupants Group**." is non-reserved and therefore appears in Arial bold font. The non-bold phrases, such as "and", "or", "affects", "exactly one of", and "consists of", are reserved OPL phrases.

A CASE tool implementation needs to automatically translate the model facts expressed by the OPD constructs into OPL sentences. To further help distinguish between things, such tools should use colors in fonts of phrases that match their colors in the OPD. For objects, the default color in OPCAT is green, for processes—blue, for states—brown, and non-reserved OPL phrase are in black font. If your book version enables seeing colors, Fig. 10.6, which is an OPCAT-generated OPM model of the process test system, exemplifies this coloring convention.

11.6 Motivation for OPM's Bimodal Expression

A legitimate question that can be raised with respect to OPL is why is text needed in addition to the diagram if we have a good graphic representation of our model? One may indeed wonder why two modalities are needed. According to the *graphics-text equivalence OPM principle*, the text and the graphics express the same contents, so there is a 100% redundancy in terms of information content! Isn't this a waste of resources? Wouldn't it make more sense to stick to just one modality—either graphics or text—and leave the other out?

11.6.1 The Dual-Channel Assumption

The graphics-text equivalence is a major source of OPM's expressive power. OPL text complements the OPD graphics. This duality implements the *dual-channel assumption* (Clark and Paivio 1991; Baddeley 1992). This is one of three major research-supported cognitive assumptions (Mayer 2003; Mayer and Moreno 2003), which stipulates that humans possess separate channels and mechanisms for processing visual and verbal representations. The combination of OPD and OPL caters directly to this dual-channel assumption (Dori 2008). Some humans are more visually inclined, while others are more text-oriented. The text and the graphics reinforce each other while the model creator or the model readers try to make sense of the semantics that model elements convey in various combinations.

The cognitive-physiological basis for this principle is that the human mind is geared to accept both visual-pictorial-graphic signals and audio-verbal-written signals. Graphics and text trigger different areas in the brain. Popularly, this is often referred to as the left brain/right brain functions. Indeed, the left hemisphere is dominant in language, processing what one hears and handling most of the duties of speaking. The right hemisphere is mainly in charge of spatial abilities, face recognition, comprehending visual imagery and making sense of what we see. Thus, catering to "both sides of the brain" through language and pictures is more likely to get the message—the conceptual model—across. Accordingly, a model that can be presented bimodally in both graphic and text is preferred over a model that can be presented in only one of the modalities. Almost all conceptual modeling languages are either textual or graphical, but not both. OPM is the first to combine the two modalities (USPTO 7,099,809, 2006).

11.6.2 Benefits of the Bimodal Representation

Individuals have different preferences regarding the way they read and write specifications. Usually, engineering-oriented people (sometimes considered to be "left-brainers") prefer diagrams, while business-oriented people ("right-brainers") favor text. Moreover, even for the same individual, the content may sometimes become clearer by looking at one modality while at other times the complementary modality is more helpful. The fact that OPL is a subset of English, the *lingua franca* natural language, makes it readable and understandable to people without the need to learn any programming or pseudo-code-like language. The syntax and semantics of OPL are well defined, eliminating the ambiguity that is often inherent in natural languages.

The syntax of OPL is designed such that the resulting text constitutes plain natural, albeit syntactically restricted, English sentences. Therefore, the bimodal graphics-text representation of the OPM model helps involve non-technical stakeholders in the requirements elicitation and initial conceptual modeling of the system under development. This involvement of such stakeholders engages them as active participants and helps detect errors soon after their inadvertent introduction.

For example, suppose that instead of using the bidirectional arrow ←→, which is the effect link, the modeler of Fig. 1.3, would use by mistake the unidirectional arrow →, which is the result link, from the process **Automatic Crash Responding** to the object **Vehicle Occupants Group** to express the fact that **Automatic Crash Responding** affects **Vehicle Occupants Group**. In this case, the following OPL sentence would have been created:

> **Automatic Crash Responding** yields **Vehicle Occupants Group**.

Obviously, this sentence, while syntactically correct, makes no sense. The modeler or the customer's representative participating in the modeling session would likely detect it on the spot. The detected error can then immediately be rectified and the correction can be verified by simply reading the newly created OPL sentence.

Any natural (and artificial) language can be selected as the target language to which the OPD constructs are converted. Moreover, the graphic representation is language-neutral and can therefore serve as a means for translating from one language to another.

11.6.3 Engaging the Customer: The Social Aspect

Using an OPM-supporting software product, OPL sentences are constructed automatically in real time in response to inputting OPD graphic symbols on the screen. This capability of any team member to provide immediate feedback about facts being modeled during the modeling process is of utmost importance, as it provides for immediate system interpretation of the human developer's intents.

The simplicity and straightforwardness of this real-time response to the modeler's graphic input in the form of a subset of English is highly valuable; not only does it provide for the ability to catch errors as soon as they are made, it also enables the active participation of the system's customer in the modeling session, where she or he can provide immediate feedback as the modeling progresses. Hence, the value of such participation is beyond just spotting errors upon their creation; it is a social process that involves the customer-side stakeholders early-on in the design, justifiably making them feel that they are part of the decision-making process and mitigating resistance to change, a common known human characteristic. The system's OPL specification resulting from an OPD set is thus amenable to being scrutinized, modified, and ultimately confirmed by the customer or domain experts acting on his behalf, who need not be software experts.

The provision of having representatives of the customer working should-to-shoulder with the developers increases the likelihood of pinpointing and catching design errors as soon as they are created, resulting in significant saving of time, money, and troubles down the road. This real-time feedback is indispensable not just in spotting errors but also in correcting them at an early stage of the system lifecycle, before they had a chance to propagate and cause costly damage. Any graphics edit (addition or removal of an element) changes the OPL script. Changes can be implemented until a satisfactory result is obtained and the customer can "sign" on the model as the blueprint of the system to be developed.

11.6.4 Closing the Requirements-Design Gap

The capability to directly and precisely translate analysis and design results to a subset of natural language has a tremendous advantage. As noted, prospective users and customers may be more comfortable with reading text than with interpreting OPDs, let alone deciphering program code. This way, the OPL text and its OPD graphic equivalent help close the gap between the original requirement specification, which is currently still expressed as free prose, and the actual system specification as expressed by the resulting OPM model. While OPL sentences are easily comprehensible to humans and thus document the system "for free," the ability to parse them provides a firm basis for automated tasks such as executable code generation, simulation, initial user interface generation, and database schema definition.

11.7 Tesperanto: A Human Readable Auto-generated Text

OPL consists of short, often disconnected sentences. While each OPL sentence is a syntactically and semantically correct English sentence, lack of fluency from one OPL sentence to the next prevents OPL from becoming a descent substitute for the free text that dominates real-life requirements and other technical specifications, such as international standards. Indeed, being mechanical and repetitive, with no text fluency, long OPL text is not natural for human reading. This has motivated the development of Tesperanto (Blekhman and Dori 2013) as the next level of automatic model-based text-from-graphics generation on top of, or instead of OPL.

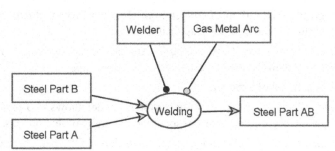

<table>
<tr><td>

Welder handles **Welding**.
Welding requires **Gas Metal Arc**.
Welding consumes **Steel Part A** and **Steel Part B**.
Welding yields **Steel Part AB**.

</td><td>

Welding is the process of creating a **Steel Part AB**, with the aid of a **Gas Metal Arc**. This process is performed by a **Welder**, consuming a **Steel Part A** and a **Steel Part B**.

</td></tr>
</table>

Fig. 11.3 OPM model of **Gas Metal Arc based Welding**. Top: OPD. Bottom left: OPL. Bottom right: Tesperanto

Tesperanto is an enhancement of OPL that follows OPM's gradual presentation principles, which cater to humans' cognitive limited capacity. It includes heuristics for sentence length adjustments, synonyms, word ordering, phrase recurrence control, and other algorithms aimed at making the

Tesperanto text look less mechanistic and more human readable. Figure 11.3 is an OPM model of **Gas Metal Arc** based **Welding**. The OPD at the top is automatically translated to both OPL and Tesperanto in the bottom left and right, respectively. This simple example demonstrates the differences in fluency of reading OPL vs. Tesperanto. While both text-from-graphics translations faithfully reflect the formal and verified OPM graphic model, Tesperanto is more humanly readable and less boring, repetitive, and mechanical. For example, while in the OPL the process **Welding** is repeated four times, once for each kind of procedural relation, in the Tesperanto translation it only appears once. Since Tesperanto is still evolving as a subject of research, it is not further used in this book.

11.8 Summary

- *Object-Process Language (OPL)* is a subset of English that expresses textually the OPM model that the OPD set expresses graphically.

- The formal syntax for OPL is expressed by a context-free grammar in Extended Backus-Naur Form (EBNF) in Annex A of ISO 19450 Publically Available Specification (PAS).

- A *model fact* is a relation between two or more things in an OPM model.

- An *OPD element* is the graphical expression of a thing or a link.

- An *OPD construct* is a collection of connected OPD elements.

- OPL serves two goals, oriented to two directions: humans and machines.

- The human-oriented OPL goal is to convert the set of OPDs comprising the OPM model into a natural language text.

- The machine-oriented OPL goal is to provide a firm basis for automatically generating the infrastructure for the application development.

- An *OPL paragraph* of an OPD is a collection of OPL sentences that express textually the same model facts that this OPD expresses graphically.

- The *graphics-text equivalence OPM principle*: Any model fact expressed graphically in an OPD is also expressed textually in the corresponding OPL paragraph.

- A *metamodel* is a model of a model.

- The metamodel of the structure of an OPM system model shows two parallel hierarchies—the hierarchy of graphic objects and the corresponding hierarchy of text objects.

- An *OPL specification* of an OPM model is the collection of OPL sentences that express textually all the model facts that the OPD set expresses graphically.

- An *OPL phrase* is a sequence of one or more words.

- A *non-reserved OPL phrase* is a modeler-defined OPL phrase that expresses a system- or domain-specific OPM model entity or relation name.

- A *reserved OPL phrase* is an OPL phrase built into the OPL EBNF syntax definition that connects two or more non-reserved OPL phrases.

- The *dual-channel assumption* is that humans possess separate systems for processing visual and verbal representations.
- The syntax and semantics of OPL are defined as a subset of English, eliminating the ambiguity that is often inherent in natural languages.
- Tesperanto is the next generation of OPL.

11.9 Problems

1. What are the pros and cons of having a textual system model specification modality alongside the graphical modality?
2. If you were to design a new modeling language with the constraint that it can use only one modality, which one would you choose? Why?
3. Which of the following three definitions of "meta", taken from dictionary.com, fits metamodel?
4. A prefix appearing in loanwords from Greek, with the meanings "after," "along with," "beyond," "among," "behind," and productive in English on the Greek model: metacarpus; metagenesis.
5. A prefix added to the name of a subject and designating another subject that analyzes the original one but at a more abstract, higher level: metaphilosophy; metalinguistics.
6. A prefix added to the name of something that consciously references or comments upon its own subject or features: a meta-painting of an artist painting a canvas, metacognition; meta-analysis.
7. Copy three OPL sentences from this chapter and reverse their bolding, that is, make each bold word not bold and vice versa. What version do you prefer—the original or the reversed? Why?

Chapter 12

SysML: Foundations and Diagrams

> *Whether it is an advanced military aircraft, a hybrid vehicle, a cell phone, or a distributed information system, these systems are expected to perform at levels undreamed of a generation ago.*
>
> Friedenthal, Moore, and Steiner (2012)

Systems Modeling Language (SysML) is a profile of the Unified Modeling Language (UML), i.e., a customized version intended for systems engineering applications. We begin the presentation of SysML with a brief description of UML, followed by an overview of SysML and its various diagram types, with reference to OPM. Recall that while OPM uses a single model that combines the various system aspects and presents them in graphics and text, SysML uses nine diagram kinds, each focusing on some particular aspect of the system. We focus on the SysML diagram kinds that have not been discussed so far: sequence diagram, activity diagram, requirements diagram, and parametrics diagram. The *sequence diagram* shows the time flow and exchange of messages among blocks. The *activity diagram* presents the activities performed by the system, their order and their control. The *requirements diagram* presents user and derived requirements that the system shall satisfy. Finally, the *parametrics diagram* models the computations that take place in the system.

12.1 UML: Unified Modeling Language

Unified Modeling Language (UML) is a standardized visual specification language for modeling of software systems. The UML specification (OMG UML 2011I, 2011S) is defined and maintained by the Object Management Group, OMG, a not-for-profit computer industry specifications consortium, which first adapted the UML specification in November 1997.

UML is a visual modeling language. As such, it specifies a graphical notation along with corresponding semantics, which are jointly used to create an abstract model of the system. UML has been designed as a language for developing software systems that are implemented using an object-oriented programming language. UML specifies multiple graphical aspect-separated views, 13 in total, to represent the system's model. Of the 13 UML types of diagrams, six types are structural diagrams and seven are behavior diagrams.

Since its introduction, UML has emerged as the dominant modeling language in the software industry. Used by large parts of the software engineering community and supported by many commercial and open-source software modeling tools, UML has evolved through several minor versions (1.x) and one major revision (UML 2).

Although UML is rooted in the software engineering domain, some efforts, e.g., (Holt 2004), have been made to apply it to the more general field of systems engineering. However, such attempts have

D. Dori, *Model-Based Systems Engineering with OPM and SysML*, DOI 10.1007/978-1-4939-3295-5_12

been recognized as problematic, primarily since UML is software-centric, so its ontology and taxonomy is limited to software artifacts. For example, physical characteristics and components of a system are hardly expressed in UML diagrams. In addition, UML does not adequately support modeling of hierarchies within a system model, an essential issue in systems engineering.

The drive to adapt UML to systems engineering applications brought about the establishment of the OMG Systems Engineering Domain Special Interest Group (SE DSIG). This OMG group, supported by the International Council on Systems Engineering (INCOSE) and ISO AP 233 workgroup, worked together on the requirements of the modeling language. The result was the UML for Systems Engineering Request for Proposal, or UML for SE RFP in short (OMG UML 2003), issued by the OMG in March 2003. SysML was the only response to the RFP. The SysML team consisted of industry users, tool vendors, government agencies, professional organizations and academia. Four and a half years after the RFP was published, version 1.0 of the SysML specification was formally released by OMG as an OMG specification in September 2007.

12.2 SysML Pillars

A general-purpose modeling language for systems engineering, SysML is intended to support specification, analysis, design, verification, and validation of complex systems. The systems may be of broad range, and can include hardware, software, data, personnel, procedures, facilities, and more. SysML reuses a subset of UML 2 and provides additional extensions in order to satisfy the RFP requirements. As a visual modeling language, SysML offers several kinds of diagrams which can reflect various aspects of a system.

SysML diagrams are commonly categorized into four "pillars"—structure, behavior, requirements, and parametric relationships. In addition, SysML provides means to cross-connect the different model elements. Figure 12.1, adapted from Friedenthal et al. (2012), shows examples of key SysML diagram types. Overall, SysML includes nine types of diagrams: four types of structure diagrams, four types of behavior diagrams, and a requirements diagram.

SysML diagram taxonomy is presented in Fig. 12.2. Using OPM notation, Fig. 12.2 shows what diagrams were adopted from UML without change, what diagrams were adopted from UML with change and what diagrams are new. Four SysML diagrams are the same as their UML counterpart: Use Case diagram, Package diagram, Sequence diagram, and State Machine diagram. Three are modified from UML 2: Block Definition diagram, Internal Block diagram, and Activity diagram. Finally, two new diagrams are added: Requirements diagram and Parametrics diagram. Each of the four SysML pillars is described next.

12.3 Requirements Diagram

Requirements are the primary input of any system or product. SysML supplies means to represent text-based requirements and to connect them to other model elements. A basic requirement, represented using the «requirement» stereotype, is composed of a unique identifier and text properties. It is also possible to extend it with additional properties (e.g., verification status property). The requirements diagram can be shown in different formats: graphical, tabular, or tree structure. Requirements can also be part of other diagrams, reflecting relationship to other model constructs. Generally, the SysML requirements constructs are not meant to replace the external requirements management tools, but rather to better integrate the system requirements with other parts of the model.

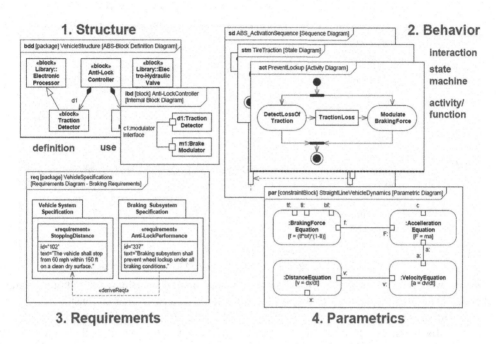

Fig. 12.1 The four pillars of SysML (Friedenthal et al. 2012)

The SysML specification provides several relationships among requirements. Requirements hierarchies, which consist of composite requirements and sub-requirements, can be described using the UML namespace containment mechanism. The «deriveReqt» dependency describes a relation between a derived requirement and its source requirement. Typically, a system-level requirement is derived into multiple subsystem requirements. The «satisfy» relationship is used to show how one or more requirements are satisfied by the model design. Other relationships are the «verify» dependency, which links between requirements and test-cases, and the «refine» dependency, which specifies that a SysML model element is a refinement of a textual requirement.

12.4 Blocks and Structure

The basic structural element in SysML is the *block*. It can be used to describe physical or logical elements of the system, such as hardware, software, data, or persons. Blocks can describe any level of the system hierarchy, from single components up to the top-level system. Block in SysML is analogous to class in UML, but rather than being a software-specific construct, it is a general-purpose structural element.

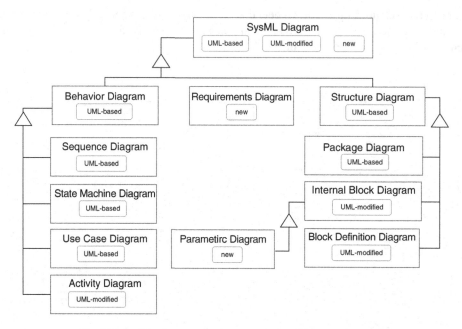

Fig. 12.2 SysML diagram taxonomy expressed as an OPM model

There are two types of structural diagrams for blocks depiction: Block Definition Diagram and Internal Block Diagram. The Block Definition Diagram (BDD) describes the relationships among blocks, such as associations, dependencies, and generalizations. It specifies system hierarchy, interconnection of parts, and classifications. The Internal Block Diagram (IBD) represents the internal structure of a block using block properties and connectors between properties. Another SysML structural diagram, the UML Package Diagram, is used to organize the model by grouping model elements.

12.5 Activity Diagram

As expressed in Fig. 12.2, SysML specifies four types of behavioral diagrams: activity diagram, sequence diagram, state machine diagram, and use case diagram.

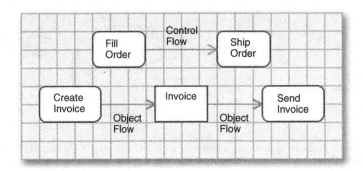

Fig. 12.3 A simple SysML activity diagram with block and action nodes and control and object flows

Activity is the fundamental behavioral element in the various SysML behavioral diagrams (excluding the use case diagram). The role of the activity diagram (see Fig. 12.3) is to represent the flow of inputs and outputs and the flow of control between actions. To this end, the activity diagram incorporates sequences and conditions for coordinating activities. Activities and activity diagrams exist also in UML, but SysML provides several extensions (Bock 2006), including means to support "continuous" flow modeling, such as rate restrictions. Support for probabilities and extensions to control (known as "control as data") were added to SysML activity diagrams. In addition, to smoothly align SysML with the widely-used classical systems engineering behavior diagram (known as EFFBD—Enhanced Functional Flow Block Diagrams; Bock, 2005), the «effbd» stereotype is specified. When this stereotype is applied to an activity, it means that the activity must conform to the constraints necessary for EFFBD.

The *use case diagram* is intended to describe basic high-level functionally by specifying the usage of the system by its actors to achieve a goal. It is often the first kind of diagram used to specify semi-formally with the customer to define the function and scope of the system to be developed.

Activity diagram is the only behavioral diagram kind that is extended in SysML with respect to UML 2, while the other three SysML behavioral diagram kinds remain unchanged or were eliminated. Sequence diagram is used to represent message-based flow of control between interacting entities, which may be actors, systems, or parts of a system. The state machine diagram models state-based behavior using object states and transitions.

An action (denoted by a rountangle) is a basic (usually atomic) unit of process in an activity diagram. As Fig. 12.3 shows, an activity diagram is composed of nodes and edges, where a node can be an action or a block (denoted by a rectangle), and an edge can be a *control flow* if it is between actions, or an *object flow* (or *block flow*) if it is between a block and an action.

12.5.1 Refining an Action into an Activity

If an action, such as **Order Processing** at the left of Fig. 12.4, has a little rake (or trident) symbol at its bottom right, this denotes a *call action* that it is elaborated into an activity with its own diagram (Fig. 12.4, right). This is a similar idea to OPM's process in-zooming. The blocks **Order**, **Invoice**, and **Product** are denoted as pins—they serve as input and output parameters.

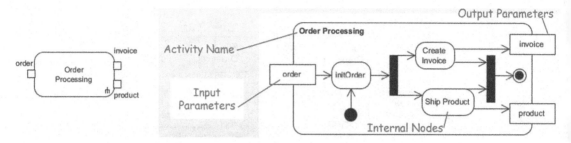

Fig. 12.4 The action Order Processing (left) has a little trident symbol, denoting it is elaborated into an activity (right). The blocks Order, Invoice, and Product are denoted as pins—input and output parameters

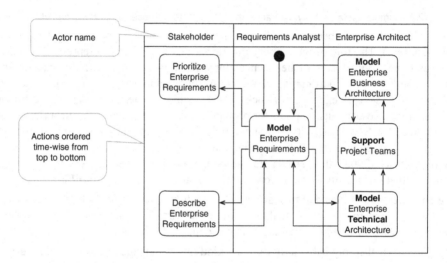

Fig. 12.5 An example of a swimlane activity diagram

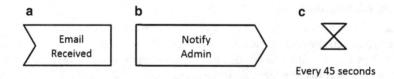

Fig. 12.6 The three special action notations: (a) accept event (b) send signal (c) time event

The **Order Processing** activity diagram has *initial* and *final pseudo nodes*—the black and black-on-white circles—to denote the activity start and end, respectively. It also has two synchronization nodes: a *fork node*—the thick vertical line from the **initOrder** action to the **Create Invoice** and **Ship Order** actions, and a *join node*—the thick vertical line from these two actions to the final pseudo node. The fork node indicates concurrent beginning of actions exiting from it, while the join node—the termination of all the actions incoming into it.

A swimlane is a kind of activity diagram that provides a way to group activities performed by the same actor or to group activities in a single thread. Figure 12.5, adapted from Agile Modeling (2015), is an example of a swimlane activity diagram. The actors are indicated in the vertical swimlanes and the diagram timeline runs from top to bottom with horizontal links crossing the swimlane borders where necessary.

12.5.2 Accept, Send, and Time Event Action Nodes

Three special actions have specific notations (see Fig. 12.6): (a) **accept event**, which waits for the occurrence of an event (signal), (b) **send signal**, which creates and sends a signal when activated, and (c) **time event**, which waits for a moment in time or a specific (possibly periodic) duration.

Figure 12.7 shows an activity diagram with an accept event, a send signal, a time event, a pin (with a "Virus alert" type), and a join node implying that scanned messages with no detected viruses are forwarded to the user every 20 seconds.

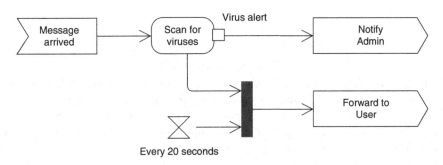

Fig. 12.7 Activity diagram with accept event, send signal, time event, pin, and a join node

12.6 **Sequence Diagram**

The sequence diagram describes the flow of control between actors and blocks. This diagram represents the sending and receiving of messages between the interacting entities called lifelines.

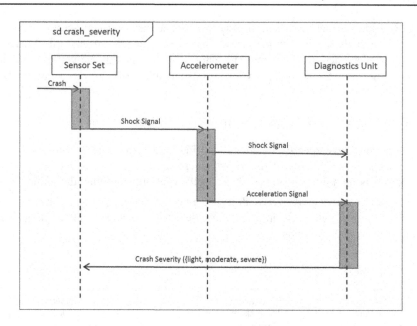

Fig. 12.8 SysML sequence diagram of crash severity

Time is represented along the vertical axis from top to bottom, like the swimlanes in an activity diagram. As specified in SysML 1.3, sequence diagrams can represent highly complex interactions with special constructs to represent various types of control logic, reference interactions on other sequence diagrams, and decomposition of lifelines into their constituent parts. Here we show only the basic symbols and construct a relatively simple sequence diagram.

Figure 12.8 is a sequence diagram of crash severity. At the top we see three blocks: **Sensor Set**, **Accelerometer**, and **Diagnostics Unit**. A corresponding *life line*, designated by a dashed line, goes down vertically from each block. Horizontal arrows designate messages between blocks. First, a **Crash** message is received by **Sensor Set**, upon which it performs some operation, called *execution occurrence* and designated as a wide line or elongated rectangle along the life line, such as the one just beneath **Sensor Set**. Upon execution completion, **Sensor Set** sends a **Shock Signal** message to the **Accelerometer**. The **Accelerometer** starts operating and sends **Shock Signal** further to the **Diagnostic Unit**, which, in turn, performs its operation and sends back to **Sensor Set** a message with the value of **Crash Severity**, which can be **light**, **moderate**, or **severe**.

As Fig. 12.9 shows, messages can be of various types. They can be *synchronous* or *asynchronous*, and can provide *return values*. Messages can start from execution occurrences, external source (gates) or unknown sources (found messages). They can end at execution occurrences, external targets (gates) or unknown destination (lost messages). Blocks, such as **Order** in Fig. 12.9, can be created and/or destroyed. A message arrow can be tilted downward rather than being horizontal to denote the fact that the passing of the message itself takes a non-zero amount of time and quantify the latency. Interactions (messages) can start or end on gates to other blocks or systems.

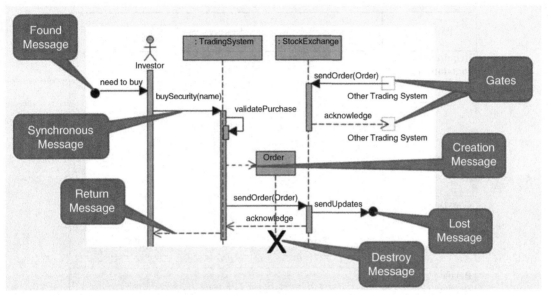

Fig. 12.9 SysML sequence diagram message kinds and their symbols

12.7 **Requirements Diagram**

The requirement diagram and the parametric diagram are two totally new kinds of diagrams that SysML has added to UML and are not part of UML. Requirement diagrams bridge typical requirements management tools and the system model. As the official OMG SysML Site indicates, SysML requirements diagram is a graphical construct for representing text-based requirements and relate them to other model elements.

The requirements diagram captures requirement hierarchies and derivations. It can be used to verify relationships between requirements and their implementation by allowing the modeler to relate a requirement to a model element that satisfies or verifies the requirement.

The main symbols of a SysML requirements diagram are presented in Fig. 12.10. A requirement is depicted as a block with the reserved word «requirement» at its top. In the SysML 1.3 document this is referred to as a stereotype of UML class that is subject to a set of constraints.

The containment relationship, depicted as a crossed circle (like the one under the Parent in Fig. 12.10) denotes that the requirement attached to the circle contains the ones linked to it. This provides for creating requirement hierarchies. Three additional main dependency relations between blocks, denoted by dashed arrows, are shown in Fig. 12.10. The stereotype «copy» denotes that the "Slave" is a copy of the "Master" (to which the arrow points). The stereotype «deriveReqt» denotes that the "Client" requirement is derived from the "Supplier" (to which the arrow points). The stereotype «satisfy» denotes that the block "namedElement" is a system component that satisfies the requirement to which the arrow points.

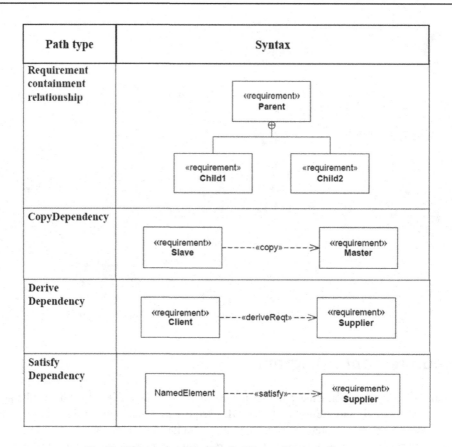

Path type	Syntax
Requirement containment relationship	
CopyDependency	
Derive Dependency	
Satisfy Dependency	

Fig. 12.10 Main symbols of the SysML requirements diagram

Three other dependencies of similar nature are «verify», «refine», and «trace». The «verify» dependency is between a requirement and a block that provides a way of verifying it. This can be a block having the stereotype «testCase». The «refine» dependency denotes that some elaborate requirement refines a more general requirement, e.g., a client's requirement. The «trace» dependency denotes that some block provide a way to trace a requirement. The «trace» dependency provides a way to keep track of where requirements are fulfilled in the system, as it is often the case that requirements are difficult to trace or it is not clear why some component was included in the model.

A standard requirement includes properties to specify its unique identifier and text requirement. Additional properties such as verification status, can be specified by the user. Indeed, requirements diagrams are depicted in a large variety of forms and styles.

Figure 12.11 presents four examples found on the Web that demonstrate this variability in styles.

The diagram in the top left is titled **req** TV Remote Control. It contains four requirements, the main of which is also called TV Remote Control. The three others, called Weight, Color, and Eco-Friendliness, are "children"—lower-level requirements that are subordinates of the parent requirement TV Remote Control.

This is designated by the lines with the crossed circles at their ends, in accord with the standard specification in Fig. 12.10. In addition to the text and ID attributes, each requirement here has the attributes source, kind, verifyMethod, risk, and status.

The diagram in the top right is titled **Requirement Diagram** Top-Level User Requirements. The standard specifies that **req** be used to designate a Requirement Diagram. The use of the black diamond, which is a symbol from block definition diagram (bdd) is another non-standard application. The containment symbol should be used instead.

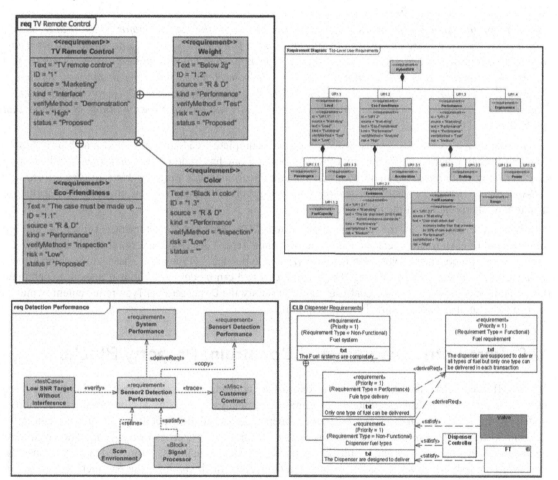

Fig. 12.11 Examples of the large variety of SysML requirement diagrams

The diagram in the bottom left, titled **req** Detection Performance, shows the use of all the six dependency kinds discussed above. For example, «testCase» Low SNR Target Without Interference «verify» «requirement» Sensor2 Detection Performance. Another example is «block» Signal Processor «satisfy» «requirement» Sensor2 Detection Performance. None of the requirements in this diagram has the feature compartment with the minimal set of features—text and ID, but the standard (Sect. 16.3.1.2) does allow to elide (leave out) this compartment.

Interestingly, Scan Environment, which is a use case, is at the origin of the «refine» dependency. This does not seem to be allowed by the standard, since according to OMG SysML v1.3 Sect. 16.3.1.1 (p.144) "The Requirement Diagram can only display requirements, packages, other classifiers, test cases, and rationale." However, this link between use cases and requirements can be useful. Trying to defend the legality of mixing symbols from various diagrams, we find that the informative Annex A—Diagrams of SysML v1.3 Standard (p. 168) states:

"Although the taxonomy provides a logical organization for the various major kinds of diagrams, it does not preclude the careful mixing of different kinds of diagram types, as one might do when one combines structural and behavioral elements (e.g., showing a state machine nested inside a compartment of a block). However, it is critical that the types of diagram elements that can appear on a particular diagram kind be constrained and well-specified. The diagram elements tables in each clause describe what symbols can appear in the diagram, but do not specify the different combinations of symbols that can be used."

This paragraph essentially grants SysML modelers complete freedom to mix and match any symbol from any SysML diagram kind with any other symbol. All one has to do is *"careful mixing"* and ensuring that *"the types of diagram elements that can appear on a particular diagram kind be constrained and well-specified."* However, what *"constrained and well-specified"* means is itself not specified, leaving it open to any interpretation of the modeler.

Finally, the diagram in the bottom right, titled **CLD** Dispenser Requirements, shows in the top compartment of each requirement, in addition to the name (e.g., Fuel Type Delivery) also the requirement's priority (e.g., {Requirement Type=Non-Functional}) and type (e.g., {Type=1}). The feature compartment contains relatively elaborate text (e.g., "Only one type of fuel can be delivered"), but it does not contain an ID. Three blocks (Valve, Dispenser Controller, and FT) satisfy the Dispenser Fuel Type requirement, which is derived from another, more comprehensive requirement.

12.8 Parametric Diagram and Constraint Property Blocks

The SysML parametric diagram provides for expressing constrains between properties, thereby enabling integration of mathematical calculations or engineering analyses, such as performance and reliability models, with SysML design models. Constraint property blocks can also specify a network of quantitative constraints stemming from mathematical expressions of physical properties of a system. The constraints are captured in constraint property blocks—ConstraintBlock constructs, expressed as equations that include the underlying parameters. For example, a ConstraintBlock can have the parameters F, m, and a, and the constraint {F=m*a}. Another example is the kinetic energy equation $E=mv^2/2$. Performance parameters and their relationships to other parameters can be tracked throughout the system life cycle.

SysML constraint property blocks enable the integration of engineering analysis, such as performance and reliability models, with other SysML models. A constraint block (see Fig. 12.12 left) includes the constraint, normally in terms of a mathematical equation, and the parameters of the constraint, such as E, m, and v for energy, mass, and velocity.

For reuse purposes, constraint blocks are defined in a Block Definition Diagram. Parametric Diagrams use constraint blocks to constrain the value properties of other blocks. Constraint blocks may thus be reused on block definition diagrams and packaged into general-purpose or domain-specific model libraries. This constraining is done by binding the constraint parameters (such as m in the example above) to specific actual value properties of a block (such as the mass of a vehicle). A parametric diagram example appears in Fig. 12.13. Figure 12.14 is an OPD representation of this parametric diagram.[1]

A parametric diagram (see Fig. 12.12 right) uses one or more constraint property blocks to constrain the properties of one or more other blocks by binding the parameters through a mathematical relation. A constraint property may be shown on a parametric diagram using a standard form of internal property rectangle with the «constraint» keyword (short for constraintProperty) preceding its name (see Fig. 12.12 left). However, a constraint property may also be shown on a parametric diagram using a rountangle (see Fig. 12.12 middle). As with the standard rectangle form, compartments and internal properties may be shown within the rountangle. Using this shape enables avoiding the need to explicitly record the «constraint» keyword.

Figure 12.13 presents a parametric diagram that constraints fuel flow rate to a car fuel demand and fuel pressure through the relation FuelFlow = Pressure/(4*(InjectorDemand)), presumably due the fact that this is a 4-cylinder engine.

Any mathematical operation, from the basic four arithmetic operations to the most complex computation, can be viewed in OPM in terms of a calculating (informatical) process that uses (but not consumes) one or more input parameters to produce an output. With this in mind, any SysML parametric diagram can be presented as an OPD where the constraint is a **Calculating** process preceded by the mathematical expression that binds and constrains the input parameters. The input parameters are instruments, unless we wish to specify that they are not kept after the **Calculating** process ends.

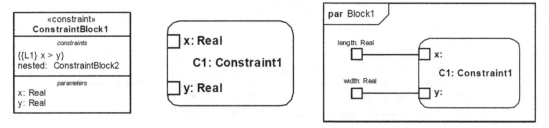

Fig. 12.12 A generic constraint block (left) and a parametric diagram (right). Source: OMG SysML v1.3, p.84

---

[1]Another, more complex example for doing calculations in appears in Fig. 22.5 and in Fig. 22.6.

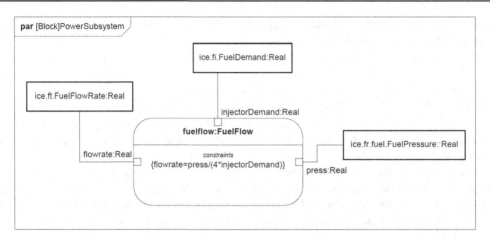

Fig. 12.13 A parametric diagram that constraints fuel flow rate to fuel demand and fuel pressure (source: OMG SysML v1.3, p.199)

Adopting this simple concept transformation, Fig. 12.14 is an OPD representation of the parametric diagram in Fig. 12.13. In addition to this compact graphic representation, we get "for free" the OPL textual representation, which can be readily translated to code in any programming language or even directly executed to compute **Pressure/(4*(Injector Demand))**. Another, more involved example for doing calculations in OPM appears in Figs. 22.5 and 22.6.

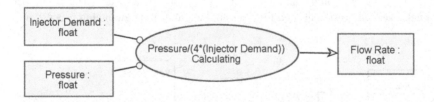

Flow Rate, Injector Demand, and **Pressure** are of type **float.**
Pressure/(4*(Injector Demand)) Calculating requires **Pressure** and **Injector Demand.**
Pressure/(4*(Injector Demand)) Calculating yields **Flow Rate.**

Fig. 12.14 An OPD representation of the parametric diagram in Fig. 12.13

12.9 SysML–OPM Comparison

In this section we compare SysML to OPM first in terms of relating to each language as a whole and then by discussing and showing how OPM can be applied to model several SysML diagram kinds. Table 12.1 provides a compact comparison between SysML and OPM in terms of various attributes.

Table 12.1 Comparison between SysML and OPM attributes

Feature	SysML	OPM
Theoretical foundation	UML; Object-Oriented paradigm	Minimal universal ontology; Object-Process Theorem
Standard documentation number of pages	~1670=700 (UML Infrastructure) + 700 (UML Superstructure) + 270 (OMG SysML)	~180=100 (ISO 19450 main standard) + 80 (appendices)
Standardization body	OMG	ISO
Number of diagram kinds	9	1
Top-level concept	Block (UML object class)	Thing (object or process)
Complexity management guiding principle	Aspect-based decomposition	Detail-level-based decomposition
Hierarchical decomposition	In some diagram kinds	Yes
Number of symbols	~120	~20
Graphic modality	Yes	Yes
Textual modality	No[2]	Yes
Built-in physical-informatical distinction	No	Yes
Systemic-environmental distinction	Partial (using boundaries)	Yes
Logical relations (OR, XOR, AND)	No	Yes
Probability modeling	No	Yes
Execution, animated simulation, validation and verification capability	Partial (in some tools for some diagram kinds)	Yes
Tool availability	Many, some free	Currently one free (OPCAT) from http://esml.iem.technion.ac.il/ Cloud-based tool under development

---

[2]It is possible to generate a textual modality using some commercial SysML tools' reporting and documentation modules but this is not part of the language standard and there is no predefined syntax for formal sentences.

12.9.1 OPM Processes as First Class Citizens

Underlying OPM is a philosophy stipulating that in order to faithfully and naturally model, analyze, and design systems in any domain, processes need to be recognized as "first class citizens." Like objects, OPM processes are considered as bona fide, stand-alone "things" rather than being encapsulated within objects, as the object-oriented (OO) approach advocates. The lack of a direct acknowledgement of process as a foundational ontological concept beside object results in a multitude of terms and symbols for process in UML and SysML: use case, activity, action, method, and sequence. All of these are processes, but each has some nuance or connotation that is not explicitly defined.

Objects in OPM are things that persist, while processes are transient things that transform objects. Processes transform objects in one of three ways: (1) affecting their state, (2) generating new objects, or (3) consuming existing objects.

12.9.2 Physical and Informatical Things

Geared for systems engineering from the outset and treating software systems as specializations of general systems, OPM has no inherent "software-oriented" language semantics. For example, OPM objects and processes can be *informatical*, or *cybernetic*, which may exist in models of both software systems and other general systems, or *physical*, which is atypical of pure software systems but obviously essential for systems in general.

Both objects and processes can be physical or informatical. Not only can objects and processes be physical or informational, they can also be systemic (part of the system) or environmental (part of the environment interacting with the system).

12.9.3 Model Multiplicity Versus Model Singularity

A major difference between SysML and OPM is the number of views (diagram types) used in each language. While OPM is based on a single diagram type—Object-Process Diagram (OPD), SysML has inherited UML's model multiplicity (Peleg and Dori 2000), i.e., it presents each one of the system's aspects in a different view, using a different diagram type. SysML includes a subset of UML diagrams, as well as two new types of diagrams for systems engineering: Requirement Diagram and Parametric Diagram.

A set of inter-related Object-Process Diagrams (OPDs), showing portions of the system at various levels of detail, constitutes the graphical, visual OPM formalism. OPD, OPM's single type of diagram, may be missing some elements that are important for systems engineering, such as the SysML parametric constraints, although these can be treated in OPM as attributes with values that are manipulated by processes that are mathematical operations.

Both languages support hierarchical representation of the model. However, in contrast to SysML, where the model is represented in separate views with partial support of hierarchy, in OPM the entire system model is based on a well-defined hierarchy of OPDs. These are but few of several dissimilarities between the languages, which make it interesting to study and compare the differences between them.

12.9.4 Graphics Versus Bimodal Graphics-Text Combination

OPM combines mathematically-grounded formal yet simple graphical language with natural language sentences to express the function, structure, and behavior of systems in an integrated, single model. The two semantically equivalent modalities, one graphic and the other textual, jointly express the same OPM model. While the visual-graphic and the verbal-textual modalities are semantically equivalent, they appeal to two different information processing channels of the brain, the visual and the lingual.

OPM is a prime vehicle for carrying out the tasks that are involved in system development. It does so in a straightforward, friendly, unambiguous manner. One important reason for this is that the design of OPM has not been influenced by what current programming languages can or cannot do, but rather, what makes the most sense when trying to represent and conceptually model systems as best as possible.

Due to the resulting intuitiveness, OPM is communicable to both technical and non-technical stakeholders of the system being developed, including peers, customers and implementers. At the same time, the formality of OPM makes it amenable to computer manipulation for generating, automatically or semi-automatically, large portions of the conceived system, notably program code and database schema.

12.9.5 Activity Diagrams Compared with OPDs

As noted, flows in an activity diagram can be of two kinds: control flow and object (or block) flow. A control flow designates the flow from one action to another without explicit mention of an object. Figure 12.7 is an example where all the flows are control flows; the message being passed from one action to the next is implicit. In contrast, an object flow has a specific object that is an output of one action and is input to the next. There are two ways to model object flow, both shown in Fig. 12.15. The one at the top is the pin notation: **Blueprint** is both the output on the pin of the **Designing** action and the input on the pin of the **Manufacturing** action. The type of the input and output must be the same. The second way to model object flow, shown at the bottom of Fig. 12.15, is the explicit object notation: The object (or block) is depicted as both the output and input.

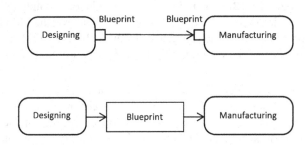

Fig. 12.15 Two ways to show an object flow. Top: pin notation. Bottom: object notation

The activity diagram at the bottom of Fig. 12.15 looks very similar to an OPD. It looks like all we need to do is replace the activity symbol—the rountangle—with the OPD symbol for process—the ellipse, we will get a semantically equivalent model. Doing this produces the OPD in Fig. 12.16. The two models really look isomorphic: just replace the shape and voila! However, to gain insight into the exact semantics of this OPD, we should read its OPL paragraph:

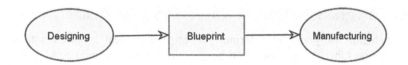

Fig. 12.16 First attempt at OPM modeling of the activity diagram at the bottom of Fig. 12.15

Designing yields **Blueprint**.
Manufacturing consumes **Blueprint**.

Is this really what we wanted to model? Is **Blueprint** really consumed by **Manufacturing**? What we really want to model is that once ready, **Blueprint** enables **Manufacturing**. However, **Manufacturing** does not consume **Blueprint**, but rather references it, so **Blueprint** is an enabler, or, more specifically, an instrument: It is required by the **Manufacturing** process, but it is not destroyed by it. Moreover, while **Blueprint** is an informatical object, **Manufacturing** is a physical process.

The OPL paragraph of this OPD is indeed more telling and it confirms our improved graphical model (Fig. 12.17):

Designing yields **Blueprint**.
Manufacturing is physical.
Manufacturing requires **Blueprint**.

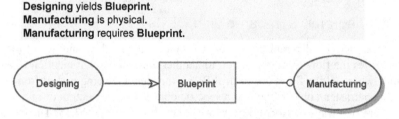

Fig. 12.17 An improved OPM model of the activity diagram at the bottom of Fig. 12.15

Contemplating on the thought process that this exercise involved, we realize that the semantics of the activity diagram is less expressive than that of the OPD. Arrows between an activity and an object in an activity diagram have *flow* semantics, while in OPM they have *transformation* semantics—creation, consumption, or state change. The **Blueprint** in the activity diagram simply "flows" between the two actions, implicitly changing its logical location as it does so, but weather **Blueprint** is consumed by **Manufacturing** or it just enables it is not specified. Conversely, the OPM arrows do not have flow semantics—they do not imply that the object involved changes its location, only that it undergoes some transformation.

The activity diagram cannot distinguish between an instrument and a consumee (neither can any other SysML diagram type, at least not directly). The distinction between the informatical essence of Designing and Blueprint on one hand and the physical essence of Manufacturing on the other hand cannot be modeled either. Neither this essence distinction nor the distinction between an enabler and a transformee can be modeled in a straightforward manner by any one of the nine SysML diagram kinds.

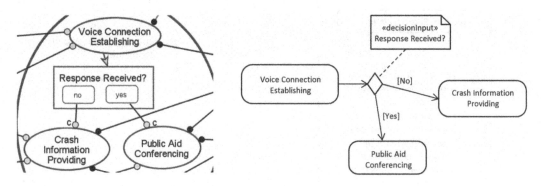

Fig. 12.18 Example of an activity diagram decision node. Left: a relevant portion of the OPD. Right: an equivalent activity diagram

12.9.6 Flow of Control in Activity Diagrams Versus OPDs

The flow of control in activity diagrams is achieved through *decision nodes*, which are diamond-shaped nodes from which two or more control flow lines emanate, as shown in Fig. 12.18. On the left hand side of Fig. 12.18 is a relevant portion of the OPD, while on the right hand side is the equivalent activity diagram.

Examining the two models, we see that OPM does not require the special decision symbol—the diamond in the activity diagram. Rather an object with two states—a Boolean object—is used. Moreover, the decision symbol often requires, as is the case here, a note (whose symbol is a piece of paper with its top right corner folded; see Fig. 12.18) with the reserved word «decisionInput» in order to be able to specify what is being decided in the decision node. Notes are informal annotations that prevent automating the model execution. Moreover, the decision variable is often an object or part of an object in and of itself (e.g., a message or the result of a function), possibly with states, attributes, and other refinees, but using a decision node does not provide for modeling that object.

12.9.7 OPM Implementation of a Requirements Diagram

As with other SysML diagrams we have seen, OPM enables modeling requirements with no need for a specialized symbol set. Consider, for example, the following requirement, called Flow Rate Regulation:

"Gasoline flow rate shall be directly proportional to the piston pressure and inversely proportional to the injector demand and to the number of pistons."

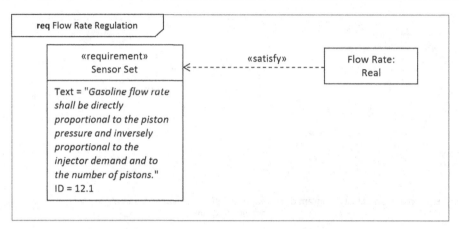

Fig. 12.19 Flow Rate Regulation requirements diagram

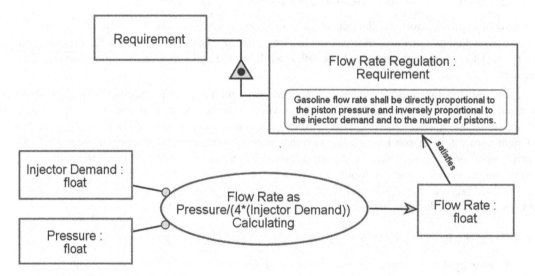

Fig. 12.20 The Flow Rate requirement from Fig. 12.19 expressed in an OPM model

This requirement is presented in the requirements diagram in Fig. 12.19. In OPM we define an informatical object class **Requirement**, which has an instance to **Flow Rate Regulation**. Since **Flow Rate** satisfies this requirement, extending the OPD in Fig. 12.14, we express this relation using OPM's tagged structural link **satisfies** in Fig. 12.20.

Another approach is to formally model the requirement and derive the textual requirement specification from the resulting OPL text, rather than writing freestyle requirements. Using the exhibition-characterization relation, we can model the **Requirement** in Fig. 12.20 as exhibiting several parts, including **Client Free Text**, **Vitality**, **Urgency**, **Satisfying Status**, and **Deriving Requirement**. The value of the attribute **Client Free Text** of the instance **Flow Rate Regulation** will be "**Gasoline flow rate shall be**

directly proportional to the piston pressure and inversely proportional to the injector demand and to the number of pistons".

To increase the generality we can model the object Piston Set whose Size attribute value is a parameter instead of the number 4 in the mathematical expression which is part of the process name "**Flow Rate as Pressure/(4*(Injector Demand)) Calculating**". Furthermore, instead of including this expression in the process name, we can in-zoom and model how the result is computed step-by-step using the parameters. This way if any one of the parameters or even the expression changes, the process name does not need to be changed.

12.10 SysML–OPM Synergies

Grobshtein and Dori (2011) evaluated aspects of SysML and OPM on the basis of a concrete sample problem, in which multiple aspects of the system were modeled in both SysML and OPM. OPM was found advantageous in presenting the system different hierarchy levels and combining structure with behavior, while SysML was found more convenient for modeling detailed views of some aspects. This finding was corroborated in a later empirical work, which pointed out that for answering particular focused questions, a certain SysML view, which was automatically generated from an OPM model, may provide a better answer quicker. Hence there is apparent potential synergy of combining advantages of these two languages.

12.11 Summary

- Activity diagrams are illustrations of workflows, which describe the flow among actions and are closest in semantics to OPDs.
- An action is a basic unit in an activity diagram, but by using the rake symbol it can be elaborated into an entire activity diagram in its sown right, providing for a refinement mechanism similar to OPM in-zooming.
- Flows in activity diagrams can be of two kinds: *control* flow and *object* flow.
- *Accept*, *send*, and *time event action nodes* have special syntax and semantics.
- *Join* and *fork nodes* are used for synchronizing actions.
- Arrows between an activity and an object in an activity diagram have *flow* semantics, while in OPM they have *transformation* semantics—creation, consumption, or state change.
- Flow of control in activity diagrams is achieved through *decision nodes*, which are diamond-shaped nodes to which a *decision input notes* are often attached. In OPM, flow of control is based in part on Boolean objects.
- Requirements diagrams bridge typical requirements management tools and the system model.
- Parametric diagrams use *constraint property blocks* to bind system parameters to each other via mathematical expressions. In OPM this can be done by expressing the mathematical formula as a computation process.

- Requirements and parametric diagrams (like all the other SysML diagram kinds) can be modeled in OPM without special symbols.

12.12 **Problems**

1. Draw an activity diagram of the OPD in Fig. 7.4.
2. Draw an activity diagram of the OPD in Fig. 8.6.
3. Using the rake symbol, connect the two activity diagrams from problems 1 and 2.
4. For each one of the two activity diagrams from problems 1 and 2, indicate the *control* flows by red and each *object* flow by green.
5. Explain the difference in the semantics of arrows between activity diagram and OPD.
6. Use the specification below to draw a requirements diagram.

> A passenger arriving at an airport deposits her baggage with the airline she is flying with. A baggage handling system manages the transfer of the baggage to the passenger's destination.

7. Compare the requirements diagram from Problem 6 with the OPD in Fig. 2.5.
8. Draw a parametric diagram for the formula $E = mC^2$.
9. Draw an OPD for the formula $E = mC^2$.
10. Compare the parametric diagram from Problem 8 with the OPD from Problem 9.

Chapter 13
The Dynamic System Aspect

Every day we are confronted with systems that have an inherent tendency to change.
The weather, the stock market, or the economic situation, are examples.

Meinhardt (1995)

Systems change over time. An important motivation in the development of OPM has been to strike a needed balance in a system's conceptual model between the structural, static and procedural, dynamic aspects of the system. The dynamic aspect of a system specifies how the system operates to attain its function, complementing its static aspect. OPM is at least process-oriented as it is object-oriented. Indeed, OPM models unify structure and behavior in one coherent frame of reference, with time being the fundamental underlying concept. This chapter addresses modeling the dynamics aspect of a system.

13.1 Change and Effect

Processes and system dynamics are closely associated with the notion of *change*. Change is such a familiar and basic concept that defining it seems both difficult and unnecessary. However, when we talk about a change in OPM, we need to be specific about what a change means.

> A **change** of an object is an alteration in the state of that object.

More specifically, a change of an object is replacing its current state by another state. The only thing that can cause this change is a process. The process causes the change by taking as input an object at some state—the input state, and outputting it in another state—the output state. Hence, a change of an object means a *change in the state* the object is at.

Stateful objects can be affected, i.e., their states can change. This change mechanism underlines the intimate, inseparable link between objects and processes. We call this change in state the *effect* of the process on the object.

> **Effect** is a change in the state of an object that a process causes by its occurrence.

While the terms "change" and "effect" seem almost synonymous, there is a subtle difference in their usage. We use *effect* to refer to what the process does to the object, and *change*—to what happens to the object as a result of the process occurrence. Later in this section we refine the above definition of effect with the notions of input and output links.

© Springer Science+Business Media New York 2016
D. Dori, *Model-Based Systems Engineering with OPM and SysML*, DOI 10.1007/978-1-4939-3295-5_13

13.2 **Existence and Transformation**

In Sect. 10.3.2, we have defined transformation of an object by a process as the generalization of construction, effect, and consumption. *Construction* is synonymous with creation, generation, or yielding. *Effect* is synonymous with change or switch, and *consumption* is synonymous with elimination, termination, annihilation, or destruction. The *effect* of a process on an object is to change that object from one of its states to another, but the object still exists, and it keeps maintaining the identity it had before the process occurred. Construction and consumption change the very existence of the object and are therefore more profound transformations than effect. When we say that a process *constructs* (yields, generates, creates, or results in) an object, we mean that the object, which had not previously existed, has undergone a radical transformation and is now a new, separate entity. When we say that a process *consumes* (eliminates or destroys) an object, we mean that the object, which had previously existed, has undergone a radical transformation so it no longer exists in the system.

13.2.1 Construction and Consumption: Extreme Object Changes

When we consider existent and non-existent as states of an object, construction and consumption become extreme cases of object state changes, as

Fig. 13.1 presents using nine OPDs. The rows in this 3×3 matrix are three stages of transformation evolution of three objects, **Constructed Object**, **Existing Object**, and **Consumed Object**. The horizontal axis (the three columns) represents the kind of object transformations, from constructive on the left to destructive on the right. Accordingly, there are three corresponding processes: **Constructing** on the left column, **Changing** in the middle, and **Consuming** on the right.

The vertical axis (the three rows) represents the level of detail, from the most detailed at the top row to the most abstract at the bottom row. In the top row, all the states of all three objects are expressed, and input-output link pairs originate from and arrive at these states. In the middle row, since the state **non-existent** of **Constructed Object** and the state **non-existent** of **Consumed Object** do not exist, they are removed along with the links connecting them. Also, edges of the remaining transforming links in all three columns have migrated from the states to the contour of the object box. This is an interim stage aimed at showing the evolution of links. Finally, in the bottom row, all the remaining states are suppressed, showing the final three transforming links: result, effect, and consumption links. The effect link (bottom center) is an abstraction of the *input-output link pair* (top center), in which the states are suppressed such that the semantics of the effect link is a change in the states of the object from some unspecified input state to another unspecified output state.

The use of the states **non-existent** and **existent** of an object is useful when we wish to explicitly model that the object is present in or missing from the system. For example, we have used it to model molecular biology concepts such as removal of a factor or gene knockdown (Somekh et al. 2014).

13.2.2 Change of State or Change of Identity?

During their life, objects can undergo a host of transformations. Transformation of an object can, by our definition, take place only when a process acts upon the object. This transformation generates, affects, or eliminates the object. The extent of the change can vary from very small to very large. If the change is small, such as a change in the location of the object or in its color, we tend to say that the object was altered from one of its states to another while keeping its identity. As the extent of the effect grows, so does the difference between the object before the process started and after it ended. At some point, the two become so conceptually different that the modeler is inclined to think of the object resulting from the process as a newly created object. The object that had existed before the process took place may have been eliminated or at least changed radically. As we show below, the issue of whether an object changed only its state or its entire identity is similar in natural and artificial systems.

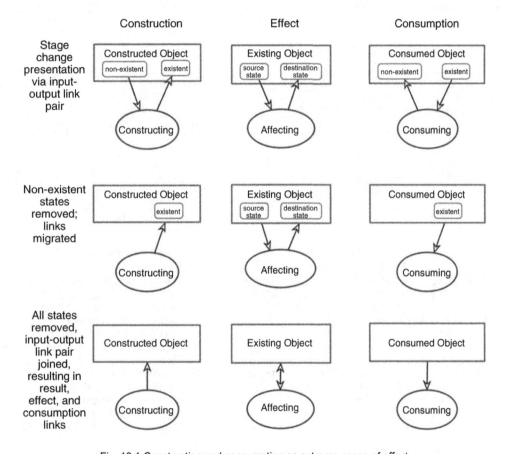

Fig. 13.1 Construction and consumption as extreme cases of effect

13.2.3 Transformations in Living Organisms

In nature, living organisms undergo a striking variety of transformations. Some of the transformations are deemed as just a change in state, while others are considered to be a change in the organism's identity. The transformation from a cub to a grown-up lion is considered a change in the state of a lion from young to adult. Similarly, growing of a baby into an adult is considered a change in the person's state. The silkworm, on the other hand, has four distinct forms of existence. It transforms from egg to larva (worm, or caterpillar) to pupa, the larva undergoes complete transformation within a protective cocoon or hardened case, to butterfly, which, in turn, lays the eggs of the next silkworm generation. Each transformation yields an object that is very distinct from its predecessor in shape and function. The difference is so profound that each such transformation is called metamorphosis. We are inclined to view each reincarnation as a separate object rather than a mere change of the same object's state. A frog, like other amphibians, transforms from spawn to egg to tadpole to legged tadpole to froglet to adult, providing an example similar to the silkworm.

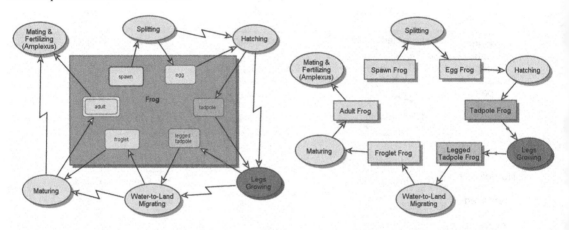

Frog can be **spawn, egg, tadpole, legged tadpole, froglet,** or **adult**.
Frog is initially **spawn** and finally **Adult**.
Mating & Fertilizing (Amplexus) is physical.
Mating & Fertilizing (Amplexus) changes **Frog** from **adult** to **spawn**.
Mating & Fertilizing (Amplexus) invokes **Splitting**.
Splitting changes **Frog** from **spawn** to **egg**.
Splitting invokes **Hatching**.
Hatching changes **Frog** from **egg** to **tadpole**.
Hatching invokes **Legs Growing**.
Legs Growing changes **Frog** from **tadpole** to **legged tadpole**.
Legs Growing invokes **Water-to-Land Migrating**.
Maturing changes **Frog** from **froglet** to **adult**.
Maturing invokes **Mating & Fertilizing (Amplexus)**.
Water-to-Land Migrating changes **Frog** from **legged tadpole** to **froglet**.
Water-to-Land Migrating invokes **Maturing**.

Mating & Fertilizing (Amplexus)
consumes **Adult Frog**.
Splitting consumes **Spawn Frog**.
Splitting yields **Egg Frog**.
Hatching consumes **Egg Frog**.
Hatching yields **Tadpole Frog**.
Legs Growing consumes **Tadpole Frog**.
Legs Growing yields **Legged Tadpole Frog**.
Maturing consumes **Froglet Frog**.
Maturing yields **Adult Frog**.
Water-to-Land Migrating consumes **Legged Tadpole Frog**.
Water-to-Land Migrating yields **Froglet Frog**.

Fig. 13.2 Two concurrently simulated models of Frog lifecycle. Left: Change of object state. Right: Change of object identity

Figure 13.2 shows an OPCAT screenshot of two OPM models that are simulated concurrently. The model on the left shows **Frog** as a single object with six states: **spawn, egg, tadpole, legged tadpole, froglet,** and **adult**. Thanks to the invocation links, once invoked by externally activating **Splitting**, this model completes a whole cycle from **spawn** to **adult**.

The model on the right shows six different stateless objects of the various incarnations of frog: **Spawn Frog, Egg Frog, Tadpole Frog, Legged Tadpole Frog, Froglet Frog,** and **Adult Frog** (here each process needs to be invoked separately; this can be avoided if we replace each consumption link, e.g., the one from **Egg Frog** to **Hatching**, with an event consumption link). At this point of the simulation the process **Legs Growing** is active (as the dark color and points along the arrows show). The pertinent OPL sentence for the model on the left is:

> **Legs Growing** changes **Frog** from **tadpole** to **legged tadpole**.

The pertinent OPL sentences for the model on the right is:

> **Legs Growing** consumes **Tadpole Frog**.
> **Legs Growing** yields **Legged Tadpole Frog**.

The frog and silkworm examples are conveniently thought of as changes of object although genetically they are the same organism, because the various incarnations of these creatures are profoundly different from each other in both appearance and behavior. The human and lion examples, on the other hand, are more naturally modeled as a change of the object's state.

13.2.4 Transformations of Artificial Objects

The situation with transformations of artificial objects is similar to natural ones: If the change is profound, objects change identity, otherwise, the same object just alters its state. What transformation is "profound" is subjective and context-sensitive. Consider, for example, two processes from a manufacturing realm: **Molding** and **Testing**. **Molding** acts on the object **Raw Material** (e.g., plastic), converting it to another object, that we call **Product**. The identity of **Raw Material** changed as a result of the **Molding** process to the extent that we need to refer to the process outcome by a different name. Hence, the object **Raw Material** has been eliminated or consumed, while a new object, called **Product**, has been created (or constructed, or generated). We can model the relation between the two objects, for example by adding a tagged structural relation from **Product** to **Raw Material** with the tag "**is made of**", which will result in the OPL sentence **Product is made of Raw Material**.

Suppose **Product** now undergoes the process of **Testing**, in which its shear strength is measured. If the test succeeds, **Product** is **approved**, otherwise it is **rejected**. Unlike the **Molding** process, which altered the identity of the processed object from **Raw Material** to **Product**, **Testing** does not change **Product** to the extent that we would be inclined to say that it lost its identity. Instead, the only effect of the **Testing** process is to alter the state of **Product** (from **untested** to **tested**). While there is a difference between **Product** before and after the **Testing**, (since after the test we have information about the product's strength, which we did not have before), this difference is not profound enough to justify change of identity. However, it does cause a change in state. Hence, transformation can be thought of as a general term that encompasses creation, effect (change of state) and elimination of an object. We will elaborate on this when discussing system dynamics.

The criterion for whether the process changes the object's state or the object's identity is whether it is possible and makes sense to create an attribute which the object in question exhibits with the same values as the states of the object. In our case the attribute of **Product** would be **Testing Status** object with the same values, **pre-tested** and **tested**. If this is possible, as is the case here, then the change is only in the state of the object but not in its identity. If not, as is the case in the **Raw Material** to **Product** example—the change is in the object identity.

Generalizing the natural and artificial examples, when the change is not profound or drastic, we are inclined to think that the object only alters its state while retaining its identity. When the transformation is extreme, a change in object identity takes place. As is the case in similar situations, the borderline between "drastic" and "non-drastic" is not well-defined. Analyzing the same system, different modelers may provide different viewpoints on whether a particular object should lose its identity and become a new object. Indeed, we will see instances where it makes sense to model changes in objects either as a change in their state (or attribute value), or as a change in their identity, and both versions would be acceptable.

13.3 Procedural Links

Procedural links are the indispensable "mortar" between processes and objects or their states. They provide for integration of the system's structure and behavior within a single model. Procedural links are of utmost importance.

> A **procedural link** is a link between a process and an object or its state, or between two processes.

The majority of procedural links are between a process and an object or its state. The only three procedural link kinds between two processes are the invocation link and the overtime and undertime exception links discussed in Chap. 22. As discussed in Sect. 10.10.3 an invocation link may replace a transient, short-lived physical or informatical object that a source process creates to initiate the destination process, which immediately consumes the transient object. This is also true for the exception links (where the object may be a message). Therefore we often omit the last part of the procedural link definition and say that a procedural link is a link between a process and an object or its state.

The structure-behavior integration that procedural links provide is one of the most important features of OPM. This integration within a single model eliminates in the first place the inherent diagram kind multiplicity problem (Peleg and Dori 2000) that are characteristic of object-oriented methods such as UML and SysML, whose ontology is far from being minimal.

13.3.1 Transforming Versus Enabling Procedural Links

The definition of OPM process requires that the process transforms at least one object. In addition to the object(s) being transformed, the process can also require one or more objects that *enable* that process, but are not transformed by it. Hence, from the viewpoint of a given process, OPM distinguishes between two types of objects: a *transformee*—an object that the process transforms (generates, affects, or consumes), and an *enabler*—an object that enables the process but is not transformed by that process. Accordingly, there are two types of procedural links: *transforming links* and *enabling links*.

13.3.2 Transformees

We have defined transformee of process P is an object B that P transforms as a result of its occurrence. The transformation can be construction, effect (change of state) or consumption. Transformee is a *role* that the object B assumes *with respect to the particular process P*. so B can be a transformee with respect to some process P_1 and an enabler with respect to another process P_2. A transformee can be one of three types defined below.

> *A **consumee** of a process **P** is a transformee of **P** that **P** consumes as a result of the occurrence of **P**.*
>
> *A **resultee** of a process **P** is a transformee of **P** that **P** creates as a result of the occurrence of **P**.*
>
> *An **affectee** of a process **P** is a transformee of **P** that that **P** affects as a result of the occurrence of **P**.*

In the bottom line of Fig. 13.1, **Consumed Object**, **Constructed Object**, and **Existing Object** are the consumee, resultee, and affectee, respectively. A consumee can be thought of as an *input* to the process, as the process consumes it, and a resultee—an *output* of the process, as the process creates it. An affectee is both *input* and *output*: the process takes it in its input state and outputs it in its output state.

These analogies are definitely true for physical objects. However, an informatical object can serve as input to a process without being consumed in whole or in part. For example, suppose in Fig. 13.3 a **File** in a database is erased by an **Erasing** process, then **File** is a consumee of as well as an input to **Erasing**. If **File** is created by a **Creating** process, then **File** is a resultee as well as an output of **Creating**. If the **File** is edited (such that data is added to, changed, or removed from the file) by an **Editing** process, then **File** is an affectee of **Editing**, as well as both input and output.

If the **File** is read from via a **Reading** process, then **File** is an input to this process, but it is not consumed or changed in any other way—it serves as an instrument for **Reading**, as we discuss below. A physical object, such as a resource, which is an input to a process, is consumed by the process, at least in part. There are many physical objects, such as a **Hammer**—a tool for the process of **Nail Driving**, that are instruments and are essentially unchanged by the process which they enable.

13.4 Transforming Links

Transforming links are unidirectional or bidirectional arrows connecting the transformee to the process which transforms it.

> *A **transforming link** is a procedural link that connects a process with a transformee of that process.*

Figure 13.3 shows the links between **File** on one hand and **File Creating**, **File Editing**, and **File Deleting** on the other hand as examples of result, effect, and consumption links, respectively. These are specializations of a transforming link, as defined below.

In Fig. 13.4, **Processing** is linked to three **Transformee** specializations: **Consumee**, **Affectee**, and **Resultee** via their corresponding transforming links—consumption, effect, and result links.

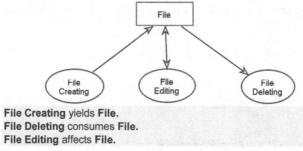

File Creating yields **File**.
File Deleting consumes **File**.
File Editing affects **File**.

Fig. 13.3 Result, effect, and consumption link between **File** and **File Creating**, **File Editing**, and **File Deleting**, respectively

*A **result link** is a unidirectional transformation link from a process to the resultee that this process creates.*

*An **effect link** is a bidirectional transformation link that connects a process with an affectee of that process.*

*A **consumption link** is a unidirectional transformation link from a consumee to the process that consumes it.*

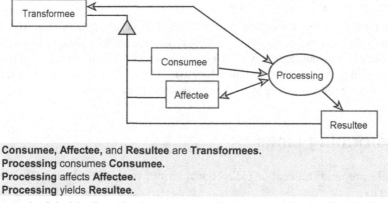

Consumee, Affectee, and **Resultee** are **Transformees.**
Processing consumes **Consumee.**
Processing affects **Affectee.**
Processing yields **Resultee.**

Fig. 13.4 Processing linked the three transformee types by their corresponding transforming links Enablers

13.4.1 Consumption and Result Timing

Existence of a consumee is a precondition, or part of the precondition, for process activation. If the required amount of consumee instances (usually 1) does not exist at the time of process initiation, then process activation shall wait for that amount of consumee instances to become existent. The consumption of the consumee instance(s) is immediate upon process activation, unless the model expresses consumption of the object over time, in which case consumption rate, a specialization of transformation rate, is used, as explained below.

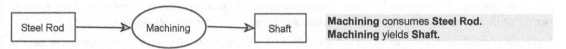

Fig. 13.5 Consumption and result timing: **Steel Rod** is consumed and disappears as soon as **Machining** starts. **Shaft** is created only when **Machining** ends

In Fig. 13.5, **Steel Rod** is a consumee for the process **Machining**, which generates the resultee **Shaft**. Once **Machining** has started, it consumes **Steel Rod**. However, **Shaft** is considered to be created only upon termination of **Machining**. During the process, **Steel Rod** does not exist anymore, but neither does **Shaft**.

13.4.2 The Evolution of Effect Link

Explicitly expressing the states of an object in the diagram often yields an OPD that is too detailed, crowded or busy, making it hard to read. This is a manifestation of the comprehensiveness-clarity tradeoff: these two desired qualities of complex system models are in constant conflict.

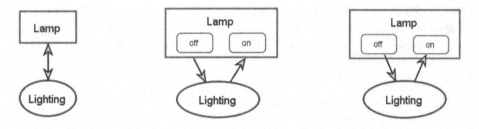

Lighting affects **Lamp**.   **Lighting** changes **Lamp** from **on** to **off**.

Fig. 13.6 The evolution of the effect link

Figure 13.6 shows state suppression and the evolution of the effect link, similar to the middle column in Fig. 13.1. In the middle OPD, the input and output links, which on the right OPD are attached to the state rountangles, migrate to the boundary of the **Lamp** object box. They now link the process and the object directly, going from and to the object itself rather than from and to its states. This interim representation is not valid in OPM. To reduce the graphic clutter, the input and output links, denoted by two opposite unidirectional arrows, have been superimposed by joining them into one bidirectional arrow, yielding the symbol of the effect link. Finally, on the left, the states of Lamp have been suppressed, because they are no longer vital since the links are not attached to them.

13.5 **Enablers**

Suppose you wish to move from your place to an apartment in another city. To do this, you need a moving truck, which you rent from a moving truck rental company. You return the truck to the same place where you took it and with the same amount of gasoline as you took it. Hence, ignoring the amortization of the truck, nothing in it has changed. However, you would not be able to carry out the moving without it. We say that the **Truck** is an *enabler* of the **Moving** process. Moreover, since some of your furniture are very heavy, you need a **Friend** as a second enabler of the **Moving** process.

An enabler of a process is an object that enables the process execution. Its presence is needed throughout the duration of the process, but when the process is over, the enabler exists at the same state as it was when the process started. In other words, an enabler of a process is an object that must be present throughout the process duration in order for that process to occur and terminate successfully, but is not transformed as a result of the occurrence of the process.

> An **enabler E** *of a process **P** is an object that must exist and be available in order for **P** to start, and remain present throughout the occurrence of **P** in order for **P** to terminate normally, with **E** ultimately unaffected.*

The enabler might undergo state change during the process, but, as the enabler definition states, when the enabled process is over, the enabler is at the same state at which it started. For example, the enabler **Oven** in Fig. 13.7 will change state from **off** to **on** at the beginning of the enabled **Baking** process, and from **on** back to **off** just prior to the end of **Baking**.

As the **Moving** example has shown, some enables are human, while others are inanimate. Hence, an enabler has two specializations: an agent or an instrument, as defined below.

13.5.1 Agent: A Human Enabler

The term *agent* is reserved for a human enabler.

> An **agent** *is an enabler who is a human or a group of humans.*

An agent is an intelligent enabler, who can control the process it enables by exercising common sense or goal-oriented considerations, implying that it must consist of one or more humans. Usually, it is a single person—the system's user or beneficiary. An agent can also be an organization, or a unit within a man-made organization, such as department, city council, government, group, team, etc.

The notion of agent is important because it provides for modeling the "human in the loop", i.e., how people interact with the system. This is a clear indication to the system designer of points of interaction with the system where *human interface* needs to be developed. Moreover, the hierarchy of processes that the agent is involved in provides an excellent guideline for the arrangement of a friendly graphic user interface, and creation of such interface can even be automated to some extent based on this model.

In the world of software and embedded systems, robots are often referred to as agents, and software agents are common in the Internet, capitalizing on evolving agent technologies. In OPM, which is geared to model all kinds of systems, including complex socio-technical systems and systems where humans are users and beneficiaries, humans (as individuals or groups) are privileged and distinguished from all the other inanimate enablers, so the term *agent* is reserved for humans only.[1] This enables focusing the attention of system architects and designers to care for humans' safety and special needs and desires

---

[1]A robot can still be called an *embedded-software agent*, and programs acting in the Internet on behalf of humans can still be called *software agents*. *Agent* without any qualification is reserved for individuals or groups of humans.

while interacting with the rest if the system—the system's usability and the users' experience and delight from using a well-designed and human-friendly and accommodating system.

The agent link is somewhat analogous to the *actor*—the "stick figure" in UML's or SysML's use-case diagram. In OPM, however, no separate kind of diagram is needed, as modeling the user is incorporated into the single OPM model. Use cases in SysML notation can automatically be extracted from the OPM model, as can other SysML models (Grobshtein and Dori 2011).

Not any human or organization is necessarily only an agent. For example, if a **Student** is engaged in the process of **Studying**, his or her **Knowledge Level** attribute change, say from **shallow** to **deep**. In this case, **Student** is not only an agent, but also a transformee. Likewise, if a department in an enterprise is undergoing business process reorganization, its structure and/or behavior changes as a result of this process, so in addition to being an agent, it is also a transformee.

The procedural link uniqueness OPM principle states that at any level of detail, an object and a process can be connected with at most one procedural link. Semantic strength and link precedence are defined and discussed in detail in Chap. 21. Here we note only that transforming links are semantically stronger than enabling links, because the transforming links denote creation, consumption, or change of the linked object, while the enabling links only denote enablement. A transforming link has precedence over an enabling link as shown in Fig. 21.15, therefore if we need to choose between an agent link and an effect link, as in the examples above, effect link shall be chosen.

13.5.2 Instrument: A Non-Human Enabler

An instrument of a process is any non-human, physical or informatical object, which does not change as a result of the execution of the process.

An instrument is a non-human enabler.

Examples of instruments include machines, tools, computers, robots, controllers, hardware, software, documents, orders, recipes, algorithms, prescriptions, files, commands, information, and data. Algorithms and recipes are prime examples of informatical instruments that can be used repeatedly, ideally without wearing out (in practice we may witness "software amortization" as well…).

Physical instruments usually change to some extent as they enable a process. In particular, they can wear out or degrade as they are being used as process enablers. Yet, from the viewpoint of the system under development, such objects would still be considered instruments, as these changes are either not significant enough to be accounted for, or they are out of the system's scope.

In other cases, wear and tear are factors to be considered. For example, in developing a **Manufacturing System**, a system architect may be required to account for **Maintaining** a **Machine** that wears out due to the **Metal Cutting** process it enables. In this case, the **Machine** should not be assigned the role of an instrument. Rather, it will be modeled as an affectee. The attribute of the **Machine** that changes as a result of its operation can be, for example, its **Amortization Level**, or hours of operation since the last overhaul. We will have to take this **Machine Wearing** process in account if our system encompasses the maintenance aspect of the **Machine**. The distinction in an OPD among the two types of enablers—agents and instruments—is made possible by their connection to the process they enable through the different enabling links, defined next.

13.5.3 Enabling Links: Agent and Instrument Links

Enables are linked to processes through enabling links.

> *An **enabling link** is a procedural link that connects a process with an enabler of that process.*
>
> *An **agent link** is an enabling link that connects a process with an agent of that process.*
>
> *An **instrument link** is a procedural link that connects a process with an enabler of that process.*

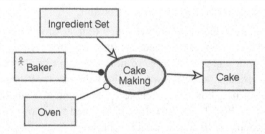

Baker handles **Cake Making**.
Cake Making requires **Oven**.
Cake Making consumes **Ingredient Set**.
Cake Making yields **Cake**.

Fig. 13.7 Enabling links example: The agent link from Baker and the instrument link from Oven

Graphically, as Fig. 13.7 shows, an enabling link is a "lollipop", a line leading from the enabler (**Baker**) to the process (**Cake Making**) it enables, which ends with a circle touching the process side. If the enabler is a human or a group of humans, the enabling link is an agent link, denoted as a "black lollipop", i.e., its ending circle is filled in (black).

The distinction between a human and a non-human enabler is important, since for humans to interact with the system, a dedicated interface needs to be designed. Hence, an optional stick figure can be added at the top-left corner of the agent's object symbol, as shown in Fig. 13.7. This optional stick figure is especially useful when the human in the model is an affectee, i.e., she or he is affected by the process to which it is linked, in which case we must use the effect link rather than the agent link. In this case, the stick figure retains the information that a human is involved.

If the enabler is an instrument, the enabling link is a "white lollipop", i.e., its ending circle is blank (white). The two OPL sentences associated with these links are:

Agent handles **Processing**.
Processing requires **Instrument**.

The OPL syntax of the first (agent) sentence is designed such that the agent appears first, followed by the reserved OPL phrase handles, followed by the process name. For the instrument sentence, the OPL syntax is such that the process name appears first, followed by the reserved OPL phrase requires, followed by the instrument name. This difference in both the OPL phrases and the order of the enablers in the sentences underlines that being humans, agents are more important than instruments.

All the process enablers must be present throughout the execution of the process which they enables. For example, in Fig. 13.7 both the agent **Baker** and the instrument **Oven** must be present throughout a **Cake Baking** process.

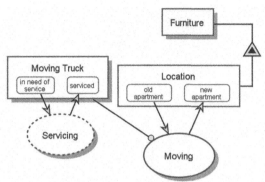

Moving Truck can be **in need of service** or **serviced**.	**Servicing** changes **Moving Truck** from **in need of service** to **serviced**.
Furniture exhibits **Location**.	**Moving** requires **Moving Truck**.
Location of **Furniture** can be **old apartment** or **new apartment**.	**Moving** changes **Location** from **old apartment** to **new apartment**.

Fig. 13.8 The same object playing the roles instrument and affectee: **Moving Truck** is an instrument of **Moving** and an affectee of **Servicing**

13.5.4 Enabler Versus Affectee

Enabler and affectee are possible roles that an object plays with respect to some processes. The same object can be an enabler for one process but not for another, or it can be an enabler for one process and an affectee for another. For example, the (environmental) process **Servicing** in Fig. 13.8, which the moving company applies periodically to its **Moving Truck**, changes the state of **Moving Truck** from **in need of service** to **serviced**, hence **Moving Truck** is an affectee of **Servicing**. However, with respect to the (systemic) process **Moving**, **Moving Truck** is an enabler—an instrument for **Moving**, while **Location** of **Furniture** is an affectee, as **Moving** changes the value (attribute state) of the **Location** attribute of **Furniture** from **old apartment** to **new apartment**.

13.6 The Preprocess and Postprocess Object Sets

Recall that the involved object set is the union of the preprocess object set and postprocess object set. As Fig. 13.9 shows, if the involved object-set contains enablers (agents and/or instruments), they are common to the preprocess and postprocess object sets, because their presence is required throughout the duration of the process they enable. Each process has its own involved object set, preprocess object set, and postprocess object set, and each can contain any number of objects.

Affectees are also common to the pre-process and post-process object sets, because they had existed before the affecting process started and remain existent after this process ended. Consumees disappear, so they belong only to the pre-process object set, while resultees are created, so they belong only to the post-process object set.

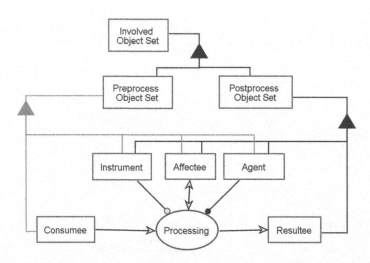

Involved Object Set consists of **Preprocess Object Set** and **Postprocess Object Set.**
Preprocess Object Set consists of **Consumee, Affectee, Agent,** and **Instrument.**
Postprocess Object Set consists of **Resultee, Affectee, Agent,** and **Instrument.**

Fig. 13.9 The Involved Object Set partitioned into Preprocess Object Set and Postprocess Object Set

The **Preprocess Object Set** and the **Postprocess Object Set** are not necessarily disjoint—they may be overlapping. Indeed, in Fig. 13.9, the overlapping members are the two enablers—**Agent** and **Instrument**, and one transformee—the **Affectee**. **Agent** and **Instrument** might belong to both object sets, because, by their definition, being enablers, they are required throughout the process (and are not supposed to change as a result of the occurrence of the process they enable). **Affectee** belongs to both the preprocess object set and postprocess object set, because it continues to exist after the process occurred, albeit in a different state. **Consumee** is the only involved object which is not in the **Postprocess Object Set**, because the **Processing** process consumed it, so it does not exist after **Processing** terminated. In an anti-symmetric manner, **Resultee** is the only involved object which is not in the **Preprocess Object Set**, because **Processing** generated it, so it did not exist prior to the beginning of **Processing**. The procedural links are summarized in Table 13.1.

13.7 **State-Specified Procedural Links**

It is often the case that we wish to specify in our model not just that an object is transformed or that it enables a process, but also at what state an enabler has to be in order for it to enable the process. We may also wish to be able to specify not just the object that a process generates, but also the particular state at which that object is generated as a result of the occurrence of a process. Likewise, one may wish to specify not just what object a process consumes, but also the particular state that the object needs to be at in order for the process to be able to consume it. State-specified procedural links provide for this.

> A **state-specified procedural link** is a procedural link that connects a process to a state of an object.

For each procedural link there is a state-specified version. State-specified procedural links differ from their non-state-specified version in that rather than connecting the (transforming or enabled) process to the involved object (transformee or enabler), they connect the process to one of the involved object's states. Thus, state-specified procedural links are elaborate versions of their regular procedural counterparts.

Table 13.1 Procedural links, their semantics, symbols, source, and destination

Link Type	Name	Semantics	Sample OPD & OPL	Source	Destination
Transforming link	Consumption	The process consumes the object.	Food → Eating **Eating** consumes **Food.**	Consumee	Process
	Result	The process generates the object.	Mining → Copper **Mining** yields **Copper.**	Process	Resultee
	Effect	The process affects the object by changing it from one unspecified state to another.	Purifying ⇄ Copper **Purifying** affects **Copper.**	Object and Process are both source and destination.	
Enabling link	Agent	The agent—a human—handles the process and is required to be there throughout the process, but it is not transformed.	Miner ●— Copper Mining **Miner** handles **Copper Mining.**	Agent	Process
	Instrument	The process requires the instrument—a non-human object— throughout the process, but not transformed.	Drill ○— Copper Mining **Copper Mining** requires **Drill.**	Instrument	Process

13.8 **State-Specified Enabling Links**

State-specified enabling links—agent link and instrument link—are defined as follows.

> A **state-specified agent link** is an agent link that originates from a specific state **s** of an agent **G** to process **P**, denoting that in order for **G** to handle **P**, **G** must be at state **s** throughout the duration of **P**.

Like its state-specified consumption link and result link counterparts, the state-specified instrument link originates from a specific state and terminates at a process. The semantics of this link is that the process is enabled if and only if the object exists and is at the state from which the link originates. This is contrasted with the "regular" instrument link, which originates from the enabling instrument but not from any particular state of that instrument. For example, a **pilot** must be **sober** in order to qualify as an agent for the **flying** process of an **Airplane**. In OPL: **Sober Pilot** handles **Flying.**

> *A **state-specified instrument link** is an instrument link that originates from a specific state **s** of the instrument **I** to process **P**, denoting that in order for **P** to execute, **I** must be at state **s** throughout the duration of **P**.*

The difference between the two instrument link types is demonstrated in Fig. 13.10, where on the left hand side, the object **Moving Truck** is the instrument for **Moving**, implying that the state at which this **Moving Truck** is does not matter. On the right hand side, the instrument link originates from the state **serviced** of **Moving Truck**, implying that only if **Moving Truck** is **serviced**, **Moving** can take place.

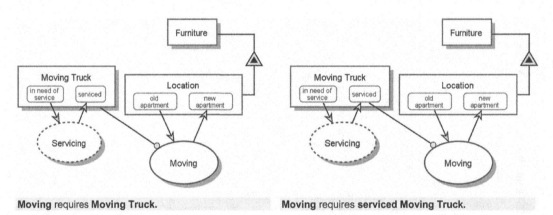

Moving requires **Moving Truck.**   **Moving** requires **serviced Moving Truck.**

Fig. 13.10 Instrument link vs. state-specified instrument link: Left: Instrument link—**Moving Truck** is an instrument of **Moving**. Right: State-specified instrument link—serviced **Moving Truck** is an instrument of **Moving**

Table 13.2 summarizes the semantics, symbols, source, and destination of the two state-specified enabling links.

13.9 **State-Specified Transforming Links**

State-specified transforming links differ from their corresponding regular, non-state-specified versions in that rather than connecting the transformee (consumee, affectee, or resultee) to or from the transforming process, they connect one of the transformee states to or from that process.

Table 13.2 State-specified enabling links: semantics, symbols, source, and destination

Name	Semantics	Sample OPD & OPL	Source	Desti-nation
State-specified Agent Link	The human agent enables the process provided she is at the specified state.	Miner [sick] [healthy] → Copper Mining **Healthy Miner handles Copper Mining.**	Agent state	Process
State-specified Instrument Link	The process requires the instrument at the specified state.	Drill [faulty] [operational] ⊸ Copper Mining **Copper Mining requires operational Drill.**	Instrument state	Process

Each one of the three transforming links—consumption, effect, and result—has a state-specified version, as defined below. The three transformees—consumee, transformee and resultee—are also roles with respect to the corresponding processes associated with them, as are agent and instrument. Similarly, the terms "input state" and "output state" refer to roles of two states of an affectee with respect to the affecting process. The input state is the state just before the affecting process starts, while the output state is the state the object is at just as that process ends.

An **input state** of object **B** is a state s_i of **B** at which **B** is when process **P** starts.

An **input link** is a link from the state s_i to process **P**.

An **output state** of object **B** is a state s_o of **B** at which **B** is when process **P** ends.

An **output link** is a link from process **P** to the state s_o.

A **state-specified consumption link** is a consumption link that originates from an input state s_i of the consumee **C** and ends at process **P**, denoting that in order for **C** to be consumed by **P**, it must be in state s_i.

The state-specified consumption link expresses the fact that the consumee is consumed by the process if and only if the consumee is in the specified state—the one to which the consumption link is connected.

> *A **state-specified result link** is a result link that originates from process **P** and ends at a state **s** of the resultee **R**, denoting that when **P** terminates, it creates **R** in state **s**.*

The state-specified result link expresses the fact that the resultee is generated by the process only at the specified state—the one to which the result link is connected.

> *A **state-specified effect link** is an in-out (input-output) link pair, whose input link originates from an input state s_i of the affectee **A** and ends at process **P**, and whose output link originates from **P** and ends at an output state s_o of A, denoting that in order for A to be affected by **P**, A must be in s_i, in which case when P terminates A will be at s_o.*

Figure 13.11 shows two examples of state-specified consumption and result links. **Machining** can only consume **Raw Metal Bar** in state **cut** and generate **Part** in state **pre-tested**. The corresponding OPL sentences follow. The OPL syntax for a state-specified object is "state name" followed by "Object Name". This syntax is demonstrated in the two OPL sentences in Fig. 15.13 by **cut Raw Metal Bar** and by **pre-tested Part**. When naming a state, one should therefore test its expressiveness by evaluating whether the phrase that results from this concatenation makes sense and reads well in OPL sentences where it appears.

Since the function of this system is **Machining**, **Cutting** and **Testing** are environmental processes.[2] **Cutting** must precede **Machining** in order to change **Raw Metal Bar** from its **pre-cut** to its **cut** state, while **Testing** changes **Part** from **pre-tested** to **tested**. Additional examples of state-specified transforming links appear in Table 13.3.

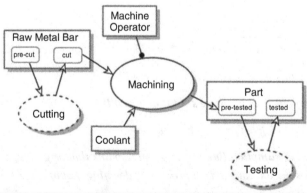

Machining consumes **Coolant** and **cut Raw Metal Bar**.
Machining yields **pre-tested Part**.

Fig. 13.11 State-specified consumption and result links: **Machining** can only consume **Raw Metal Bar** in state **cut** and generate **Part** in state **pre-tested**

---

[2]In a system with a larger scope of **Manufacturing**, the three processes **Cutting**, **Machining**, and **Testing**, in that sequence, would all be systemic subprocesses of **Manufacturing**.

13.9.1 State Change Versus Object Consumption and Generation

We have noted that object consumption and generation can be thought of as extreme cases of state change, when the states are implicitly non-existent and implicitly existent. For example, in Fig. 13.11, the **Machining** process consumes an object—**Raw Material Bar**—and generates a different object—**Part**. However, the **Cutting** and **Testing** processes change only the states of **Raw Material Bar** and **Part**, respectively, but not their identity. This is so because the **Machining** process is more drastic—it changes the input object profoundly such that its identity as **Raw Material Bar** is lost, and a new object, **Part**, is born.

As a result of the occurrence of the **Machining** process, **Raw Material Bar** has changed its state from **existent** to **non-existent**. In other words, it was consumed. **Part** has changed its state from **non-existent** to **existent**. In other words, it was generated. Conversely, **Testing** does not consume **Part**. It merely adds information about the part, indicating whether it can pass to the next production stage. **Cutting** is not such a clear-cut case, as one can justifiably argue that this process takes as input a long **Raw Material Bar** object and outputs several shorter **Raw Material Bar Segment** objects, each of which is separately input to **Machining**.

13.10 **State-Specified Effect Links**

Each of the five procedural links presented in Table 13.1 has a state-specified counterpart, which is shown in Table 13.3. The single stateless effect link from Table 13.1 gives rise to three kinds of state-specified effect link pairs, shown in Table 13.4.

Table 13.3 Consumption and result state-specified procedural links: semantics, symbols, source, and destination

Name	Semantics	Sample OPD & OPL	Source	Destination
State-specified consumption link	The process consumes the object if and only if the object is in the specified state.	Eating consumes edible Food.	consumee state	consuming process
State-specified result link	The process generates the object in the specified state.	Mining yields raw Copper.	generating process	resultee state

Instead of the single effect link in Table 13.1, when states were not present, in Table 13.4 there are three types of state-specified effect link pairs. Each link pair consists of an input link and an output link.

The difference between them stems from the origin of the input link and the destination of the output link. We use the word ***in-out*** as a shorthand notation for input-output.

> An ***in-out-specified effect link pair*** *of process P is a pair of links consisting of an input link from the input state s_{in} of object B to P and an output link from P to the output state s_o*

Table 13.4 Input output state-specified procedural links: semantics, symbols, source, and destination

Name	Semantics	Sample OPD & OPL	Source	Destination
In-out-specified effect link pair (consisting of one state-specified *input link* and one state-specified *output link*)	The process changes the object from a specified input state via the *input link* to a specified output state via the *output link*.	**Purifying** changes **Copper** from **raw** to **pure**.	affectee input (source) state	affecting process
			affecting process	affectee output (destination) state
Input-specified effect link pair (consisting of one state-specified *input link* and one state-unspecified *output link*)	The process changes the object from a specified input state to any output state.	**Testing** changes **Sample** from **awaiting test**.	affectee input (source) state	affecting process
			affecting process	affectee
Output-specified effect link pair (consisting of one state-unspecified *input link* and one state-specified *output link*)	The process changes the object from any input state to a specified output state.	**Cleaning & Painting** changes **Engine Hood** to **painted**.	affectee	affecting process
			affecting process	affectee output (destination) state

In the example for the in-out-specified effect link in Table 13.4, the OPL sentence is:

Purifying changes **Copper** from **raw** to **pure.**

Here, **raw** and **purified** are the input (source) and output (destination) states of **Copper**, respectively.

An **input-specified effect link pair** of process P is a pair of links consisting of an input link from the input state s_{in} of object B to P and an output link from P to B.

In the example for the output-specified effect link in Table 13.4, the OPL sentence is:

Testing changes **Sample** from **awaiting test.**

Here, **awaiting test** is the input state of **Sample**. The output state of **Sample** is not specified, implying that (depending on the outcome of **Testing**) it can be any one of the three of **Sample** states.

> *An **output-specified effect link pair** of process P is a pair of links consisting of an input link from object B to P and an output link from P to the output state s_{out} of B.*

In the example for the output-specified effect link in Table 13.3, the OPL sentence is:

Cleaning & Painting changes **Engine Hood** to **painted.**

Here, **painted** is the output state of **Engine Hood**. The input state of **Engine Hood** is not specified, implying that it can be any one of the three **Engine Hood** states.

13.10.1 Value-Specified Procedural Links

> *A **value-specified procedural link** is a link between a process and one or two values of an attribute that the process changes.*

Each state-specified procedural link in Table 13.4 has a value-specified procedural link counterpart. The three value-specified procedural links are depicted in Table 13.5. Values are states of attributes, so the semantic and syntax of value-specified procedural links are somewhat different than their state-specified counterparts, as specified in Table 13.5 and defined below.

> *A **value setting link** is a unidirectional value-specified procedural link from a process to an attribute value, which sets that value, regardless of what it was earlier.*

The value setting link is the counterpart of the state-specified result link of an object that is not an attribute. The difference is that while the state-specified result link creates an object in the specified state, the attribute is not created since it exists along with its exhibitor. What it does is to specify the value of that attribute.

> *A **value effect link** is a bidirectional value-specified procedural link from a process to an attribute value and back, which changes that value from some unspecified value to another.*

A value can be easily distinguished from a state by inspecting the object that "owns" the state in question: If that owning object is an attribute, then the state is a value, and if not—the state is just a state.

The value effect link is the counterpart of the state-specified effect link of an object that is not an attribute. The difference is that while the state-specified effect link changes an object from one unspecified state to another, the value effect link changes the value from some unspecified value to another.

> An ***in-out-specified value effect link pair*** *is a pair of a value-specified input link and a value-specified output link which change that attribute value from the input vale to the output value.*

Table 13.5 Value-specified procedural links: semantics, symbols, source, and destination

Name	Semantics	Sample OPD & OPL	Source	Destination
Value Setting Link	The process sets the value of an attribute.	**Engine** exhibits **Temperature**. The value of **Temperature** of **Engine** is **t_new**. **Heating** sets the value of **Temperature** of **Engine** to **t_new**.	process	attribute value
Value Effect Link	The process affects the value of an attribute by changing it from an unspecified input value to an unspecified output value.	**Engine** exhibits **Temperature**. The value of **Temperature** of **Engine** is **t**. **Heating** affects the value **t** of **Temperature** of **Engine**.	attribute value and process	attribute value and process
In-out-specified value effect link pair (consisting of one value-specified *input link* and one value-specified *output link*)	The process changes the value of an attribute by changing it from an input value to an output value.	**Engine** exhibits **Temperature**. The value of **Temperature** of **Engine** can be **t_old** and **t_new**. **Heating** changes the value of **Temperature** of **Engine** from **t_old** to **t_new**.	input value process	Process output value

The in-out-specified value effect link pair is the counterpart of the in-out-specified effect link pair of an object that is not an attribute. The difference is that while the in-out-specified effect link pair changes an object from one specified state to another specified state, the value effect link changes the value from some specified value to another specified value.

The names of the values are parameter names. For example, **t_new** is the new value of **Temperature** of **Engine** set by **Heating**. We can also assign actual numbers to the parameters, as demonstrated in Fig. 13.12.

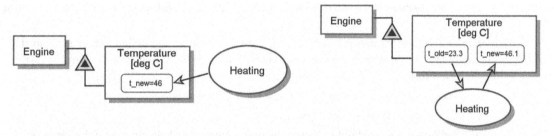

Engine exhibits **Temperature** in deg C.
The value of **Temperature** of **Engine** in deg C is **t_new**.
Heating sets the value of **Temperature** of **Engine** in deg C to **t_new=46**.

Engine exhibits **Temperature** in deg C.
The value of **Temperature** of **Engine** in deg C can be **t_old=23.3** and **t_new=46.1**.
Heating changes the value of **Temperature** of **Engine** in deg C from **t_old=23.3** to **t_new=46.1**.

Fig. 13.12 Value-specified procedural links with parameters and actual numeric values

13.11 **Summary**

- A *change* of an object is an alteration in the state of that object.
- *Effect* is a change in the state of an object that a process causes.
- *Construction* is an extreme case of object effect, where the object's input state is nonexistent and the output state is existent.
- *Consumption* is an extreme case of object effect, where the object's input state is existent and the output state is nonexistent.
- When the transformation is *extreme*, a *change in object identity* takes place.
- When the change is not profound or drastic, the object only alters its state while retaining its identity.
- A *transformee* of process P is an object B that P transforms as a result of the occurrence of P.
  - A *consumee* of a process P is a transformee of P that P consumes as a result of the occurrence of P.
  - A *resultee* of a process P is a transformee of P that P creates as a result of the occurrence of P.
  - An *affectee* of a process P is a transformee of P that that P affects as a result of the occurrence of P.

- A *transforming link* is a procedural link that connects a process with a transformee of that process.

  o   A *result link* is a unidirectional transformation link from a process to the resultee that this process creates.

  o   An *effect link* is a bidirectional transformation link that connects a process with an affectee of that process.

  o   A *consumption* *link* is a unidirectional transformation link from a consumee to the process that consumes it.

- An *enabler* E of a process P is an object that must exist and be available in order for P to start, and remain present throughout the occurrence of P in order for P to terminate normally, with E ultimately unaffected.

  o   An *agent* is an enabler who is a human or a group of humans.

  o   An instrument is a non-human enabler.

- An *enabling link* is a procedural link that connects a process with an enabler of that process.

  o   An *agent link* is an enabling link that connects a process with an agent of that process.

  o   An *instrument link* is a procedural link that connects a process with an enabler of that process.

- An *input state* of object **B** is a state s_i of **B** at which **B** is when process **P** starts.

- An *input link* is a link from the state s_i to process **P**.

- An *output state* of object **B** is a state s_o of **B** at which **B** is when process **P** ends.

- An *output link* is a link from process **P** to the state s_o.

- A *state-specified consumption link* is a consumption link that originates from an input state s_i of the consumee **C** and ends at process **P**, denoting that in order for **C** to be consumed by **P**, it must be in state s_i.

- A *state-specified result link* is a result link that originates from process **P** and ends at a state **s** of the resultee **R**, denoting that when **P** terminates, it creates **R** in state **s**.

- A *state-specified effect link* is an in-out (input-output) link pair, whose input link originates from an input state s_i of the affectee **A** and ends at process **P**, and whose output link originates from **P** and ends at an output state s_o of **A**, denoting that in order for **A** to be affected by **P**, **A** must be in s_i, in which case when P terminates A will be at s_o.

  o   An *in-out-specified effect link pair* of process **P** is a pair of links consisting of an input link from the input state s_{in} of object **B** to **P** and an output link from **P** to the output state s_{out} of **B**.

  o   An *input-specified effect link pair* of process **P** is a pair of links consisting of an input link from the input state s_{in} of object **B** to **P** and an output link from **P** to **B**.

  o   An *output-specified effect link pair* of process **P** is a pair of links consisting of an input link from object **B** to **P** and an output link from **P** to the output state s_{out} of **B**.

- A *value changing link* is a link between a process and an unspecified value of an attribute which the process changes.

13.12 **Problems**

1. Give two examples of each of the following, provide their OPM models, and verify that the resulting OPL describes your original intent.
2. Change of an objects.
3. Consumption of an objects.
4. Creation of an objects.
   The following questions relate to Figs. 13.13 and 13.14, which describe a system being simulated by animation.
5. What is the system described in this OPD?
6. What are the affectee, agent and instrument?
7. What is the OPL sentence that describes effect?
8. What is the relation between **Driver** and **Car**? What link is used to express this?
9. What is the relation between **Gasoline Tank** and **Car**? What link is used to express this?
10. What is the process within **Car Fueling** taking place at this time?
11. What object does it transform and how? What is the OPL sentence describing this?
12. What link is missing between this process and **Pump**? What is the OPL sentence that would be created if you added this link?
13. What are the five affectees in this OPD? Which one is different than the other four and why?
14. What agent link is missing?
15. Describe the state changes of **Pump**.
16. What can you tell from the colors of the states of the various objects? Please refer specifically to **Gasoline Tank**.
17. What effect link is missing? Hint: Look at the one present.
18. Suppose **Car** is the only vehicle in the **Gas Station** throughout the **Car Fueling** process. Where would you place the states called **car present** and **car absent**?
19. How would the corresponding link change as a result?
20. What process reverts **Gas Station** to its original state?

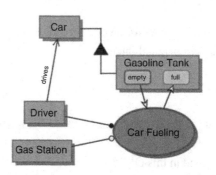

Fig. 13.13 OPD for Chapter problems

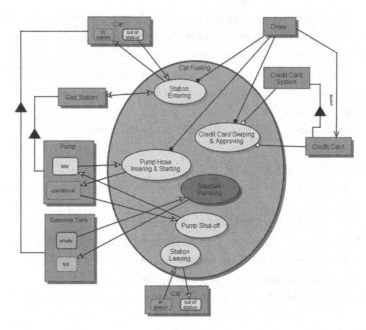

Fig. 13.14 OPD of Car Fueling from Fig. 13.13 in-zoomed

21. Based on your responses to the previous two questions, explain why is it OK that in Fig. 13.13 **Gas Station** is an instrument, while in Fig. 13.14 it is an affectee?

Chapter 14

The Structural System Aspect

> *The Piglet lived in a very grand house in the middle of a beech-tree, and the beech-tree was in the middle of the Forest, and the Piglet lived in the middle of the house. Next to his house was a piece of broken board which had: "TRESPASSERS W" on it.*
>
> Winnie-The-Pooh, by A. A. Milne

Structure pertains to the relatively fixed, non-transient, long-term relationships that exist among objects—components or parts of the system. Alternatively, structure can be viewed as a snapshot—a picture of the generally dynamic system, or part of it, at some point in time. This snapshot captures the entire system at some state, where each stateful object is at some state or in transition between two of its states, and specific relationships between objects hold. Structure is contrasted with the complementary dynamic aspect of the system, or its behavior, which has to do with the changes the system undergoes over time, along with the causes for and effects of these changes. In other words, structure is about the static aspect of the system, while behavior is about its dynamic aspect. This chapter is devoted to discussing the structure of systems and expressing it through OPM.

14.1 Structural Relations

A basic concept that is needed in order to discuss structure is structural relation.

> A **structural relation** is a linkage, connection, or association between two objects or between two processes that holds in the system for at least some time.

A structural relation in the system is not contingent upon conditions that are time-dependent. While structural relations usually exist between two objects and are less frequently used between two processes, there are processes that exhibit structural relations. For example, subprocesses inside an in-zoomed process are parts of that process, so there is structural relation, and more specifically an aggregation-participation (whole-part) relation between them, with the in-zoomed process being the whole, and the subprocesses—the parts. As we discuss below, a structural link is the graphical expression of a structural relation.

14.1.1 Binary Relations in the Focus

By its nature, a structural relation is multilateral, because every thing that participates in the association has some relation with the rest of the things. The number of things involved in the structural relation determines the *arity* of the relation: a relation of a thing to itself is a *unary* structural relation, a relation between two things is a *binary* structural relation, a relation between three things is a *ternary* structural relation, and so forth.

© Springer Science+Business Media New York 2016
D. Dori, *Model-Based Systems Engineering with OPM and SysML*, DOI 10.1007/978-1-4939-3295-5_14

A unary structural relation is possible with respect to aggregation participation, which is a structural relation. For example, as the OPD in Fig. 14.1 shows, a **Military Unit** is comprised of one or more (smaller) **Military Units**.

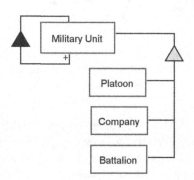

Military Unit consists of at least one **Military Unit**.
Platoon, Company, and **Battalion** are **Military Units**.

Fig. 14.1 Modeling a unary structural link as a link from the object to itself

As an example of how to model ternary or higher arity structural relations, consider modeling the following sentence: "An underwater tunnel connects the city with an airport." The relation "connects" can be thought of as ternary relation, as it involves the three objects in that sentence. Using the state-preserving process **Connecting**, we can model this system in OPM using three procedural links, as shown in Fig. 14.2.

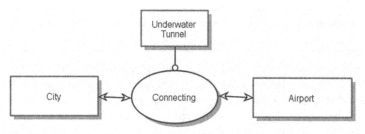

Connecting affects **City** and **Airport**.
Connecting requires **Underwater Tunnel**.

Fig. 14.2 Modeling a ternary structural link as three procedural links with the state-preserving process **Connecting**

As this example shows, *n*-ary relations with $n \geq 3$ can be analyzed as a set of structural or procedural binary links. Figure 14.3 shows the system in Fig. 14.2 using two structural links only and no process whatsoever. Moreover, as we shall see, given that the relation tagged **connected** is transitive, it is possible to conclude that "**City** and **Airport** are **connected**."

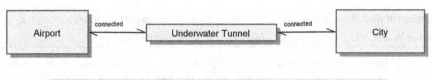

City and **Underwater Tunnel** are **connected.**
Underwater Tunnel and **Airport** are **connected.**
Fig. 14.3 The system in Fig. 14.2 specified using structure only

In view of this observation, we focus our attention on binary relations. Binary structural relations are held between two things with the same perseverance, i.e., either between two objects—things whose perseverance value is persistent, or static, or between two processes—things whose perseverance value is transient, or dynamic. For example, aggregation-participation is a fundamental structural relation that is applicable to processes just as well as it is to objects. However, in general, structural relations are more prevalent with objects than they are with processes, so in this chapter we focus on binary structural relations between objects.

14.1.2 Forward and Backward Structural Relations

A binary structural relation is bidirectional: if thing T_1 relates to thing T_2 through the relation $\mathfrak{R}$, then it is also true that T_2 relates to T_1 through another relation $\mathfrak{R}'$, and vice versa.

Symbolically, $T_1 \, \mathfrak{R} \, T_2 \Leftrightarrow T_2 \, \mathfrak{R}' \, T_1$.

$\mathfrak{R}$ is a symbol that stands for the *forward structural relation*, that is, the structural relation as T_1 views it while referring to T_2. Conversely, $\mathfrak{R}'$ is the *backward structural relation*, i.e., the relation as T_2 views it while referring to T_1. $\mathfrak{R}$ and $\mathfrak{R}'$ constitute a *structural relation pair*.

$\mathfrak{R}$ and $\mathfrak{R}'$ may be semantically identical, in which case they are symmetric. Symbolically, $\mathfrak{R} = \mathfrak{R}'$. For example, if $\mathfrak{R}$ = "**touches**" then $\mathfrak{R}'$ = "**touches**". Hence, if "**A touches B**" then "**B touches A.**" As we discuss in the sequel, a pair of symmetric relations can be converted to a single reciprocal relation.

$\mathfrak{R}$ and $\mathfrak{R}'$ may be the inverse of each other, or anti-symmetric, such that existence of a relation in one direction mandates the existence of the opposite relation in the opposite direction. Symbolically, if $\mathfrak{R}$ and $\mathfrak{R}'$ are the inverse of each other, then $(\mathfrak{R}')' = \mathfrak{R}$. For example, if $\mathfrak{R}$ = "**is parent of**", then $\mathfrak{R}'$ = "**is child of**". Hence, if "**A is parent of B**", then "**B is child of A.**" Not any pair of relations is symmetric or anti-symmetric. For example, if **A points to B**, it is not necessarily true that **B points to A**.

14.1.3 Structural Links Versus Structural Relations

Links express graphically the semantics of relations.

> A **link** is the graphical representation of a relation.

This definition of link holds for both procedural and structural relations. While a structural relation models an association between two things (usually objects) that is meaningful in the system, a *structural link* graphically represents the structural relation.

> *A **structural link** is an arrow with an open head that represents a binary structural relation in an OPD from a source object to a destination object.*

The relation between structural relation and structural link is the same as the relation between procedural relation and procedural link: In both cases, the link expresses graphically what the relation expresses verbally. For example, the procedural (instrument) link in Fig. 14.2 between **Underwater Tunnel** and **Connecting** is the graphical expression of the instrument relation between these two things. Likewise, the structural (bidirectional tagged) link in Fig. 14.3 between **Underwater Tunnel** and **City** is the graphical expression of the structural relation between these two objects, tagged **connected**.

The open head arrow, $\longrightarrow$, which symbolizes a structural link, is contrasted with the closed triangular arrowheads of the transforming links. As a reminder, transforming links include the four unidirectional links symbolized as $\longrightarrow\!\!\triangleright$ with different sources and destinations: (1) the consumption link (from object to process), (2) the result link (from process to object), (3) the input link (from state to process), and (4) the output link (from process to state). As we see, these four links share the same graphical symbol, and the only difference between them is their different sources and destinations. The only bidirectional transforming link is the effect link, $\triangleleft\!\!\longrightarrow\!\!\triangleright$, connecting a process and an object to denote an unspecified state change (when we discuss values, which are states of attributes, we will see another use for this symbol as well as for the input and output links).

14.1.4 Structure Tag and Tagged Structural Link

The structural link's open arrow points from one object to another. We have defined phrase as a combination of one or more words, separated by spaces, which constitutes a logical entity, but not a complete sentence. A meaningful *structural tag* can be recorded along a structural link, making it a *tagged structural link*.

> *A **structural tag** is a phrase that expresses the semantics—the nature, meaning, or content—of the structural relation between the two things that participate in the relation.*

Examples of structural tags (or shortly just tags) are **resembles, owns, is next to, similar to, extends, restricts, resides in, borders with, eliminates the need for, represents, is equivalent to**, and **contains**.

> *A **tagged structural link** is structural link with a structural tag recorded along the link.*

On the left of Fig. 14.4 is an example of an OPD with four objects—**Airport, City, Highway**, and **Underwater Tunnel**, and three tagged structural links. Two are unidirectional, with the tags **serves** and **surrounds**. The third is a bidirectional tagged structural link with the tags "**passes through the**" and "**provides for shortening the**".

The OPD on the right of Fig. 14.4 demonstrates that a structural relation can exist also between two processes. As the OPL sentences in Fig. 14.4 demonstrate, the syntax of a tagged structural OPL sentence is a simple concatenation of the source thing followed by the tag, followed by the destination thing. The tag is non-capitalized and is in **bold Arial** letters since it is user-defined rather than a reserved phrase.

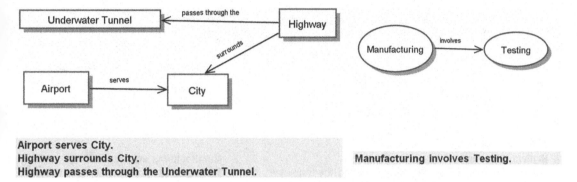

Airport serves City.
Highway surrounds City.
Highway passes through the Underwater Tunnel.

Manufacturing involves Testing.

Fig. 14.4 Examples of unidirectional tagged structural relations

14.1.5 Bidirectional Tagged Structural Link

The tagged structural relations and links defined and exemplified so far have been unidirectional. The tag is therefore a *forward tag*—a tag from the source thing to the destination thing. As discussed, for any tagged structural relation (and its graphical representation as a link) there is a corresponding tagged structural relation (and link) in the opposite direction, expressed by a *backward tag*—a tag from the destination thing to the source thing. We can express the two relations in a single bidirectional tagged structural link.

> *A **bidirectional tagged structural link** is a combination of two tagged structural links in opposite directions.*

The bidirectional structural link is depicted as a harpoon-shaped arrow, ⤆⤇ which links the two things. The tags of the relation in one direction and in the other direction are recorded such that the harpoon edges sticking out of the arrowheads unambiguously determine the direction in which each relation holds, as Fig. 14.5 demonstrates. The harpoon points to the destination thing. Consider the OPD on the left of Fig. 14.5, where the objects **Highway** and **Underwater Tunnel** are linked with a bidirectional tagged structural relation. The tag from **Highway** to **Underwater Tunnel** is "**passes through**", while the one in the opposite direction is "**provides for shortening the**". Similarly, in the OPD on the right of Fig. 14.5, the processes **Manufacturing** and **Testing** are linked with a bidirectional tagged structural relation, where the two tags are "**involves**" and "**is embedded in**".

In the OPD on the left of Fig. 14.5, the inverse relation from **City** to **Airport** is "**is served by**", and the one from **City** to **Highway** is "**is surrounded by**". Since no information is added by specifying these passive voice relations, we avoid doing so. However, we need to bear in mind that in principle any structural relation is bidirectional.

UML and SysML use the association link as something analogous to OPM's tagged structural link (either unidirectional and bidirectional), but these are applicable only to objects (in UML) or to their counterparts in SysML, called blocks. As for processes, this is possible only in use case diagrams, where tags can indicate relations between use cases.

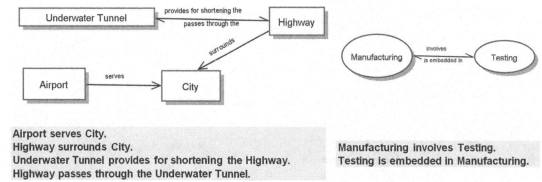

Airport serves City.
Highway surrounds City.
Underwater Tunnel provides for shortening the Highway.
Highway passes through the Underwater Tunnel.

Manufacturing involves Testing.
Testing is embedded in Manufacturing.

Fig. 14.5 Highway and Underwater Tunnel are linked with a bidirectional tagged structural relation

14.2 **Reciprocity and Transitivity of Structural Relations**

Two properties (OPM model element attributes) of structural relations are useful for inference and cause and effect determining: reciprocity and transitivity. These are discussed and defined next.

14.2.1 The Reciprocity Attribute of Structural Relation

In the examples we have seen, the anti-symmetric forward and backward structural relations between the source and destination objects differ in name and semantics. However, there are cases in which the forward and backward structural relations are identical. Consider the example in the OPD on the left hand side of Fig. 14.6 and the corresponding two OPL sentences.

A bidirectional tagged structural relation is reciprocal if the structural relation tag between objects **A** and **B** in both directions is the same. To avoid repeating the same tag twice in the OPD and getting two separate sentences in the OPL paragraph, we change the tag such that a meaningful sentence will result in from concatenating it to a sentence of the from "**A** and **B** are … .", For example, in Fig. 14.6 we need a tag to complete the sentence "**Engine** and **Gearbox** are … ." Thus, in the OPD on the right hand side of Fig. 14.6 we use the single reciprocal structural relation **attached** that is semantically equivalent to the OPD on the left. *A reciprocal structural relation* is a bidirectional tagged structural relation, in which the forward and backward structural relations are identical.

Algebraically, let $\Re$ be a structural relation from A to B such that A $\Re$ B, and let $\Re'$ be a structural relation from B to A such that B $\Re'$ A. Iff $\Re = \Re'$ then $\Re$ is reciprocal. The equality sign here is to be interpreted as "are semantically the same".

> *A **reciprocal structural relation** $\Re$ is a structural relation for which it holds that if A $\Re$ B and B $\Re'$ A then $\Re = \Re'$.*

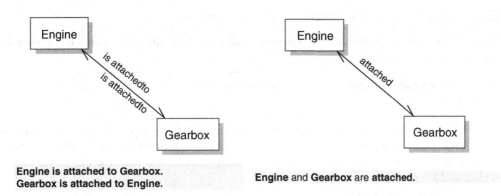

Engine is attached to Gearbox.
Gearbox is attached to Engine.

Engine and **Gearbox** are **attached**.

Fig. 14.6 Reciprocity exemplified. Left: The relation between Engine and Gearbox is reciprocal, since the two tags in the bidirectional tagged structural relation, "is attached to", are identical. Right: The equivalent, more succinct OPD, with attached as the single reciprocity tag

A reciprocal structural link—the graphical expression of the reciprocal structural relation—is defined as follows.

> *A **reciprocal structural link** is a bidirectional tagged structural link, in which the identical forward and backward tags are replaced by a single reciprocity tag.*

Additional examples of reciprocal structural relations include **mutually exclusive, in touch, siblings, relatives, linked, equivalent, adjacent, intersecting, overlapping, engaged, related, connected, in agreement,** and **in love with each other**. The addition of the prefix "**mutually**" or the suffix "**with each other**" can help render or clarify the reciprocity of many relations. As the example in Fig. 14.6 shows, an OPL sentence that expresses a reciprocal structural relation is constructed by concatenating the two objects, joined by the reserved word and between them, followed by the reserved word are, followed by the reciprocal structural relation tag.

> ***Reciprocity** is a property of a structural relation that denotes whether its forward and backward structural relations have the same semantics.*

In the metamodel of a **Structural Link**, the three possible values of its **Reciprocity** property are **positive, neutral,** and **negative**. The **Reciprocity** value is **positive** if the semantics of the link's tag in both the forward and backward directions is the same, **negative** if the tag semantics in the forward direction is the opposite of that in the backward direction, and **neutral** if the tag semantics in the forward direction is neither the same nor the opposite of that in the backward direction. The default **Reciprocity** value of **Structural Link** is **neutral**.

A bidirectional tagged structural link with positive reciprocity can be called shortly a *reciprocal structural link*, one with negative reciprocity is an *anti-reciprocal structural link*, and one with neutral reciprocity—a *non-reciprocal structural link*.

14.2.2 The Transitivity Attribute of Structural Relation

Transitivity of a structural relation has the following definition and semantics, which is the same as the definition of transitivity in algebra:

> *A **transitive structural relation** $\mathcal{R}$ is a structural relation for which it holds that if A $\mathcal{R}$ B and B $\mathcal{R}$ C then A $\mathcal{R}$ C.*

Figure 14.7 exemplifies the transitivity attribute of a structural link. The relation **contains** is transitive and can therefore be extended from any object from which the link originates to any object to which it points. Given that the structural relation **contains** is transitive, additional relations can be deduced from the OPD in Fig. 14.7, such as:

Database contains File.
Folder contains Record.
Database contains Record.

Transitive structural relations yield hierarchies. Figure 14.7 is an example of a *containment* hierarchy. We can extend this hierarchy by specifying, for example, that **Record contains Field, Field contains Character**, etc. We cannot, however, construct a similar hierarchy for the structural relation **attached**, because the structural relation **attached** is not necessarily transitive, so its transitivity is neutral.

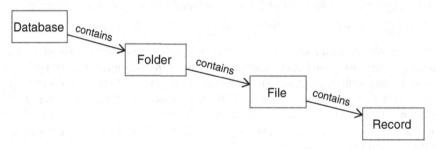

Database contains Folder.
Folder contains File.
File contains Record.

Fig. 14.7 Transitivity exemplified. The relation contains is transitive and can therefore be extended from any object from which the link originates to any object to which it points

Figure 14.8 is another example of a transitive relation. Due to the positive transitivity of the tagged structural relation **feeds**, based on the model, it is possible to deduce, for example, that "**Spring feeds Lake.**"

> ***Transitivity*** *is a property of a structural relation that determines whether the structural relation is transitive.*

Like reciprocity, the value of the transitivity property of a structural relation can be *positive, neutral,* or *negative*, as determined by the semantics of the tag. When we say that a relation is transitive, we mean that the value of the structural link's transitivity is positive.

The relation **contains** in Fig. 14.7 is an example of a structural relation whose transitivity property value is positive: it is always true that if **A contains B** and **B contains C** then **A contains C**. Since the structural relation **contains** is transitive, we say that the value of the transitivity attribute of the structural relation **contains** is positive. The structural relation **in the middle of**, which appears several times in the excerpt from Winnie-The-Pooh at the beginning of this chapter, is also transitive.

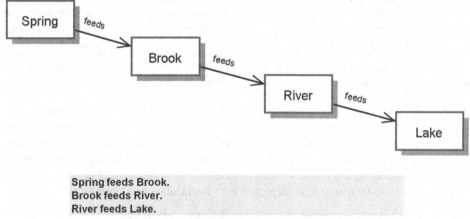

Spring feeds Brook.
Brook feeds River.
River feeds Lake.

Fig. 14.8 Transitivity symbol exemplified by the transitive relation feeds

A neutral transitive structural relation is a structural relation that may or may not be transitive. Consider the relation **is friend of** as an example of a neutral transitive structural relation. It may be true that if **Al is friend of Ben** and **Ben is friend of Chen**, then it may be the case that **Al is friend of Chen**, but this is not guaranteed. Likewise, if **A**, **B** and **C** are closed shapes in a plane, **A touches B** and **B touches C** may imply that **A touches C**, but this is not guaranteed. Hence, the transitivity value of both **is friend of** and **touches** is neutral.

An example of a structural relation with negative transitivity is "**directly contains**": If in Fig. 14.7 the relation "**contains**" is replaced by "**directly contains**", then if "**Database directly contains Folder**" and "**Folder directly contains File**", then it is false that "**Database directly contains File**". A similar example can be drawn for Fig. 14.8 if we change "**feeds**" to "**directly feeds**".

As another example, suppose **Jack is father of Jim** and **Jim is father of Jill**, then **Jack is not father of Jill**. As a final example from plane geometry, consider three points, **A**, **B**, **C**, and **D** along a straight line, such that **AB**, **BC**, and **CD** are three line segments. If **AB touches BC** and **BC touches CD**, then the sentence **AB touches CD** is always false. Hence, in this system, the transitivity of the structural relation **touches** between two line segments on a line is negative.

In the metamodel of a **Structural Link**, the three possible values of its **Transitivity** property are **positive**, **neutral**, and **negative**. The **Transitivity** value is **positive** if the semantics of the link's tag is transitive, **negative** if the tag semantics is such that the relation is never transitive, and **neutral** if the tag semantics does not enable determining if the transitivity is positive or negative. The default **Transitivity** value of **Structural Link** is **neutral**.

Table 14.1 Examples for the three values of Reciprocity and Transitivity

Value Structural relation attribute	positive	neutral	negative
Reciprocity	touches, connected, adjacent, disconnected, equivalent, congruent, related, mixed	likes, dislikes, is indifferent to	is father of, is on top of, surrounds, above, wears, consists of
Transitivity	feeds, contains, is ancestor of, surrounds, above, mixed, consists of	adjacent, is next to, is friend of, holds hand of	is father of, directly contains, directly feeds

Knowledge about the reciprocity and transitivity values of links in the model can help deduce relations that can extend beyond the link destination, and this can be automated to generate new knowledge from a complex model, where remote relations that may extend over several OPDs are not obvious by merely inspecting the model visually. Table 14.1 provides several examples for each one of the three values of the two structural relation properties—**Reciprocity** and **Transitivity**.

To enhance the analytical power of an OPM model, non-default values of a link's reciprocity and transitivity can be stored in a model by an OPM modeling tool as a property (meta-attribute) of the link, which can be made accessible, (e.g., by double-clicking the link). For example, if the OPM model contains a tagged structural relation with the tag "contains", we can store the fact that the value of the **Transitivity** property of this relation is **positive**, i.e., contains is a transitive relation. This enables the model to deduce that if **A contains B** and **B contains C**, then **A contains C**.

14.2.3 Null Tags, Null Structural Links, and Their Default OPL Phrases

The tag in both the unidirectional and the bidirectional tagged structural links may be the *null tag*, i.e., an empty tag. The OPM models in Fig. 14.9 show **Freedom** and **Justice** connected by a unidirectional (top) and bidirectional (bottom) null structural links—structural links with null tags.

The *default null tags* are the most general ones; they involve word *relation*, as defined below.

> The **unidirectional default null tag** *is the default null tag for the unidirectional structural link, and its associated OPL reserved phrase is* "relates to".
>
> The **bidirectional default null tag** *is the default null tag for the bidirectional structural link, and its associated OPL reserved phrase is* "related".

For the OPDs in Fig. 14.9, these default null tags give rise to the OPL sentences written on the right hand side of Fig. 14.9.

Freedom relates to **Justice**.   **Freedom** and **Justice** are related.

Fig. 14.9 Freedom and Justice connected by a unidirectional (top) and bidirectional (bottom) null structural links

14.2.4 Model-Specific Null Tags

The default null tags can be altered by the system modeler for each system model separately or for an entire enterprise, or an entire domain.

> *A **Model-specific null tag** is a tag defined by the system modeler that overrides the default null tags for a specific system model, an enterprise, or a domain.*

As there are two default null tags, the unidirectional default null tag and the bidirectional default null tag, there are two respective user-defined null tags: the *unidirectional model-specific null tag* and the *bidirectional model-specific null tag*.

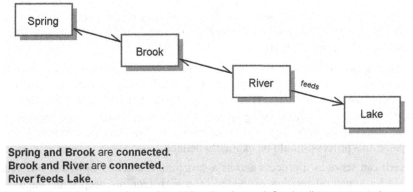

Spring and Brook are **connected**.
Brook and River are **connected**.
River feeds Lake.

Fig. 14.10 Example of use of the bidirectional user-defined null tag connected

For example, suppose for the system represented by Fig. 14.9, the system modeler sets the user-defined unidirectional null tag to "**leads to**" and the user-defined bidirectional null tag to "**equivalent**". The two OPL sentences corresponding to the two OPDs in Fig. 14.9 would then be:

Freedom leads to Justice.
Freedom and Justice are equivalent.

Since user-defined null tags are, by definition, user-defined, they are bolded by default, but the user can define them to be non-bold. The minimal scope of user-defined tags is the entire OPM model, but, as noted, it can be extended to a group of models or to an enterprise or to an entire domain.

One of the most useful bidirectional user-defined null tag is **connected**. For example, suppose in the OPM model in Fig. 14.10 the bidirectional user-defined null tag has been defined to be **connected**, the OPL paragraph would change accordingly to the two first OPL sentences in Fig. 14.10.

14.3 **Structural Relations as State-Preserving Processes**

Many of the tags of the structural relations are some verb forms of *state-preserving processes,* discussed in Chap. 13 above. Some examples are **surrounds, precedes, follows, contains, holds, maintains, remains, supports, owns, possesses, connects, surrounds, fastens, aggregates,** and **comprises.** What, then, is the difference between these verbs and bona fide processes? The difference lies in their semantics: state-preserving processes convey a message of continuity, stability, detachment from time, or steady state. Indeed, such verbs do not pass the process test, which stipulates three conditions for a thing to qualify as a process:

(1) Object transformation: A process must transform at least one of the objects in the preprocess object set.

(2) Association with time: A process must represent some happening, occurrence, action, procedure, or activity that takes place along the timeline.

(3) Association with verb: A process must be associated with a verb.

Of these conditions, state-preserving processes do not fulfill the first and second conditions. The verb in the tag of the structural relation does not (and should not) carry out any object transformation, and therefore no happening, occurrence, action, procedure, or activity takes place along the timeline. Rather, a verb representing a structural relation has the notion of static, steady state that is true as long as no process acts upon any of the objects involved.

We can think of a state-preserving process as a process that acts against some force that attempts to change the status quo. For example, *supporting* of a physical object on earth is a process that keeps an object in its current place. Without that support, the object would fall due to gravity. Similarly, *containing* of liquid in a vessel prevents it from being spilled. Conversely, if some non-trivial process must take place to hold an object static against gravity or another force, such as the propelling of a helicopter to keep it in one place, this process should be explicitly defined.

The same verb can serve as a process and as a structural relation. Telling the difference between an actual process and a structural relation expressed by a verb requires deep understanding of the model semantics. For example, in the OPL sentence "**Highway surrounds City**", the word **surrounds** is a structural relation. Once the highway has been built, for as long as it exists, it is static and keeps surrounding the city regardless of the time element. However, in the sentence "**Police surrounds House.**" the phrase **Surrounding** is a process that changes the object **House** from **non-surrounded** to **surrounded.** It fulfills all the conditions of the process test: It requires **Police** activity that takes place along the time line.

14.4 **Summary**

- A ***structural relation*** is a linkage, connection, or association between two objects or between two processes that holds in the system for at least some time.
- A binary structural relation is bidirectional.

- A *structural link* is an arrow with an open head that represents a binary structural relation in an OPD from a source object to a destination object.
- A *structural tag* is a phrase that expresses the semantics—the nature, meaning, or content—of the structural relation between the two things that participate in the relation.
- A *tagged structural link* is structural link with a structural tag recorded along the link.
- A *bidirectional tagged structural link* is a combination of two tagged structural links in opposite directions.
- *Property* is an attribute of an OPM model element.
- A *reciprocal structural relation* $\mathcal{R}$ is a structural relation for which it holds that if A $\mathcal{R}$ B and B $\mathcal{R}'$ A then $\mathcal{R} = \mathcal{R}'$.
- A *reciprocal structural link* is a bidirectional tagged structural link, in which the identical forward and backward tags are replaced by a single reciprocity tag.
- *Reciprocity* is a property of a structural relation that denotes whether its forward and backward structural relations have the same semantics.
- A *transitive structural relation* $\mathcal{R}$ is a structural relation for which it holds that if A $\mathcal{R}$ B and B $\mathcal{R}$ C then A $\mathcal{R}$ C.
- *Transitivity* is a property of a structural relation, which determines whether the structural relation is transitive.
- The *values* of both the reciprocity and the transitivity properties of a structural relation can be *positive, neutral,* or *negative.*
- The *unidirectional default null tag* is the default null tag for the unidirectional structural link, and its associated OPL reserved phrase is "relates to".
- The *bidirectional default null tag* is the default null tag for the bidirectional structural link, and its associated OPL reserved phrase is "related".
- A *user-defined null tag* is a tag defined by the system modeler that overrides the default null tags for a specific system model, an enterprise, or a domain.

  State-preserving processes convey a message of continuity, stability, detachment from time, or steady state.

14.5 **Problems**

1. In Fig. 14.2, is Connecting a state-preserving process? Explain.
2. What is the difference between a structural relation and a structural link?
3. In Fig. 14.5, change each one of the two unidirectional tagged structural relations to a bidirectional one.
4. Update the OPL to reflect the changes you made in response to the previous question.
5. In Table 15 add three examples in each one of the six cells.

6. Give three examples of state-preserving processes that are not provided in this chapter.
7. Write six English sentences that express binary structural relations. For each sentence draw the corresponding OPD and write the OPL sentences.
8. Draw three OPDs that express unidirectional binary structural relations and three OPDs that express bidirectional binary structural relations. For each OPD write the corresponding OPL sentence(s).
9. Pick up a book, a newspaper or a magazine you have handy and open it at a random page.

    a. Find 7–10 structural relations expressed in this page.
    b. Write their OPL sentences.
    c. Draw their OPDs.

10. Draw an OPD of a real product in your house or one that you are familiar with that has at least three levels of aggregation. Write the corresponding OPL paragraph (the OPL sentences that are equivalent to the OPD).
11. Find examples of three relations, one with a positive transitivity, one with a neutral and one with a negative transitivity. Draw their OPDs and write their OPL sentences.
12. When Don turns his laptop on, using the power button, his Internet browser is set to open with the URL of his favorite comics site, which he reads on a daily basis. A button near the top of his browser opens his email account. After reading both, he shuts down the computer.

    a. Apply OPM to model this description in three different ways:
    (1) Using only objects and structural relations;
    (2) Using as many processes and states as possible, and only procedural relations; and
    (3) Using a combination of the two ways above.
    b. Reflecting on the three models you built, answer the following questions.
    (1) Which model most faithfully described the system?
    (2) Which model conveys the most details?
    (3) Which model captures best what Don was doing? Why?
    (4) Which model do you prefer? Explain and point to likes and dislikes in each.

Chapter 15

Participation Constraints and Forks

Fork: the point or part at which a thing, as a river or a road, divides into branches.

Dictionary.com

In all the examples and discussions so far we have tacitly assumed that each thing, be it object or process, participates in the relation singly, i.e., in a quantity of exactly 1. Indeed, the convention in OPDs is that when no quantity is explicitly recorded by the side of a structural link, it is taken to be 1, which is the default value. In general, however, we may wish to specify a certain number or a range of numbers of instances of the same class of things that participate in the relation. Similarly, our models so far have tacitly assumed that a process involves one object instance of each object class to which it is linked. Indeed, this is the default. However, it is sometimes required to model the fact that more than one object takes part in a process. Process participation constraints and link cardinalities are designed to take care of this. We then turn to another useful notation—the fork—which is based on the observation that structural relations are distributive in a sense analogous to the distributive law in algebra. This is graphically represented via forks, as defined, discussed and demonstrated in this chapter.

15.1 Structural and Procedural Participation Constraints

When more than one object is involved in a relation, a participation constraint needs to be specified to denote this.

> *A **participation constraint** is a property of a link expressing the number or a mathematical expression recorded along a link next to an object, which denotes the multiplicity (number of repetitions) of that object in that relation.*

Since a relation and the link denoting it can be structural or procedural, there are two corresponding kinds of participation constraints: structural and procedural.

> *A **structural participation constraint** is a participation constraint recorded along a structural link.*
>
> *A **procedural participation constraint** is a participation constraint recorded along a procedural link.*

The *default participation constraint* is 1, and it is implicit. Thus, if exactly one thing participates in the relation, no participation constraint needs to be specified. When the participation constraint on the

© Springer Science+Business Media New York 2016
D. Dori, *Model-Based Systems Engineering with OPM and SysML*, DOI 10.1007/978-1-4939-3295-5_15

destination side of the structural link is different than 1, it has to be specified explicitly, as shown in Fig. 15.1 for a structural relation.

15.2 **Structural Participation Constraints**

Structural participation constraints can be one- or two-sided.

> *A **one-sided participation constraint** is a participation constraint on either the source or the destination link side.*

A source participation constraint is a one-sided participation constraint on the source side of the link. A destination participation constraint is a one-sided participation constraint on the destination side of the link.

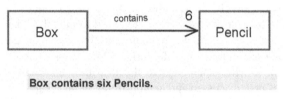

Box contains six Pencils.

Fig. 15.1 A destination participation constraint example

The OPD in Fig. 15.1 is an example of a destination participation constraint—a tagged structural link, for which the participation constraint is on the destination (link target) object. In this example, it is expressed as a specific number, 6. The destination object **Pencil** in the OPD of Fig. 15.1 has the participation constraint **6**, while the object **Box** has the implicit default participation constraint, which is 1. If the participation constraint is explicit, as it is for **Pencil** in the OPL sentence "**Box contains six Pencils**", it means that the participation constraint is greater than 1. In this case, while generating the OPL sentence from the OPD, the numeric or symbolic value or mathematical expression of the participation constraint is put before the object name and the object name becomes plural.[1]

To keep up with English grammar, the verb for any tag, including the null tag, has to conform to the plurality of source and destination things in the sentence. For example, if the source **Bedroom** of a unidirectional null tag has a participation constraint of 3, and the destination is **Apartment**, the OPL sentence is: "**Three Bedrooms** relate to **Apartment.**" To follow the rule to "spell small numbers out", the numerals (symbols) of numbers from zero to nine should be written in letters or as digits (figures), so "**Three Bedrooms** relate to **Apartment.**" is preferable. Therefore the OPL sentence in Fig. 15.1 has in it **six** rather than **6**.

Ignoring the participation constrain in Fig. 15.2, the OPL sentence would be simply "**Bolt fasten Flange.**" Since the source object **Bolt** has the participation constraint **8**, while the destination object **Flange** has the implicit default participation constraint, we get OPL sentence in Fig. 15.2.

---

[1]Usually that means concatenating the letter **s**, but a program that generates OPL sentences from OPDs should also account for exceptions of converting a noun from singular to plural. Indeed OPCAT handles most of the irregularities associated with plurals.

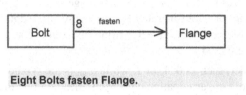

Eight Bolts fasten Flange.

Fig. 15.2 A source participation constraint example

15.2.1 Parameterized Structural Participation Constraints

By default, a participation constraint is *numeric*, i.e., it is specified as a number, usually an integer, as shown in the OPDs in Figs. 15.1 and 15.2. However, a participation constraint can also be *parameterized*, i.e., it can be a mathematical expression containing one or more symbols.

> *A **parameterized participation constraint** is a participation constraint which is a mathematical expression with one or more parameters.*

Figure 15.3 is an example of a parameterized participation constraint. Here, **n** is a natural number and the modeler expresses the fact that the number of **Cylinders** in **Engine** is even.

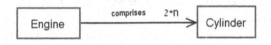

Engine comprises 2*n Cylinders.

Fig. 15.3 A parameterized participation constraint example

When numbers, even small ones, are involved in a sentence with parameters, as in Fig. 15.3, or in a range (as in Fig. 15.4, see next section), then the numbers are expressed as digit numerals and not in letters. The syntax of participation constraint expressions and more elaborate example of parameterized participation constraints are provided in Chap. 17 below on aggregation-participation.

15.2.2 Range Participation Constraints

A participation constraint can be more than just a single number or a single expression. It can also be a range.

> *A **range participation constraint** is a participation constraint with lower and upper bounds, each possibly an expression, on the number of possible objects that can take part in the relation.*

A compound participation constraint can be any combination of numbers, expressions, and ranges. A range is denoted as "$q_{min} .. q_{max}$". A single number or parameter can be thought of as a special case of range with $q_{min} = q_{max}$.

Two compound participation constraints are exemplified in Fig. 15.4. In the left OPD, the compound participation constraint comprises two ranges. In the first range, q_{min} = 3 is the lower bound and q_{max} = 5 is the upper bound. The two quantities are separated by two consecutive dots. The second range is 8..10. In the right OPD of Fig. 15.4, the compound participation constraint comprises one number, 2, and one parameterized range, 3*n, where n ≤ 4.

Often, q_{min} is a small number, such as 0, 1, or 2, while q_{max} is the symbol *, which stands for **many**. The symbol * is a "reserved symbol" in participation constraint, meaning that the exact value of "many" is not fixed as in an algebraic equation. A letter stands for a parameter—a particular, yet unspecified number.

Machine Center controls 3 to 5 or 8 to 10 Machines.   **Machine Center controls 2 or 3*n Machines,** where n ≤ 4.

Fig. 15.4 A one-sided cardinality with a range participation constraint of 3..5

15.3 **Shorthand Notations and Reserved Phrases**

The reserved phrase "q_{min} to q_{max}" can be used for any of the participation constraints, where both q_{min} and q_{max} can be any real number. However, it frequently makes more sense to use different phrases that express the participation constraint more naturally.

As in UML and SysML, the asterisk symbol * stands for "many", so "0..*" means zero or more, or, in other words, "optional", abbreviated as *. The range "1..*", abbreviated as +, means one or more, and as an OPL reserved phrase: "at least one".

The four abbreviated participation constraint symbols are:

- "?" for 0..1,
- "*" for 0..*,
- nothing for 1..1, and
- "+" for 1..*.

Each such abbreviation has a corresponding OPL reserved phrase. The abbreviated participation constraint symbols, their bounds, OPL reserved phrases, and sample OPDs with corresponding OPL sentences are shown in Table 15.1.

Combining particular values is also allowed. For example, the participation constraint "?, **3**..*" is legal and is translated in OPL as "**optional** or at least **3**". Finally, while all the examples so far referred to objects, they can be applied to processes as well.

Table 15.1 The abbreviated participation constraint symbols, their bounds, phrases, and sample OPDs with corresponding OPL sentences

Lower & Upper Bounds q_{min} .. q_{max}	Symbol	OPL Phrase	OPD Example & OPL Sentence
0..1	?	an optional	Car —has—?→ Sunroof **Car has** an optional **Sunroof.**
0..*	*	optional (+ plural)	Car —is equipped with—*→ Airbag **Car is equipped with** optional **Airbags.**
1..1	(none)	(none)	Car —is steered by→ Steering Wheel **Car is steered by Steering Wheel.**
1..*	+	at least one	Car —carries—+→ Spare Tire **Car carries** at least one **Spare Tire.**

15.4 Cardinality

In a structural relation, each link edge—one on the source side and the other on the destination side—can have a participation constraint that is in general independent of the participation constraint on the other edge.

> **Source participation constraint** *is the participation constraint on the source side of the (structural or procedural) link.*
>
> **Destination participation constraint** *is the participation constraint on the destination side of the (structural or procedural) link.*

The definition refers equally to structural and procedural links. The combination of the two participation constraints is the link's *cardinality*, which also applies to structural and procedural links alike.

> **Cardinality** *is a property of a link whose value depends on the combination of the source and destination participation constraints of the structural link.*

We denote the cardinality as $[q_{min} .. q_{max}, q'_{min} .. q'_{max}]$, where q_{min} and q_{max} are the lower and upper bounds of the participation constraint on the source side of the link, while q'_{min} and q'_{max} are the corresponding parameters on the link's destination side.

15.4.1 The Four Common Cardinality Kinds

Cardinality is an important factor in database schema design, which takes place during the design phase of information systems development. The various kinds of participation constraints on the two structural link edges give rise to a number of combinations. Traditionally, these combinations were thought of as yielding four possible cardinality kinds: one-to-one, one-to-many, many-to-one and many-to-many. These are exemplified in Fig. 15.5.

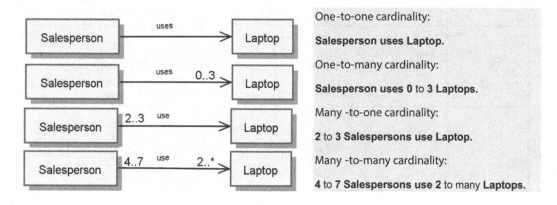

Fig. 15.5 The four cardinality kinds exemplified

As the top OPD in Fig. 15.5 shows, a one-to-one cardinality exists when no participation constraint is recorded on either side of the structural link, in which case the default value 1 is assigned to both sides. A one-to-many cardinality exists when there is an explicit participation constraint with $q_{min} > 0$ and $q_{max} > 1$ on exactly one side of the structural link and 1 on the other. This is exemplified in the second OPD in Fig. 15.5, while the third is an example of many-to-one cardinality. Finally, a many-to-many cardinality exists when the participation constraints on both sides of the structural link are explicit, and in both $q_{max} > 1$, as exemplified in the bottom OPD of Fig. 15.5.

15.4.2 The 16 Cardinality Kinds

Combining pairs of the four symbols "?", "*", "1", and "+", we get 16 cardinality kinds. These are listed in the 4×4 array in Table 15.2. The array cells with the four customary cardinalities, [1, 1], which is "one-to-one", [1, +], which is "one-to-many", [+,1], which is "many-to-one", and [+, +], which is "many-to-many", are greyed at the bottom-right part of the table. These cardinality kinds are the ones recognized in entity relationship diagrams (ERDs), proposed by Chen (1976), which are used to design databases. Here we see that they comprise one quarter of the 16 possible combinations.

Table 15.2 The 16 cardinality types obtained by combinations of pairs of the four participation constraint kinds

Source symbol / Destination symbol	?	*	1	+
?	[?, ?]	[?, *]	[?, 1]	[?, +]
*	[*, ?]	[*, *]	[*, 1]	[*, +]
1	[1, ?]	[1, *]	[1, 1]	[1, +]
+	[+, ?]	[+, *]	[+, 1]	[+, +]

15.5 Procedural Participation Constraints

By its definition, a process must transform *at least* one object, but there could be more. Moreover, we want to be able to model the fact that an enabler, be it an agent or an instrument, is optional or is required in a certain amount. A procedural participation constraint, defined above as a number or an expression recorded along a procedural link next to the source or destination object, denotes the multiplicity of that object in that procedural relation. The quantity of processes is always assumed to be one, so *there is no participation constraint next to the process end of the procedural link.*

Figure 15.6 shows two procedural participation constraints, one on an agent link and the other—on an effect link. As with the structural participation constraints, the + (plus) symbol stands for "at least one", while the * (asterisk) symbol—for "optional". Following the grammatical rule that numbers up to ten should be spelled out in text rather than as digits, the number **3** in the OPD is written as **Three** in the corresponding OPL paragraph sentence. This is an optional convention and it is not used in conjunction with parameters, as Fig. 15.7 demonstrates.

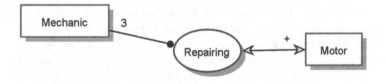

Three Mechanics handle **Repairing.**
Repairing affects at least one **Motors.**

Fig. 15.6 Examples of two participation constraints on procedural links

15.5.1 Parameterized Procedural Participation Constraints

Figure 15.7 shows the use of a variety of participation constraints in procedural links with parameters, ranges, and parameter constraints.

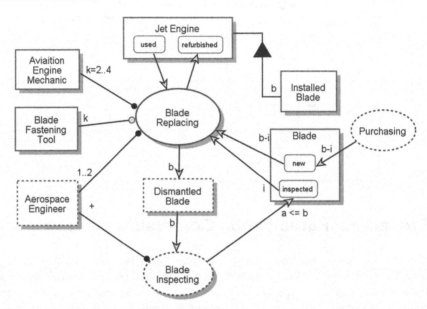

k=2 to **4 Aviation Engine Mechanics** handle **Blade Replacing**. **Jet Engine** can be **used** or **refurbished**. **Jet Engine** consists of **b Installed Blades**. **1** to **2 Aerospace Engineers** handle **Blade Replacing**. An optional **Aerospace Engineer** handles **Blade Inspecting**. **Blade** can be **inspected** or **new**.	**Blade Replacing** requires **k Blade Fastening Tools**. **Blade Replacing** changes **Jet Engine** from **used** to **refurbished**. **Blade Replacing** consumes **i inspected Blades** and **b–i new Blades**. **Blade Replacing** yields **b Dismantled Blades**. **Blade Inspecting** consumes **b Dismantled Blades**. **Blade Inspecting** yields **a<=b inspected Blades**. **Purchasing** yields **b–i new Blades**.

Fig. 15.7 Participation constraints in procedural links with parameters, ranges, and parameter constraints

As both the OPD and the OPL express, in this **Blade Replacing** system, a **Jet Engine** has b **Installed Blades**. Two to four (a number set to k) **Aviation Engine Mechanics** handle the process, for which they use k **Blade Fastening Tools**. The **Blade Replacing** process is also handled by one or two **Aerospace Engineers**. This process yields b **Dismantled Blades**, which undergo **Blade Inspecting**, an environmental process that yields a number a (which is at most b) of **inspected Blades**. The process consumes a total of b **Blades**, of which i are **inspected** and $b–i$ are **new**. This is the number of **new Blades** obtained by **Purchasing** them. This example shows not only how parameterized participation constraints are used with procedural links, but also how they can serve to express *parameter constraints*—constraints among the parameters. Additional constraints can be added. For example we could specify that $i{\leq}b$ to avoid getting a negative number for $b–i$.

15.5.2 Enabler and Transformee Participation Constraints

A process must contain at least one transformee and it can have one or more enables. This is expressed in the OPD in Fig. 15.8, showing a metamodel of the kinds of objects involved in **Processing**, classified into **Enablers** and **Transformees**.

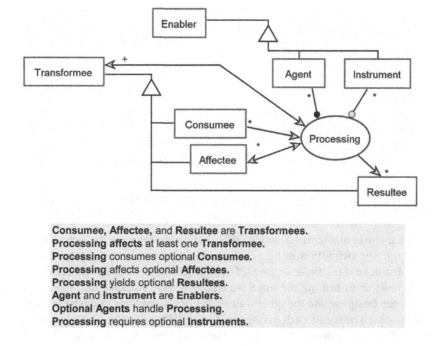

Consumee, Affectee, and Resultee are Transformees.
Processing affects at least one Transformee.
Processing consumes optional Consumee.
Processing affects optional Affectees.
Processing yields optional Resultees.
Agent and Instrument are Enablers.
Optional Agents handle Processing.
Processing requires optional Instruments.

Fig. 15.8 Participation constraints on **Enablers** and **Transformees**

15.6 The Distributive Law of Structural Relations

In algebra, when we have an expression of the form $ab + ac$, we can factor it out and write it as $a(b+c)$. In a similar vein, the distributive law of structural relations is as follows.

> *If A, B, and C are all objects or are all processes, and $\Re$ is a structural relation, then $A \Re B, A \Re C \Leftrightarrow A \Re (B, C)$.*

This is not just a law in mathematics and in OPM, but, as we see next, the same idea is applicable also in natural languages. The two OPDs in Fig. 15.9 provide an example of the graphical application of the distributive law of structural relations. In the OPD on the left hand side of Fig. 15.9 there are two disjoint tagged structural links, both bearing the same tag **employs**. One **employs** tag is recorded along the link from **Firm** to **Graphic Designer** and the other—along the link from **Firm** to **Systems Engineer**. This OPD has exactly two graphic sentences, each giving rise to one OPL sentence. Denoting the relation **employs** by $\Re$, **Firm** by A, **Graphic Designer** by B and **Systems Engineer** by C, ignoring the added participation constraints, this is like writing $A \; \Re \; B, \; A \; \Re \; C$.

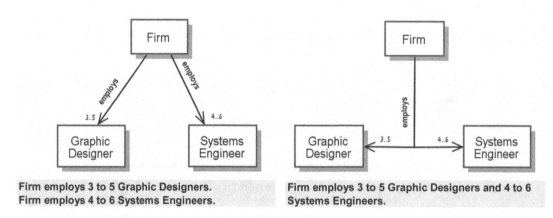

Firm employs 3 to 5 Graphic Designers.   Firm employs 3 to 5 Graphic Designers and 4 to 6
Firm employs 4 to 6 Systems Engineers.   Systems Engineers.

Fig. 15.9 The distributive law of structural relations applied in OPDs. Left: disjoint links. Right: joint links

This is not just a law in mathematics and in OPM, but, as we see next, the same idea is applicable also in natural languages. The two OPDs in Fig. 15.9 provide an example of the graphical application of the distributive law of structural relations. In the OPD on the left hand side of Fig. 15.9 there are two disjoint tagged structural links, both bearing the same tag **employs**. One **employs** tag is recorded along the link from **Firm** to **Graphic Designer** and the other—along the link from **Firm** to **Systems Engineer**. This OPD has exactly two graphic sentences, each giving rise to one OPL sentence. Denoting the relation **employs** by $\Re$, **Firm** by A, **Graphic Designer** by B and **Systems Engineer** by C, ignoring the added participation constraints, this is like writing $A \; \Re \; B, \; A \; \Re \; C$.

In the OPD on the right hand side of Fig. 15.9, the two **employs** tagged structural links are joined at their origin and fork (diverge) somewhere along the link. Since now only one structural link emanates from the source object, the two OPL sentences become one. Using our notation, again ignoring the added participation constraints, this is like writing $A \; \Re \; (B, \; C)$. The expressions representing the left and right OPDs are the same as those in the algebraic formula of the distributive law above (with the addition of the participation constraints). Indeed, they are semantically equivalent both graphically and textually. Processes can also be related by structural relations that are distributive, but since the use of structural relations is much more prevalent for objects, we focus on objects.

Graphically, joining of the origin of the two structural links in Fig. 15.9 having the same tag **employs** has the same function as the algebraic parentheses. The parentheses in the distributive law expression $A\Re(B, \; C) \Leftrightarrow A\Re B, \; A\Re C$ enable using $\Re$ just once. Analogously, the joint tagged link enables using **employs** just once in both the OPD and is corresponding OPL sentence. Finally, the OPL reserved word **and** is analogous to the comma in the distributive law expression. Joining structural relations with the same tag gives rise to forks, which are discussed next.

15.7 **Fork, Handle, and Tine**

In algebra, the distributive law $A\Re(B, C) \Leftrightarrow A\Re B, A\Re C$ is extensible to any number n of elements. Thus, $A\Re(B_1, B_2, \ldots B_n) \Leftrightarrow A\Re B_1, A\Re B_2, \ldots A\Re B_n$. The same is true for OPM and natural languages. To express this in OPM we define fork below.

> *A **fork** is a combination of two or more structural links with the same semantics expressed by the same tag.*

A fork has a common joint edge on the origin side of the link, called *handle*, which splits into two or more edges on the destination side of the link, each of which is a *tine*.

> ***Handle** is the joint origin-side edge of the fork.*
>
> ***Tine** is the split destination-side edge of the fork.*
>
> ***Handle thing** is the thing linked to the handle of the fork link*
>
> ***Tine thing** is a thing linked to a tine of the fork link.*
>
> ***Object fork** is a set of objects connected by a fork.*
>
> ***Process fork** is a set of processes connected by a fork.*

Since a structural relation is between objects or between processes, if the handle thing is an object, all the tine things are also objects, and the same applies to processes. The two OPDs in Figs. 15.10 and 15.11 exemplify the value of using fork relations. The OPD in Fig. 15.10 contains 10 separate structural links, all having the tag **passes through**. It is therefore equivalent to the OPL paragraph in Fig. 15.10, which has 10 OPL sentences. This OPL paragraph reflects the redundancy of links in its corresponding OPD. Though syntactically and semantically correct, the 10-sentnece paragraph is mechanical, repetitive, and not suitable for human reading.

The application of the distributive law provides for aggregating the ten links into a fork. Using the expression $A\Re B_1, A\Re B_2, \ldots A\Re B_n \Leftrightarrow A\Re(B_1, B_2, \ldots B_n)$, and substituting $A=$ **Danube River**, $B_1=$ **Germany**, $B_2=$ **Austria**, etc., the result is presented in Fig. 15.11, where only one structural link, labeled **passes through**, emanates from **The Danube River**, forking into ten tine. The OPL paragraph of this OPD shrinks from ten sentences to just one *fork OPL sentence*—a single perfect and more humanly readable English sentence. The handle of the fork in Fig. 15.11 is the segment emanating from the handle object **Danube River**, while each of the 10 tines is the line segment with the arrowhead reaching to a tine object (a country box in this example) and the segment connecting this line segment to the handle.

The participation constraints on the various tines may be different from the default, 1, for each tine object separately. Since the handle is common to all the tines, its participation constraint is also common. If a different participation constraint is required on the handle side for some link, then this link needs to be separated from the fork.

Danube River passes through Moldova.
Danube River passes through Romania.
Danube River passes through Serbia.
Danube River passes through Slovakia.
Danube River passes through Ukraine.

Danube River passes through Germany.
Danube River passes through Hungary.
Danube River passes through Austria.
Danube River passes through Bulgaria.
Danube River passes through Croatia.

Fig. 15.10 The 10 countries through which the Danube River passes through

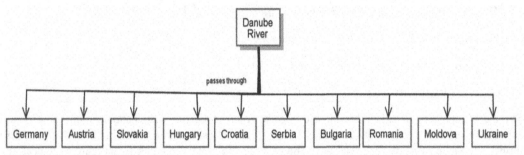

Danube River passes through Germany, Austria, Slovakia, Hungary, Croatia, Serbia, Bulgaria, Romania, Moldova, and Ukraine.

Fig. 15.11 The 10 "passes through" tagged links in Fig. 15.10 are replaced by a single fork with the same tag

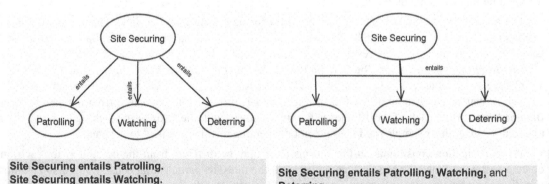

Site Securing entails Patrolling.
Site Securing entails Watching.
Site Securing entails Deterring.

Site Securing entails Patrolling, Watching, and Deterring.

Fig. 15.12 An example of a fork with processes

Figure 15.12 is an example of a fork in which all the linked things are processes, demonstrating that all the things connected by a fork are of the same persistence: either all are object or all are processes. This is so because structural relations are between things of the same persistence, i.e., between two objects or between two processes. Therefore, if the handle thing is an object, the tine things are all objects too, and vice versa.

15.8 The Tine Thing Set

A *set* is an abstract collection of things (also called *elements* or *members*). Each thing in the set is unique.

> *The **tine thing set** of a fork is the set of all the things linked to the tines of the fork.*

The *tine object set* of a fork is the set of all the objects linked to the tines of the fork, while the *tine process set* of a fork is the set of all the processes linked to the tines of the fork.

The tine object set of the fork labeled **employs** in the OPD in Fig. 15.9 includes the two types of occupations that the **Firm** employs. The tine object set of the fork labeled **employs** in the OPD in Fig. 15.9 is {**Graphic Designer, Systems Engineer**}. The tine object set of the fork labeled **passes through** in the OPD Fig. 15.11 is {**Germany, Austria, Slovakia, Hungary, Croatia, Serbia, Bulgaria, Romania, Moldova, Ukraine**}.

Frequently, showing all the fork things overloads the OPD both graphically and mentally, as is the case in Fig. 15.11. If the tine object set is significantly greater than 2, as in Fig. 15.11, it may be convenient to omit some of the objects in the tine object set that are not relevant for what that particular OPD is designed to convey. Indeed, recall that the model fact representation OPM principle stipulates that an OPM model fact needs to appear in at least one OPD in order for it to be represented in the model; objects that are not relevant in a particular OPD do not need to be shown in it. Following this principle, not each OPD in a system's OPD set that contains the handle thing must contain all the things in the tine thing set. Suffice it that each one of the tine things appears once in a relation ℜ to the handle thing in order for it to be part of the set of tine things. We exemplify and elaborate on this when we define and discuss the fork degree and comprehensiveness properties next. One OPD may contain one subset of the tine thing set, while in other OPDs that belong to the same OPD set, other subsets of things connected to tines can be hidden to alleviate cognitive load and enhance the diagram readability.

Three fork properties help refine the OPM model: degree, comprehensiveness, and orderability. These are discussed next in this section.

15.8.1 Fork Degree

The size (number of elements) of the tine object set is equal to the fork degree.

> ***Fork degree** is a property of fork whose value is the size of the tine object set.*

For example, the degree of the fork in Fig. 15.9 whose handle is **Firm** is 2.The degree of the fork from **Danube River** in Fig. 15.11 is 10, as the tine object set of the fork labeled **passes through** in the OPD in Fig. 15.11 includes all ten countries through which the **Danube River** passes.[2]

> *The **tine thing set** of a fork is the union of the tine sets emanating from the same handle and having the same tag in all the OPDs in the OPD set.*

For example, suppose another OPD in the OPM model to which the OPD in Fig. 15.9 belongs has the following tine object set of size 4: {**Systems Engineer, Programmer, Software Engineer, Project Leader**}. Suppose also that these are the only two OPDs in the OPD set of that OPM model where the object **Firm** appears with the tagged structural link labeled **employs**. The tine object set of the fork labeled **employs** would then be: *Tine-object-set* (**Firm employs**) = {**Graphic Designer, Systems Engineer**} ∪ {**Systems Engineer, Programmer, Software Engineer, Project Leader**} = {**Graphic Designer, Systems Engineer, Programmer, Software Engineer, Project Leader**}. The fork degree of the OPD that shows all the occupations that the firm employs is 5—the size of the tine object set.

15.8.2 Fork Comprehensiveness

While omission of irrelevant tine things helps eliminate the excess clutter frequently caused in OPDs of real life systems, it may also mislead the reader of an individual OPD into thinking that the tine thing set presented in that particular OPD is comprehensive, i.e., all the tine things that can be linked to the handle thing are indeed linked. To avoid such confusion, it is important to indicate whether all the things in the tine thing set that can be linked to the handle are indeed linked. To this end, we define the fork's *comprehensiveness* property value as follows.

> ***Fork comprehensiveness*** *is a Boolean property of a fork which is positive if all the things in the tine thing set are attached to the fork's handle and negative otherwise.*

Being a Boolean property, **Comprehensiveness** has two values: **positive**, if the fork is comprehensive, i.e., all the things in the tine thing set are attached to the fork's handle, and **negative** otherwise. Using the fork's comprehensiveness property, one can indicate whether the structure implied by the fork is comprehensive or non-comprehensive. The importance of fork comprehensiveness is that it tells the diagram reader whether all the tine things that can potentially be linked to the handle object are indeed linked. A non-comprehensive fork is marked by a short bar perpendicular to the fork near the handle thing.

Continuing the example in Fig. 15.11, suppose in some OPD we wish to show only those countries or areas that were historically "behind the iron curtain". Examining the OPD in Fig. 15.13, we see that **Germany** and **Austria** were removed. Graphically, the non-comprehensiveness of this fork is marked by the non-comprehensive fork symbol—the short bar perpendicular to the fork near the handle object. This non-comprehensive fork symbol expresses the fact that not all the countries through which the **Danube River** passes are represented in this OPD. The OPL reserved phrase that expresses the fact that the fork is non-comprehensive is "and more", which is appended at the end of the list of fork objects, as the OPL sentence in Fig. 15.13 demonstrates.

---

[2]For trivia lovers: The Danube river passes across the most national borders (askville.amazon.com).

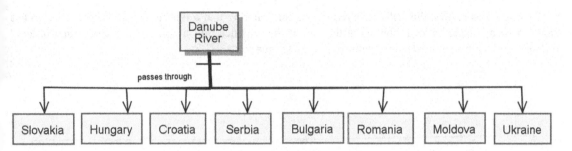

Danube River passes through Slovakia, Hungary, Croatia, Serbia, Bulgaria, Romania, Moldova, Ukraine, and at least one more.

Fig. 15.13 A non-comprehensive fork is marked by the short bar perpendicular to the fork near the handle object

The default value of the fork's **Comprehensiveness** property is **positive**, meaning that the fork is comprehensive and indicating that all the objects in the tine set of the fork are attached to the fork's handle. In this default case the handle will not be marked with the non-comprehensive fork symbol. The other value of **Comprehensiveness** is **negative**, so the fork is non-comprehensive, implying that the tine set is incomplete, as at least one tine thing is missing. The OPL reserved phrase "and at least one more" at the end of the OPL sentence in Fig. 15.13 expresses this. A non-comprehensive fork can be made comprehensive by completing the missing things in the forks' tine thing set while removing the non-comprehensive fork symbol, thereby changing its **Comprehensiveness** state from **negative** to **positive**.

15.8.3 Fork Orderability

The elements of a set in general, and the things in the tine thing set of a fork in particular, can be *ordered* or *unordered*. This is determined by the fork's *orderability* property.

> *Orderability is a Boolean property of a fork's thing tine set, which is positive if the things in the tine thing set are ordered and negative otherwise.*

Like **Comprehensiveness**, **Orderability** is a Boolean attribute of the **Tine Set** of a **Fork**, whose values are **positive** and **negative**. A **Tine Set** with **negative Orderability** is an **Unordered Tine Set**, and this is the default, so it requires no special indication.

For a thing tine set with positive orderability, there often (but not always) exists some logical relation $\Re$ of the things in the tine thing set $\{T_1 \ldots T_N\}$ such that $T^{(j)} \Re T^{(j+1)}$ for each $T^{(j)}$ in $\{T^{(1)}, T^{(2)}, \ldots, T^{(N)}\}$. For example, if T_i; $1 < i < N$ is a set of N natural numbers, and $\Re$ is the $<$ inequality symbol, then the orderability of the tine thing set is positive. If the tine thing set is the parts of a scientific paper {header, body, footer} there is no $\Re$ that determines this order.

A **Tine Set** with **positive Orderability** is an **Ordered Tine Set**. To denote that a fork's tine set is ordered, the word ordered appears next to the handle of the fork, as demonstrated in the OPD in Fig. 15.14. The word ordered is a graphic symbol rather than a reserved OPL phrase, because it is part of the OPD just like the non-comprehensiveness fork symbol.

As Fig. 15.14 shows, the OPL reserved phrase for denoting that a tine thing set is ordered, is "in this order", which is added after a comma at the end of the sentence. For a non-comprehensive and ordered fork, the OPL phrase is "and at least one more, in that sequence".

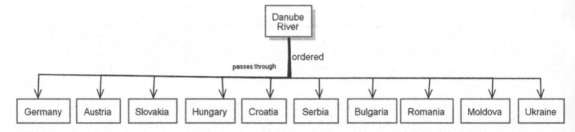

Danube River passes through Germany, Austria, Slovakia, Hungary, Croatia, Serbia, Bulgaria, Romania, Moldova, and Ukraine, in that sequence.

Fig. 15.14 An ordered tine set of a fork relation is marked by the word "ordered" next to the fork's handle

To express the order graphically, the things in the tine thing set must be arranged either horizontally from left to right, as in Fig. 15.15, or vertically, from top to bottom. The object boxes may not be ordered nicely even though the orderability of the tine thing set is positive.

To resolve this potential ambiguity, the ordering algorithm is to arrange the objects by the left-to-right order of their leftmost side of the object box (increasing x coordinate), and for those with the same left side coordinate, arrange by top-to-bottom order of the topmost side of the object box (decreasing y coordinate, or increasing if we consider the coordinates of pixels in a monitor). The same applies to processes, where the box is the one that encloses the process ellipse.

15.8.4 Tine Thing Set Order Rule

The order of the things in the tine thing set can be based on some rule.

> **Order rule** *is a property of an ordered tine thing set, which specifies textually in the OPD the rule or criterion according to which the things in the tine thing set are ordered.*

The **Order Rule** can be null, which is the default, or any other phrase written in lower-case letters. **Order Rule** whose value is null means that there is no order criterion, and nothing (if there is no order) or "ordered" (if there is order but the rule is trivial, such as the order of the days of the week) is written next to the handle.

If there is an ordering rule that needs to be specified, the phrase "ordered by" rather than "ordered" is used in the OPD next to the fork, and recorded below it is the order criterion itself. For example, the OPD in Fig. 15.15 indicates an ordered tine set with the order rule "**river flow**", implying that the countries are ordered by following the flow of the Danube River.

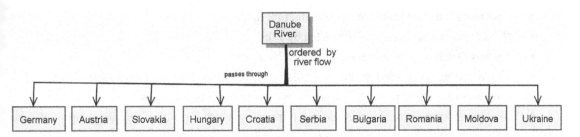

Danube River passes through Germany, Austria, Slovakia, Hungary, Croatia, Serbia, Bulgaria, Romania, Moldova, and Ukraine, ordered by **river flow.**

Fig. 15.15 Order criterion marked by the phrase "ordered by", followed by the order criterion "river flow" below it

15.9 **Summary**

- A *participation constraint* is a number or a mathematical expression recorded along a link next to an object, which denotes the multiplicity (number of repetitions) of that object in that relation.
- A *structural participation constraint* is a participation constraint recorded along a structural link.
- A *procedural participation constraint* is a participation constraint recorded along a procedural link.
- The *default participation constraint* is 1, and it is implicit.
- A *parameterized participation constraint* is a participation constraint which is a mathematical expression with one or more parameters.
- A *range participation constraint* is a participation constraint with lower and upper bounds, each possibly an expression, on the number of possible objects that can take part in the relation.
- *Source participation constraint* is the participation constraint on the source side of the (structural or procedural) link.
- *Destination participation constraint* is the participation constraint on the destination side of the (structural or procedural) link.
- *Cardinality* is a property of a link whose value depends on the combination of the source and destination participation constraints of the structural link.
- The *distributive law of structural relations*: If A, B, and C are all objects or are all processes, and $\Re$ is a structural relation, then $A \, \Re \, B$, $A \, \Re \, C \Leftrightarrow A \, \Re \, (B, C)$.
- A *fork* is a combination of two or more structural links with the same semantics expressed by the same tag.
- *Handle* is the joint origin-side edge of the fork.
- *Tine* is the split destination-side edge of the fork.
- *Handle thing* is the thing linked to the handle of the fork link

- *Tine thing* is a thing linked to a tine of the fork link.
- *Object fork* is a set of objects connected by a fork.
- *Process fork* is a set of processes connected by a fork.
- The *tine thing set* of a fork is the set of all the things linked to the tines of the fork.
- *Fork degree* is a fork property that specifies the size of the tine object set.
- *Fork comprehensiveness* is a Boolean fork property which is positive if all the things in the tine thing set are attached to the fork's handle and negative otherwise.
- *Orderability* is a Boolean fork property which is positive if the things in the tine thing set are ordered and negative otherwise.
- *Order criterion* is a property of an ordered tine thing set, which specifies textually in the OPD the criterion according to which the things in the tine thing set are ordered.

15.10 Problems

1. Model a system in which three cranes are used to lift an elevator to the top of a new building.
2. Change the objects, the tag in the tagged structural relations, and the participation constraints in each of the four OPDs in in Fig. 15.5 such that meaningful sentences are obtained.
3. Select from Table 15.2 3 of the 16 cardinality types. For each, create and OPD that demonstrates it.
4. Model a library comprised of n shelves, each of which can hold up to 20 books.
5. For the library in the previous question, model a process **Maximal Number of Books Computing** that does what its name says.
6. Model two object forks with objects and two process forks, and write their OPL paragraphs.
7. For each fork in the previous problem, draw an OPD assuming that the distributive law of structural relations does not exist. Which option is more compact? Why?
8. Specify the tine thing set and the fork degree for each one of the four forks in the previous problem.
9. For one object fork or one process fork from the previous question add a new fork whose tine thing set has a non-empty intersection with the old fork.
10. Add a non-comprehensiveness fork symbol where appropriate in the forks of the previous question.
11. Draw the comprehensive fork of the two forks from the previous question.
12. Is there any potential order criterion in any one of the four forks from the first question? If so, pick one and add to it is orderability criterion. If not—design a new ordered fork and specify its order criterion.
13. Write the OPL sentences for all the OPDs in your answers to the questions in this chapter.

Chapter 16

Fundamental Structural Relations

Four structural relations are most prevalent and play an especially important role in specifying and understanding systems. Termed the *fundamental structural relations*, these relations are:

- *Aggregation-participation*, which denotes the relation between a whole and its parts,
- *Exhibition-characterization*, which denotes the relation between an exhibitor—a thing exhibiting a one or more features (attributes and/or operations) and the things that characterize the exhibitor,
- *Generalization-specialization*, which denotes the relation between a general thing and its specializations, giving rise to inheritance, and
- *Classification-instantiation*, which denotes the relation between a class of things and an instance of that class.

This chapter is devoted to discussing these structural relations, while subsequent chapters deal with each of them separately.

16.1 Relation Symbols and Participants

Due to the prevalence of the fundamental structural relations, in order to avoid writing their tags over and over again and make them readily graphically identifiable, each one of the four fundamental structural relations is assigned with a unique triangular symbol. Table 16.1 lists the fundamental structural relations with their respective triangular symbols as they appear linked in an OPD, and the OPL sentence that corresponds to each OPD. While all the OPD examples are of objects linked to objects (except for **Operation B**), being structural relations, the four fundamental structural relations exist between processes and can be depicted also linking processes. To begin, we next define refineable and refinee.

> **Refineable** *is a thing amenable to refinement via a fundamental structural relation.*

Each **Refineable** is the ancestor (parent) of the two-level hierarchy induced by the fundamental structural relation. Hence, as Table 16.1 presents in brackets in the leftmost column, a **Refineable** can be a **Whole**, an **Exhibitor**, a **General**, or a **Class**. Each of the four refineables corresponds to one of the four fundamental structural relation.

> **Refinee** *is a thing that refines a refineable.*

Each **Refinee** is the descendant (child) of the two-level hierarchy induced by the fundamental structural relation. Table 16.1 presents in brackets in the second-from-left column the four **Refinees** corresponding to the refineables in the structural relations: a **Part**, a **Feature**, a **Specialization**, and an **Instance**. As we discuss later, **Feature**, in turn, specializes into **Attribute** (a structural feature) and **Operation** (a procedural feature).

© Springer Science+Business Media New York 2016

D. Dori, *Model-Based Systems Engineering with OPM and SysML*, DOI 10.1007/978-1-4939-3295-5_16

Table 16.1 The fundamental structural relation names, OPD symbols, and OPL sentences

Structural Relation Name [Participant Name]		Graphic Symbol with OPD usage	OPL Sentence(s)	
Forward [Refineable]	Backward [Refinee]		Forward	Backward
Aggregation **[Whole]**	Participation [Part]	Whole / Part A / Part B	**Whole** consists of **Part A** and **Part B**.	
Exhibition [Exhibitor]	**Characterization** **[Feature:** **Attribute** or **Operation]**	Exhibitor / Attribute A / Operation B	**Exhibitor** exhibits **Attribute A** as well as **Operation B**.	
Generalization **[General]**	Specialization [Specialization]	General Thing / Specialization A / Specialization B		**Specialization A** and **Specialization B** are **General Things**.
Classification **[Class]**	Instantiation [Instance]	Class / Instance A / Instance B		**Instance A** and **Instance B** are instances of **Class**.

16.2 Relation Names and OPL Sentences

The name of each fundamental structural relation consists of a pair of dash-separated words.[1] As Table 16.1 presents, the first word in each such pair is the *forward relation name*, i.e., the name of the relation as seen from the viewpoint of the thing up in the hierarchy—the ancestor, or parent—while looking down the hierarchy. The second word is the *backward (or reverse) relation name*, i.e., the name of the relation as seen from the viewpoint of the thing down in the hierarchy—the descendant, or child—of that relation while looking up the hierarchy.

The first fundamental structural relation, aggregation-participation, denotes the relation between a whole thing and its parts. Exhibition-characterization denotes the relation between a thing and its features (attributes and operations). Generalization-specialization denotes the relation between a general thing and its specializations. Finally, classification-instantiation denotes the relation between a class of things and the instances of that class.

Since the full names of these relations are rather long, each has a short version, which is either the forward or backward structural relation name only. The short name, denoted in Table 16.1 by bold letters,

---

[1]The pair of words "dash-separated" is a pair of dash-separated words (pun intended).

is selected to be the more meaningful of the two: **Aggregation, Characterization, Generalization**, and **Classification**.

As Table 16.1 shows, all the four fundamental structural relation symbols are equilateral triangles linked via orthonormal polylines, i.e., lines whose segments are parallel to either one of the diagram axes (also called Manhattan lines). The tip of the triangle is linked through an orthonormal polyline to the root of the hierarchy tree—the aggregate or whole in our case (**Whole**, in the first row of Table 16.1, for example). The triangle's base is linked through other orthonormal polylines to each one of the parts of the aggregate (**Part A** and **Part B** in our example). The fact that the links of the fundamental structural relations run horizontally or vertically but not diagonally (like all the procedural links) helps differentiate them visually from procedural links. Using different colors for different links that cross each other (which should be avoided as much as possible) is also helpful in crowded OPDs.

The OPL sentences of the fundamental structural relations are also either in the forward or the backward direction. The direction was similarly determined by how natural the sentence sounds in plain English. The forward direction is used for aggregation and characterization:

> **Whole** consists of **Part A** and **Part B**.
> **Exhibitor** exhibits **Attribute A**, as well as **Operation B**.

The backward direction is used for generalization and classification:

> **Specialization A** and **Specialization B** are **General Things**.
> **Instance A** and **Instance B** are instances of **Class**.

As usual, the multiple versions of these two OPL sentences, which include three or more refinees, are:

> **Specialization A, Specialization B,** and **Specialization C** are **General Things**.
> **Instance A, Instance B,** and **Instance C** are instances of **Class**.

16.3 Structural Hierarchies, Transitivity, User-Defined Symbols

The special graphic symbols assigned to the four fundamental structural relations due to their prevalence and usefulness do not make them particularly special; diagramming convenience, avoiding multiple tags, and ease of diagram reading have motivated the introduction of these symbols. Yet, the first three of these four relations do have in common the hierarchy and transitivity they induce (examples are given in the relevant chapters that follow, discussing each relation separately):

In **Aggregation**, a part can be the whole of yet smaller parts, creating an aggregation-participation hierarchy. This hierarchy is transitive: If A consists of B (and other parts) and B consists of C (and other parts), then A (indirectly) consists of C (and other parts).

In **Characterization**, a feature (attribute or operation) can be the exhibitor of lower-level features, creating an exhibition-characterization hierarchy. This hierarchy is transitive: If A exhibits B and B exhibits C, then A (indirectly) exhibits C.

In **Generalization**, a specialization can generalize lower-level specializations, creating a generalization-specialization hierarchy. This hierarchy is transitive: If A generalizes B (and possibly other specializations) and B consists of C (and possibly other specializations), then A (indirectly) generalizes C (and possibly other specializations). With respect to **Classification**, as explained in Chap. 20, an instance can only be a leaf in a generalization-specialization hierarchy. Therefore, the classification-instantiation relation cannot be transitive.

Complex hierarchies can be created by mixing combinations of the four relations. Following this idea of denoting a frequently used relation by a special symbol, it is possible to add a symbol for one or more structural relations that are widely used within a specialized domain. Consider an example from the domain of chemical laboratory testing of industrial lots. In this domain, the phrase "**is a sample of**" is a very prevalent and useful structural relation between a sample and the lot from which it was taken. A dedicated graphic symbol and a corresponding reserved phrase "**is a sample of**" can be introduced in this domain to enable quicker and easier modeling. The symbol selected in a real case in work done at ISCAR Ltd.—an enterprise operating in the domain of metal cutting tool manufacturing by sintering technology—was a piece cut out of a cake, symbolizing that the taste of the piece of cake—the sample— is the same of the entire cake—the lot from which the sample was taken. The four fundamental structural relations are so central to conceptual modeling that the next chapters are devoted to discussing each one of them.

16.4 **Summary**

- Four structural relations are fundamental and therefore are assigned graphic symbols.
  - *Refineable* is a thing amenable to refinement via a fundamental structural relation.
  - *Refinee* is a thing that refines a refineable.
- The four fundamental structural relations are:
  - Aggregation-participation;
  - Exhibition-characterization;
  - Generalization-specialization; and
  - Classification-instantiation.
- Each fundamental structural relation has a unique triangular symbol.
- The symbol replaces the tag, making the OPD more graphic and more quickly comprehensible.
- Each fundamental structural relation induces a hierarchy.
- Complex hierarchies can be created by mixing the four relations.

In certain domains, additional structural relations might be fundamental and user-defined dedicated symbols can be allocated for them.

16.5 **Problems**

1. For each thing in Table 16.1 indicate whether it is a refineable or a refinee.
2. For each OPD in Table 16.1 draw an alternative OPD without using a fundamental relation.
3. For each OPL sentence in Sect. 16.2 provide a concrete OPL example and its corresponding OPD.

Part III

Structure and Behavior:

Diving In

Having laid down in Part II the fundamentals and foundations of model-based systems engineering in both OPM and SysML, Part III goes to the heart of conceptual modeling. In the first four chapters of this Part, we delve into the details and usage of each one of the four fundamental structural relations. Chapters 17 and 18 discuss aggregation-participation and exhibition-characterization, respectively. Chapter 19 is about states and values, concepts that are needed for the two remaining fundamental structural relations—generalization-specialization and classification-instantiation, both elaborated on in Chap. 20. Chapter 21 concerns complexity management. It defines and describes the four refinement and abstraction mechanisms of OPM while also discussing complexity management in SysML. Chapter 22 is about OPM operational semantics and control links—the way control is managed during execution of the system. In Chap. 23 we specify how to model logical operators and probabilities. Finally, Chap. 24 is an overview of ISO 19450 Publically Available Specification (PAS)—*Automation Systems and Integration—Object-Process Methodology*, adopted by the International Organization for Standardization (ISO) in 2015.

Chapter 17
Aggregation-Participation

The whole is more than the sum of its parts.
Aristotle, *Metaphysica*

This large four-wheel chariot ... consists of a number of parts joined together by leather straps and wooden nails. ... Each of the four large wheels has 34 spokes ...
Description of a wood and leather Chariot, Eastern Altai, Russia (The State Hermitage Museum, 2001)

This chapter discusses the first fundamental structural relation, possibly the most important one: aggregation-participation—the relationship between the whole and its parts. Any interesting system can be described as a whole decomposed into parts. The system as a whole and any one of its parts can then be described separately using natural language adjectives to assign attribute values to objects and adverbs to assign attribute values to processes. Without the ability to mentally take things apart and examine their features, our ability to study systems would be greatly hindered. Aggregation-participation is also known as whole-part (Coad and Yourdon 1991), composition (Kilov and Simmonds 1996), or the part-of relationship (Fowler 1996).

17.1 Underlying Concepts

Aggregation-participation is a fundamental structural relation which denotes the fact that a refineable—a relatively high-level, ancestor, parent thing (object or process) aggregates (i.e., consists of, composed of, contains, or comprises) one or more refinees—lower-level, descendant, child things. The higher-level thing is called the *whole*, or *aggregate*, while the lower-level things that comprise it are the *parts*. This relationship is very central in conceptual modeling, and at least at a superficial level, is relatively easy to comprehend. Aggregation-participation is a means to describe the composition of every non-trivial thing by enumerating its parts in the whole-part hierarchy.

17.1.1 Gestalt Theory

Relating to the famous saying attributed to Aristotle quoted above that *"The whole is more than the sum of its parts"*, Koffka (1935, p. 176) rephrased this observation as follows: *"the whole is something else than the sum of its parts"*, arguing that the operation of summing up is often meaningless, but what is always meaningful in a whole is its relationships with its parts.

© Springer Science+Business Media New York 2016
D. Dori, *Model-Based Systems Engineering with OPM and SysML*, DOI 10.1007/978-1-4939-3295-5_17

In 1924, Wertheimer and Reizler (1944) introduced the gestalt theory, which basically claims that "*what is happening in the whole cannot be deduced from the characteristics of the separate pieces*" and that what happens to parts of the whole is determined by laws relating to the structure of that whole. A configuration or pattern of elements in any domain is unified as a whole so much that its properties cannot be derived from a simple summation of its parts. In psychology, Rescher and Oppenheim (1995) have provided a conceptual framework for the precise explication of the gestalt concept of "whole" and summarized the intuitive requirements or conditions of talking about a whole and its parts:

> *The whole must possess some attribute in virtue of its status as a whole, an attribute peculiar to it and characteristic of it as a whole. The parts of the whole must stand in some special and characteristic relation of dependence with one another; they must satisfy some special condition in virtue of their status as parts of a whole.*

17.1.2 Holism and Emergence

To specify the concept of part, it is necessary at the very outset to state the conditions under which some object is to be considered part of another whole thing. The specification of a particular part-whole relation thus determines for a given thing, the whole, which things are its parts. (Latimer and Stevens 1997). From a system's viewpoint, the "special condition" that things must fulfil as parts of a whole is *holism*. Holism, in turn, is the condition for *emergence*—the emerging function of a system that stems from the particular whole-part relations and the way the parts are aggregated, which none of the parts alone exhibits.

We tend to think of aggregation as a relation between a whole object and its object parts. Indeed, this is the usual context. However, unlike most trains of though, which attribute holism to object parts and the whole to the aggregate object, in OPM the same relation is used with analogous semantics for processes as it is for objects: A process can consist of parts, which are the subprocesses of that whole process, and the outcome of the aggregate process is not a mere sum of the outcomes of its subprocess parts, but a process with an emergent transformation of an object, which none of its subprocesses alone, nor their simple "arithmetic" sum could have delivered.

Thus, an OPM object may consist of other, lower-level objects (and exhibit, but not consist of, processes, which are its operations, as we discuss in Chap. 18). Analogously, an OPM process may consist of other, lower-level processes (and exhibit, but not consist of, objects, which are its attributes, as we discuss in Chap. 18). We elaborate on this idea while discussing refinement in Chap. 21.

17.1.3 Decomposition Depth

A question that arises frequently during modeling is: How far should the decomposition go? How deep down should it continue? Naturally, most things can be decomposed further than the deepest decomposition specified in a model of the system. In particular, physical objects can be decomposed all the way down to the molecular and atomic or even sub-atomic levels. However, the specification of yet deeper participation hierarchy levels always should stop at a point that is deemed sufficient by the system modeler, architect, engineer, or analyst for the purpose of specifying the system under development or study. That level of detail shall be sufficient to explain the function, structure, and behavior of the system under study (as is typical in science) or prescribe how to go about its detailed design (typically in engineering).

17.1.4 Why Use "consists of" and not "has a"?

Some early object-oriented (OO) methods referred to the aggregation-participation relation as the "has-a" relation (as opposed to the "is-a" relation for the generalization-specialization relation, which is the subject of Chap. 20). It may indeed seem natural to use some form of the verb "to have" to denote the relation between the whole and its parts, as in "*A car has a body, an engine, and four wheels.*" However, we avoid the use of this verb to denote aggregation because it is overloaded and may have[1] various interpretations. To see this, suffice it to look at the sentence examples "*Dave has a step mother.*", "*Jack has a yellow motorcycle.*", "*We are having a discussion.*" "*I am having hard time understanding.*" "*The patient has cold.*" and "*The object has an attribute.*" OPM's choice of the reserved phrase consists of for denoting the aggregation-participation relation is explained below.

17.2 Aggregation-Participation as a Fork

Like all structural relations, aggregation-participation is a pair of forward and backward structural relations. *Aggregation* is the forward structural relation—the relation as seen from the aspect of the aggregate, the whole, or the ancestor, when it refers to its parts—the descendants. The backward structural relation, i.e., the relation as seen from the aspect of each part, is *participation*.

Aggregation and participation are inverse relations: Aggregating can be thought of as the process of creating a whole from its parts, while participating is being one of the parts that comprise the aggregate. However, as we have noted in the discussion on structural relations in Sect. 14.3, *aggregating* is a state-preserving process. Its semantics is of parts being held together to create the whole, with time having little or no relevance to this relation.

The forward (or hierarchically downward) direction of the aggregation-participation relation, from the whole to its parts, is the *aggregation* direction. The reserved phrase used to express the forward direction of the relation is "consists of." The backward, (or upward, or reverse) direction, from each part to the whole, is the *participation* direction. The phrase used to express the backward direction of the relation is "is part of", but this is not an OPL reserved phrase.

The two OPDs in Fig. 17.1 exemplify how the aggregation-participation relation replaces the tagged structural relation. In the OPD on the left, the relations between **Lamp** and its three parts are expressed using three bidirectional tagged structural link, as we have been using so far. All three forward tags are "**consists of**", with the source object **Lamp** being the whole and the destination objects—**Base**, **Light Bulb**, and **Electric Chord**—the parts. The tag in the backward direction for each one of these three links is "**is part of**". Thus we get six OPL sentences—one forward and one backward for each of the three links.

The phrase "**consists of**" in the OPL paragraph on the left hand side of Fig. 17.1 is bolded since it is not reserved—it comes from a user-defined tag, put on a bidirectional tagged structural link, rather than from a dedicated aggregation symbol. The opposite is true for the reserved phrase "consists of" in OPL

---

[1]Already in this sentence, as well as in this footnote, we *have* a built-in example that shows the multiple uses of "have."

paragraph on the right hand side of Fig. 17.1, in which one OPL sentence, "**Lamp** consists of **Light Bulb, Base,** and **Electric Cord**." replaces six OPL sentence on the left.

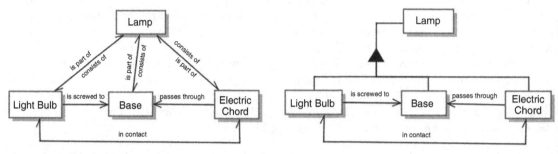

Lamp consists of Light Bulb.
Light Bulb is part of Lamp.
Lamp consists of Base.
Base is part of Lamp.
Lamp consists of Electric Cord.
Electric Cord is part of Lamp.
Light Bulb is screwed to Base.
Electric Cord passes through Base.
Light Bulb and Electric Cord are in contact.

Lamp consists of Light Bulb, Base, and Electric Cord.
Light Bulb is screwed to Base.
Electric Cord passes through Base.
Light Bulb and Electric Cord are in contact.

Fig. 17.1 Aggregation expressed by three tagged structural links (left) and the aggregation-participation symbol (right)

The solid black triangle ▲—the aggregation-participation relation symbol—replaces the pair of forward and backward textual tags of the bidirectional structural link that express textually the aggregation-participation relation. Like the rest of the fundamental structural relation symbols, the aggregation-participation relation symbol is a helpful shorthand graphic notation convention for this important and widely used structural relation. The symbol helps identify the relation easily in the OPD, saving graphic clutter and excessive text typing and reading.

Being a structural relation, the aggregation-participation relation abides by the distributive law, two or more structural links can be represented as a fork. In the OPD at the right of Fig. 17.1, the relations between **Lamp** and its three parts are expressed using the specific symbol designated for the aggregation-participation relation, a solid black equilateral triangle, ▲, whose base is horizontal. The whole is linked to the top of the triangle and the parts—to its base. This enables replacing the first six OPL sentences on the left with a single one—the first on the right. Unlike the tag "**consists of**" in Fig. 17.1, which, being user-defined, is bold, the phrase "consists of" in Fig. 17.1 is a reserved OPL phrase and therefore it is not bold.

17.3 **A Semantic Web Example**

RDF, the Resource Description Framework (W3C Consortium 2014), integrates a variety of applications from library catalogs and world-wide directories to syndication and aggregation of news, software, and content to personal collections of music, photos, and events using XML as interchange syntax. The RDF specifications provide a lightweight ontology system to support the exchange of knowledge on the Web.

An example of the use of the aggregation-participation fundamental structural relation can be found in the following excerpt taken from Sect. 2.2 of the RDF Primer (Manola and Miller 2004):

"*...each statement consists of a subject, a predicate, and an object.*"

The use of the phrase "*consists of*" is a clear indication of the existence of a whole-part, or aggregation-participation relation between the whole and its part. Indeed, as we have seen, OPM uses this as a reserved phrase to denote this relation. The OPD that is equivalent to this OPL sentence (and should be generated from it by any OPM-supporting tool such as OPCAT) is depicted in Fig. 17.2. Indeed, this OPL sentence is almost identical to the original one above.

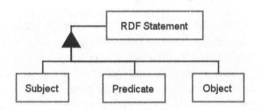

RDF Statement consists of **Subject**, **Predicate**, and **Object**.

Fig. 17.2 OPD of the sentence "RDF Statement consists of Subject, Predicate, and Object"

The black triangle, which denotes the aggregation-participation fundamental structural relation, has its tip is linked to the aggregate (the whole, which is the object **RDF Statement**), while its (always horizontal) base is linked to its three parts: **Subject**, **Predicate**, and **Object**. This is a fork, in which **RDF Statement** is the handle object, and the set {**Subject**, **Predicate**, **Object**} is the tine object set. If forks did not exist, the OPD would have required three separate aggregation links, each with its own black triangle symbol. As we will soon see in Fig. 17.4, since UML and SysML do not have the notion of fork, we would indeed need three separate aggregation (diamond symbols) to express the same three model facts.

17.3.1 Different Phrases, Same Semantics

In the case of the **RDF Statement** analyzed above, we were lucky to find out that the phrase in the natural language sentence "*...each statement consists of a subject, a predicate, and an object,*" contained the reserved OPL phrase **consists of**. This made it easy to deduce that a whole-part relationship exists between an object **RDF Statement** and a set of other objects. There are, however, many other syntactical expressions with the same whole-part semantics. These include "*has parts,*" "*comprised of,*" "*is made of,*" and "*comprises.*" Other expressions, such as "*is divided into,*" "*make up,*" or "*contains,*" may, under some interpretation, also be considered as having the same whole-part relation semantics, while in a different context they may convey a somewhat different meaning. Consider, for example, the following definition of an RDF triple, found in Sect. 3.1 of the W3C Proposed Recommendation *Resource Description Framework (RDF): Concepts and Abstract Syntax* (Klyne et al. 2004):

"*Each triple has three parts: a subject, an object, and a predicate (also called a property) that denotes a relationship.*"

In Sect. 6.1 of the same document, we find that:

*"An **RDF triple** contains three components: the **subject**, which is an RDF URI reference or a blank node, the **predicate**, which is an RDF URI reference, and the **object**, which is an RDF URI reference, a literal or a blank node."*

Comparing these two excerpts from the same document, we must deduce that *"has three parts"* has the exact same meaning as *"contains three components,"* as both relate to the composition or structure of an RDF triple. Moreover, if we accept that the semantics of the verbs *"contains"* and *"has parts"* in this context is the same as *"consists of,"* then we can summarize the two citations above in the following OPL sentence:

RDF Triple consists of Subject, Predicate, and Object.

The problem of multiple words, idioms, or phrases that have the same or almost the same semantics, which is demonstrated here, is a major issue in natural language processing (NLP) and understanding. Using their natural human intelligence, human beings normally have no problem assigning the same semantics to such different syntactic entities, and grasp subtle differences when they exist and are relevant. The example above shows that even in highly formal documents, such as one defining the semantic Web, in which semantics is the issue of discourse, free use is made of equivalent idioms and phrases, justifiably counting on the human intelligence to resolve it.

Indeed, people interpret meaningful sentences effortlessly all the time without even paying attention to the fact that other words and a totally different syntax was used to express the same semantics. When NLP techniques are considered, this issue becomes of prime importance, and has to be dealt with meticulously. OPL solves this problem by being a subset of English that is defined formally via a context-free grammar. Future developments in automated sematic sentence understanding can be key to model evolution of ground-truth, humanly validated kernel OPM models, such as the one developed by Somekh et al. (2014) for the mRNA lifecycle.

17.4 Aggregate Naming

Frequently during the analysis, we encounter situations in which we need to name an aggregate, which has no single word in natural language. To illustrate the point of aggregate naming and the importance of appropriate phrase generation, consider a transportation, civil, and systems engineering development team, whose assignment is to improve the traffic in a city. After some thought and discussion, the team agrees that an essential object in the system is the composition of a car and the person that drives it in the city streets. This object is much more central to the system than a car alone or a driver alone.

The role a car without a driver plays is restricted to parking issues, while the driver without the car should be considered a pedestrian. Nonetheless, having agreed that the car along with its driver is a major object that needs to be accounted for in the system, our team still lacks an elegant way of referring to it. Since there is no single word in English (and most likely in any other natural language) for this object, the team has come up with the name **Car-Driver Complex**, as illustrated in Fig. 17.3. As we will see, these situations are not unique to aggregates; they are also encountered in a variety of other circumstances, such as naming an attribute when only the names of its values are explicit.[2] In cases like these, we must exercise our creativity to generate an appropriate phrase that best captures the essence of what we wish to express.

The capability of inventing meaningful names, or generating expressive phrases, is a very important component of the analysis process. It provides us with the power to abstract into a whole a collection of things that would otherwise be very difficult to think about and relate to as a unity. Recall that indeed the first OPM principle—the Function-as-a-Seed OPM Principle—calls for starting the process of modeling a system by defining, naming, and depicting the function of the system. The name of the function shall express what the system is designed to do, and what value its beneficiaries will gain from using it.

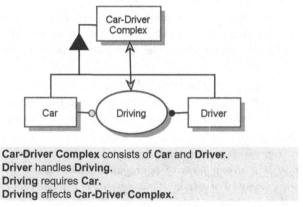

Car-Driver Complex consists of **Car** and **Driver**.
Driver handles **Driving**.
Driving requires **Car**.
Driving affects **Car-Driver Complex**.

Fig. 17.3 Naming an aggregate which has no single word in natural language

17.5 Composite and Shared Aggregation in UML and SysML

SysML adopted from UML 2 all the definitions related to class diagram (and several other diagram kinds) "as is." SysML block diagram inherits the same semantics as UML 2 class diagram. Hence, in UML 2 and SysML class diagrams there are two types of aggregation: *composite aggregation* and *shared aggregation* (Object Management Group 2010, p. 39).

- **Composite aggregation**, depicted as a black diamond next to the whole end of the link, (see Fig. 17.4) "*indicates that the composite object has responsibility for the existence and storage of the composed objects (parts).*" Composite aggregation, also referred to as *strong aggregation*, or the *composition relationship*, or *standard composite aggregation*, or *non-shared association*, is considered a "strong" form of containment or aggregation: A part can belong to just one aggregate, and if the aggregate is consumed, all its parts are consumed along with it. Originally defined for UML, *responsibility* and *storage* in the composite aggregation definition are software-related concepts. SysML, which is supposed to accommodate systems of any kind, not just software, has inherited this definition, as is the case with many other definitions.

---

[2]For example, what is the name of the attribute the values of which are **wide** and **narrow**? **Width**? **Narrowness**? Something in-between? Such a neutral word does not exist. Section 18.7 contains a detailed discussion on this topic.

- **Shared aggregation**, also called simply *aggregation*, denoted as a white (blank) diamond next to the whole end of the link, is a loose, "weak" type of whole-part relationship. Unlike composite aggregation, in shared aggregation, the part has "life of its own," and it can be part of more than one whole. According to Object Management Group (2010, p. 39), "*precise semantics of shared aggregation varies by application area and modeler.*" While usually, in shared aggregation each part can exist independently of the whole, leaving the semantics of a relation vague is not a good idea to begin with. The tagged structural relation in OPM is user-defined, and this would be a better way to express specific semantics by application area or modeler, rather than leaving the semantics of a language symbol open to a variety of interpretations by various modelers even in the same domain and even if all of them relate to the same system model.

The connecting lines of the aggregation relation in UML need not be orthonormal and are usually diagonally straight, as Fig. 17.4 demonstrates. UML and SysML do not have the fork construct, so as Fig. 17.4 shows, each part in a UML (and SysML) class diagram needs to be connected with a dedicated aggregation symbol.

Composition is stronger than aggregation in that the whole is "responsible" for its parts, so when the whole is consumed so are all the objects of which it is composed. Hence, the part cannot be owned by more than one whole. Here is what the UML 2.0 Superstructure document v 2.2 (2005) says about composite aggregation (p. 41):

"*An association may represent a composite aggregation (i.e., a whole/part relationship). ... Composite aggregation is a strong form of aggregation that requires a part instance [to] be included in at most one composite at a time. If a composite is deleted, all of its parts are normally deleted with it. Note that a part can (where allowed) be removed from a composite before the composite is deleted, and thus not be deleted as part of the composite.*"

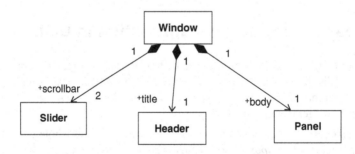

Fig. 17.4 The symbol of composite aggregation in UML and SysML

In OPM the distinction between composite and shared aggregation is not necessary, since one can model exactly what part or parts are consumed when the whole is consumed and what parts remain, as the OPM model in Fig. 17.5 demonstrates: After **Crashing**, the whole **Car** and its **Chassis** are gone, but the **Powertrain** remains (and can be reused).

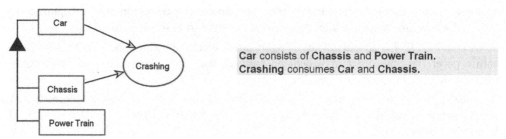

Car consists of **Chassis** and **Power Train**.
Crashing consumes **Car** and **Chassis**.

Fig. 17.5 OPM model demonstrating how UML/SysML shared and composite aggregation can be modeled in tandem

17.6 **Expressing Parts Order**

Sometimes, the order of the parts that comprise the whole is significant. Sets are abstract collections of things that consist of *elements* or *members*. A set may therefore be thought of as an aggregate (whole) and its elements—as parts. Each element in the set is unique. Since aggregation-participation is a structural relation, everything that applies to a fork is true for aggregation-participation, including the way orderability is indicated. Being a fork, the **Aggregation-Participation** relation exhibits the Boolean **Orderability** property, which denotes whether or not the set of parts is ordered. The two values of **Orderability** are ordered and unordered, with the default value being unordered. Let us again consider the RDF triple case (Klyne et al. 2004):

An RDF triple is conventionally written in the order subject, predicate, object.

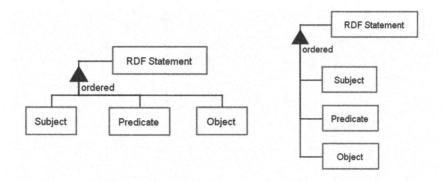

RDF Triple consists of **Subject, Predicate,** and **Object,** in that sequence.

Fig. 17.6 The OPD label "ordered" and the OPL reserved phrase "in that sequence" indicate the order of the parts of RDF Triple from left to right (in the OPD on the left) or top-down (in the OPD on the right)

We model graphically the fact that the three elements of an RDF triple are ordered by adding the label ordered next to the black triangle symbolizing the aggregation-participation relation, as shown in the OPD in Fig. 17.6. The parts can be ordered with no sematic difference either from left to right, as the OPD on the left shows, or top-down, as the OPD on the right shows. The corresponding OPL phrase is "in that sequence", which follows a comma after the name of the last part in the ordered list.

The OPD in Fig. 17.7 is an example of an aggregation hierarchy, which specifies the reading order of a scientific paper, i.e., the order in which the parts of the paper should be read, with participation constraints, which are discussed in Chap. 15.

When dealing with processes, orderability is intimately related to the top-to-bottom timeline within an in-zoomed process, which dictates the process execution order. We elaborate on this in Chap. 21 while discussing complexity management.

17.7 Aggregation and Tagged Structural Relations

In the next example, we illustrate an OPM model that combines aggregation-participation with tagged structural relations. Consider the sentence extracted from the RDF Primer (Manola and Miller 2003):

RDF models statements as nodes and arcs in a graph.

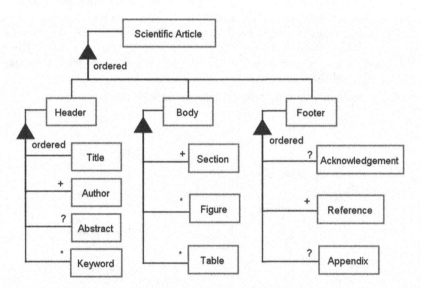

Scientific Paper consists of Header, Body, and Footer, in that sequence.
Header consists of Title, at least one Author, an optional Abstract, and optional Keywords, in that sequence.
Body consists of at least one Section, optional Figures, and optional Tables.
Footer consists of an optional Acknowledgement, at least one Reference, and an optional Appendix, in that sequence.

Fig. 17.7 The ordered aggregation hierarchy of a scientific paper with participation constraints

In order to model this sentence in OPM, using our prior knowledge about graphs and assuming that a graph has at least two nodes and one arc (which is the case with RDF graphs), we break the sentence above into the following three simpler, more explicit sentences:

1. A graph consists of at least two nodes and one arc.
2. RDF graph is a graph.
3. An RDF graph models at least one RDF statement.

Sentence (1) above is modeled in Fig. 17.8. As in the previous example, the black triangle denotes aggregation, where the object **Graph** is the whole, while **Node** and **Arc** are the parts. The plus (+) symbol above **Arc** denotes the "at least one" (+) participation constraint, while the "**2..***" symbol above **Node** denotes the participation constraint "**2 to many**".

The fact that has been added in the second OPL sentence is that an **RDF Graph** is a (specialization of) **Graph**. As such, it inherits the structure of **Graph**. To express the fact that an **RDF Graph** models at least one **RDF Statement**, a unidirectional tagged structural relation is used, and the tag reads "**models**".

We ended up with two similar OPL sentences, obtained from two W3C proposed recommendations:

"*RDF Statement consists of Subject, Predicate, and Object.*" (Manola and Miller 2003), and

"*RDF Triple consists of Subject, Predicate, and Object.*" (Klyne et al. 2004)

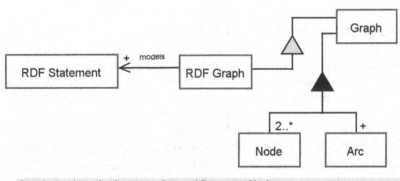

Graph consists of at least one **Arc** and **2** to many **Nodes**.
RDF Graph is a **Graph**.
RDF Graph models at least one **RDF Statement**.

Fig. 17.8 The OPM model of a graph consisting of at least one node and optional arcs

Under the assumption that if two things consist of exactly the same set of parts, or components, they are equivalent (if not the same), one can deduce that **RDF Triple** and **RDF Statement** are equivalent. This statement is expressed in the OPM model depicted in Fig. 17.9 by the (vertical) null tag bidirectional structural link between these two objects, which combines model facts from Figs. 17.6 and 17.8. This OPD also expresses that **Subject** and **Object** in an **RDF Graph** are **Nodes** in a general **Graph**, and that **Predicate** in an **RDF Graph** is an **Arc** in a **Graph**.

Another example for the use of the null tag bidirectional structural relation is when we model the sentence from Sect. 6.1 of (Klyne et al. 2004)

*The predicate is also known as the **property** of the triple.*

This is expressed in the OPD of Fig. 17.9, where **Property** is linked to **Predicate** with a null tag bidirectional structural link to indicate that they are equivalent, assuming that the null tag default is "equivalent". This translates to the OPL sentence "**RDF Triple** and **RDF Statement** are equivalent."

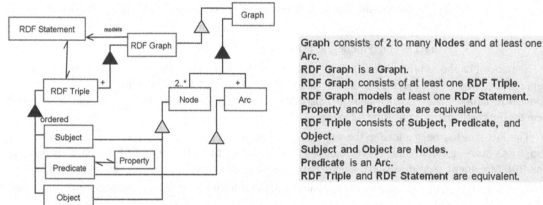

Fig. 17.9 An OPM model demonstrating a bidirectional tagged structural link with one tag

17.8 Non-Comprehensive Aggregation

Being a specialization of fork, aggregation inherits the Boolean **Comprehensiveness** property just as it inherits the Boolean **Orderability** property. The default aggregation **Comprehensiveness** value is **comprehensive**: we assume that if nothing is indicated, then all the parts are specified in the model. If we wish to denote that the aggregation is **non-comprehensive**, we add the non-comprehensiveness symbol— a short horizontal bar below the aggregation black triangle symbol, as shown in Figs. 17.10 and 17.11. The corresponding OPL phrase is "and at least one other part", used in the last OPL sentence in Fig. 17.10.

If an aggregation symbol is both ordered and non-comprehensive, the OPL phrase for non-comprehensiveness precedes that for the orderability. For example, if in Fig. 17.10 the aggregation symbol attached to **Body**, which is non-comprehensive, would also be ordered, the resulting OPL sentence would be:

Body consists of at least one **Section,** optional **Figures,** and at least one other part, in that sequence.

17.8.1 Partial Aggregation Consumption

When we wish to specify that the whole and a specific subset of its part are consumed, we can model this succinctly using partial aggregation consumption, as exemplified in Fig. 17.12. In the OPM model on the left of Fig. 17.12, the **Consuming** process consumes **Whole** along with its **Part B** and **Part D**, while **Part A** and **Part C** remain intact as separate objects. This is similar to the car crashing example in Fig. 17.5. In the OPM model on the right of Fig. 17.12, the terse version using partial aggregation shows that the **Consuming** process consumes **Whole** and only **Part B** and **Part D**, while all the other parts of **Whole**, which are not shown in the partial aggregation, remain as distinct, unchanged objects.

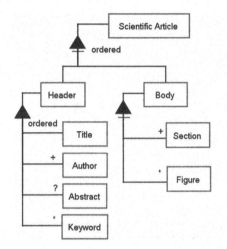

Scientific Paper consists of Header, Body, and at least one other part, in that sequence.
Header consists of Title, at least one Author, an optional Abstract, and optional Keywords, in that sequence.
Body consists of at least one Section, optional Figures, and at least one other part.

Fig. 17.10 The non-comprehensive aggregation symbol is a short vertical line below the aggregation triangle expressing that not all the parts are shown

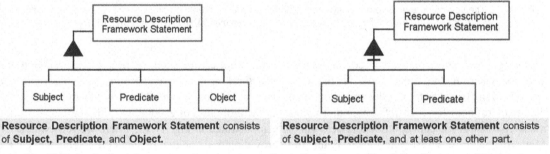

Resource Description Framework Statement consists of Subject, Predicate, and Object.

Resource Description Framework Statement consists of Subject, Predicate, and at least one other part.

Fig. 17.11 Application of non-comprehensive aggregation in the Resource Description Framework Statement

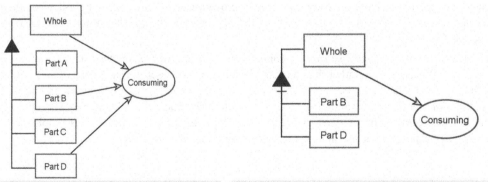

Whole consists of Part A, Part B, Part C, and Part D.
Consuming consumes Whole, Part B, and Part D.

Whole consists of Part A, Part D, and at least one other part.
Consuming consumes Whole, Part B, and Part D.

Fig. 17.12 Partial aggregation consumption exemplified

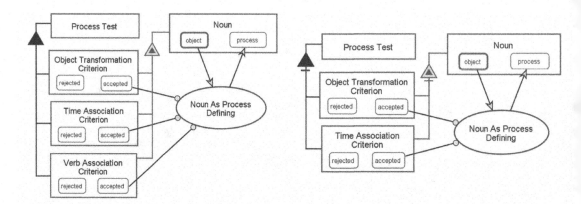

Process Test consists of Object Transformation Criterion, Time Association Criterion, and Verb Association Criterion.
Noun exhibits Object Transformation Criterion, Time Association Criterion, and Verb Association Criterion

Process Test consists of Object Transformation Criterion, Time Association Criterion, and at least one other part.
Noun exhibits Object Transformation Criterion, Time Association Criterion, and at least one other feature.

Fig. 17.13 The non-comprehensivemness symbol demonstrated for aggregation and characterization. Left: Original **Process Test** model. Right: Updated model after removing **Verb Association Criterion**

Being a fork property, the non-comprehensiveness symbol can be used not only for aggregation, but also for each of the other three fundamental structural relations—exhibition, specialization, and classification. To correctly use the non-comprehensive symbol, an OPM modeling tool must keep track of the set of refinees for each refineable and adjust the symbol and corresponding OPL sentences as the modeler changes the collection of refinees. This is demonstrated in Fig. 17.13, where we reuse the OPM Model of the Process Test from Fig. 10.6, this time providing only the two relevant OPL sentence. On the left is the original model, while on the right the object **Verb Association Criterion**, which is both a part of **Process Test** and an attribute of **Noun**, has been removed, causing an automatic update of the OPD to include the non-comprehensive symbol for both the aggregation and the exhibition. The OPL sentences were updated as well.

As we can see, the OPL phrase for non-comprehensive exhibition-characterization is "and at least one other feature". We use feature rather than attribute because, as we discussed in Chap. 16 and will elaborate in Chap. 18, feature can be an attribute (object) or an operation (process), both of which can be attached to the base of the same exhibition symbol, ⚠. Similarly, the OPL phrase for non-comprehensive generalization-specialization is "and at least one other specialization", and the OPL phrase for non-comprehensive classification-instantiation is "and at least one other instance".

17.9 The Parameterized Participation Constraints Mini-Language

The use of participation constraints in the aggregation-participation relation is similar to their use in a general tagged structural relation. A different participation constraint can be attached to each one of the parts in the tine set of the whole. As with the general tagged structural relation, the implicit default for the number of parts of a whole is 1. A participation constraint other than 1 is recorded outside the part next to the point connecting the part with the orthonormal line from the solid triangle's base.

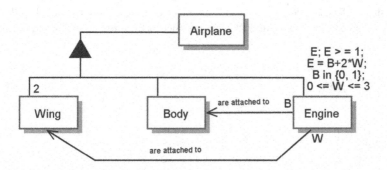

Airplane consists of Body, 2 Wings, and E Engines, where E>=1, E = B+2*W, B in {0, 1}, and 0<=W<=3.
B Engines are attached to Body.
W Engines are attached to Wing.

Fig. 17.14 Parameterized participation constraints applied to aggregation-participation links

The OPD in Fig. 17.14 and the OPL that follows it exemplify this. Since an **Airplane** consists of two **Wings**, the participation constraint **2** is recorded next to the object **Wing**. **Airplane** also consists of a certain number of **Engines**, the exact number of which is determined by a couple of parameters. The example in Fig. 17.14 uses three parameters, **E**, **B**, and **W**, to express the number of **Engines** in an **Airplane**, the number of **Engines** attached to the **Body**, and the number of **Engines** attached to a **Wing**, respectively.

As exemplified in Fig. 17.14, there is a specific syntax of parameterized participation constraints as they are recorded in an OPD. This syntax defines a small-syntax language, called Parameterized Participation Constraints (PPC) mini-language. It draws from, and is similar to, the syntax of arithmetics and set notation in conventional third-generation and OO programming languages, such as C, C++ and Java. This syntax, specified informally next using this example, must not be confused with the much more complex syntax of OPL, which is presented formally in EBNF in the OPM ISO 19450 PAS (see Chap. 24). The PPC mini-language must also not be confused with UML's OCL, which is also designed as an add-on to UML to specify constraints that cannot be expressed graphically in UML, as Sect. 22.10 discusses briefly.

To demonstrate the PPC mini-language syntax, let us follow the example in Fig. 17.14. The set of four constraints, each expressed in a line of text in Fig. 17.14 above the object **Engine** are the **E** *parameter constraint set*—the set of four constraints for **E**, where **E** is the parameter for the number of **Engines** in the **Airplane**. The parameter (**E** in our case) appears first, followed by semicolon, followed by zero or more (four in our case) constraints separated by semicolons. Each constraint is an equality or inequality, or a set membership notation. The left hand side is the parameter name, the right hand side is a mathematical expression, and the two sides are separated by one of the equality or inequality symbols =, $\neq$ (or != when only the ASCII character set is available), <, >, $\leq$ (or <=), $\geq$ (or >=), or by the membership notations $\in$ (or "in"), or $\notin$ (or "not in").

As noted, the symbols and syntax used in the constraint expressions are based on common conventions of programming languages. For example, multiplication is denoted by an asterisk, as in **E = B+2*W**. The reserved phrase in is the set-theoretic symbol $\in$, so "**b** in **{0, 1}**" is the same as "b $\in$ {0, 1}". In our example, the first constraint, **E >= 1**, constrains the number of **Engines** in the **Airplane** to be at least one. The second constraint, **E = B+2*W**, is the total number of **Engines**, which is equal to the number of **Engines** in the **Body** (which can be **0** or **1**), and **W** is the number of **Engines** in each **Wing** (which can be **0**, **1**, **2**, or **3**).

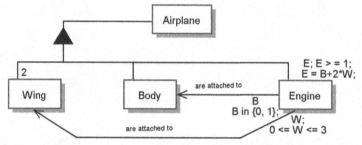

Airplane consists of **Body**, **2 Wings**, and **E Engines**, where E>=1 and E = B+2*W.
B Engines are attached to Body, where B in {0, 1}.
W Engines are attached to Wing, where 0<=W<=3.

Fig. 17.15 The parameterized participation constraints from Fig. 17.14 expressed differently

As this example shows, the OPL syntax for the parameterized constraints set is such that the main parameter precedes the name of the object to which it relates, followed by a comma and the reserved phrase where, followed by a comma-separated list of constraints with the reserved phrase **and** preceding the last constraint.

Figure 17.15 presents another way to specify the parameterized participation constraints, which is different than that in Fig. 17.14, but it uses the same parameterized constraint syntax and has the same semantics. The PPC mini-language is compared in Sect. 22.10 with Object Constraints Language (OCL) that augments UML.

17.10 **Summary**

- Aggregation-participation is a fundamental structural relation which denotes the fact that a refineable—the whole—aggregates one or more refineables—the parts.
- Aggregation-participation is a pair of forward and backward structural relations.

- The solid black triangle, ▲, is the aggregation-participation relation symbol. It replaces the pair of forward and backward textual tags of the aggregation-participation relation.

- Aggregating is the process of creating a whole from its parts, while participating is enumerating the parts that comprise the aggregate.

- In UML 2 and SysML, there are two types of aggregation in class diagrams: shared—weak aggregation, marked as a white diamond, and composite—strong aggregation, marked as a black diamond.

- In OPM the distinction between composite and shared aggregation is not necessary, since one can model exactly what part or parts are consumed when the whole is consumed and what parts remain.

- Orderability is a Boolean property of the aggregation relation, inherited from fork.

- To denote that the aggregation is ordered, we add the symbol ordered next to the aggregation triangle.

- Comprehensiveness is another Boolean property of the aggregation relation, inherited from fork.

- To denote that the aggregation is non-comprehensive, we add a short horizontal bar below the aggregation triangle.

- The Parameterized Participation Constraints (PPC) mini-language has a small syntax that determines how to phrase a set of constraints for a parameter in a participation constraint.

17.11 **Problems**

1. Draw two OPDs of a two-story house and its major parts, one without and one with the aggregation participation link.
2. Which OPD was easier to draw? Why?
3. Use the second OPD from the first problem to demonstrate the use of orderability in terms of vertical location of the parts of the house, the highest one being the first. Add parts as needed.
4. Demonstrate non-comprehensiveness by removing one or more parts from the OPD in the previous question.
5. Add at least two participation constraints to an OPD from one of the previous question.
6. Draw OPDs describing two objects for which the parts are ordered and two for which they are not.
7. Draw two OPDs for an object consisting of at least eight different parts at the first participation level, with non-comprehensive aggregation. A subset of the parts should appear in one OPD and another subset in the other OPD such that the union of the subsets is comprehensive.
8. According to Figs. 17.13 and 17.14 what are the possible numbers of engines in an **Airplane**?

9. Use parameterized participation constraints to create the aggregation hierarchy of a high rise building. The building has a certain number of floors, each having two types of apartments, standard and luxury. In each floor from floor 4 and above there are three standard and two luxury apartments. In the first three floors, there is one small and two large offices. Decide how many floors there are and how many faucets are required for each unit, and create the appropriate OPD with participation constraints. Complete details as you see fit. Using your OPD, compute the number of faucets the contractor needs to order for a 22 story building.

Chapter 18
Exhibition-Characterization

I must be able to attribute properties to the objects.
Kant (1787)

To define and describe things in the world, natural languages use adjectives and adverbs. Without these types of words, which describe objects and are also interchangeably called attributes, features, qualities, characteristics, or properties, neither objects nor processes can be adequately distinguished and understood. Exhibition-characterization is the fundamental structural relation that binds a refineable (object or process)—the *exhibitor*, with a refinee—another object or process, called *feature*, which characterizes the exhibitor.

18.1 Feature and Exhibitor

Exhibition-characterization is a fundamental structural relation. Like any binary structural relation, it involves two things: the exhibitor and the feature.

> **Feature** *is a refinee that characterizes (describes) a thing.*
>
> **Exhibitor** *is a refineable that exhibits (is characterized by) a feature.*
>
> **Exhibition-Characterization** *is a fundamental structural relation which denotes the fact that a feature characterizes an exhibitor (and conversely, the exhibitor exhibits the feature).*

To be consistent with the naming convention of the fundamental structural relations, the first word in the exhibition-characterization relation pair describes the forward direction of the relation, from the exhibitor to the feature, while the inverse direction goes from the exhibitor to the feature.

The relationship between feature and exhibitor in the exhibition-characterization relation is analogous to that between a part and a whole in the aggregation-participation relation: Part is a refinee that comprises a refineable—the whole, which aggregates the parts. Like aggregation-participation, exhibition-characterization is transitive, giving rise to an exhibition hierarchy. The forward direction, then, is also the downward direction: from a thing higher in the hierarchy—the exhibitor—to one or more things lower in the hierarchy—the features.

The forward (downward) direction of the exhibition-characterization relation, from the exhibitor to its features, is the *exhibition* direction, while the reverse (upward) direction, from each feature to the exhibitor, is the *characterization* direction. The above definition assumes the forward direction of the exhibition-characterization relation. Viewed in the backward direction, the feature is said to *characterize* the exhibitor. Figure 18.1 expresses on the left the exhibition-characterization relation as a bidirectional tagged structural link, yielding two OPL sentences, while on the right, the relation's designated symbol is used, resulting in a single OPL sentence with the (non-bold) reserved OPL word exhibits.

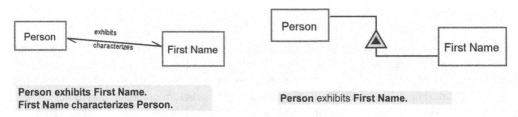

Person exhibits First Name.
First Name characterizes Person.

Person exhibits **First Name.**

Fig. 18.1 The exhibition-characterization relation expressed as a bidirectional tagged structural link (left) and with the relation's designated symbol (right)

The word for the backward relation, *characterization*, is much more commonly used in the context of the relation than its forward counterpart, *exhibition*. *Characterization* is therefore the short name of the relation. Based on this, we may occasionally drop the "exhibition" part of the name of this fundamental structural relation and abbreviate it to *characterization*, bearing in mind that this is the direction up the hierarchy level.[1]

18.1.1 Primary and Secondary Qualities

Many philosophers who discussed epistemology and metaphysics, including Galileo, Descartes, and Locke, have made the conceptual distinction between primary and secondary qualities (or properties, or attributes). Primary qualities are "independent" properties of objects, such as shape or mass, which convey facts about the thing and do not rely on subjective judgments. Secondary qualities are properties such as color, taste, smell, and sound, which depend on and produce sensations in observers and do not provide objective facts about things.

As Galileo (1623) wrote in The Assayer, "*… tastes, odors, colors, and so on are no more than mere names so far as the object in which we locate them are concerned, and that they reside in consciousness.*" Further, Descartes (1647) wrote about secondary qualities that "*we are not aware of their being anything other than various arrangements of the size, figure, and motions of the parts of these objects which make it possible for our nerves to move in various ways, and to excite in our soul all the various feelings which*

---

[1]This concession exemplifies the kind of design tradeoff decisions that need to be made while conceiving OPM names. On one hand, consistency and orderliness are imperative, but on the other hand, clarity and expressive power are enhanced when the language is as natural and as terse as possible. Since English, like all natural languages, has its idiosyncrasies, compromises such as this must often be made after weighing the pros and cons of each alternative. It may also be somewhat odd that we spend so much intellectual effort in choosing good names for abstract ideas. However, a meaningful name can make the great difference between a well-understood and appropriately used concept, and one that misses the point due to a term that while being formally correct, is poorly understood.

they produce there." Similar observations were made by Newton (in *Optica*, 1721) about the color of rays, and by Leibnitz (in *Discourse on Metaphysics*, 1686) about size, figure and motion.

This distinction was criticized by Berkeley (1710) in his "immaterialism" theory, which denied the existence of material substance altogether. According to Berkeley, familiar objects, like a table, are only ideas in the human perceiver's mind, and cannot exist without being perceived. The ideas created by sensations are all that people can know for sure. When an object is stripped of all its secondary qualities, the idea that there is some object has no support, since without qualities one cannot give any content to the idea of the object existence. Kant (1783) also went against this distinction, claiming that both primary and secondary, qualities are subjective, as they are located in the brain of a knowing observer. This discussion complements our previous treatment in Sect. 10.3 of object identity.

18.2 Attribute and Operation: The Two Kinds of Feature

Perseverance is a thing's property with two values: static and dynamic. Perseverance is the property that enables distinction between an object and a process. It determines that the thing is an object when the perseverance value is persistent (static), and a process—when the perseverance value is transient (dynamic). A feature—a thing that characterizes a thing—is also classified into two types based on whether its perseverance value is static or dynamic.

> *An **attribute** is a feature whose perseverance value is static.*
>
> *An **operation** is a feature whose perseverance value is dynamic.*

An attribute is a static feature—an *object* that characterizes a thing, while operation is a dynamic feature—a *process* that characterizes a thing. Being an object, the perseverance value of attribute is *persistent* (static). Being a process, the perseverance value of operation is *transient* (dynamic).

The OPL sentence that relates an **Exhibitor** to two features, **Feature 1** and **Feature 2**, is:

Exhibitor exhibits **Feature 1** and **Feature 2**.

The OPL sentence that relates an **Exhibitor** to three features, **Feature 1**, **Feature 2**, and **Feature 3**, is:

Exhibitor exhibits **Feature 1, Feature 2**, and **Feature 3**.

All the features on the list must be of the same perseverance, i.e., all are attributes (object features) or all are operations (process features). If some of the features are attributes while others are operations, we divide the features into two lists, one of attributes and the other—of operations. If the exhibitor is an object, then the first list of features is of (one, two, or more) attributes, and the second—of operations. The list of attributes is connected to the list of operations by the reserved OPL phrase as well as. As an example, the following OPL sentence specifies an **Object** exhibitor with three attributes and two operations:

Object exhibits **Attribute 1, Attribute 2**, and **Attribute 3**, as well as **Operation 1** and **Operation 2**.

If the exhibiting thing is **Process**, the list of operations precedes the list of attributes:

Process exhibits **Operation 1** and **Operation 2**, as well as **Attribute 1, Attribute 2**, and **Attribute 3**.

18.3 **Features in UML and SysML Versus OPM**

Attributes and operations are concepts that exist also in the object-oriented (OO) approach. In OO terminology, an attribute is also referred to as a *data member*, while an operation is also referred to as a *method* or a *service*. All these words are meant to express *"something that the object can do"* or *"a way in which the object behaves."* In traditional procedural third generation programming languages, operation is also referred to as a *function*, a *procedure*, or a *routine*. Table 18.1 summarizes the definitions of attribute and operation as specializations of feature along with similar concepts in OO and traditional programming languages.

Table 18.1 The specializations of thing and feature by perseverance and similar concepts in OO and traditional programming languages

Perseverance value	Thing	Feature	OO similar concepts	Traditional similar concepts
persistent (static)	Object	Attribute	Data member	Variable, Parameter
transient (dynamic)	Process	Operation	Method, Service	Procedure, Routine, Subroutine, Function,

OPM treats features as things that have their own right of existence, regardless of the fact they may also characterize higher-level things. While aggregation-participation and generalization-specialization are recognized relations in SysML (as in UML) and have their own symbols (black or white diamond for the former, white triangle for the latter), exhibition-characterization is not an explicit relation and does not have a symbol. Rather, an attribute is recognized as such in UML by its location in the second of the three vertically-arranged compartments that comprise the UML object class symbol. In SysML there can be an arbitrary number of compartments in a block, so each compartment must be labeled. For example, in Fig. 18.2, the label is "values".

Paradoxically, although OPM does not attempt to be "purely" object-oriented, it is more object-oriented in its treatment of characterization than the OO paradigm. In OO, attributes and methods are encapsulated, or embedded, within objects. Are attributes not objects, but rather "different animals" that reside within the object? If an attribute is not an object, then what is it? Does the world consist not only of objects but also of attributes (and methods)? OPM does not encounter this dilemma, since it defines feature generically as a thing that describes a thing and as one that specializes into an attribute—an object—and an operation—a process.

To demonstrate the problem caused by not treating attributes as objects, consider a "classical" example of **Name** and **Address** as attributes of the object class **Person**, and **Moving** as an operation of **Person**.[2] As Fig. 18.2 shows on the left, in SysML this is done by assigning a title to each compartment. The top compartment has the «Block» stereotype title, which is analogous to Object in UML and OPM, with the name of the block, Person, underneath it. Below this top compartment are the "values" (attributes) compartment, with Name and Address as the values, and at the bottom is the operations

---

[2]We assume here that **Person** is capable of **Moving** without the need for external objects, such that **Moving** can be considered an operation of **Person**.

compartment, with Moving as the listed operation. In UML and many of its predecessors, such as Object Modeling Technique, OMT (Rumbaugh et al. 1991) the attributes and operations are listed always in the second and third class box compartments, respectively, so no titles are needed.

On the right hand side, Fig. 18.5 shows the corresponding OPM notation: **Name** and **Address** are separate objects, and **Moving** is a process. Since **Name** and **Address** are linked to **Person** with the exhibition-characterization symbol, they are also attributes of **Person**. For the same reason, **Moving** is an operation of **Person**. A side benefit of this notation is that we can connect **Moving** to **Address** with an effect link to denote the fact that **Moving** has an effect on the **Address** of **Person**, already combining structure and behavior in this simple OPD.

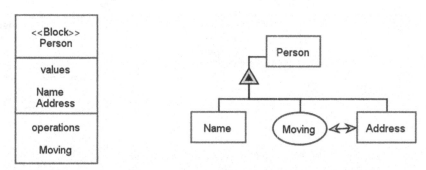

Person exhibits **Name** and **Address, as well as Moving.**
Moving affects **Address.**

Fig. 18.2 Expressing attributes (values) and operations in SysML (left) and in OPM (right)

Outside the context of **Person**, both **Name** and **Address** are bona fide objects in their own right. Moreover, as shown in Fig. 18.3, each one of them consists of parts: **Name** consists of **First Name** followed by **Last Name**; **Address** consists of **Street**, **City**, **Zip Code**, **State** and **Country**, in that sequence.

18.4 OPM Thing and Feature Name Uniqueness

Different things in an OPM model must have different names in order for them to be distinguishable and to avoid confusion. However, when it comes to features, which are things that describe things, it becomes difficult to come up with a different name for each feature. For example, in Fig. 18.3, there is an attribute of **Person** called **Name**, but **Street** and **City** might, in turn, also have an attribute called **Name**. Hence, features of things are allowed to have the same name as features of other things.

The uniqueness of features is maintained by adding "of **Exhibitor**", where of is a reserved OPL phrase (word in this case) and **Exhibitor** is the name of the thing that exhibits the feature. Thus, a feature of a feature shall have two "of" reserved OPL words, as in **Length** of **Name** of **Person**. The following *name uniqueness OPM principle* summarizes this.

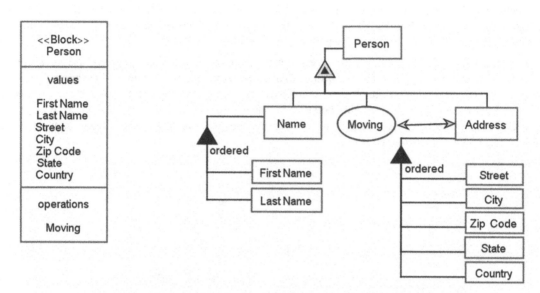

Person exhibits **Name** and **Address**, as well as **Moving**.
Moving of **Person** affects **Address** of **Person**.
Name of **Person** consists of **First Name** and **Last Name**, in that sequence.
Address of **Person** consists of **Street, City, Zip Code, State**, and **Country**, in that sequence.

Fig. 18.3 Expressing parts of attributes in SysML (left) and in OPM (right)

The Thing Name Uniqueness OPM Principle

Different things in an OPM model which are not features must have different names. Features are distinguishable by appending to them the reserved word "of" and the name of their exhibitor.

18.5 The Four Thing-Feature Combinations

Exhibition-characterization is unique among the structural relations in that it is the only one that allows relating objects to processes and processes to objects. All the other structural relations, including in particular the remaining three fundamental structural relations, allow linking things with the same perseverance value only: objects (things whose perseverance value is persistent, or static) can be linked only to objects and processes—(things whose perseverance value is transient, or dynamic) only to processes. Thus, objects can be parts or specializations or instances only of objects, and processes can be parts or specializations or instances only of processes. However, when it comes to exhibition-characterization, all the four object-process (exhibitor-feature) combinations are possible. In other words, as shown also in Fig. 18.4, since both thing and its feature can be an object or a process, the 2×2 Cartesian product yields a state-space of four different combinations of a thing and the feature that characterizes it, namely, from left to right and from top to bottom in Fig. 18.4: (1) an attribute of an object, (2) an operation of an object, (3) an attribute of a process, and (4) an operation of a process.

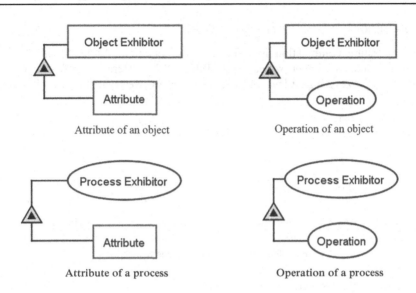

Fig. 18.4 The four thing-feature combinations

As an example of an object-attribute combination, **Address** is an object in its own right, but it is also an attribute of **Person**, as it is one of the things that characterize it. As an example of an object-operation combination, **Printing** is a process, which is also an operation of **Printer**, as it is a thing that characterizes what a **Printer** is capable of—what its function is. All four combinations are discussed and further demonstrated in this section. In the following subsections we elaborate on each one of these combinations.

18.5.1 The Object-Attribute Combination

The first thing-feature combination—object and its attribute—is the customary attribute of classical OO approaches. Here we refer to an object B_2—the attribute—that *characterizes* (describes) a higher level object B_1. Conversely, we say that B_1 *exhibits* B_2. A few examples for such pairs of objects and their attributes are **Material—Specific Weight, Person—Age, Chemical Element—Atomic Weight, Laptop—Manufacturer, Book—Author, Officer—Rank**, and **Dog—Breed**. The first four of these examples are depicted in the four OPM models in Fig. 18.5.

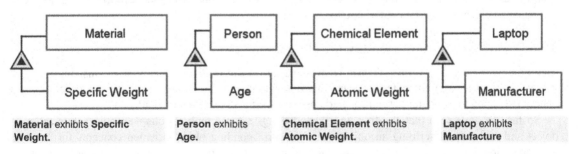

Fig. 18.5 Examples of attributes of objects

18.5.2 The Object-Operation Combination

The second thing-feature combination is object and its operation. As noted, in OO approaches an operation is also called *method* or *service* (see Table 18.1). Here we refer to a process P_1—the operation—that characterizes a higher level object B_1. Conversely, we say that B_1 exhibits the operation P_1.

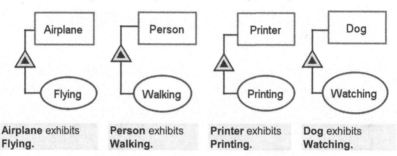

Fig. 18.6 Examples of operations of objects

An operation of an object is a process that is internal to the object: it can be performed by the object or its part(s) and affects only objects that are parts, features, or specializations of that object. In other words, an operation of an object B_1 has no side effect on, nor does it require any object that is outside of B_1. Under this condition, the operation can be identified as being "owned" by B_1. The OO approach, and consequently UML and SysML, view *all* processes as operations that are encapsulated within and owned by objects. This encapsulation is a major source of confusion and an impediment to faithful system modeling. In OPM, encapsulation is valid only when the process is internal to the object. In cases like this, the process is defined as an operation of the encapsulating object.

A few examples of pairs of an object and its operation are **Airplane—Flight, Person—Walking, Printer—Printing, Officer—Commanding**, and **Dog—Watching**. Figure 18.6 presents four OPM models that correspond to these pairs. As these examples show, an operation is a specialization of a process. As such, a name given to an operation should be a gerund, i.e., a verb form ending with the "**ing**" suffix.

Many objects, in particular physical and artificial ones, exhibit a major operation that expresses the main *function* that the object is designed to perform; the *service* it is expected to provide. Such objects are systems. A system (which is artificial) provides value to the system's beneficiary. For example, the function that the object **Printer** supplies is **Printing**, the function of **Airplane** is **Flying**, the function of **Crane** is **Lifting**, and the function of **Dryer** is **Drying**. This is in line with our definition of an artificial system as an object that carries out a function.

18.5.3 The Process-Attribute Combination

Like objects, processes require adequate representation in the model of any system. Just like objects, processes might require attributes—objects that describe them. The idea of attributes for processes is a natural extension to attributes for objects and poses no special conceptual difficulty.

So far, we have seen that the first and second thing-feature combinations—an object describing an object and a process describing an object—are the corresponding object-oriented concepts for attribute and operation (or service, or method). However, the third thing-feature combination—an object describing a process—is not explicitly defined in the OO approach. Here we refer to an object B_1—the attribute—that characterizes a higher level process P_1. Conversely, we say that the process P_1 *exhibits* the attribute B_1. Few examples of pairs of a process and its attribute are **Diving—Depth, Commanding—Language, Printing—Quality, Striking—Duration, Manufacturing—Quantity, Watching—Effectiveness, Singing—Volume, Skiing—Location,** and **Flying—Speed.**

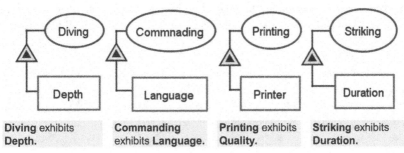

| Diving exhibits Depth. | Commanding exhibits Language. | Printing exhibits Quality. | Striking exhibits Duration. |

Fig. 18.7 Examples of attributes of processes

Figure 18.7 presents OPM models that correspond to the first four process-attribute pairs. Each of these process-attribute pairs can be embedded in a natural language sentence. Here are possible examples, where the processes are bold and their attributes are italicized:

(1) **Diving** at a *depth* of 30 meters or more requires the diver to make decompression stops.
(2) The *language* the office was using for **commanding** was foreign and strange.
(3) The **printing** of this device is of poor *quality*.
(4) The employees have been **striking** for *duration* of over two weeks.

While all the processes in these examples are nouns having the gerund form, they can be easily converted into sentences where the processes are verbs, with the same semantics as before:

(1) A diver who **dives** at a *depth* of 30 meters or more is required to make decompression stops.
(2) The officer **commands** in a foreign *language*.
(3) This device **prints** with poor *quality*.
(4) The employees **strike**, and this has been lasting for a *duration* of over two weeks.

As these examples show, this OPM extension of the OO, UML and SysML attribute and operation concepts is a direct consequence of recognizing processes as bona fide independent kind of things besides, rather than being necessarily subordinates of objects, or second-class citizens that are owned objects.

18.5.4 The Process-Operation Combination

The fourth and last thing-feature combination—process and its operation—is the second one that is not explicitly defined in the object-oriented (OO), UML and SysML approaches. It is the least prevalent combination and may be somewhat difficult to grasp. Here we refer to a process P_2—the operation—that characterizes a higher level process P_1. Conversely, we say that the process P_1 exhibits the operation P_2. Following OPM definition of a process, only a process can change a thing. In other words, the process is the thing, which is "responsible" for this change. That process can be an operation. An operation of an object changes the object that exhibits ("owns" in OO terms) that operation. Likewise, an operation of a process changes the exhibiting process—the process that exhibits that operation.

In daily life we do not think so much about operations of processes. The best way to understand the meaning of an operation of a process is to look at time. A change of an object along the timeline means that the state of an object (or its value, in case that object is an attribute) inspected at time t is different from its state at a later time $t + \Delta t$. Extending this idea from objects to processes, if we sample a process at two different points in time, we may notice a change in that process, manifested as a difference in the value of one of the attributes of that process, which is caused by an operation of that process.

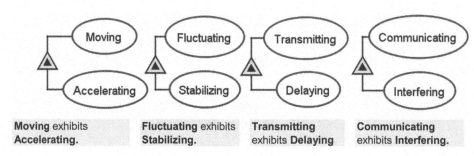

Moving exhibits   **Fluctuating** exhibits   **Transmitting**   **Communicating**
Accelerating.   **Stabilizing.**   exhibits **Delaying**   exhibits **Interfering.**

Fig. 18.8 Examples of operations of processes

Figure 18.8 contains four partial OPM models, each showing a process and its operation. In the model on the left, **Accelerating** is an operation that changes the value of the attribute **Velocity** of the **Moving** process. Similarly, the operation **Stabilizing** of the **Fluctuating** process changes the value of the **Amplitude** attribute of **Fluctuating**. Next, **Delaying** is an operation of **Transmitting** that changes its **Duration** attribute. Finally, **Interfering** is an operation of the **Communicating** process, which changes the value of the **Signal-to-Noise Ratio** attribute of the **Communicating** process.

In mathematical terms, a change of an object along the timeline is a *first derivative* of some quantity (which is an attribute value of that object) *with respect to time*. In an analogous manner, since a process is a pattern of transformation (responsible for transforming an object), an operation of a process is a transformation of a transformation, or a *change of a change*. In mathematical terms, this is a *second derivative* (derivative of the derivative) of some quantity with respect to time. Indeed, the examples of pairs of a process and its operation shown in Fig. 18.8 have the notion of changing a process and can be quantified mathematically using second order derivatives. For example, in the OPM model on the left of Fig. 18.8, if we denote the attribute **Velocity** of the process **Moving** of an object as a function of time by $v(t)$, then we know that $v(t)$ is the first derivative of the attribute **Position** s of the object as a function of time: $v(t) = s'(t)$. Denoting by $a(t)$ the attribute **Acceleration** of the **Accelerating** process, we have $a(t) = v'(t) = s''(t)$, where $a(t)$ is the first derivative of **Velocity** and the second derivative of **Position**.

18.6 Fundamental Structural Hierarchies

Feature is a relative term. A thing is a feature if it describes another thing. This feature itself can have parts or be further described by another, lower level feature. Since both exhibition-characterization and aggregation-participation are fork relations, structural hierarchies of these relations (as well as generalization-specialization, discussed in a couple of chapters) can be formed.

Consider the object **City**, whose feature hierarchy is depicted in Fig. 18.9. Three important attributes of **City**, in addition to its **Name**, are **Location**, **Population**, and **Climate**. Besides being attributes of **City**, **Location**, **Population** and **Climate** are objects in their own right, so each may have its own set of features or parts. **Location** has the attributes of the **Continent**, **Country**, **Region**, and **Coordinate Set**. **Population** exhibits the attributes **Size** and **Demographics** and the operations **Aging** and **Earning**. **Demographics**, in turn, consists of **Average Age** and **Average Income**. **Aging** and **Earning** are two operations that respectively affect the two parts of **Demographics**, and **Precipitating** is an operation of **Climate** that affects **Average Precipitation**.

18.7 The Attribute Naming Problem

Natural languages often provide us with a definite noun for naming the attribute. For example, the attribute whose two extremes are the adjectives "**short**" and "**long**" is called **Length**. The attribute whose two extreme adjectives are "**narrow**" and "**wide**" is called **Width**, and the attribute whose two extremes are "**heavy**" and "**light**" is called **Weight**. Sometimes, the attribute name (the noun) is from the same radical (root word) as one of the (often extreme) values (the adjective) along the spectrum of possible values for that attribute. Examples for such attribute-value (noun-adjective) pairs are **Length—long**, **Width—wide**, **Readiness—ready**, and **Beauty—beautiful**. Of these pairs, the radical (root) may be either the name of the attribute—the noun (e.g., **Beauty**) or the name of one of the values of that attribute—the adjective (e.g., **ready**).

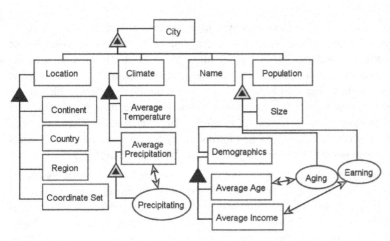

City exhibits **Location, Name, Climate**, and **Population**.
Location of City consists of **Continent, Country, Region**, and **Coordinate Set**.
Climate of City consists of **Average Temperature** and **Average Precipitation**.
Average Precipitation exhibits **Precipitating**.
Precipitating affects **Average Precipitation**.
Population of City exhibits **Size** and **Demographics**, as well as **Aging** and **Earning**.
Demographics of **Population** consists of **Average Age** and **Average Income**.
Aging affects **Average Age**.
Earning affects **Average Income**.

Fig. 18.9 A structural hierarchy example of **City**

The names of some attributes are neutral nouns, while others are taken from one of the extreme values of the attribute and are biased towards it. The attribute **Shape**, for example, is a neutral noun. Its values may be the adjectives **round, square, elliptic**, etc. There is no bias in **Shape** toward any of its values. Conversely, **Length** is biased towards the **long** extreme of the **short**—**long** value spectrum. Picking up **Shortness** instead would tilt the bias to the other extreme. Hence, a sentence such as "The shape of the house is square." makes perfect sense, whereas "The length of the stick is long," while syntactically correct, is semantically awkward. Skipping the name of the attribute, we would rather say "The stick is long." In this case, the attribute **Length** is implicit in the sentence. We could also skip the attribute name of the attribute **Shape** in the sentence "The shape of the house is square." and say "The house is square." We call such an attribute *implicit*. Implicit attribute sentences are usually used when the attribute name is taken from one of its extreme values. Examples are **Length**, taken form the pair **long**–**short**, **Beauty**, taken from the pair **beautiful**–**ugly**, and **Width**, taken from the pair **wide**–**narrow**. Interestingly, the choice of which of the extremes is chosen as the name of the attribute tends to favor the one that is considered better or larger. Thus, it is much less natural to respectively name these attributes **Shortness**, **Ugliness**, and **Narrowness**, although these words are legal nouns.

The use of implicit attribute sentences in natural language is the rule rather than the exception. Skipping the name of the attribute to which the value belongs and make direct reference to the object that exhibits the value is most prevalent. Implicit attributes are so widespread, that in many cases the natural language does not have a dedicated noun for the attribute itself, while the adjectives, which are the values or states of that attribute, do have widely recognized and used names.

As an example, consider the implicit attribute sentence "This book is interesting." The adjective interesting refers to an attribute of this book, whose possible values may be "**interesting**" and "**boring**." There is no single noun for an attribute whose values are **interesting** and **boring**. Plausible names of this attribute may be either **Interest Level** or **Boredom Level**. However, each is biased toward one of the extremes of the spectrum or the other. Ideally, we would like a word that is neutral and not biased toward any one of the possible attribute values.

In other cases, it is obvious that the name of the attribute was invented after the value was already in use. For example, **Laziness** is a name of an attribute which has **lazy** as one of its values (and **energetic** or **industrious** or **hardworking** as another), and the suffix "ness" hints to its later introduction into the language. Obviously, if we attach to a **Person** an attribute called **Laziness**, we would expect the value of this attribute to be **lazy** rather than **hardworking**. More simply and more naturally, we would like to say that "**Person** is **lazy**." This sentence is much shorter, clearer, and straightforward compared with the two OPL sentences "**Person** exhibits **Laziness**." and "**Laziness** of **Person** is **lazy**." Indeed, as discussed Sect. 18.8 OPM has the option of implicit attribute, where **lazy** and **hardworking** are directly modeled as states of **Person** rather than values of its **Laziness** attribute, which, in this case, becomes redundant.

However, in the general case, in OPM, where modeling is formal, we often have to explicitly model the attribute before we can model its states or values, and if there is no word for the attribute, we have to invent it. Indeed, in OPM there is the problem of finding adequate names for properties (metamodel attributes) of **Thing**. The name of the property of **Thing** whose values are **natural** and **artificial** is **Origin**. We have also called **Essence** the property of **Thing** whose values are **physical** and **informatical**. **Perseverance** has been chosen as the name for the property whose values are **persistent** (in which case the thing is an object) and **transient** (in which case the thing is a process). The choice of these property names points to the difficulty in finding the right word to name an attribute (or property) whose values are prevalent. For example, **transient** and **persistent**, which are the values of the property **Perseverance**, are widely used, while **Perseverance** is not recognized in conjunction with these adjectives. **Origin** and **Essence** are neutral. **Perseverance** is less neutral; the American Heritage Dictionary (1996) defines perseverance as "steady persistence in adhering to a course of action, a belief, or a purpose; steadfastness." *Steady persistence* inclines toward the notion of **Object**, since its **Perseverance** value is indeed **persistent**. However, *course of action* has the notion of a process…

18.8 Properties of Features and Links

Features and **Links** have several properties (metamodel-level attributes), which are discussed in this section. These include **Explicitness**, **Mode**, **Touch**, and **Emergence**. Some of these properties are relevant to **Feature** in general, i.e., to both **Attribute** and **Operation**, while others—just to **Attribute**.

18.8.1 Explicitness

OPM caters to the natural language tendency to skip attributes and jump directly to their values, as Sect. 18.7 discusses, by providing the option to model attributes implicitly, as Fig. 18.10 demonstrates.

> An attribute is ***implicit*** *if its values are assigned as states directly to the exhibitor with no specification of the attribute name.*
>
> An attribute is ***explicit*** *if it is a separate object that is linked to the exhibitor with an exhibition-characterization relation.*
>
> ***Explicitness*** *is an attribute of an attribute whose values are explicit (the default) and implicit.*

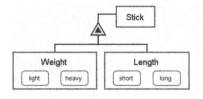 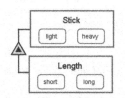 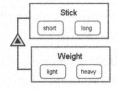

Stick exhibits **Weight** and **Length**. **Weight** can be **light** or **heavy**. **Length** can be **short** or **long**.

Stick can be **light** or **heavy**. **Stick** exhibits **Length**. **Length** can be **short** or **long**.

Stick can be **short** or **long**. **Stick** exhibits **Weight**. **Weight** can be **light** or **heavy**.

Fig. 18.10 Explicit and implicit attribute modeling

It is easy to identify an implicit attribute: If an object has states that are placed directly inside its rectangle rather than in its attribute, then the attribute whose values are within the object is implicit. By default, an attribute is explicit—its **Explicitness** value is **explicit**. It often makes sense to use an **implicit** attribute, as this circumvents the attribute naming problem discussed in the previous section—the need to invent a name for the attribute. We saw the example of **Laziness** in the previous section. As another example, **Lamp** can be **on** or **off**. It would be cumbersome to define a dedicated explicit attribute for these states and difficult to find a good name for it: "**Onness**"? "**Offness**"? "**Operational Status**"? None of these makes sense.

It is not possible to have more than one implicit attribute for the same thing, because this would mix values of different attributes in the same sentence without affiliating them with the proper "owning" attributes. For example, examining Fig. 18.10, we observe that sentences such as "**Stick** can be **light, heavy, short,** or **long**" do not make sense, because values of the **Weight** and **Length** of **Stick** are mixed. We can have either **Weight** or **Length** as implicit attributes, but not both. In the OPM model on the left of Fig. 18.10, both **Weight** and **Length** are explicit attributes of **Stick**. In the middle, **Length** is an explicit attribute, with values **long** and **short**, while **Weight** is implicit, with states **light** and **heavy**. Finally, in the OPM model on the right, the opposite is true: **Weight** is an explicit attribute, with values **light** and **heavy**, while **Length** is implicit.

18.8.2 Mode

Some attributes are **qualitative** while others are **quantitative**. We have seen the example of the attribute **Shape** of **House**, where possible values can be **round**, **square**, and **rectangular**. These values cannot be quantified by a numeric value. They are just qualitatively different from each other. We say therefore that **Shape** is a qualitative attribute. Other examples of qualitative attributes include **Mood**, with states **happy, sad, angry,** etc., **Health**, with states **healthy** and **sick**, and **Marital Status**, with states **single, married, divorced,** etc. Examples of quantitative attributes are **Weight** [Kg] and **Height** [m]. As these examples show, quantitative attributes need to be followed by the unit of measurement in brackets, as discussed in Chap. 22. Since an attribute can be qualitative or quantitative, **qualitative** and **quantitative** are values of a property of **Attribute** called **Mode**.

> *An attribute is **quantitative** if its values are numerical or parametric.*
>
> *An attribute is **qualitative** if its values are non-numerical.*
>
> *An operation is **quantitative** if it transforms a quantitative attribute, otherwise it is* **quantitative**.
>
> **Mode** *is a property of a feature that determines whether it is qualitative (the default) or quantitative.*

The definition of *numerical* here includes *parametric*—a parameter is a symbol that stands for some numerical value. We could assign numeric values, or "codes" to values of a qualitative attribute, for example, **single** = 1; **married** = 2. Indeed, this was a common practice in early information processing systems and is still often the practice, especially when data has to be analyzed statistically. However, semantically this does not render a qualitative attribute quantitative.

An example of quantitative operations is **Height Measuring**, which creates a value for the quantitative attribute **Height**. Another example is **Weighing**, which creates a value for the quantitative attribute **Weight**. Section 13.10 discusses how to model setting or updating values using value-specified procedural links.

18.8.3 Touch: A Property of a Quantitative Attribute

A quantitative attribute can be **hard** or **soft**, depending on whether it can be computed from other attributes or not. For example, **Date of Birth** of a **Person** is a hard attribute, while **Age** of **Person** is a soft attribute. By knowing the **Date of Birth** of a **Person** and the current value of **Date**, **Age** of **Person** can be computed. As another example, the **Weight** of each part of **Airplane** is a hard attribute, while the total **Weight** of **Airplane** is a soft attribute since it can be computed by summing the weights of the individual parts. The name of the property of **Attribute** whose values are **hard** and **soft** is **Touch**.

> *A quantitative attribute is **hard** if its value cannot be deduced or computed from other attributes.*
>
> *A quantitative attribute is **soft** if its value can be deduced or computed from other attributes.*
>
> ***Touch** is a property of a quantitative attribute which determines whether it is hard (the default) or soft.*

Deciding whether a soft attribute should be pre-computed has practical implications during the detailed design stage of an information system. Pre-computed values can be stored for quick response time at the cost of storage space. Alternatively, soft attributes can be computed on demand, saving space but also delaying the response time of the information system. This is a common tradeoff in databases, where the need for high response speed is weighed against storage overhead.

18.8.4 Emergence

Depending on whether a feature is exhibited only by the object as a whole or only by one or more (but not all) of its parts, a **Feature** (an **Attribute** or an **Operation**) can be **inherent** or **emergent**.

> *A feature of an object is **inherent** if a least one of the object's parts exhibits it.*
>
> *A feature of an object is **emergent** if no one of the object's parts alone exhibits it.*
>
> ***Emergence** is a property of an object whose values are inherent (the default) and emergent.*

To understand the difference between emergent and inherent features, consider **Airplane**'s attribute **Weight** and its operation **Flying**. **Weight** of **Airplane** is the sum of the individual **Weight** values of each one of the parts that make up the **Airplane**. **Flying**, on the other hand, was not an operation that any part of **Airplane** could exhibit on its own. Rather, this feature emerges from the unique ensemble of the parts of **Airplane** that endows **Airplane** with the ability to carry out the **Flying** operation. Hence, **Flying** is an *emergent* feature (operation in this case) of **Airplane**, while **Weight** is an *inherent* feature (attribute in this case) of the **Airplane**.

In systems, operations are frequently emergent, because systems are built with the intent of achieving some function that is not localized in or achievable by any part of the system alone. **Flying** of **Airplane** is an excellent example. Bar-Yam (1997) distinguishes between simple and complex systems and claims that complexity can emerge from a collection of simple parts that comprise a system. The converse can be true as well: a system composed of complex parts may exhibit simple behavior at a larger scale. For example, planet Earth is a highly complex system, but when viewed from the perspective of its movement around the sun, it is relatively simple, pointing to the relativity of the term complexity.

18.8.5 The Link Homogeneity Property

The property that specifies whether a link connects things with the same **Perseverance—static** (persistent, defining an object) or **dynamic** (transient, defining a process) is called **Homogeneity**. The values of **Homogeneity** are **homogeneous**, which applies if the two things that the link connects exhibit the same **Perseverance** (either both are objects or both are processes), and **non-homogeneous** otherwise (one is an object and the other—a process). Since most structural links are between two objects or between two processes, the **Homogeneity** value **homogeneous** is the default for structural links. Conversely, since most procedural links are between an object and a process, the **Homogeneity** value **non-homogeneous** is the default for procedural links.

> *A link is **homogeneous** if it connects two things that exhibit the same perseverance value.*
>
> *A link is **non-homogeneous** if it connects two things that exhibit opposite perseverance values.*
>
> ***Homogeneity** is a property of a link whose values are homogeneous (the default for structural links) and non-homogeneous (the default for procedural links).*

Almost all the structural links are only **homogeneous**: they either connect two objects or two processes. The only exceptional structural link that is **Exhibition-Characterization**, which can be both **homogeneous** (in case it connects an object with an attribute or a process with an operation) or **non-homogeneous** (in case it connects an object with an operation or a process with an attribute). All the other structural links, and in particular the remaining three fundamental structural relations, are **homogeneous**. Analogously, almost all the procedural links are **non-homogeneous**, as they connect an object to a process. The only procedural links that are **homogeneous** are the invocation link discussed in Sect. 10.10.3 and the overtime and undertime exception links discussed in Chap. 22.

18.9 Summary

- *Exhibition-characterization* is a relation between a thing and the features that characterize it.
- The shorthand name of this relation is *characterization* and its symbol is △.
- Characterization is the only fundamental structural relation for which all four combinations of an object and a process, as an exhibitor and a feature, are possible.
- A feature which is an object, is called an *attribute*, while a feature which is a process is an *operation*.

- An attribute is *implicit* if its values are assigned directly to the exhibitor with no specification of the attribute name.
- An attribute is *explicit* if it is a separate object that is linked to the exhibitor with an exhibition-characterization relation.
- *Explicitness* is an attribute of an attribute whose values are explicit (the default) and implicit.
- An attribute is *qualitative* if its values are non-numerical.
- An attribute is *quantitative* if its values are numerical.
- An operation is *quantitative* if it transforms a quantitative attribute, otherwise it is *quantitative*.
- *Mode* is a property of a feature that determines whether it is qualitative (the default) or quantitative.
- A quantitative attribute is *hard* if its value cannot be deduced or computed from other attributes.
- A quantitative attribute is *soft* if its value can be deduced or computed from other attributes.
- *Touch* is an attribute of a quantitative attribute which determines whether it is hard (the default) or soft.
- A feature of an object is *inherent* if a least one of the object's parts exhibits it.
- A feature of an object is *emergent* if no one of the object's parts alone exhibits it.
- *Emergence* is a property of an object whose values are inherent (the default) and emergent.
- A link is *homogeneous* if it connects two things that exhibit the same perseverance value.
- A link is *non-homogeneous* if it connects two things that exhibit opposite perseverance values.
- *Homogeneity* is a property of a link whose values are homogeneous (the default for structural links) and non-homogeneous (the default for procedural links).

18.10 **Problems**

1. For each one of the four exhibitor-feature combinations, draw an OPD that is not provided as an example in this chapter.
2. "**The quick brown fox jumps over the lazy dog**" is an English-language sentence called pangram—a phrase that contains all of the letters of the alphabet. Create an OPM model of this sentence in which **Jumping** is an operation of **Fox**.
3. In the model you created in the previous question change each explicit attribute to an implicit one and vice versa.
4. Provide two examples of inherent features and two of emergent features.
5. Create an OPM model of the structure—parts and features—of the Pazyryk burial mounds chariot in the Hermitage Museum in St. Petersburg according to the following description (image available in URL).

This large four-wheel chariot is one of the striking finds of the Pazyryk burial mounds. It consists of a number of parts joined together by leather straps and wooden nails. The trunk is made of two frames joined by means of short carved poles and leather straps. The frames constitute the basis for the canopy. Each of the four large wheels has 34 spokes. The axles do not have a rotary device, and the distance between the back and front wheels is only 5 cm, which meant that the chariot could only be used on flat ground. It could, however, be easily disassembled and transported on horses. Thanks to the permafrost, the chariot is in an excellent state of preservation.

Chapter 19
States and Values

The Caterpillar ... got down off the mushroom and crawled away into the grass merely remarking as it went, "One side will make you grow taller, and the other side will make you grow shorter."

Alice in Wonderland. Lewis Carroll, 1899

To be able to talk explicitly about a change in an object over time, we assign to it a number of possible, "legal" *states*. Hence, a state is a situation an object can be at. States and values add expressiveness to OPM. A value is a state of an attribute. As such, it is a specialization of state: Whereas objects can have states, only states of attributes, which are objects that describe other object, are called values. States and values enable modeling change in an object while that object retains its identity. We have been using the terms states and values quite intuitively since the early chapters of this book. If objects and processes are the building blocks of OPM, and links are the mortar, states can be considered as the finish of the house: the paint job, the furniture, and architectural elements. At any time in the life of the object, when no process is acting on it, that object is at one of its states. Cause and effect are tightly linked with the concepts of change of state over time. This chapter formalizes the concepts of states and values, and shows how they can be used to enhance model expressiveness.

19.1 State Defined

To be able to talk explicitly about a change in an object, we assign to it a number of mutually exclusive situations, positions, or values, which we refer to as *states*.

> A **State** is a situation or position at which an object can exist for some period of time during its existence.

19.1.1 State Enumeration

An example of valid states of a **Planet** is **visible** and **invisible**, and the OPL sentence specifying it is "**Planet** can be **visible** or **invisible**." A **Planet** can change its **invisible** state to a **visible** state by rising above the horizon and when there are no clouds. A state enumeration OPL sentence such as "**Planet** can be **visible** or **invisible**." enumerates all the states that the object can be at. It starts with the object name, followed by the reserved phrase "can be" (or "is" in the case of just one state) followed by a list of states, which are comma-separated in the case of three or more states, and ending with the reserved phrase "or" between the last and second to last states. An object cannot be at more than one state at a time. Therefore, the semantics of the state enumeration sentence is that of the logical exclusive OR, called XOR for short. The default capitalization of a state name is lower-case letter.

© Springer Science+Business Media New York 2016
D. Dori, *Model-Based Systems Engineering with OPM and SysML*, DOI 10.1007/978-1-4939-3295-5_19

19.1.2 Initial, Final, and Default States

It is often convenient or desirable to specify what the *initial state*, the *final state*, and the *default state* of an object are.

> The **initial state** *of an object B is the state at which B is upon its generation or as the system starts executing.*
>
> The **final state** *of an object B is the state at which B is upon its consumption or as the system finishes executing.*
>
> The **default state** *of an object B is the state at which B is expected to be when its state is not specified.*

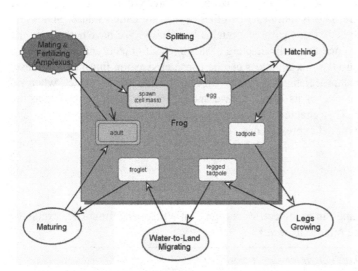

adapted from www.tooter4kids.com/Frogs/lifecycle.jpg

Frog is physical.
Frog can be **spawn (cell mass), egg, tadpole, legged tadpole, froglet,** or **adult.**
Frog is initially **spawn** and finally **Adult.**
State **adult** of **Frog** is default.
Mating & Fertilizing (Amplexus) changes **Frog** from **adult** to **spawn (cell mass).**
Splitting changes **Frog** from **spawn (cell mass)** to **egg.**

Hatching changes **Frog** from **egg** to **tadpole.**
Legs Growing changes **Frog** from **tadpole** to **legged tadpole.**
Maturing changes **Frog** from **froglet** to **adult.**
Water-to-Land Migrating changes **Frog** from **legged tadpole** to **froglet.**

Fig. 19.1 Initial, final, and default states demonstrated in the lifecycle of a Frog with simulation. The initial state is spawn (bold frame) and adult is both the final state (double frame) and the default state (the open arrow pointing at adult). The simulation emphasizes closing the lifecycle

An object can have zero or more initial states, zero or more final states, and at most one default states. The same state can be any combination of initial, final and/or default. The initial and final states are especially useful for objects that exhibit a lifecycle pattern, such as a product, a system, or our familiar frog from Chap. 13. The default state is useful for specifying the state at which an object is when no state is specified. The symbols for initial, final, and default states are a bold state frame, a double state frame, and a state frame pointed to by an open arrow, respectively. These are demonstrated in the simulated lifecycle of **Frog** in Fig. 19.1: The initial state of **Frog** is **spawn (cell mass)**, denoted by the bold state frame. The state **adult** is both the final state, denoted by the double frame, and the default state—the open arrow pointing at the **adult** state frame.

The conceptual simulation in Fig. 19.1 shows the process **Mating & Fertilizing (Amplexus)**—the highlighted solid ellipse—operating on **Frog** to change it from the state **adult** to the state **spawn (cell mass)**. The corresponding OPL sentence is:

Mating & Fertilizing (Amplexus) changes **Frog** from **adult** to **spawn (cell mass)**.

This state transition emphasizes the cyclical nature of **Frog**, as the final (and default) state of **Frog**, **adult**, yields **Frog** in the initial state, **spawn (cell mass)**, through the **Mating & Fertilizing (Amplexus)** process.

19.2 **State Suppression and Expression**

The elimination of the state symbols from the object is termed *state suppression*. State suppression is one of several abstracting options. Abstracting is a means to simplify the OPD at the cost of hiding details related to things in the OPD. Expectedly, as both the OPDs and in their equivalent OPL sentences demonstrate, state suppression eliminates the information about how exactly the process affects the object. This information can be provided in lower-level OPDs, where the states of the process are made explicit.

The reverse of state suppression is *state expression*: refining the OPD by adding relevant states. As Fig. 19.2 shows, whereas state expression is accompanied by splitting the effect link into its input link and output link components, state suppression is accompanied by merging the input-output link pair into a single effect link.

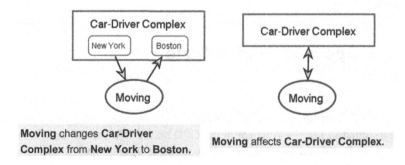

Moving changes **Car-Driver Complex** from **New York** to **Boston**.

Moving affects **Car-Driver Complex**.

Fig. 19.2 State suppression example

19.2.1 State Specializations and Their Participation Constraints

Figure 19.3 is a metamodel of **Object** showing the specializations of **State**—**Initial State**, **Final State**, and **Default State**, and their participation constraints. This is also specified in the OPL to the right of the OPD.

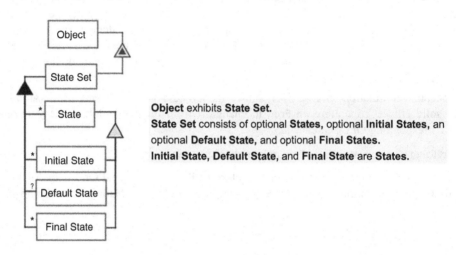

Object exhibits **State Set**.
State Set consists of optional **States**, optional **Initial States**, an optional **Default State**, and optional **Final States**.
Initial State, Default State, and Final State are **States**.

Fig. 19.3 A metamodel of **Object** showing the specializations of **State**: **Initial State**, **Final State**, and **Default State**, with their participation constraints

In the metamodel in Fig. 19.3, **State** and its three specialization—**Initial State**, **Default State**, and **Final State**—are all objects. This metamodel specifies the participation constraints for the three **State** specializations. The OPL on the right states that **State Set** can consist of "optional **Initial States**" and "optional **Final States**", i.e., zero, one, or more than one initial states and zero, one, or more than one final states. Indeed, while usually an object has at most one initial state, it can have more than one. For example, some process can create the object in one initial state while another process can create the same object in a different initial state. Alternatively, as we show below, the same process can create an object stochastically at one of two or more initial states. An object may also have more than one final state, from which it cannot exit. However, **State Set** can consist of "an optional **Default State**", i.e., there may be at most one default state.

19.3 **Value: A Specialization of State**

> ***Value*** *is a state of an attribute.*

Since value is a state of an attribute, it is a specialization of state. The nuance in semantics between state and value is demonstrated in Fig. 19.4, where in the OPD on the left, **off** and **on** are states of the object **Lantern**, while on the right, **off** and **on** are values of the attribute **Operational Status** of the object **Lantern**.

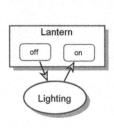

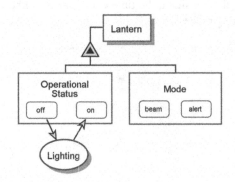

Lantern can be off or on.
Lighting changes Lantern from off to on.

Lantern exhibits **Operational Status** and **Mode**.
The values of **Operational Status** can be **off** or **on**.
The values of **Mode** can be **beam** or **alert**.
Lighting changes the value of **Operational Status** of **Lantern** from
off to **on**.

Fig. 19.4 Example of the difference between state and value. Left: off and on are states of the object Lantern. Right: off and on are values of the attribute Operational Status of the object Lantern

19.4 State Transition: When a Process Is Active

At any point in time, an object can be in at most one of its states. We say "at most", because the object can also be in transition between two states—the input state and the output state of the affectee with respect to the process currently affecting that affectee. During the time at which the process affecting the object takes place, the object has already left its input state, but it has not yet entered its output state. This is an unstable situation of an object which occurs when a process is changing the object from being at its input state—the state at which the object was before the process started, to being at its output state—the state where it is going to be once the process is over. During this time the object undergoes *state transition*.

> *State transition is an unstable period of time for an object, which takes place when a process acts on it to change its state.*

Consider the following car painting example. When a **white Car** is painted **red**, its input state (the value of its **Color** attribute when it enters the body shop for painting) is **white**. This is shown in the top left OPD in Fig. 19.5 by the state **white** of **Color** highlighted. The output state of **Car** (the value of its **Color** attribute when it leaves the body shop) is **red**. This is shown in the bottom right OPD in Fig. 19.5 by the state **red** of **Color** highlighted. In-between these two stable states, **Painting** takes place. During this time interval, when the **Car** is being painted, i.e., throughout the **Painting** process, which may be a couple of days, the value of its **Color** attribute is not completely white any more, but it is not yet red either. Indeed, while the **Car** is being painted, it is in *transition* between two **Car** states. We say that while undergoing the **Painting** process, the **Color** of **Car** is *unstable*. This is shown in the top right and bottom left OPDs in Fig. 19.5, where the highlighting of the **red** and **white** states gradually change from **red** and **white**. The duration of the transition, the time when **Car** is neither completely **red** nor **white**, is equal to the duration of the painting process.

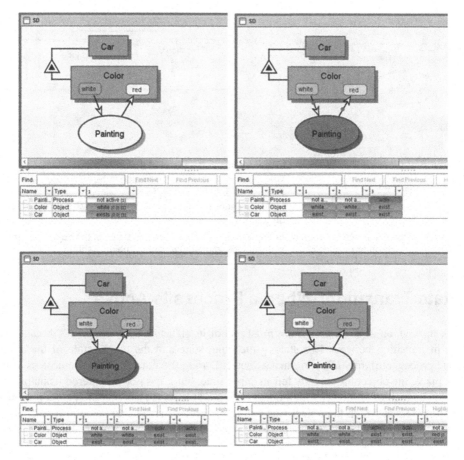

Fig. 19.5 The Car Painting system in action: The Car starts as white (top left) and ends as red (bottom right). The diagrams at the bottom of each OPD are the lifespan diagrams

As the car painting example demonstrates, objects and processes in the system have *history*, which is accumulated as the system performs its function. The history of an object begins at the time when it is created and becomes an identifiable entity, and it ends at the time when it is consumed so it is no longer the same identifiable entity. The history includes a time record of when the object was created, by what process, the state changes the object went through while it maintained its identity, when the object was consumed, and by what process.

History is meaningful only with respect to a particular system execution, i.e., the system at the operational level, or instance level, but not the conceptual level, or class level, because only when a system executes its function, it is possible to track and record what process instance started and ended when, and what object instance was transformed, whether it was created or consumed, or whether its state was changed.

The history of a process includes, for each execution of each process in the system, the time at which it started and ended. A particular process execution constitutes a process instance. The history also includes the transformee and enabler instances in the involved object set. A useful tool to view, trace, and analyze the history of objects and their states, and of processes in a system is the *lifespan diagram*, which OPCAT indeed includes.

> *A **lifespan diagram** is a diagram which, for any point in time during the life of the system, shows what objects exists in the system, what state each object is at, and what processes are active.*

The four lifespan diagrams shown at the bottom of each one of the four OPDs in Fig. 19.5 record the history of the car painting system as time progresses. In the diagram below the OPD in the top-left, only the first time period is displayed. **Painting** is not active, and the **Car** is **white**. In the second diagram, the first three time periods are displayed. In the third period, **Painting** is active, and the **Car** is no longer **white**. The same happens in the fourth period, as shown in the third diagram. Finally, in the fifth period, shown in the bottom diagram, **Painting** is no longer active, and the **Car** is **red**.

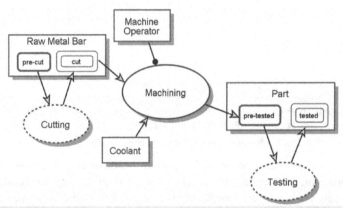

Raw Metal Bar can be **pre-cut** or **cut**.
Raw Metal Bar is initially **pre-cut** and finally **cut**.
Machining requires **Coolant**.
Machine Operator handles **Machining**.
Part can be **pre-tested** or **tested**.
Part is initially **pre- tested** and finally **tested**.

Cutting changes **Raw Metal Bar** from **pre-cut** to **cut**.
Machining consumes **Raw Metal Bar**.
Machining yields **pre-tested Part**.
Testing changes **Part** from **pre-tested** to **tested**.

Fig. 19.6 **Raw Metal Bar** and **Part** are objects that can be in transition between states

As another example, in the OPD in Fig. 19.6, **Cutting** takes **Raw Metal Bar** from its **pre-cut** to its cut state. As long as **Cutting** is active, the state of **Raw Metal Bar** is in transition and bound to the **Cutting** process: **Cutting** takes it out of its **pre-cut** state but has not yet brought it to its **cut** state with process completion. During **Cutting**, the state of **Raw Metal Bar** is unstable and therefore indeterminate: it could be partly cut and reusable or mostly cut and unusable. In either case, it is not available for **Machining**, since it is not in its **cut** state. Likewise, during **Testing**, **Part** is already not **pre-tested**, yet it is still not **tested**.

If an active affecting process stops prematurely or takes too long, the state of any affectee remains indeterminate, unless exception handling resolves the object to one of its permissible states. This can be done using overtime or undertime exception link, discussed in the chapter on OPM operational semantics.

19.5 Path Labels and Flip-Flop

When two or more procedural links exit from the same process, it is not possible to know what link to follow unless the links are labeled.

Following path **carnivore, Food Preparing** consumes **Meat.**
Following path **carnivore, Food Preparing** yields **Stew** and **Steak.**
Following path **herbivore, Food Preparing** consumes **Cucumber** and **Tomato.**
Following path **herbivore, Food Preparing** yields **Salad.**

Fig. 19.7 Path labels demonstrated on consumption and result links

Figure 19.7 demonstrates the problem and the use of path labels on consumption and result links which solves this problem. If **Tomato**, **Cucumber** and **Meat** all exist, then the result is the generation of **Salad**, **Stew**, and **Steak**. However, we cannot tell what ingredients went into what dish. And what if we want to model that for vegetarians we wish to prepare only **Salad** and for meat eaters only **Stew** and **Steak**?

This is solved by using the path labels carnivore and herbivore, recorded along the procedural links, as shown in Fig. 19.7 and expressed by the OPL. Path labels uniquely determine which link to follow on exiting the process: The link to be followed is the one having the same label as the one with which we entered the process. Using path labels, it is possible to follow a specific scenario in the model that span multiple consecutive procedural links. As this example demonstrates, path labels remove the logical AND requirement from the objects in the preprocess object set. Here, only all the objects in the preprocess object set whose links have the same label must exist in order for the precondition to be met. Thus, **Tomato** and **Cucumber** alone, or **Meat** alone, meet the precondition for **Food Preparing**, and the outcome is dictated by the path label.

> *A **path label** is a label on a procedural link which specifies that the link to be followed is the one with the same label as the one with which the process was entered.*

Path labels remove the ambiguity arising from multiple outgoing procedural links, and they can also be used for state-specified links. For example, in Fig. 19.8 there are two output links: one from **Heating** to the state **liquid** of **Water** and the other to state **gas**. Entering this process from state **ice**, it is not clear whether the flow of control should go to state **liquid** or to state **gas**, unless we use path labels. An alternative would be to have two separate processes, one called "Ice-to-Liquid Heating" and the other— "Liquid-to-Gas Heating". A similar solution can be applied to Fig. 19.7. Without path labels, every pair of incoming and outgoing procedural links must have its own process.

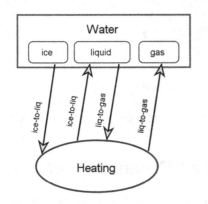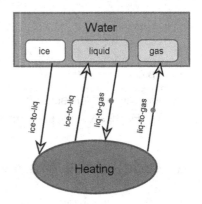

Water can be **ice, liquid,** or **gas.**
Following path **ice-to-liq, Heating** changes **Water** from **ice** to **liquid.**
Following path **liq-to-gas, Heating** changes **Water** from **liquid** to **gas.**

Fig. 19.8 Path labels demonstrated on an in-out link pair

Path labels provide a *memory mechanism*, which is required for *state machines*, where the next state transition depends on the state of the system and on the previous move. When the process precondition involves an object or state connected via a path-labeled procedural link, and the postprocess object set has more than one possibility for destination object or state, the appropriate postprocess object set destination shall be the one obtained following the link with the same path label as the link connecting one or more objects and/or states from the preprocess object set.

From a metamodel perspective, **Path Label** is an (optional) property of **Procedural Link**. The memory mechanism dictates that if the scenario unfolded through a path with some path label, then it must proceed to the next step following the direction marked with same path label.

Fig. 19.9 presents an animated simulation of a simple **Push Button**, which when pushed shuts **off** a lamp that is turned **on** and turns it **on** if it is shut **off**. The **Push Button** "remembers" its state, so whenever it is pushed, it switches states. We can use the same idea to model a "flip-flop", a two-state device which offer basic memory for sequential logic operations and used for digital data storage of binary numerical data. This OPM model mechanism can also be used to achieve the "NOT" logical operator, as discussed in Sect. 23.2.

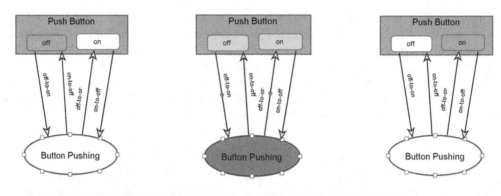

Push Button can be **off** or **on.**
Following path **off-to-on, Button Pushing** changes **Push Button** from **off** to **on.**
Following path **on-to-off, Button Pushing** changes **Push Button** from **on** to **off.**

Fig. 19.9 A simple **Push Button** with memory based on the flip-flop mechanism

19.6 A Model of the Brain's "Self-Organized Criticality"

As Ouellette (2014) wrote, based on Bak et al. (1987), in 1999, Bak proclaimed that perhaps the brain functions properly in a critical state between too much order and total disorder. This "self-organized criticality" works based on the same fundamental principles as a simple sand pile, in which avalanches of various sizes help keep the entire system stable. For example, if the brain is deprived of sleep, its organization gets off the "sweet spot" that is at or near the self-organized criticality, and therefore cannot function properly.

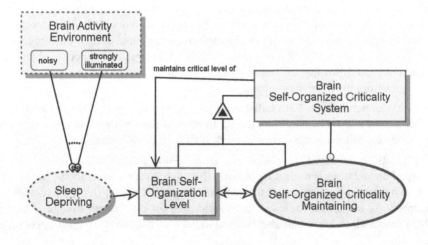

Fig. 19.10 Top-level OPD (SD) of the **Brain Self-Organized Criticality System**

Figure 19.10 is SD, the top-level OPD of the **Brain Self-Organized Criticality System**. It demonstrates a feedback loop: A **noisy** or **strongly illuminated Brain Activity Environment** invokes **Sleep Depriving**. Moving on to Fig. 19.11, SD1, where **Brain Self-Organized Criticality Maintaining** is in-zoomed, we see an animated simulation of the system model. What has happened until this frozen moment in the simulation is that **Brain Self-Organization Level**, initially at state **critical**, changed to **too chaotic**, and the process **Brain Self-Organized Criticality Maintaining** was initiated, starting with the first subprocess — **Order Level Monitoring**. Since (following path **chaotic**) the observation is that the **Brain Self-Organization Level** is **too chaotic**, the value of **Observed Brain Organization Level** changes to **too chaotic**. Note that **Brain Self-Organization Level** is an attribute of the process **Brain Self-Organized Criticality Maintaining** since it is an object within the scope of that process that needs to be maintained within a nominal value range or within a certain tolerance.

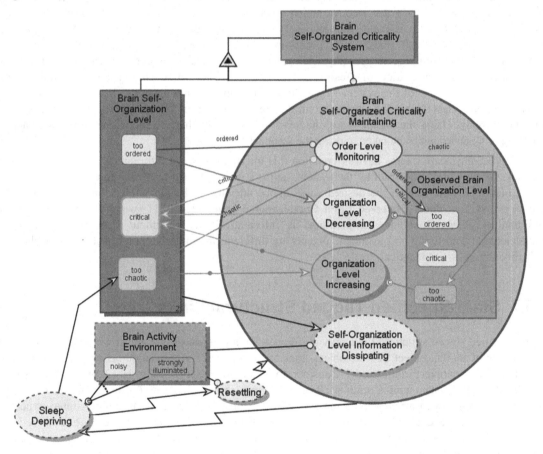

Fig. 19.11 SD1—**Brain Self-Organized Criticality Maintaining** in-zoomed

For example, the **Human Body** needs to maintain a temperature within a narrow range of 36.4-37.0 degrees Celsius. Similarly, an air conditioning system needs to maintain the **Room Air** temperature of 69-

72 degree Fahrenheit. The **Temperature Maintaining** process starts with the subprocess **Temperature Monitoring**, which can be **too low**, **within range**, or **too high**. If the **Observed Temperature** it is **too low**, **Heating** occurs (in a **Human Body** this can be done by **Body Fat Burning**; in an **Air Conditioning System**— by **Furnace Igniting**), changing the **Temperature Level** of the **Human Body** or the **Room Air** from **too low** to **within range**. If the **Observed Temperature** is **within range**, no corrective action is needed, so no subprocess occurs, and if the **Observed Temperature** it is **too high**, **Cooling** occurs (by **Perspiring** or **Condensing**), again restoring the value of the **Temperature Level** attribute to **within range**. As some time passes by, the **Environment**, being **hot** or **cold**, tends to shift the **Temperature** value from it desired range to **too high** or **too low**, respectively, and a new cycle of **Temperature Marinating** occurs.

The similarity between maintaining temperature in a biological system and in an artificial one demonstrates that complex systems, be they biological or man-made, are subject to the same underlying feedback principle of taking a corrective action when necessary to maintain a desired attribute value. What is common to both is the "cyber-physical" control mechanism that involves both *physical* and *informatical* ("cybernetic") objects and processes: While **Temperature** is a physical attribute, the **Temperature Monitoring** process uses physical means (**Thermometer** or **Skin Nerve Cells**) to generate an informatical object—the value of **Observed Temperature**. This value is transmitted to the control mechanism—the "brain" of the system—by a passing through a communication channel. This can be an electronic signal via a wire in the air conditioning system or an electric signal from the skin to the brain in the human body. Using the signal value, the control mechanism then determines what physical action (**Heating** or **Cooling**) has to be taken, closing the feedback loop.

All cyber-physical systems have in common this interplay between informatical objects that signify the state of the world, as sensed by the system, and systemic physical processes to counter the adverse effect of the environment on the desired value of the attribute to be maintained. Indeed, as the OPM model shows, the object **Observed Brain Organizational Level** Fig. 19.11 (which is analogous to the informatical object **Observed Temperature**) is informatical—it is without shadow. Although the implementations in living and inanimate objects are different, the underlying cyber-physical mechanism is highly similar, if not identical.

19.7 State-Specified Tagged Structural Links

State-specified tagged structural links provide for associating a state of one object with another object or with a state of another object. A state-object association link enables association between a state of some object and another object in the model. Consider, for example the OPD in Fig. 19.12, where **Oven** is both an object in the system and a state of **Product**—a possible location of **Product**. This is expressed graphically by the open arrow—the same symbol used for a with the null tag unidirectional structural link, from the state **oven** of **Product** to the object **Oven**. The difference between the unidirectional structural link and the state-specified tagged structural link is that while the former connects an object to an object, the latter connects a state to an object or to a state of another object. The state-specified structural links are presented in Table 19.1.

As another example, in a **Check-Based Paying** system, described in Fig. 19.13, the **Check** has an attribute called **Keeper**, which describes the entity that keeps the check at a given point in time during its processing. **Keeper** has three states: **payer**, **payee**, and **bank**. These three states are respectively associated with the three objects **Payer**, **Payee**, and **Bank**. This is denoted in the OPD by the three corresponding links from the state to the associated object.

Table 19.1 State-specified structural relations and links summary

Directionality \ Source/Destination	source state-specified	destination state-specified	source-and-destination state-specified
unidirectional	![A s → tag-name → B] **S A tag-name B.**	![A s ← tag-name ← B] **B tag-name s A.**	![A sa → tag-name → B sb] **Sa A tag-name sb B.**
bidirectional	![A s ← f-tag-name / b-tag-name → B] **S A f-tag-name B.** **B b-tag-name s A.**		![A sa ← f-tag-name / b-tag-name → B sb] **Sa A f-tag-name sb B.** **Sb B b-tag-name sa A.**
reciprocal	![A s ← recip-tag-name → B] **B and s A are recip-tag-name.**		![A sa — recip-tag-name — B sb] **Sa A and sb B are recip-tag-name.**

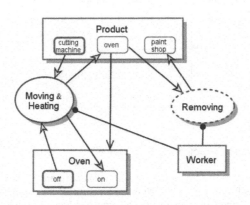

State oven of **Product** relates to **Oven.** *(Remaining OPL omitted)*

Fig. 19.12 Associating states with objects via the state-object association link exemplified: Oven is both an object in the system and a state of Product

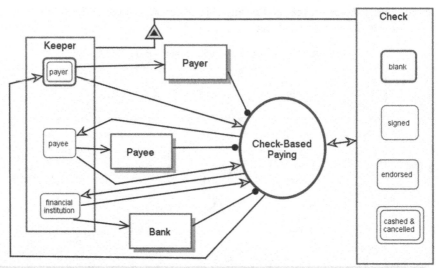

Check can be **blank, signed, endorsed,** or **cashed & cancelled.**
Check exhibits **Keeper.**
Keeper of **Check** can be **payer, payee,** or **financial institution.**
State **payer** of **Keeper** relates to **Payer.**
State **payee** of **Keeper** relates to **Payee.**
State **Financial institution** of **Keeper** relates to **Bank.** *(Remaining OPL omitted)*

Fig. 19.13 Associating attribute values with objects via state-specified structural link

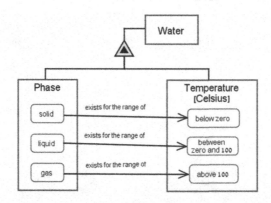

Water exhibits **Phase** and **Temperature** in **Celsius.**
Phase can be **solid, liquid,** or **gas.**
Temperature in **Celsius** can be **below zero, between zero and 100,** or **above 100.**
Solid Phase exists for the range of below zero Temperature in **Celsius.**
Liquid Phase exists for the range of between zero and 100 Temperature in **Celsius.**
Gas Phase exists for the range of above 100 Temperature in **Celsius.**

Fig. 19.14 Source-and-destination state-specified tagged structural link

As an example of a source-and-destination state-specified link, in Fig. 19.14, each one of the three **Phase** values of **Water** is associated with its corresponding **Temperature** value range via three source-and-destination state-specified tagged structural links whose tag is "**exists for the range of**".

19.8 Compound States and State Space

The examples we have seen so far are of states that are *atomic*, i.e., states that are not combined of other states. While the majority of states in OPM models are atomic, *compound* states may exist as well.

> An **atomic state** is a state that is not combined of other states.
>
> A **compound state** is a state that combines at least two other states.

As an example, one attribute of **Car** in Fig. 19.15 is **Location**, with values **New York** and **Boston**. Another attribute is **Car**'s **Drivability** (its ability to move on the road), with values **operational** and **broken**.

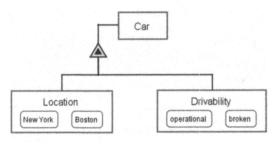

Fig. 19.15 The Location-Drivability state space of Car

Since **Location** and **Drivability** are orthogonal (independent of each other), **Car** can be in one of four *compound* states: **operational** in **New York**, **operational** in **Boston**, **broken** in **New York**, and **broken** in **Boston**. The 2×2 Cartesian product of **Location** and **Drivability** values constitutes the *state space* of **Car**.

> The **state space** of an object is the Cartesian product of the sets of states of all the attributes and parts of the object.

Moving on to a more complex example, **Airport** in Fig. 19.16 exhibits four attributes with two states each: **Weather Conditions**, **Tower Services**, and **Radar Coverage**, as well as **Pilot Familiarity** with three states. The Cartesian product of the sets of states of each attribute enumerates the object's state space. For our **Airport** example, this Cartesian product is **Weather** × **Tower Service** × **Radar Coverage** × **Pilot Familiarity** = {**fair, hazardous**} × {**available, unavailable**} × {**nonexistent, existent**} × {**poor, fair, excellent**} Thus, there are 2×2×2×3 = 24 states of **Airport**.

In general, if an object has n attributes (including an implicit one, if it exists) and stateful parts, each having v_i values, then the size of the state space is:

$$S = \prod_{i=1}^{n} v_i$$

In this context, each attribute can also be referred to as a *dimension*, analogous to the way that vectors can serve as dimensions (e.g., the three orthogonal vectors called X, Y, and Z that span a 3-dimensional Cartesian point space). For example, one of the 24 states of **Airport**, obtained by listing the first state in each of the four attributes of **Airport** above, is:

(Weather = fair, Tower Service = available, Radar Coverage = strong, Pilot Familiarity = poor).

Each such point can be the precondition for some process. Figure 19.16 shows the preconditions for two alternative subprocesses of **Landing Decision Making** that **Air Traffic Controller** makes: **Landing Permission Granting** and **Landing Permission Denying**. The preconditions for these two processes are expressed in the OPL sentences.

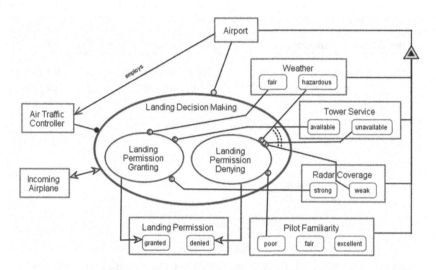

Landing Permission Granting occurs if **Weather Condition** is **fair**, **Tower Service** is **available**, and **Radar Coverage** is **strong**.
Landing Permission Denying occurs if **(1) Weather Condition** is **hazardous**, **Tower Service** is **unavailable**, or **Radar Coverage** is **weak**, and **(2) Pilot Familiarity** is **poor**.

Fig. 19.16 Examples of compound states (points in the state space) of Airport required for Landing Permission Granting and Landing Permission Denying

This example includes the use of condition links, discussed in the chapter on OPM operational semantics, and of OR and XOR (X-OR) logical operators, which are discussed in another separate chapter, dedicated to these operations.

19.8.1 Multiple Condition Clause OPL Sentence

The second OPL sentence in Fig. 19.16, which is a multiple condition clause OPL sentence, shows how complex conditions can be expressed unequivocally in an OPM model. A multiple clause condition OPL sentence consists of $n > 1$ (two or more) X-OR clauses. Each X-OR clause expresses an OR condition or a XOR condition, and it starts with a parenthesized clause number "(i)", where $i = 1, 2, \ldots n$. The clause numbers enable OPL to create any number of groups of OR or XOR conditions, all of which are related by logical AND.

19.8.2 Using Processes to Determine Compound States

Processes can be used to determine compound states. In Fig. 19.17, **Table Lamp**, which can have the compound states **dark** and **lit**, consists of three parts: **Switch**, **Power Plug**, and **Light Bulb**, each having two states.

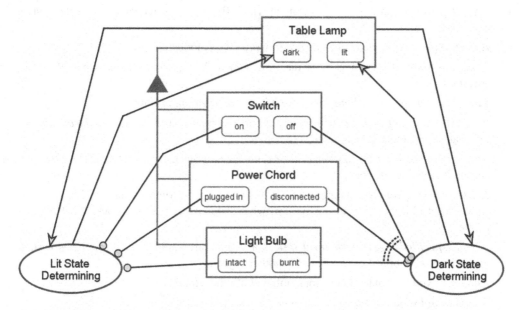

Table Lamp can be **dark** or **lit**.
Table Lamp consists of **Switch, Power Chord, and Light Bulb**.
Switch can be **off** or **on**.
Power Chord can be **plugged in** or **disconnected**.
Light Bulb can be **intact** or **burnt**.
Lit State Determining requires **on Switch, plugged in Power Chord, and intact Light Bulb**.
Dark State Determining changes **Table Lamp** to **dark Table Lamp**.
Lit State Determining changes **Table Lamp** to **lit Table Lamp**.
Dark State Determining requires **burnt Light Bulb, disconnected Power Chord, or off Switch**.
Lit State Determining yields **lit Table Lamp**.

Fig. 19.17 Determining the compound states **dark** and **lit** of **Table Lamp** with processes

Some of the points in the object's state space are not feasible, for example: (**Table Lamp = dark**, **Switch = on**, **Power Chord = plugged in**, **Light Bulb = intact**). The processes determine what points in the object state space are feasible. For two dimensions, this can be also presented in a table, possibly as a two-dimensional array inside an in-zoomed object. However, a table does not express the reasoning behind the feasibility or infeasibility of each point.

19.9 **Summary**

- A *State* is a situation or position at which an object can exist, or a value an attribute can assume, for some period of time during its existence.
- An *initial state* of an object B is a state at which B is upon its generation or as the system starts executing.
- A *final state* of an object B is a state from which B cannot exit.
- A *default state* of an object B is the state which B is expected to be when its state is not specified.
- *Value* is a state of an attribute, therefore it is a specialization of state.
- In addition to being at some state, an object can also be unstable, when it is *in transition* between two states—the input state and the output state.
- *State transition* is an unstable period of time for an object, which takes place when a process acts on it to change its state.
- A *lifespan diagram* is a diagram which, for any point in time during the life of the system, shows what objects exists in the system, what state each object is at, and what processes are active.
- A *state-specified tagged structural link* is a tagged structural link that connects a state of an object to another object or to a state of another object.
- An *atomic state* is a state that is not combined of other states.
- A *compound state* is a state that combines at least two other states.
- The *state space* of an object is the Cartesian product of the sets of states of all the attributes and parts of the object

19.10 **Problems**

1. A car can be driven if it has fuel, the battery is charged, and the car keys are found. Draw an OPD with attributes and states that specify these conditions.
2. Enumerate the state space of the car in the previous question: (1) as a list, (2) in a table.
3. Draw OPDs and write the OPL sentences of three objects having initial and final states.
4. Draw OPDs and write the OPL sentences of three objects having a default state.
5. The **Car-Driver Complex** requires not only the states of car enumerated in problem 1, but also a sober, awake, and licensed driver.
6. Incorporate these requirements in an OPD of the Car-Driver Complex.
7. Write the OPL paragraph of this OPD.
8. Suggest an alternative way to display the OPD of (a).

9. An ordered set of values of **Size** of some object can be **Miniature, Tiny, Small, Medium, Big, Large, Extra Large, Great, Giant**, and **Colossal**. Alternatively, one can have a range of numbers of some specified measurement unit (e.g., meters for length or kilograms for mass) that indicate a more accurate and "objective" specification of the same **Size** attribute. Pick up an object with two sets of attributes, one qualitative and the other quantitative. Use the textual values of **Size** above and map them in an OPD to numeric ranges of your choice.

Chapter 20
Generalization and Instantiation

> *As this term is most commonly used, a generalization is an "all" statement, to the effect that all objects of a certain general kind possess a certain property.*
>
> Lowe (1983)

While discussing aggregation and exhibition, we talked about entire groups of objects or processes—any scientific paper, any employee, any running. However, what if we wanted to consider the example of a specific paper, written by a certain John Doe? Or if we wanted to consider a group of employees, namely managers, who receive a certain salary out of the range of salaries available for the company? Perhaps we would like to discuss running in a marathon, as opposed to just any kind of running? We need to be able to pay particular attention to a specialized group, which belongs to a more general group, or even a specific instance out of a class of objects. As its name clearly points out, generalization-specialization is the relation between a general and a special case of a thing. Classification-instantiation is the relation between a class of things and a unique instance from the class. Since these two concepts are important to systems modeling, we consider them two of the four fundamental relations; and since they are intimately related, they are discussed and explained together in this chapter.

20.1 Generalization-Specialization: Introduction

Let us first consider several simple examples to set the stage for discussing generalization-specialization, or "gen-spec."[1]

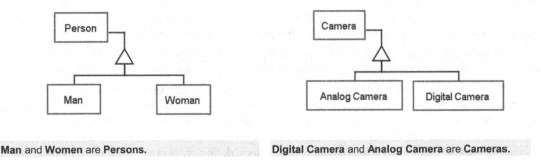

Man and **Women** are **Persons**.   **Digital Camera** and **Analog Camera** are **Cameras.**

Fig. 20.1 Generalization-specialization examples

Person in the left OPD of Fig. 20.1 is the general case, while **Man** and **Woman** are its special cases. Other examples are "**Dog** and **Cat** are **Pets**.", "**Pascal**, **Java**, and **C++** are **Programming Languages**.",

---

[1]The shorthand term "gen-spec" is borrowed from Coad and Yourdon (1991).

© Springer Science+Business Media New York 2016

D. Dori, *Model-Based Systems Engineering with OPM and SysML*, DOI 10.1007/978-1-4939-3295-5_20

"**Airplane** and **Car** are **Vehicles**.", "**Flying** and **Sailing** are **Transporting**.", and "**Ketchup** and **Mustard** are **Condiments**."

> *Generalization-specialization is a fundamental structural relation between a general thing G and one or more things S_1, S_2, ... S_n, which are specializations of G.*

An alternative way of expressing the OPL sentence might have been "**Digital Camera** and **Analog Camera** specialize **Cameras**." However, sticking to the principle of keeping the OPL language as natural and as simple as possible, OPL uses the clearer and more intuitive reserved phrases "is a" (or "are" for plural) rather than "specializes" or "specialize" for denoting the gen-spec relation from the reverse, or bottom-up direction, from the specialized thing—the specialization—to the generalizing thing—the general. Any number of specializations is possible. The following example is of three specializing objects.

Cucumber is a **Vegetable**.
Tomato is a **Vegetable**.
Carrot is a **Vegetable**.

We combine the three specialization sentences above into one:

Cucumber, **Tomato**, and **Carrot** are **Vegetables**.

Generalization-specialization is a transitive relation, meaning that if **A** is a **B**, and **B** is a **C**, then **A** is a **C**. More concretely, consider the following two specialization sentences:

Tomato is a **Vegetable**.
Vegetable is a **Plant**.

Since generalization-specialization is transitive, we can deduce that:

Tomato is a **Plant**.

Generalization-specialization means that a refineable, the general, generalizes two or more **refinees**, which are specializations of the general. The generalization-specialization relation binds one or more specializations with the same perseverance as the general, such that both the general and all its specializations are objects (in metamodel terms, if the **Thing's Perseverance** is **persistent**) or the general and all its specializations are processes (if the **Thing's Perseverance** is **transient**).

Graphically, an empty triangle with its apex connecting by a line to the general and the specializations connecting by lines to the opposite base denotes the generalization-specialization relation link.

UML and SysML use a white (blank) triangle to denote generalization-specialization, (as in OPM), but in UML and SysML the triangle's tip is linked directly to the generalizing object, and the white triangle base is not necessarily horizontal, but rather perpendicular to the line connected to the specialization. Moreover, similar to the case with aggregation, since there is no fork in UML, each specialization in a UML class diagram and SysML block definition diagram must have its own symbol. Since UML and SysML do not have processes in class diagrams, the aggregation and specialization relations in UML and SysML apply to objects only.

20.1.1 Process Specialization

Not only objects are subject to generalization-specialization. The same relation applies to processes as well. Figure 20.2 shows two simple examples.

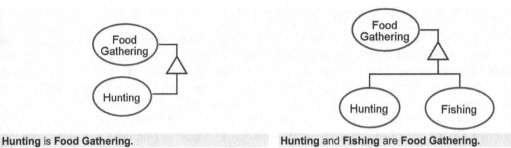

Hunting is **Food Gathering.**   Hunting and Fishing are **Food Gathering.**

Fig. 20.2 Single and plural process specializations

In order to comply with the English grammar, the process specialization sentence is slightly different than the (object) specialization sentence in that (1) instead of the reserved phrase "is a," the reserved word "is" is used, and (2) while the generalizing object is plural, as in **Vegetables**, in multiple process specialization sentence it is singular, as in **Cooking**. Consider the following OPL sentences.

Boiling is **Cooking.**
Frying is **Cooking.**
Grilling is **Cooking.**

The three OPL sentences above become:

Boiling, Frying, and **Grilling** are **Cooking.**

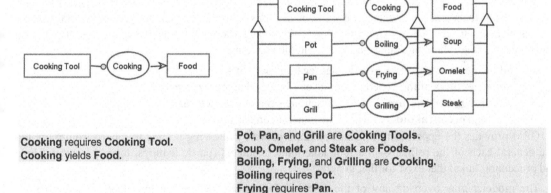

Cooking requires **Cooking Tool.**
Cooking yields **Food.**

Pot, Pan, and **Grill** are **Cooking Tools.**
Soup, Omelet, and **Steak** are **Foods.**
Boiling, Frying, and **Grilling** are **Cooking.**
Boiling requires **Pot.**
Frying requires **Pan.**
Grilling requires **Grill.**
Boiling yields **Soup.**
Frying yields **Pan.**
Grilling yields **Steak.**

Fig. 20.3 Left: A general pattern of Cooking. Right: The specializations of **Cooking Tool**, **Cooking**, and Food, and the specialized links between these specializations

Specializations of objects and processes can be combined to specify specialized procedural links between the object and process specializations. Figure 20.3 shows on the left a pattern of **Cooking**, which uses **Cooking Tool** as an instrument and yields **Food**. On the right are three specializations of **Cooking Tool**, **Cooking**, and **Food**. Each **Cooking Tool** specialization is an instrument of a specialization of **Cooking**, yielding a specialization of **Food**.

20.1.2 Link Under- and Over-Specification

Link under-specification would occur if on the right OPD of Fig. 20.3 we would have left the two links as in the OPD on the left and not specify the six procedural links on the right. This would mean that any tool can be used for any cooking. Link over-specification would occur if, in addition to the six procedural links in the OPD on the right, we would have added the two links as in the OPD on the left. Both should be avoided. In under-specification, leaving the single instrument link from **Cooking Tool** to **Cooking** on the right means that any **Cooking Tool** could be considered as instrument of any **Cooking** process and to yield any **Food**. On the other hand, in over-specification, the two generalizing links, left along with the six specialized links, become redundant. Under- and over-specification can occur also with structural links.

20.2 Inheritance

The most prominent and immediate benefit gained from using the gen-spec relation is the inheritance it induces.

> **Inheritance** *is assignment of OPM elements—things and links—of a general to its specializations.*

In OO design, the meaning of inheritance is that attributes, and to some extent also operations, of the generalizing object are inherited to the specialized objects. In OPM, the effect of inheritance is stronger, as, in addition to inheriting features and parts, it includes inheriting structural and procedural links, as well as states. Through the generalization-specialization relation, each specialization inherits from the general each of the following four kinds of inheritable elements:

- all the **parts** of a general from its aggregation-participation link,
- all the **features** of the general from its exhibition-characterization link,
- all the **tagged structural links** to which the general connects, and
- all the **procedural links** to which the general connects.

OPM provides the opportunity for multiple inheritance by allowing a thing to inherit from more than one general each of the refinees—the four inheritable elements (parts, features, tagged structural links, and procedural links) that exist for that general.

The modeler may override any of the parts of the general, which are by default inherited by the specialization, by specifying for any participant inherited from a general, a specialization of that participant with a different name and a different set of states.

20.2.1 Creating a General from Candidate Specializations

To create a general from one or more candidate specializations, the inheritable elements common to each of the candidates migrated "upward" to a generalizing thing. The manipulation of inheritable elements shall be as follows:

- Combine all of the common features and common participants of the specializations into one newly created general;

- Connect the new general using the generalization-specialization relation link to the specializations;
- Remove from the specializations all of the common features and common parts that the specializations now inherit from the new general; and
- Migrate any common tagged structural link and any common procedural link that connects a thing T to each one of the specializations from the specializations to the general, such that there will be a single link from T to the general.

20.2.2 Feature Inheritance

A general thing inherits its features—attributes and operation—to each one of its specializations. For example, Fig. 20.4 is an OPD of a **Camera**, which has two features: The attribute **Optical Zoom** and the operation **Image Capturing**. This OPD has the following corresponding OPL paragraph, where the last OPL sentence expresses the unidirectional tagged structural relation.

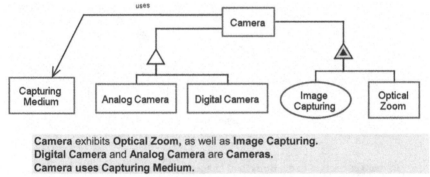

Camera exhibits **Optical Zoom**, as well as **Image Capturing**.
Digital Camera and **Analog Camera** are **Cameras**.
Camera uses **Capturing Medium**.

Fig. 20.4 Left **Camera** and its **Analog Camera** and **Digital Camera** specializations

Since **Digital Camera** and **Analog Camera** are specializations of **Camera**, we can replace **Camera** with its **Digital Camera** and its **Analog Camera** specializations. This has indeed been done in Fig. 20.5, which demonstrates the basic semantics of inheritance: the specialization—the refinee— inherits features (attributes and operations) from the general—the refineable.

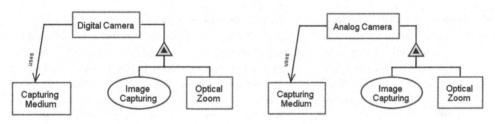

Fig. 20.5 Digital Camera and Analog Camera are specializations of Camera, therefore each can substitute Camera from Fig. 20.4

In OPM not only features are inherited; links and states are inherited as well. The inheritor can therefore replace the ancestor. **Digital Camera** and **Analog Camera** inherit not only the features of **Camera**, which are the attribute **Optical Zoom** and the operation **Image Capturing**; they also inherit the tagged structural relation **uses** from **Camera** to **Capturing Medium**. Moreover, not only structural relations are inherited; procedural relations are inherited as well. The inheritor, however, may have more features, links, or states.

20.2.3 Inheritance of Structural Relations

Consider the OPD in Fig. 20.6, in which we specify the parts of **Camera** and the specializations of **Capturing Medium**.

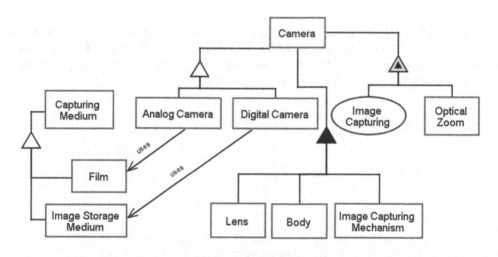

Camera consists of **Lens, Body,** and **Image Capturing Mechanism.**
Image Storage Medium and **Film** are **Capturing Mediums.**
Digital Camera uses **Image Storage Medium.**
Analog Camera uses **Film.** (Other sentences omitted.)

Fig. 20.6 The parts, specializations and features of **Camera** are specified along with the specializations of **Capturing Medium**

This implies that the parts **Camera** consists of are inherited to the two **Camera** specializations:

Digital Camera consists of **Lens, Body,** and **Image Capturing Mechanism.**
Analog Camera consists of **Lens, Body,** and **Image Capturing Mechanism.**

Not only aggregation is inherited. Any tagged structural relation, such as **uses**, is inherited. Since the tagged relation **uses** links **Camera** to **Capturing Medium**, when we specify the specializations of both **Camera** and **Capturing Medium** without taking care of the structural relation **uses**, we introduce link under-specification. This under-specification, encountered earlier, stems from the fact that the structural relation **uses** from **Camera** to **Capturing Medium** does not specify which **Camera** specialization (**Analog Camera** or **Digital Camera**) uses which **Capturing Medium** specialization (**Image Storage Medium** or **Film**). To set this straight, we specify which **Camera** specialization **uses** which **Capturing Medium** specialization.

20.2.4 State and Link Inheritance

In OPM, states and links are inherited too. Prior to the **Image Capturing** process in the **Camera** example, the **Capturing Medium**, which the **Camera uses**, is blank. After the process **Image Capturing** occurs, **Capturing Medium** is **recorded**. Hence, **blank** and **recorded** are two states of **Capturing Medium**. The OPD in Fig. 20.7 has two generalization links, one for **Camera** and the other for **Capturing Medium**. These two relations induce the two OPDs in Fig. 20.8.

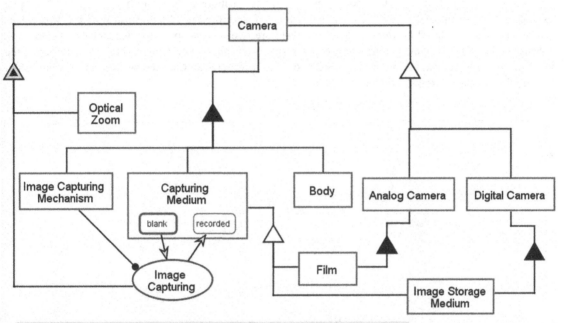

Analog Camera and Digital Camera are Cameras.
Capturing Medium can be blank or recorded.
Camera consists of Body, Image Capturing Mechanism, and Capturing Medium.
Film and Image Storage Medium are Capturing Mediums.
Image Capturing requires Image Capturing Mechanism.
Image Capturing changes Capturing Medium from blank to recorded.

Fig. 20.7 State inheritance: **Film** and **Image Storage Medium** inherit the states and the input and output links to and from **Image Capturing**

20.3 **Specialization Through a Discriminating Attribute**

Quite often, a general has specializations that are distinguished from the general in that there is a certain attribute of the general whose restricted value defines the specialization.

> *A **discriminating attribute** is an inherited attribute whose different values define corresponding specializations.*

Figure 20.10 shows an OPD in which **Vehicle** exhibits the attribute **Travelling Medium** with values **ground, air,** and **water surface. Travelling Medium** is the discriminating attribute of **Vehicle,** because the three values of **Travelling Medium** define the three specializations of **Vehicle.** These are **Car, Aircraft,** and **Ship,** with the corresponding **Travelling Medium** values **ground, air,** and **water surface.**

A general may have more than one discriminating attribute. The maximum number of specializations with more than one discriminating attribute is the Cartesian product of the number of possible values for each discriminating attribute, where some combination of attribute values may be invalid. For example, extending the content of Fig. 20.10, another attribute of **Vehicle** might be **Purpose** with the two values **civilian** and **military.** Based on these two values, there are two **Vehicle** specializations: **civilian Vehicle** and **military Vehicle.** Due to multiple inheritance, the result is an inheritance lattice where the number of the most detailed specializations would be 3 × 2 = 6 as follows: **civilian Car, civilian Aircraft, civilian Ship, military Car, military Aircraft,** and **military Ship.**

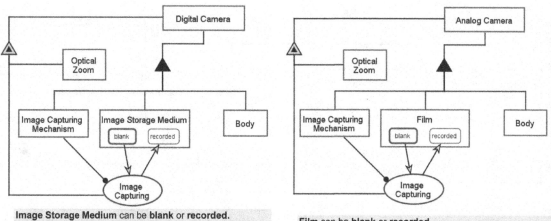

Image Storage Medium can be **blank** or **recorded.**
Digital Camera consists of **Body, Image Storage Medium,** and **Image Capturing Mechanism.**
Image Capturing requires **Image Capturing Mechanism.**
Image Capturing changes **Image Storage Medium** from **blank** to **recorded.**

Film can be **blank** or **recorded.**
Analog Camera consists of **Body, Film,** and **Image Capturing Mechanism.**
Image Capturing requires **Image Capturing Mechanism.**
Image Capturing changes **Film** from **blank** to **recorded.**

Fig. 20.8 State inheritance induced by the OPD in Fig. 20.9. Left: **Camera** is substituted by **Digital Camera,** and **Capturing Medium**—by **Image Storage Medium.** Right: **Camera** is substituted by **Analog Camera,** and **Capturing Medium**—by **Film**

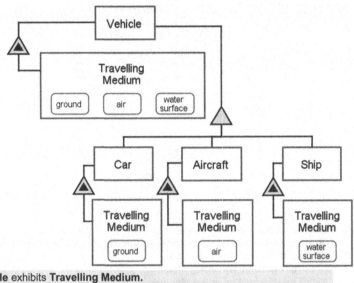

Vehicle exhibits **Travelling Medium.**
Travelling Medium of **Vehicle** can be **ground, air,** and **water surface.**
Car, Aircraft, and **Ship** are **Vehicles.**
Travelling Medium of **Car** is **ground.**
Travelling Medium of **Aircraft** is **air.**
Travelling Medium of **Ship** is **water surface.**

Fig. 20.10 The discriminating attribute **Travelling Medium** and its specializations

20.4 **State-Specified Characterization Link**

> *A **state-specified characterization link** is an exhibition-characterization link from a specialization to a specific value of a discriminating attribute of its general, which expresses the fact that the specialization can have only that value for that discriminating attribute.*

Graphically, the state-specified characterization link is the triangular exhibition-characterization symbol, with its apex connected to the specialization and its base—to the specific value. Using the state-specified characterization relation link, the OPD in Fig. 20.11 is significantly more compact than its equivalent OPD in Fig. 20.10. Here, the discriminating attribute **Travelling Medium** of **Vehicle** with values **ground, air,** and **water surface** appears only once, as opposed to four times in Fig. 20.10. The model expresses **Car, Aircraft,** and **Ship** as specializations of **Vehicle**, connecting each specialization with a state-specified characterization relation link to the corresponding **Travelling Medium** value of **ground, air,** and **water surface**, respectively.

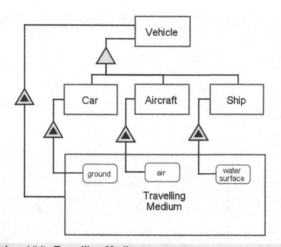

Vehicle exhibits **Travelling Medium.**
Travelling Medium of **Vehicle** can be **ground, air,** and **water surface.**
Car, Aircraft, and **Ship** are **Vehicles.**
Car exhibits **ground Travelling Medium.**
Aircraft exhibits **air Travelling Medium.**
Ship exhibits **water surface Travelling Medium.**

Fig. 20.11 State-specified characterization link example

20.5 **Classification-Instantiation**

An instance is an actual thing of some class of things, all having the same set of features, same structure, and same behavior. For example, **Lassie** and **Blackie** in Fig. 20.12 are instances of **Dog**. **Dog** is the class of all the dogs, and **Lassie** is an actual exemplar of that class. The symbol of instantiation is a black inverted triangle inside a larger white triangle.

In spoken English, the sentence "Lassie is a dog" is more natural, but the phrase "is a" is reserved for the specialization sentence, so to avoid conflicts and be explicit, the phrase "is an instance of" links an instance with its class in an OPL sentence that expresses instantiation. The plural version, used for more than one instance, is "are instances of," as in "**Bach, Beethoven** and **Brahms** are instances of **Composers.**"

20.5.1 Classes and Instances

The things we have encountered while discussing generalization-specialization are *classes* of things, either object classes or process classes. When we talked about objects, we were actually referring to a typical example of its object class, a pattern of objects from which objects could be generated.

> A **class** is a template of a thing.
>
> An **instance** of a class is an incarnation of a particular identifiable member of that class.

The definitions of class and instance are more general than their OO counterparts, as they refer to things rather than to objects. In metamodel terms, since a **Thing** is an **Object** or a **Process**, **Class** specializes into an **Object Class** and a **Process Class**. Likewise, **Instance** specializes into an **Object Instance** and a **Process Instance**: An **Object Instance** is an incarnation of the pattern specified by the **Object Class** and a **Process Instance** is an incarnation of the pattern specified by the **Process Class**.

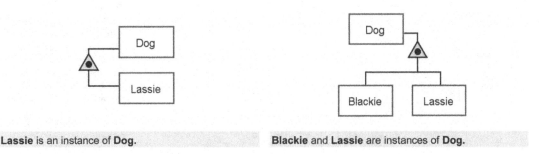

Lassie is an instance of **Dog**.   **Blackie** and **Lassie** are instances of **Dog**.

Fig. 20.12 The instantiation symbol links a class (**Dog**) to one or more of its instances

The template that the class defines includes everything that is inherited. As we have seen, in OPM it means that not only features, but also structural relations and procedural relations are inherited, and for object classes states are also inherited. Unlike a specialized class, an instance cannot exhibit any feature that its class does not exhibit, nor can an instance of an object be at a state that is not a state of its class. An object instance can be uniquely identified in the system, so at any given point in time it is possible to observe whether it exists, and if so—what its states and attribute values are.

20.5.2 Instantiation Versus Specialization

Generalization-specialization is a transitive structural relation that gives rise to a hierarchy tree. Each level in the hierarchy contains specializations of the level above it. The "leaves" of that hierarchy are the *instances* of the class. Thus we can say that instantiation is a special case of specialization, which, in the context of the system under study or development, cannot be specialized further. Figure 20.13 shows a specialization hierarchy that starts with **Car** as its top level and presents increasingly specialized object classes until it gets to **Jack's Car**. This is the first object that is physical and unique. It has a **VIN** (vehicle identification number) that uniquely identifies it, and at any given moment the values or states of all its attributes, such as **Color**, **Location**, **Mileage** and **Speed**, can be specified.

Instance is a leaf in the generalization-specialization hierarchy—it is not possible to have specializations of an instance. Inheritance of features from a class to its instances is exactly the same as the inheritance of features from a super-class to its sub-class anywhere along the generalization-specialization hierarchy. The only differences are that (1) an instance cannot have further specializations, because it is at the bottom of the hierarchy, and (2) only an instance has concrete values of its attributes, as Fig. 20.13 demonstrates.

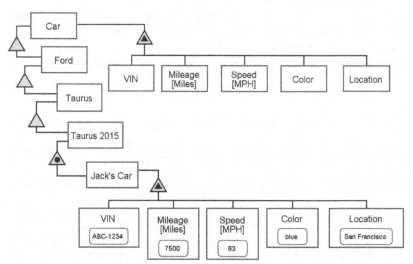

Fig. 20.13 The specialization hierarchy of **Car** all the way to the instance **Jack's Car** and its specific attribute values at the time of observing it

20.6 **The Relativity of Instance**

Like many other concepts we have encountered, the term instance is relative to the system of discourse. What for a certain system is considered instance of a class, can for another system be just a sub-class of a super-class. An instance in one system may be a class that has instances or that further recursively specializes into more refined classes, which ultimately have instances.

To demonstrate this, let us look at a few examples from the world of cars. We have seen that **Taurus 2015** is an object class of all the instances of cars made by **Ford** of model **Taurus** manufactured in the year **2015**. Suppose that the system we are now concerned with is a system for comparing and evaluating cars of model year 2015. One of the instances in this system is **Taurus 2015**, and it is an instance of the object class **Model Year 2015 Car**. Physical cars with specific **VIN** do not exist and have no meaning in this system. In the gen-spec hierarchy tree, **Taurus 2015** is one of the leaves: it has no further specializations beneath it.

As another example, consider a national highway system, in which the system architects are interested in the various types of vehicles that use the roads. What matters to them about the vehicles are their size, weight, average speed, and average annual distance that each type of vehicle travels. The designers of this system therefore decided to categorize vehicles into three types: cars, trucks and buses. While these three types are specializations of vehicle, for the system under consideration they are also the three instances of the object class vehicle. The architects are not interested in each individual car, bus or truck, so the number of each vehicle type, its average speed, mileage, etc. are attributes of vehicle that are inherited to its three instances.

Consider now a different system of the **Motor Vehicles Taxation Office** in some country, which, for taxation purpose differentiates between **Taxation Classes** of **Motor Vehicles** as follows: **Commercial Van, Sedan, Collector Car, Sports Utility Vehicle,** and **Luxury Car.** For this system, cars are differentiated into these types based on their **Market Value** and **Application.** Furthermore, the system maintains and constantly updates a list of each **Vehicle Manufacturer** and each **Vehicle Model** by **Year Model,** with an indication of which **Vehicle Model** belongs to which **Taxation Class.** Here, the **Taxation Class** is an attribute of **Vehicle. Commercial Van, Sedan,** etc., are values of the **Taxation Class** attribute of **Vehicle.** The instances of the class **Vehicle** in this system are the various **Year Models,** because the system is only concerned with setting tax levels on cars by **Taxation Class** and does not care about individual cars.

Finally, consider a car dealership. Here, of course, each individual car has its own record, including its VIN, make, model, year, owner, etc. This is the "classical" case of instance, similar to the one presented in Fig. 20.13, where each instance is a physical entity with its unique identifier. However, as we have seen, instances can be informatical, such as car models, vehicle types or records in a file.

20.7 Constraining Attribute Values

A class can be used to constrain the possible range of attribute values. In Fig. 20.14, **Adult** is a class with three attributes: **Gender,** with possible values **female** and **male, Height** in **cm,** with possible values **120..240** (120 through 240), and **Weight** in **Kg,** with possible values **40..240. Jack Robinson** is an instance of **Adult,** with **Gender** value **male, Height** value **185 cm,** and **Weight** value **88 Kg.** As Fig. 20.14 demonstrates, the name of the instance of Adult, Jack Robinson in this case, can be followed by the semicolon symbol ":" followed by the name of the class. This is useful when only the instance appears in an OPD without being attached to this class.

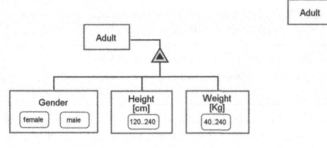
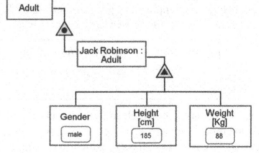

Adult exhibits **Gender, Height** in cm, and **Weight** in Kg.
Gender of **Adult** can be **female** or **male.**
Height of **Adult** in cm ranges from **120** to **240.**
Weight of **Adult** in Kg ranges from **40** to **240.**

Jack Robinson is an instance of **Adult.**
Gender of **Jack Robinson** is male.
Height in cm of **Jack Robinson** is **185.**
Weight in Kg of **Jack Robinson** is **88.**

Fig. 20.14 The attribute values of the calss **Person** are constrained with value ranges (class on left and instance on right)

The OPD in Fig. 20.15 presents the class **Metal Powder Mixture**, indicating that its **Specific Weight** attribute value can range from **7.545** to **7.537 gr/cm3.** An operational (runtime) instance of **Metal Powder Mixture** is Mixture Lot #7545 with Specific Weight attribute value is 7.555 gr/cm3. This value is within the allowable range.

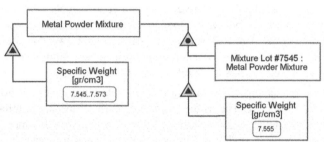

Metal Powder Mixture exhibits **Specific Weight** in gr/cm3.
Specific Weight in gr/cm3 of **Metal Powder Mixture** ranges from **7.545** to **7.537**.
Mixture Lot #7545 is an instance of **Metal Powder Mixture**.
Specific Weight in gr/cm3 of **Metal Powder Mixture** is **7.555**.

Fig. 20.15 Constrsaining attribute value. Left: The class and it attribute value range. Right: the instance and its actual value, which is in the constrained range

The OPL sentence "**Mixture Lot #7545** exhibits **Specific Weight** in **gr/cm3.**", is not present in the OPL of Fig. 20.15, because that sentence is implicit from the expressed fact "**Mixture Lot #7545** is an instance of **Metal Powder Mixture**, and therefore **Mixture Lot #7545** inherits this attribute from **Metal Powder Mixture**.

20.8 **Process Instances**

OPM instantiation applies not just to objects but also to processes. The processes we have encountered so far are actually *process classes*: they are *patterns of happenings that involve object classes*.

> *A **process class** is a pattern of happening (the sequence of subprocesses), which involves object classes that are members of the involved object set of that process class.*

A process occurrence, which follows this pattern and involves particular object instances in its preprocess and postprocess object sets, is a process instance. Hence, a process instance shall be a particular occurrence of a process class to which that instance belongs. Any process instance is therefore associated with a distinct set of preprocess and postprocess object instance sets.

> *A **process instance** is a particular occurrence of a process class to which that instance belongs.*

The power of the process class concept is that it enables the modeling of a process as a template or a protocol for some transformation that a class of objects undergoes. That transformation includes neither the spatio-temporal framework nor the particular set of object instances with which the process instance is associated; these can be identified only when we are at the instance level, or operational level of the system.

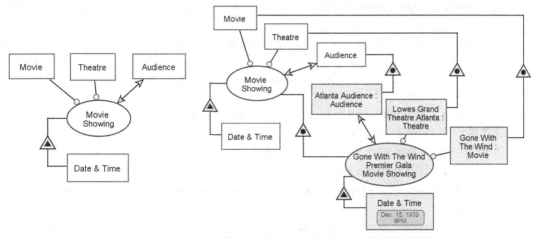

Movie Showing exhibits Date & Time.
Movie Showing requires Movie and Theatre.
Movie Showing affects Audience.

Lowes Grand Theatre Atlanta is an instance of Theatre.
Gone With The Wind is an instance of Movie.
Atlanta Audience is an instance of Audience.
Gone With The Wind Premier Gala Movie Showing is an instance of Movie Showing.
Gone With The Wind Premier Gala Movie Showing exhibits Date & Time.
Date & Time of Gone With The Wind Premier Gala Movie Showing is Dec. 15, 1939 8PM.
Gone With The Wind Premier Gala Movie Showing requires Gone With The Wind and Lowes Grand Theatre Atlanta.
Gone With The Wind Premier Gala Movie Showing affects Atlanta Audience.

Fig. 20.16 **Movie Showing** as an example of a process class (left) and its instace (right)

A process instance is a concrete occurrence of a process class, whose preprocess and postprocess object sets are sets of object instances. In particular, a process instance has a time stamp, a specific date and time at which the process started or ended. Figure 20.16 depicts on the left **Movie Showing** as an example of a process class, with **Movie**, and **Theatre** as instruments of this process class, **Date & Time** as its attribute, and **Audience** as the class' affectee. In the OPD on the right, **Gone With The Wind Premiere Gala Movie Showing** is a process instance of the **Movie Showing** process class. All the instances are greyed out to distinguish them from their classes. **Gone With The Wind** is an instance of **Movie**, **Atlanta Theatre** is an instance of **Theatre**, **Atlanta Audience** is an instance of **Audience**, and **Dec. 15 1939 8PM** (Dirks 2015) is the value of **Date & Time** at which the process instance took place. The same objects instance can participate in two or more process instances. For example, the same is an instance of **Movie**, identified by its name as **Gone With The Wind**, can participate in all the process instances of **Gone With The Wind Movie Showing** (other than the premier gala one), but each **Atlanta Audience** is a different instance of **Audience**, since it is comprised of a different set of movie goers.

20.9 **Summary**

- *Generalization-specialization* is the relation between a general thing and a specialization of that thing.
- *Classification-instantiation* is the relation between a class of things and a unique instance that belongs that class.
- Generalization-specialization gives rise to **inheritance** from the generalized thing to the specialized one(s).
- Inheritance is of features (attributes and operations), structural relations and procedural relations. For objects, states are inherited too.
- OPM processes specialize in a manner similar to objects.
- States of specialized objects can override inherited states.
- A class is a template, from which things that instantiate the class can be generated as members of that class.
- Instance is a relative term. A specialization in one system can be an instance in another.
- A process instance is a particular occurrence of a process at a given point in time and whose involved object set is a set of object instances.

20.10 **Problems**

1. Provide two examples of object specializations and two of process specializations. Specify them in OPDs and OPL.
2. Create a specialization hierarchy of sports games, which would include as a minimum volleyball, basketball, soccer, football, tennis, and baseball. Apply OPM to show what features are common and inherited, and what are game-specific.
3. Repeat the previous problem for a specialization hierarchy of track and field sport types, which would include at least three types of running, three types of swimming and three types of throwing.
4. Considering the inheritance of procedural links, are the effect links redundant? Why or why not?
5. Draw the OPD expressed in the OPL paragraph below.

    Pilot, Sailor, and **Driver** are **Occupations.**
    Airplane, Vessel, and **Truck** are **Transportation Systems.**
    Flying, Sailing, and **Driving** are **Transporting.**

6. Complete the OPD from the previous question with the following model facts: (1) Pilot, Sailor, and Driver handle Flying, Sailing, and Driving, respectively. (2) Flying, Sailing, and Driving require Airplane, Vessel, and Truck, respectively.

7. Give examples of two systems where instances in the first system are specializations in the second. Draw the OPD and write the OPL of these systems.

8. The main types of welding are: (1) Gas—Uses gas flame over metals until molten puddle is formed. Most popular fuels used with oxygen include acetylene and hydrogen. (2) Arc—Two metals are joined by generating an electric arc between a covered metal electrode and the base metal. (3) Oxygen and Arc Cutting—Metal cutting in welding is the severing or removal of metal by a flame or arc. Use OPM to describe these welding types.

9. Specify three instances of electrical appliances at your home. For each one describe its object class with at least three levels of aggregation-participation hierarchy and the operations it performs. Use the instantiation symbol to denote your appliance and provide an attribute that uniquely identifies it.

Chapter 21

Complexity Management: Refinement and Abstraction

The human mind, after all, can only juggle so many pieces of data at once before being overwhelmed.

C. Downton (1998)

The very need for systems analysis and design strategies stems from complexity. If systems or problems were simple enough for humans to be grasped by merely glancing at them, no methodology would have been required. Due to the need for tackling sizeable, complex problems, a system development methodology must be equipped with a comprehensive approach, backed by set of reliable and useful tools, for controlling and managing complexity. OPM provides four refinement-abstraction mechanisms to manage systems' inherent complexity: (1) unfolding–folding, (2) in-zooming–out-zooming, (3) state-expressing–state-suppressing, and (4) view creating. These mechanisms, defined and discussed in this chapter, make possible the specification of contextualized model segments as separate, yet interconnected OPDs. Taken together, they provide a complete model of the functional, value providing system. These mechanisms enable presenting and viewing the modelled system, and the elements it contains, in various contexts that are interrelated by the common objects, processes and relations. The set of clearly specified and compatible interconnected Object-Process Diagrams completely specify the entire system to an appropriate extent of detail and provide a comprehensive representation of that system with a corresponding textual statement of the model in OPL. This chapter elaborates on complexity management issues and specifies the various abstracting-refining mechanisms.

21.1 The Need for Complexity Management

Analyzing is the process of gradually increasing the human analyzer's knowledge about and understanding of the system's architecture—the system's structure and behavior combination, which enables it to attain its function. This is typical of a scientist's work, who, in a sense, is engaged in reverse-engineering nature and systems in it. Analogously, designing—a major engineering task—is the process of gradually increasing the amount of details about the system being architected. Complexity is inherent in real-life systems: Soon enough during this architecting process, the sheer amount of details contained in any real-world system of reasonable size overwhelms the system analyzer or architect, who must be equipped with a concept and tools to tackle this detail explosion problem. We cannot do much about the inherent complexity of the system, but by using a simple modeling framework, we can significantly reduce the system's complicatedness—how complicated it is perceived by a person looking at the model that specifies the system. OPM strives to minimize complicatedness through simplicity of the language.

© Springer Science+Business Media New York 2016
D. Dori, *Model-Based Systems Engineering with OPM and SysML*, DOI 10.1007/978-1-4939-3295-5_21

Requirements analysis and conceptual design are first steps in the lifecycle of a new system, product or project. Creating (sometimes unconscious) resistance on the side of the prospective audience—the various stakeholders—to accept the analysis and design results, because they look too complex and thus intimidating, may have the adverse effect of jeopardizing the likelihood of success of subsequent phases of the product development.

The severity and frequency of the detail explosion problem calls for an adequate solution to meet the needs of the systems modeling and analysis community. A major test of any analysis methodology is therefore complexity management—the extent to which it provides reasonable tools for managing the ever-growing complexity of the modeling outcomes in a coherent, clear, and useful manner. Such complexity management tools are extremely important for organizing the knowledge that the system architects and designers accumulate and generate during the system architecting and design process. Equally important is the role of complexity management tools in facilitating the communication of the analysis and design results to other humans, including customers, beneficiaries, peers, superiors and system developers down the development cycle road—implementers, testers, operators, etc.

Trying to incorporate the details into one big diagram, the amount of drawn symbols gets very large, and their interconnections quickly become an entangled web. Because the diagram has become so cluttered, it is increasingly unwieldy and difficult to comprehend. System architects experience this detail explosion phenomenon on a daily basis, and anyone who has tried to model a non-toy system of even modest complexity will sympathize with and endorse this description. This information overload happens even if the language (such as UML and SysML) advocates using multiple diagram kinds for the various system aspects. While some of the diagram kinds might be simpler than one kind (as in OPM), combining them all to obtain a holistic system view is cognitively much more difficult. A system modeling language must include integral mechanisms for controlling and managing this complexity. This entails being able to present and view the system at various levels of detail that are consistent with each other.

21.2 **The Model Complexity Assertion**

The basic principle of OPM complexity management is the following *detail hierarchy OPM principle*.

The Detail Hierarchy OPM Principle

Whenever an OPD becomes hard to comprehend due to an excessive amount of details, a new, descendant OPD shall be created.

The creation of the new OPD is done by one of the first two complexity management mechanisms—in-zooming or unfolding—taking advantage of the model fact representation OPM principle. This principle states that *an OPM model fact needs to appear in at least one OPD in order for it to be represented in the model*. Based on this principle, we can omit from the descendant, newly created OPD, in which a specific thing was refined, any model fact that already appeared in the ancestor OPD and is not needed to make some point in the new OPD, without losing that fact from the model. This way, new OPDs can be kept simple as they need not carry all the "baggage" of their ancestors. This provides for maintaining any OPD sufficiently simple so it does not overwhelm the limited human cognitive capacity.

The determination of when an OPD becomes too complex due to excessive amount of details is left to the discretion of the modeler, because it cannot be defined by merely fixing a maximal number of model elements in the OPD. There are other factors, such as regularity, layout, and link crossings that affect comprehension Nonetheless, a modeling tool such as OPCAT should limit the size of the canvas on which a single OPD is drawn. This indirectly limits the number of entities and enforces periodic use of in-zooming and unfolding.

Since this refinement and detail removal can be done recursively and at any required number of times, we can tackle highly complex systems and still keep the model humanly accessible and comprehensible. Hence we can make the following OPM model complexity assertion:

The OPM Model Complexity Assertion

Applying refinement mechanisms of in-zooming and unfolding to stateful objects or processes, OPM can conceptually model systems at any level of complexity.

21.3 Aspect-Based Versus Detail-Level-Based Decomposition

UML and SysML address the problem of managing systems complexity primarily by *aspect decomposition*—dividing the system model into 14 (UML) and 9 (SysML) different diagram types for modeling various aspects of the system – structure, dynamics, state transitions, timing, etc.

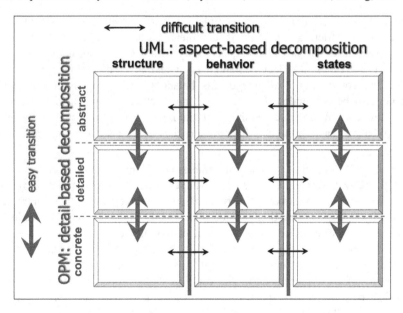

Fig. 21.1 The two orthogonal divide-and-conquer strategies

Advocating the integration of the various system aspects into a single model, the approach OPM takes is orthogonal, ***detail-based decomposition***: Rather than applying a separate model for each system aspect, OPM handles the inherent system complexity by decomposition of the system into a hierarchy of self-similar diagrams of the same single kind—OPDs—via its abstracting-refining mechanisms. These enable presenting and viewing the system, and the things that comprise it, at various detail levels. The entire system is completely specified through its OPD set—a set of compatible OPDs, each providing a partial view of the system being investigated or developed, which together provide a full picture of the system. Each OPD is accompanied by its automatically generated OPL paragraph.

Figure 21.1 shows the two orthogonal complexity management strategies. In the aspect-based decomposition, two thick, solid, vertical lines separate the structure, behavior and state transition aspects from each other. The thin bidirectional horizontal arrows across these lines symbolize difficult transition among the various models. The detail-based decomposition is represented by the two thin, dashed, horizontal lines that separate the various levels of detail—abstract, detailed and concrete, from each other. The thick bidirectional vertical arrows symbolize easy transition among the detail levels. The diagram is schematic; it by no means implies that horizontally there are only three levels of abstraction in OPM. In fact, this number is not bounded. The diagram should also not be interpreted as if vertically there are only three diagram types in a multi-diagram-type approach.

21.4 **The Completeness-Clarity Trade-off**

Like most classical engineering problems, complexity management entails a tradeoff that must be balanced between two conflicting requirements: completeness and clarity. *Completeness* means that the system must be specified to the last relevant, necessary detail. *Clarity* means that to communicate the analysis and design outcomes, the documentation, be it textual or diagrammatic, must be legible and comprehensible. The complexity challenge entails balancing these two forces that pull in opposite directions and need to be reconciled: On one hand, completeness requires that the system details be stipulated to the fullest extent possible. On the other hand, the need for clarity imposes an upper limit on the level of complexity of each individual diagram and does not allow for a diagram that is too cluttered or loaded.

Figure 21.2 is an OPM model of the parts of **Complexity Managing** and its effect on the **System Model**'s **Completeness** and **Clarity** attributes. Complexity management must address and solve this problem of completeness-clarity tradeoff by striking the right balance between these two contradicting demands. OPM achieves clarity through abstracting and completeness through refining. Abstracting, the inverse of refining, saves space and reduces complexity, but it comes at the price of completeness. Conversely, refining, which contributes to completeness, comes at the price of loss of clarity. There are "no free meals"; as is typically the case with engineering problems, there is a clear tradeoff between completeness of details and clarity of their presentation. The solution OPM proposes is to keep each OPD simple enough, and to distribute the system specification over a set of consistently inter-related and mutually-aware OPDs that contain things at various detail levels. Abstracting and refining are the analytical tools that provide for striking the right balance between clarity and completeness.

21.5 **State Expression and State Suppression**

Explicitly depicting the states of an object in an OPD may result in a diagram that is too crowded or busy, making it hard to read or comprehend. OPM enables state suppression—hiding the appearance of some or all the states of an object as represented in a particular OPD when those states are not necessary in that OPD's context. In Fig. 21.4, the two states of each one of the two attributes form the OPD in Fig. 21.2 were suppressed, so the input-output link pair changes to an effect link (Fig. 21.3).

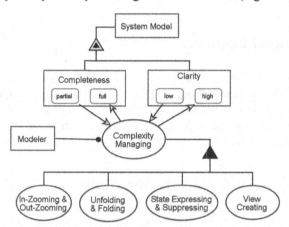

System Model exhibits **Completeness** and **Clarity**.
  Completeness of **System Model** can be **partial** or **full**.
  Clarity of **System Model** can be **low** or **high**.
Modeler handles **Complexity Managing**.
Complexity Managing consists of **In-Zooming & Out-Zooming, Unfolding & Folding, State Expressing & Suppressing,** and **View Creating**.
Complexity Managing changes **Clarity** from **low** to **high** and **Completeness** from **partial** to **full**.

Fig. 21.2 The parts of **Complexity Managing** and its effect on the **System Model's Completeness** and **Clarity** attributes

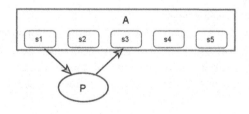

A can be **s1, s2, s3, s4,** or **s5**.
P changes **A** from **s1** to **s3**.

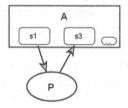

A can be **s1, s3,** or at least one other state.
P changes **A** from **s1** to **s3**.

Fig. 21.3 A stateful object with all states expressed (left) and a suppressed version (right)

The inverse operation of state suppression—state expression—exposes one or more hidden object states. The modeler may suppress any subset of states. The complete set of states of an object is the union of the set of states of that same object appearing in all of the OPDs in the OPD set—the set of OPDs of the entire OPM model.

Graphically, the annotation indicating that an object presents a proper subset (i.e., at least one but not all) of its states, shall be a small state suppression symbol in the object's right bottom corner. This symbol appears as a small state with an ellipsis label, which signifies the existence of one or more states that the view is suppressing, The textual equivalence of the state suppression symbol shall be the OPL reserved phrase "or at least one other state".

21.6 **Unfolding and Folding**

Unfolding is a mechanism for refinement, elaboration, or decomposition. Unfolding reveals a set of things that relate to the unfolded thing—the refineable. The result of unfolding is a hierarchy tree, the root of which is the refineable. Linked to the root are the refinees—one or more things—parts, specializations, features, or instances—that adds details about the refineable through one or more of the four fundamental structural relations. Any refinee can, in turn, be the refineable for the next level of unfolding.

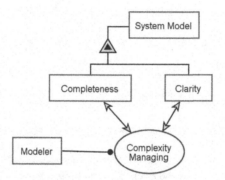

> **System Model** exhibits **Completeness** and **Clarity**.
> **Modeler** handles **Complexity Managing**.
> **Complexity Managing** affects **Clarity** and **Completeness**.

Fig. 21.4 The OPD from Fig. 21.2 after state suppression of the two attributes and folding of **Complexity Management**

Folding is the inverse operation of unfolding. It is a collapsing and abstracting mechanism, which can be applied to a hierarchy of an unfolded refineable. Folding is applied from the bottom of the hierarchy upward. Each folding operation hides some or all of the refineables. Folding all the refineables leaves just the refineable—the root of the tree hierarchy.

Since each of the four fundamental structural relation links may undergo unfolding and folding, the four kinds of unfolding-folding pairs are the following.

- aggregation unfolding—exposing the parts of a whole, and participation folding—hiding the parts of the whole,

- exhibition unfolding—exposing the exhibitor's features, and characterization folding—hiding the features of the exhibitor,
- generalization unfolding—exposing the specializations of the general, and specialization folding—hiding specializations of the general, and
- classification unfolding—exposing the class instances, and instantiation folding—hiding the instances of the class.

21.7 In-Diagram and New-Diagram Unfolding

Unfolding can be done either in the current OPD or in a new OPD.

> ***In-diagram unfolding*** *is unfolding in which the refineable and its refinees appear unfolded in the same OPD in which the refinee was originally.*

Since unfolding uses one of the four the fundamental structural links, in-diagram unfolding is graphically, syntactically, and semantically equivalent to using the corresponding fundamental structural links. While in-diagram unfolding increases the load of the diagram, it saves the need to create a new diagram, but if there are many refinees, or the current OPD is already busy, we will prefer new-diagram unfolding.

> ***New-diagram unfolding*** *is unfolding in which the refineable and its refinees appear unfolded in a new OPD.*

Both in- and new-diagram unfolding can be applied to both objects and processes. Graphically, in new-diagram unfolding, the unfolded refineable is denoted by a thick contour in both the more abstract OPD in which the refineable appears folded, without refinees, and in the new, more detailed OPD, in which the refineable appears unfolded and connected to its refinees with one or more fundamental structural link.

The modeler should make a decision as to whether to use in-diagram or new-diagram unfolding based on clarity considerations: If the current OPD is already crowded and tends to be cluttered, a new OPD should be created to prevent the current OPD from becoming unwieldy. If in-diagram unfolding had been applied and later the OPD became too crowded, the modeler can then switch from in-diagram to new-diagram unfolding, thereby alleviating the complicatedness of the current OPD (at the price of an additional OPD in the OPD set). Thus, the modeler decision whether to use in-diagram or new-diagram unfolding should account for the trade-off between the clutter added to the current OPD and the need to create a new OPD for displaying the refinees and associated links amongst them.

Partial unfolding may be depicted using the non-comprehensiveness symbol for aggregation, exhibition, and classification. To satisfy a particular contextual relevance for an OPD, a modeler may choose which refinees appear unfolded.

While unfolding and folding can be applied to both objects and processes, it is more prevalent for objects, while processes can be refined via in-zooming, discussed next, or via unfolding. Process unfolding is useful for functional decomposition which is very important in complex systems. Such systems have many more auxiliary functions, in addition to the core function, that are concurrent or independent of the core function's flow. There is usually at least one more function—system setup and management, a set of many services. Service-oriented systems offer several parallel or concurrent services that cannot be thought of as working serially. Real-time systems perform several functions in parallel rather than serially, while each component continuously samples its input from the other components and acts upon it.

21.8 Port Folding

A procedural link from an operation of an object exhibitor to another object is lost during the operation unfolding, because two objects cannot be directly connected by a procedural link. Similarly, a procedural link from an attribute of a process exhibitor to another process is lost during the operation unfolding, because two objects cannot be directly connected by a procedural link. However, it is often desirable to maintain these links (Fig. 21.5).

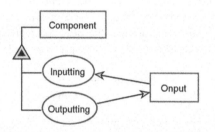
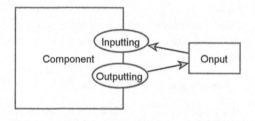

Component exhibits **Inputting** and **Outputting**.
Inputting consumes **Onput**.
Outputting yields **Onput**.

Component exhibits **Inputting** and **Outputting** as ports.
Inputting consumes **Onput**.
Outputting yields **Onput**.

Fig. 21.5 Port folding. Left: the unfolded model. Right: The port-folded version

Based on Mordecai and Dori (2013), a possible solution is *port folding*, shown in Fig. 21.6. Port folding is a specialization of folding, an intermediate state between complete folding and complete unfolding, in which we shift the process refinee—the operation—to the contour of the object refineable—the exhibitor. Graphically, this looks similar to a SysML activity diagram port on the folded exhibitor.

Port folding is a useful representation if the modeler wants to use the object rectangles to give an idea about the physical layout and relative sizes of the various system components. The reserved phrase "as ports" (or "as a port" for singular) at the end of the exhibition sentence indicates port folding. Port folding can also be applied to attributes of processes.

21.9 In-Zooming and Out-Zooming

In-zooming is a refinement operation, usually applied to processes, which specifies the subprocesses of the process being in-zoomed, as well as their (possibly partial) performance or execution order. As an example, in Fig. 21.6, the process **Check-Based Paying** from Fig. 19.13 is in-zoomed in the descendant OPD on the right, showing its four subprocesses, as expressed in the OPL sentence:

Check-Based Paying zooms into **Writing & Signing, Delivering & Accepting, Endorsing & Submitting,** and **Cashing & Cancelling,** in that sequence.

The execution order of these four processes follows the *timeline OPM principle*, repeated here:

The Timeline OPM Principle

The timeline within an in-zoomed process is directed by default from the top of the in-zoomed process ellipse to its bottom.

The execution order is expressed in OPL by the reserved phrase in that sequence at the end of the in-zooming sentence. The exposition of the four subprocesses in the context of the **Check-Based Paying** process provides for explicitly specifying how the states of both **Check** and **Keeper** change throughout the lifecycle of check, as also expressed in the OPL sentence to the left of the OPD.

Within the context of the in-zoomed process there may be partial order: overall there is an order dictated by the timeline, but two or more processes can be performed in parallel. As an example, suppose a process P zooms into seven subprocesses, **SP1, SP2 … SP7,** such that **SP1** executes first, then **SP2** and **SP3** in parallel, then **SP4**, and finally **SP5, SP6,** and **SP7** in parallel. Then the OPL sentence will be:

P zooms into **SP1,** parallel **SP2** and **SP3, SP4,** and parallel **SP5, SP6,** and **SP7,** in that sequence.

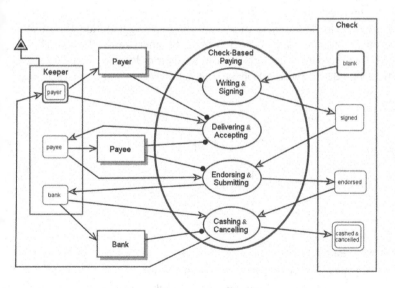

Check-Based Paying zooms into **Writing & Signing, Delivering & Accepting, Endorsing & Submitting,** and **Cashing & Cancelling,** in that sequence. **Writing & Signing** changes **Check** from **blank** to **signed.** **Delivering & Accepting** changes **Keeper** from **payer** to **payee.** **Endorsing & Submitting** changes **Check** from **signed** to **endorsed.** **Cashing & Cancelling** changes **Check** from **endorsed** to **cashed & cancelled** and **Keeper** from **bank** to **payer.** *(Rest of OPL suppressed.)*

Fig. 21.6 The process **Check-Based Paying** from Fig. 19.13 is in-zoomed, showing the details of the state changes that **Check** and **Keeper** undergo, as well as the agents involved in each subprocess

OPM can be considered process-oriented from the aspect of giving priority to modeling processes first (initially the system's function, the process that delivers the external value) and recursively zooming into this function while modeling the objects that are relevant to each process at the corresponding detail level.

21.9.1 In-Diagram and New-Diagram In-Zooming

Like unfolding, in-zooming can be done either in the current OPD or in a new OPD.

> ***In-diagram in-zooming*** *is in-zooming in which no new OPD is created, and the refineable appear in-zoomed along with its refinees in the same OPD.*
>
> ***New-diagram in-zooming*** *is in-zooming in which the refineable and its refinees appear in-zoomed in a new OPD.*

All the examples so far were of new-diagram in-zooming. Indeed this is the more prevalent way of in-zooming, since in-zooming requires a lot of "real estate" to specify the internal subprocesses and the process being in-zoomed, as well as for depicting the additional relevant objects with links to these new subprocesses, making the current OPD often too crowded. However, as Fig. 21.12 shows, in-diagram in-zooming is also useful.

21.9.2 In-Zooming and Out-Zooming of Objects

Just like process in-zooming has the aggregation-participation semantics between the in-zoomed process and its temporally-ordered subprocesses, so does object in-zooming has the aggregation-participation semantics between the in-zoomed object and its spatially-ordered parts. In other words, the spatial order according to the top-down or left-to-right layout of the parts determines their order. This is demonstrated in the metamodel in Fig. 21.7: **Whole** from **SD** zooms in **SD1** into **Part A** and **Part B,** in that vertical sequence.

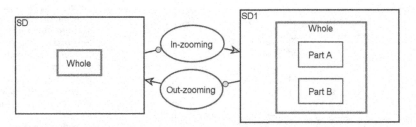

SD is refined by in-zooming **Whole** in **SD1.**
Whole from **SD** zooms in **SD1** into **Part A** and **Part B,** in that vertical sequence.

Fig. 21.7 A metamodel of in-zooming and out-zooming of objects

If **Part A** and **Part B** in Fig. 21.7 would be arranged horizontally, the OPL sentence would be: **Whole** from **SD** zooms in **SD1** into **Part A** and **Part B,** in that horizontal sequence. The ability to define order within objects opens the way to modeling tables and matrices of any dimension. For example, we can rename **Whole** in Fig. 21.7 to be **Table**, and **Part A** and **Part B** can be called **Row 1** and **Row 2**, respectively. In the next in-zoom level, each row can be in-zoomed to expose its elements, arranged horizontally, e.g., **Row 1** zooms into **Element (1,1)**, **Element (1,2)**, and **Element 1,3)**, in that horizontal sequence. Thus, **Element (1,2)** will be the second element in the first row of the matrix. A third dimension can be achieved by zooming into each element, this time vertically, and this can proceed recursively. Each in-zooming operation, applied to all the elements at the current level, adds one more dimension. Since each element can have a value, we can use OPM to do matrix operations, such as addition or multiplication, and OPM tables can be used for relational databases.

Time is one-dimensional and flows only forward, so to determine process execution order—the timing—we only needed the vertical axis to specify the order of the subprocesses in an in-zoomed process. Physical objects, however, are three-dimensional, so for object in-zooming we can at least schematically model the relative layout of object parts in two dimensions, taking advantage of the fact that the paper or computer screen used for conceptual modeling are two-dimensional. The limitation here is that objects are rectangular rather than arbitrarily shaped, but we can still get a schematic, albeit rough, 2D layout. Moreover, if the in-zoomed object is an informatical object, such as a table or a matrix, zooming into it can expose the actual cells of the table or matrix as individual objects.

21.10 **Synchronous Versus Asynchronous Process Refinement**

Unlike unfolding, which can be applied to each of the four the fundamental structural links, in-zooming has the semantics of aggregation-participation only: The refineables are parts of the in-zoomed refinee; they cannot be features, specializations, or instances. However, in addition to the whole part semantics, the layout of the subprocesses within the in-zoomed process determines their execution order. Conversely, when processes are unfolded, as are the four subprocesses of **Complexity Managing** in Fig. 21.2, there is no implied order to them (unless they have positive orderability, which must be denoted by the ordered symbol next to the aggregation black triangle). The of aggregation unfolding of **Complexity Managing** in Fig. 21.2, rather than in-zooming of **Complexity Managing**, is correct, because there is no predetermined order of applying the four refinement operations while modeling a system. Rather, the modeler applies them in an arbitrary order as needed. This is an example of an asynchronous process. On the other hand, **Check-Based Paying**, shown in Fig. 21.6, is an example of a synchronous process.

> A **synchronous process** is a process whose subprocesses have a predefined, fixed order.
>
> An **asynchronous process** is a process whose subprocesses do not have a predefined, fixed order.

Due to the difference between aggregation and in-zooming as far as processes are concerned, in-zooming is suitable for modeling synchronous processes, while aggregation unfolding—for modeling asynchronous processes. A system can have a blend of both synchronous and asynchronous processes. Moreover, if a process has several synchronous subprocesses and others that are not, the same process can be both in-zoomed, showing its synchronous subprocesses ordered in the in-zoomed process ellipse and its asynchronous ones—aggregation unfolded, either in the same or in a separate OPD.

Since the aggregation-participation fundamental structural relation does not prescribe any partial order of process performance, the modeling of synchronous process refinement must use in-zooming, in which order can be defined. The system in Fig. 10.5 is synchronous: there is a fixed, well-defined order of each subprocess within the in-zoom context of **Dish Washing**.

To model asynchronous process refinement we use the aggregation-participation fundamental structural link, either through in-diagram aggregation unfolding or as a new-diagram aggregation unfolding of the process. Figure 21.8 depicts a portion of a **Home Safety System** that carries out the function **Home Safety Maintaining**, which includes the subprocesses **Burglary Handling**, **Fire Protecting**, and **Earthquake Alarming**. Since the order of these three subprocesses is unknown, the OPD uses in-diagram aggregation unfolding with an aggregation-participation link from this function rather than an in-zoomed version of **Home Safety Maintaining**. **Home Safety Maintaining** in-zooms to a recurring systemic process, **Monitoring & Detecting**, for which **Detection Module** is an instrument and **Threat Appearing** is an environmental process.

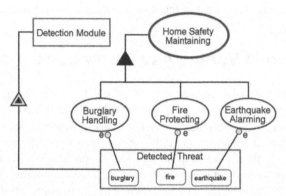

Home Safety Maintaining consists of **Burglary Handling**, **Fire Protecting**, and **Earthquake Alarming**.
Detection Module exhibits **Detection Treat**.
Detection Treat can be **burglary**, **fire**, or **earthquake**.
Burglary Detected Threat initiates **Burglary Handling**, which requires **burglary Detected Threat**.
Fire Detected Threat initiates **Fire Protecting**, which requires **fire Detected Threat**.
Earthquake Detected Threat initiates **Earthquake Alarming**, which requires **earthquake Detected Threat**.

Fig. 21.8 Home Safety Maintaining is an asynchronous system

21.11 **The Equivalence between In-Zooming and Unfolding**

One can express the details of a synchronous process via both in-zooming and unfolding. Figure 21.9 presents a process P in-zoomed, in the OPM model on the left, and its equivalent OPM model on the right, in which P is unfolded. However, as we can see in Fig. 21.9, in-zooming is preferable as it requires less symbols and yield a shorter OPL paragraph. Using in-zooming rather than unfolding, we can use instrument and result links instead of instrument event link and result event link, because the events within an in-zoomed context are implicit.

Importantly, when a process is in-zoomed, its subprocesses are its parts, while the objects exposed as a result of this in-zooming are the process' attributes. Symmetrically, when an object is in-zoomed, its internal objects are its parts, while its internal processes are its operations. The latter fact provides for depicting processes as operations of an object by putting them inside the in-zoomed view of that object.

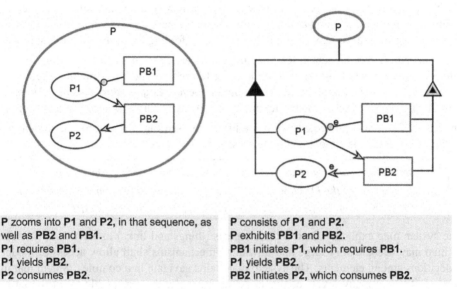

P zooms into **P1** and **P2**, in that sequence, as well as **PB2** and **PB1**.	P consists of **P1** and **P2**.
P zooms into **P1** and **P2**, in that sequence, as well as **PB2** and **PB1**.	P exhibits **PB1** and **PB2**.
P1 requires **PB1**.	**PB1** initiates **P1**, which requires **PB1**.
P1 yields **PB2**.	**P1** yields **PB2**.
P2 consumes **PB2**.	**PB2** initiates **P2**, which consumes **PB2**.

Fig. 21.9 The eqivalence between in-zooming (left) and unfolding (right)[1]

21.12 **The System Map and the Ultimate OPD**

There is exactly one System Diagram, SD—the top-level OPD, the level 0 OPD. It often contains one main, core systemic process, which is the value-delivering function of the system. Recursive new-diagram process in-zooming iterations result in a set of OPDs that are organized in a (hierarchical) tree structure, with SD being the root (detail level 0) of the OPD tree, SD1, SD2, etc. being at detail level 1 of the OPD hierarchy, SD1.1, SD1.2, ... SD 2.1, SD2.2... being at detail level 2 of the OPD hierarchy, and so on.

> *An **OPD tree** is a directed tree graph whose nodes are OPDs obtained by recursive refinement (in-zooming and/or unfolding) of processes in the system, starting with the function—the process in SD.*
>
> *The **OPD set** is the set of all the nodes in the OPD tree.*

---

[1]The red contour is assigned by OPCAT automatically to a thing that is both in-zoomed and unfolded.

> **Detail level** *of an OPD is the number of nodes in the OPD tree that need to be traversed from that OPD to the root, SD, including SD itself.*

The OPD tree is a tree of processes—a graph whose nodes are OPDs. The root is SD, the System Diagram, and the other nodes are the descendant OPDs, marked with their OPD labels, such as SD1, which is at detail level 1, SD2.3, which is at detail level 2, etc. The directed edges of an OPD tree have labels with each edge pointing from the parent OPD, which contains the refineable element, to a child OPD containing refinees, which elaborates a process in the parent OPD via new-diagram in-zooming for synchronous subprocesses or new-diagram aggregation unfolding for asynchronous subprocesses.

Since in-zooming has the semantics of aggregation-participation, each in-zooming in the hierarchy is also interpreted as aggregation-participation in order to preserve the tree structure. Figure 21.10 shows at the top the OPD tree—the hierarchy of the **Product Lifecycle Engineering** system OPM model (Dori and Shpitalni 2005). The OPD set of the model in Fig. 21.10 has 11 OPDs spanning 4 levels of detail.

While the OPD tree is presented like a file hierarchy (see Fig. 21.10 top), the system map, shown at the bottom of Fig. 21.10, is a more elaborate presentation of the OPD tree.

> *The **system map** is an elaborate OPD tree, in which each node in the tree is a miniaturized icon of the OPD, with thick grey arrows pointing from each process in one OPD to its refined (in-zoomed or unfolded) version in the child OPD.*

The system map explicitly depicts the elements (things and links) in each OPD (node). Because the system map may become very large and unwieldy, mechanisms shall allow access to model content and the associations among elements. The system map helps navigate in a complex system that may comprise hundreds of OPDs at many levels of detail. As an example, the executable OPM model of the mRNA decay model in Somekh et al. (2014) contains hundreds of objects and processes in over 40 OPDs at 9 levels of detail, with hyperlinks from a thing in the model to the paper from which the model fact was extracted.

Figure 21.11 is a screenshot of a simulated execution of the **mRNA Decay** OPM model (Somekh et al. 2014), showing it being at an OPD SD2.4.2.2.1.2.4.2 – **eIF4F Dissociates Cap and Decaysome** in-zoomed, as indicated also by the frame around this process in the OPD tree on the left. This OPD demonstrates the self-similarity of OPDs: regardless of what detail level an OPD is at, it used only stateful objects, processes, and relations among them.

Currently, the system in Fig. 21.11 is executing in parallel four subprocesses (in dark blue), after having completed the subprocess **eIF4F Dissociates Cap** above them. The dissociation is manifested in each of these four subprocesses by consuming a link, modeled as an object in its own right, between two objects, e.g., the factor **Xrn1** and the protein **eIF4E** at the bottom are dissociated by the process **eIF4E and Xrn1 Dissociation**. Below the OPD is the lifespan diagram, enabling inspection of each object and process at each point in time. The browser on the left is open on the relevant paper, one of the 43 papers from which the model facts in this OPD were taken, obtained by clicking on the in-zoomed process.

This example demonstrates the indispensability of the refinement mechanisms, and in particular in-zooming. Without it, it would be impossible to comprehensibly show the hundreds of things in the model and the thousands of links among them in a single OPD or in any other kind of diagram.

In addition, an OPM tool set should provide a mechanism for creating views, as OPDs with associated OPL sentences, of objects and processes that meet specific criteria. These views may include the critical path for minimal system execution duration, or a list of system agents and instruments, or an OPD of objects and processes involved in a specific kind of link or set of links. For example, an OPD can be created by (1) refining (unfolding or in-zooming) an object or (2) collecting and presenting in a new OPD things that appear in various OPDs for expressing assignment of system sub-functions to system-module objects.

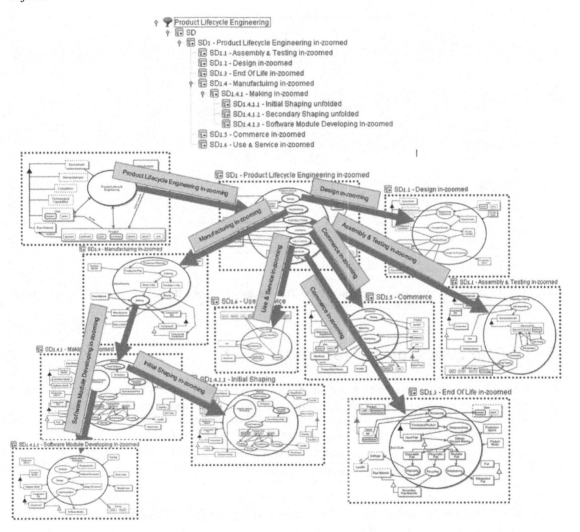

Fig. 21.10 The tree hierarchy (top) and system map (bottom) of the **Product Lifecycle Engineering** system OPM model

> *The **ultimate OPD** is single flat representation of the OPM system model.*

The ultimate OPD is obtained by recursively flattening the OPD tree from the bottom up all the way to the OPD tree toot, such that the entire model is represented in this single OPD. Except for very small system models, the ultimate OPD is definitely unfit for use by humans due to our limited cognitive capacity. However, for computer processing—knowledge management, navigation, querying, etc., the ultimate OPD is very useful.

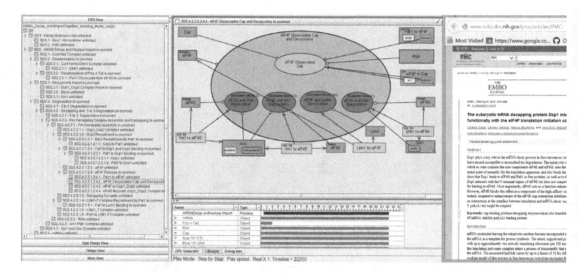

Fig. 21.11 A screenshot of simulated execution of the **mRNA Decay** OPM model (Somekh et al. 2014), showing detail level 8—**SD2.4.2.2.1.2.4.2—eIF4F Dissociates Cap and Decaysome in-zoomed**

21.13 The OPD Object Tree and Forest

Unlike the OPD (process) tree, which results from process refinement and has a single root, there can be many OPD object trees, at least one from each refineable object, which together constitute a forest.

> *An **OPD object tree** is a tree whose root is an object B and whose nodes are things that result from recursively refining B via unfolding and in-zooming, where each in-zooming is converted to aggregation-participation.*

Each tree stems from a distinct refineable object that unfolds or in-zooms to reveal its details—not necessarily just parts as in the process in-zooming, but possibly also features, specializations, or instances. Rather than identifying the possible flow of execution control as in the OPD (process) tree, each OPD object tree encapsulates the information about an object as a hierarchical structure. Since in-zooming has the semantics of aggregation-participation, like the OPD tree, each in-zooming in the hierarchy of the OPD process is also interpreted as aggregation-participation in order to preserve the tree structure. Complete or partial OPD object trees can be presented as views (see Sect. 21.18). The root of each OPD object tree can be attached as a child of the node in the OPD (process) tree, creating the system map (see Sect. 21.12).

21.14 **Out-Zooming**

Out-zooming is the inverse operation of in-zooming. A scenario in which the need for out-zooming arises is when the modeler observes that the current OPD is already over-crowded, making it necessary to hide the content of an in-zoomed process in the current OPD. In-diagram out-zooming does not create a new OPD, which implies removing and losing the subprocesses and objects inside the process being out-zoomed. Therefore, unless the modeler decides that these subprocesses are too detailed for the purpose at hand and is ready to delete them, in-diagram out-zooming does not make a lot of sense.

New-diagram in-zooming elaborates a refineable in an existing OPD, say **SDn**, where **n** is the current level of detail, by creating a new OPD, **SDn+1**, which elaborates the refineable at the next detail level by adding subprocesses, associated objects, and relevant links. Figure 21.12 is a metamodel of the **New-Diagram In-Zooming** and **New-Diagram Out-Zooming** processes. The OPM model on the right uses in-diagram in-zooming of the model on the left to elaborate the two processes: **New-Diagram In-Zooming**, for creating a new-diagram in-zoomed context, filled in with subprocesses and objects, and **New-Diagram Out-Zooming**, for creating a new-diagram out-zoomed (empty) context. **New-Diagram In-Zooming** begins with **Content Showing**, followed by **Link Refining**. **New-Diagram Out-Zooming** begins with **Link Abstracting**, the inverse process of **Link Refining**, followed by **Content Hiding**, the inverse process of **Content Showing**.

Semi-Zoomed OPD is an interim object, which is created and subsequently consumed during both **New Diagram In-Zooming** and **New-Diagram Out-Zooming**. This interim object appears only within the contexts of both **New-Diagram In-Zooming** and **New-Diagram Out-Zooming**.

In Fig. 21.13, the metamodel on the left hand side of Fig. 21.12 is elaborated by embedding an actual OPDs inside its objects **SDn**, **SDn+1**, and **Semi-Zoomed OPD**. In this particular OPM model example, **SDn**, presented in Fig. 21.13 at the top middle, includes the process **P**, which is a refineable about to be in-zoomed, as well as four objects: the consumee **C**, the agent **A**, the instrument **D**, and the resultee **B**, connected to **P** with the corresponding different procedural links. This OPD inside the meta-object **SDn** is instrument for the **New-Diagram In-Zooming** on the left.

Content Showing is the first of the two **New-Diagram In-Zooming** subprocesses. During **Content Showing**, the boundary of **P** expands to make room for showing its content—the model subprocesses **P1**, **P2**, and **P3**, as well as the interim model object **BP**. The result of **Content Showing** is presented as the content of the interim object **Semi-Zoomed OPD**. This interim object is recognizable only in the context of **New-Diagram In-Zooming**. The second subprocess, **Link Refining**, done by the modeler, consumes it while creating **SDn+1** presented in Fig. 21.13 at the bottom in the middle.

During **Link Refining**, the procedural links attached to the contour of **P** migrate to the appropriate subprocesses as determined by the modeler. Thus, since **P1** consumes **C**, the consumption link arrowhead migrates from **P** to **P1**. The agent **A** handles both **P1** and **P2**, so in **SDn+1** two agent links, one to **P1** and the other to **P2**, replace the single one in **SDn** from **A** to **P**. **P3** requires **D**, so the instrument link migrates from **P** to **P3**. Finally, since **BP** results from **P1**, and **P3** consumes it, the corresponding result and consumption links are added, making **BP** an interim, internal object of **P**, recognizable only within the context of **P**. Likewise, **P1**, **P2**, and **P3** are internal processes of **P**, and as such they are recognizable only within the context of **P**. The OPD inside the meta-object **SDn+1** is instrument for the **New-Diagram Out-Zooming** on the right. What happens next is the exact inverse of what we have seen, both in the order of the subprocesses and what each of them does.

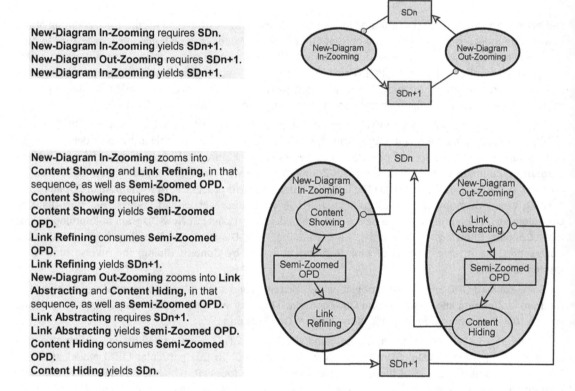

Fig. 21.12 A metamodel of new-diagram in-zooming and new-diagram out-zooming

Link Abstracting is the first of the two **New-Diagram Out-Zooming** subprocesses. During **Link Abstracting**, the links connected to subprocesses and interim objects of P migrate to (the boundary, the ellipse circumference of) P itself, resulting in exactly the same **Semi-Zoomed OPD** that is depicted inside **New-Diagram In-Zooming**. This **Semi-Zoomed OPD** interim object is consumed by **Content Hiding**, creating **SDn** presented in Fig. 21.13 at the top in the middle. The boundary of **P** can now shrink, as it is empty and there is no need for making room to show its content (the model subprocesses **P1**, **P2**, and **P3**, as well as the interim model object **BP**), which is now hidden. The result of **Content Showing** is presented as the content of the interim object **Semi-Zoomed OPD**.

21.15 **Simplifying an OPD**

In-diagram out-zooming—the elimination of an in-zoomed process content—followed by new-diagram in-zooming can simplify an already-modeled OPD that the modeler deems overly complicated or overloaded with details. In-diagram out-zooming reduces the cognitive load necessary to understand the complicated OPD at the expense of adding a new OPD to the OPD set, which is the result of the subsequent new-diagram in-zooming, which creates a new OPD at an interim level of detail, as explained next.

Figure 21.14 demonstrates simplifying an OPD by in-diagram out-zooming followed by new-diagram out-zooming. On the left is the original OPD set with three OPDs: **SD**, **SD1** and **SD1.1**. Realizing that **SD1** is overly complicated, in order to simplify the model, the modeler decides that a set TO (Things to be Out-zoomed), comprising four things in **SD1—P1**, **P2**, and **P3**, along with **BP**—shall be replaced by a single new process **P123** via new-diagram out-zooming.

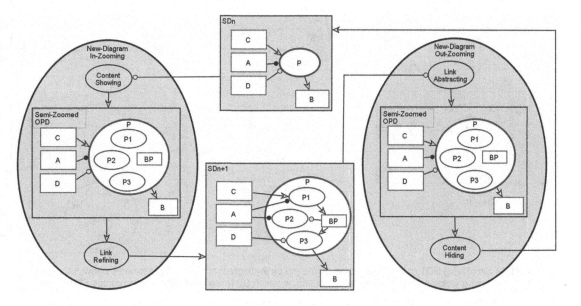

Fig. 21.13 The metamodel on the left in Fig. 21.12 elaborated with an example of an actual OPM model inside it

In the middle of Fig. 21.14, **P123** undergoes new-diagram out-zooming, resulting in **SD1.1[new]** (in a real implementation, the new OPDs shall not be marked with [new]; this label only helps the explanation here).

Here is how this is done. The modeler indicates the things in the set TO (things to be out-zoomed) and the name of the new interim process to be created (**P123** in our case). The grey background denotes these candidate elements. The process-to-be **P123** now undergoes new-diagram out-zooming, following the two subprocesses described earlier: link abstracting and content hiding. As a result of link abstracting, the links that were connected to subprocesses of the future **P123** process migrated to the contour of the now-created **P123**, and as a result of content hiding, **P123** becomes empty, as shown in **SD1[new]**.

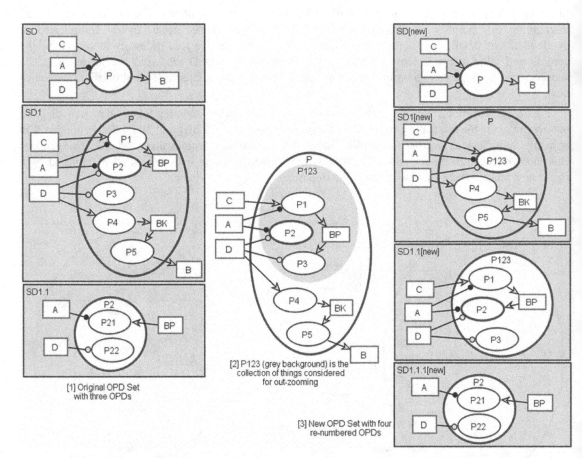

Fig. 21.14 Simplifying SD1 of the OPM model on the left by in-diagram out-zooming followed by new-diagram in-zooming yields a new OPM model on the left, in which SD1[new] and SD1.1[new] replace SD1

In order to preserve the model facts that were eliminated (such as the model facts that **A** is agent to **P1** and **P2**), a new OPD, **SD1.1[new]**, was created with these facts. Hence, on the right of Fig. 21.14 is the new OPD set, which now has four OPDs: **SD[new]**, **SD1[new]**, **SD1.1[new]**, and **SD1.1.1[new]**, renumbered to reflect the new OPD hierarchy, In this augmented hierarchy, the complicated OPD **SD1** has been replaced by two simpler OPDs – **SD1[new]** and **SD1.1[new]**.

Examining **SD1[new]**, we see that it is indeed less complicated and less crowded than the original **SD1**, since it has a net of five fewer elements: three removed processes, **P1**, **P2**, and **P3**, one removed object, **BP**, two removed links, and one added process, **P123**. This new OPD is inserted into the process hierarchy, pushing the old **SD1.1**, which remains unchanged, one detail level down, from detail level 2 to detail level 3. Due to the addition of **SD1.1[new]**, **SD1.1**is renumbered to be **SD1.1.1[new]**.

21.16 Abstraction Accounts for Procedural Link Precedence

Recall that the *procedural link uniqueness OPM principle* asserts that at any level of detail, an object and a process can be connected with at most one procedural link, which uniquely determines the role of the object with respect to the process at that detail level.

When the modeler performs abstraction via state suppression, folding, or out-zooming, the procedural links between refinees and other things in the OPD that are not refinees, migrate to the context (graphically the contour, or circumference) of the refineable. For example, suppressing the states in Fig. 10.4, the pair of input-output links migrates from the two states to **Person** to become an effect link. Another example is **P123** in Fig. 21.14.

This migration may cause a conflict, in which two or more procedural links of different kinds link an object and a process. According to the procedural link uniqueness OPM principle an object or an object state can link to a process only by a single, unique procedural link. Figure 21.15 demonstrates the problem of procedural link abstraction. In **SD1**, the result link from **P1** to **B** is more significant, or is semantically stronger, than the effect link from **P2** to **B**, so when the process **P** in **SD1** is out-zoomed in **SD**, the result link prevails.

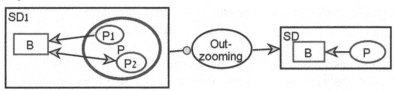

Fig. 21.15 Abstracting different procedural links invokes the link precedence

To sustain this principle, OPM resolves the conflict between candidate links by determining, based on the links' semantic strength, which link remains or which new link replaces the candidates in the abstract OPD. The loss of detail information is consistent with the notion of abstraction. Semantic strength and link precedence are two concepts to guide the determination of which links to retain and which to hide when an OPD is out-zoomed or folded.

> **Semantic strength** *of a procedural link is the significance of the information that the link carries.*

Information concerning a change in existence, either creation or elimination, is more significant than information about change to an existing thing. The relative semantic strength of the two conflicting procedural links determines the link precedence. When two or more procedural links compete to remain represented in an OPD that is being abstracted (out-zoomed, folded, or state-suppressed), the link that prevails is the one with the highest semantic strength.

21.16.1 Precedence Among Transforming Links

Transforming links include result, effect, and consumption links, and their variants having the event or condition control modifiers.

> ***Link precedence*** *is an ordered list of procedural links with diminishing sematic strength.*

Table 21.1 Link precedence among the transforming links

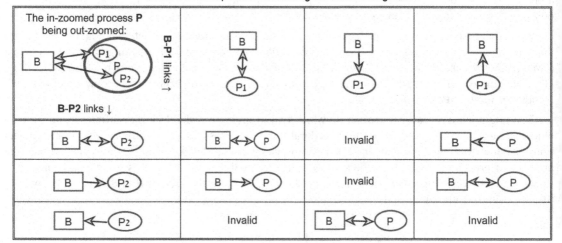

Table 21.1 shows link precedence among the transforming links: **P** in the upper left corner is out-zoomed. The column headings show the three possible transforming links between **P1** and **B**, while the row headings show the three possible links between **P2** and **B**. The table cells show the prevailing link between **B** and **P** after **P** is out-zoomed. Cells marked as "Invalid" indicate the impossibility of the combination. For example, inspecting the center cell, if **P1** consumes **B**, then **B** no longer exists when **P2** later tries to consume it again. Since object creation and consumption are semantically stronger (i.e., they have higher semantic strength) than affecting the object by changing its state, result and consumption links have precedence over effect links, as demonstrated in Table 21.1. However, since result and consumption links are semantically equivalent, when they compete, the prevailing link shall be the effect link because the effect link allows both creation and elimination as effects.

21.16.2 Precedence Among Transforming and Enabling Links

Transforming links are semantically stronger than enabling links, because the transforming links denote creation, consumption, or change of the linked object, while the enabling links only denote enablement. A transforming link therefore has precedence over an enabling link as shown in Fig. 21.16.

Within the enabling links, an agent link has precedence over an instrument link, because in artificial systems the humans are central to the process, they handle the system and must ensure its proper operation. In addition, wherever there is human interaction, an interface should exist and this information should be available to the modeler of a refineable so that they can design the human-system interface according to the conceptual model specification.

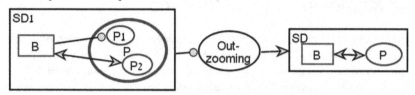

Fig. 21.16 Link precedence among transforming and enabling links

Summarizing the semantic strength of the procedural non-control links, the primary link precedence is as follows:

Consumption = Result > Effect > Agent > Instrument

Here, the = and > symbols refer to the semantic strength of the links. State-specified links have higher precedence than basic links that do not specify states.

21.16.3 Precedence Among Same-Kind Non-control Links and Control Links

Each non-control link kind has a corresponding event and condition link that are useful for determining finer, secondary precedence distinction within each kind of procedural link. A secondary link precedence exists within each procedural link in the primary link precedence. The event link has higher semantic strength than its corresponding non-control link, while the condition link has a weaker semantic strength than its corresponding non-control link. The semantic strength of an event link is stronger than the semantic strength of its corresponding non-control link, because any event link has semantics of both its corresponding non-control link plus the event capable of initiating a process. The semantic strength of a conditional link is weaker than the semantic strength of its corresponding non-control link, because the condition modifier weakens the precondition satisfaction criteria for the connecting process.

21.16.4 Summary of the Procedural Link Precedence

Summarizing the semantic strength of the procedural links based on the distinction between primary and secondary precedence, the complete order of precedence is as follows:

1.	consumption event	>	consumption
2.	consumption	=	result
3.	result	>	consumption condition
4.	consumption condition	>	effect event
5.	effect event	>	effect
6.	effect	>	effect condition
7.	effect condition	>	agent event
8.	agent event	>	agent
9.	agent	>	agent condition

10.	agent condition	>	instrument event
11.	instrument event	>	instrument
12.	instrument	>	instrument condition

21.17 Link Migration upon In-Zooming

The context (graphically, the outer circumference) of a process **P** acts as parentheses in algebra that are used to express the distributive law: Any procedural link attached to **P** is thus viewed as is it is attached to each one of **P**'s subprocesses. An example appears in Fig. 8.2, where **crashed Vehicle** is instrument to all the four subprocesses inside **Automatic Crash Responding**.

As the modeler adds subprocesses, she or he often fails to manually migrate procedural links to the specific subprocesses, causing them to be implicitly attached to superfluous procedural links that invalidate the model. To help avoid these situations, as soon as a modeler draws the first subprocess **P1** inside and in-zoomed process **P**, a modeling tool should automatically move to **P1** all the procedural and control links that were attached to **P** in the parent OPD. An example is Fig. 5.1, which shows the **Automatic Crash Responding** process after it was in-zoomed and after its first subprocess, **Crash Severity Measuring**, was drawn inside it near the top of the enclosing ellipse of the **Automatic Crash Responding** process. The links that were attached to **Automatic Crash Responding** have migrated to be attached to **Crash Severity Measuring**.

It is the modeler's role to see to it that the various transforming links that are now attached to **P1** will be put back to **P** or moved to subsequent subprocesses. Similarly, enabling links may need to be migrated to one or more specific subprocesses, where the linked enabler is really needed. As an alternative to the automatic link migration, the tool can check the validity of the links after the insertion of each new subprocess and alert the modeler as needed.

21.18 View Creating: The Fourth Refinement Mechanism

View creating—the fourth refinement mechanism after state expression, in-zooming and unfolding, is achieved by collecting model facts from various OPDs in the OPD set and putting them together in a new OPD called View for the purpose of demonstrating a specific aspect. Examples include (1) a process tree—a complete or partial tree of the process hierarchy of the system, which is a purely procedural view of the system, (2) an object tree—a complete or partial tree of the object hierarchy of the system, which is a purely structural view of the system, (3) an allocation view, showing what objects are allocated to perform what functions (processes) in the system model, and (4) an animated simulation motivated view, aimed at easing the concurrent inspection of how certain objects and processes from disparate OPDs interact. In a modeling tool, views shall not be edited to add, remove, or change any model fact. Rather, this should be done in the non-view OPDs and reflected automatically in the pertinent views. The inverse of view creating is view deleting.

21.19 **Middle-Out as the De-facto Architecting Practice**

Ideally, analysis and design start at the top and make their way gradually to the bottom—from the general to the detailed. In real life, however, analysis typically starts at some arbitrary detail level and is rarely linear. The design is not linear either. Usually, these are iterative processes, during which knowledge, followed by understanding, is gradually accumulated and refined. The system architect cannot know in advance the precise structure and behavior of the very top of the system—this requires analysis and becomes apparent at some point along the analysis process. Step by step, the analyst builds the system specification by accumulating and recording facts and observations about things in the system and relations among them.

Due to the non-linear nature of the analysis and design processes, linear, unidirectional "bottom-up" or "top-down" approaches, while seeming highly methodical, are rarely applicable to real-world systems. Rather, it is frequently the case that the system under construction or investigation is so complex and unexplored, that neither its top nor its bottom is known with certainty from the outset. More commonly, analysis and design of real-life systems start in an unknown place along the system's detail level hierarchy. The analysis proceeds "middle-out" by combining top-down and bottom-up techniques to obtain a complete comprehension and specification of the system at all the detail levels.

It thus turns out that even though architects usually strive to work in an orderly top-down fashion, more often than not, the de-facto practice is the middle-out mode of analysis and design. Rather than trying to fight it, system modeling approaches and tools must provide facilities to handle this middle-out architecting mode along with support for top-down and bottom up approaches.

21.19.1 OPM Caters to the Mixed Approach

Using OPM, the accumulated knowledge is documented and represented as interconnected model facts through a set of OPDs and their corresponding OPL paragraphs. If the OPD that is being augmented becomes too crowded, busy, or unintelligible, a new OPD is created. This descendant OPD repeats one or more of the things in its ancestor OPD in a refined form. These repeated things establish the link between the ancestor and descendant OPDs. The descendant OPD does not usually replicate all the details of is ancestor, as some of them are abstracted, while others are simply not included. This new OPD is therefore amenable to refinement of new things to be laid out in the space that was saved by not including things from the ancestor OPD. In other words, there is room in it to insert a certain amount of additional details before it gets too cluttered. When this happens, a new cycle of refinement takes place, and this goes on until the entire system has been completely specified. As we have seen in this chapter, OPM caters not only to this top-down approach, but also to bottom-up and middle-out via abstracting and OPD simplifying along with the addition of an interim detail level.

21.19.2 When Should a New OPD Be Created?

An OPD set has to be readable and easy to follow and comprehend. The following rules of thumb are helpful in deciding when a new OPD should be created so OPDs are as easy to read and grasp as possible.

- The OPD should not stretch over more than one page or one average-size monitor screen.
- The OPD should not contain more than 20–25 entities (objects, processes or states).

- Things (objects or processes) must not occlude each other. They are either completely contained within higher-level things, in case of zooming, or have no overlapping area. An exception to this guideline is when port folding (See Sect. 21.8) is applied.
- The diagram should not contain too many links.
- A link should not cross the area occupied by a thing.
- The number of links crossing each other should be minimized.

21.20 Navigating Within an OPM System Model

Since, as we have seen, an OPM model can be very large navigation inside the model and orientation becomes an issue.

21.20.1 OPM Diagram Labels and Tree Edge Labels

The OPM system name is the name of the OPM model that specifies the system. An OPD name is the name that identifies each OPD in the OPD process tree. SD shall contain one and only one systemic process, which represents the overarching system function that delivers functional value to stakeholders. It may, in addition, to contain one or more environmental processes. SD is the label of the root OPD in the OPD tree. The OPD tree root, SD, occupies level (tier) 0 in the OPD tree and it is the single node at this level. Higher numbered tiers, i.e., those corresponding to successive refinements, may have more than one OPD.

Not only the nodes in the OPD tree are labeled; the edges are too. Each edge (an arc connecting two nodes—two OPDs) in the OPD tree has a unique label. The label expresses a refinement relation that corresponds to the implicit invocation link or unfolding relation. Considering each OPD to be an object and the entire OPD process tree to be a single OPD, each edge is a unidirectional tagged structural link with a tag that reads: "is refined by in-zooming **<Refineable Name>** in ", or "is refined by unfolding **<Refineable Name>** in ". An OPD refinement OPL sentence is an OPL sentence describing the refinement relation between a refineable present in a tier$_N$ OPD and its refining OPD in tier$_{N+1}$. The syntax of an in-zoomed OPD refinement OPL sentence is:

<Tier$_N$ OPD label> is refined by in-zooming **<Refineable Process Name>** in **<Tier$_{N+1}$ OPD Label>**.

Similarly, the syntax of an unfolded OPD refinement OPL sentence is:

<Tier$_N$ OPD label> is refined by unfolding **<Refineable Process Name>** in **<Tier$_{N+1}$ OPD Label>**.

21.20.2 Whole System OPL Specification

An OPL paragraph is the collection of OPL sentences that together specify in text what the corresponding OPD specifies graphically. An OPL paragraph name, using the OPD name, may precede the first OPL sentence of each OPL paragraph.

> An **OPD model specification** is the collection of successive OPDs in the system's OPD tree.

> An **OPL model specification** is the collection of successive OPL paragraphs corresponding to the OPDs in the system's OPD tree, from which duplicate OPL sentences were removed.
>
> An **OPM model specification** is a side-by-side presentation of the OPD model specification and the corresponding OPL paragraph is presented to the right of each OPD.

An example of an OPM model specification is presented in Table 21.2, which contains the entire OPM model of the Dish Washing system in Fig. 10.5.An OPM model specification of a system begins with a starting title, as in **Dish Washing System** *OPM model specification*.

The left column contains the OPDs in the OPM system's OPD set in a breadth-first order, but the modeler may override this default order. The corresponding OPL paragraphs are listed on the right column, such that each OPL paragraph is to the right of its OPD.

21.21 Summary

- *Complexity management* is essential for taming the complexity of real-world systems, both man-made and natural.

- The **OPM Model Complexity Assertion** is that applying refinement mechanisms of in-zooming and unfolding to stateful objects or processes, OPM can conceptually model systems at any level of complexity.

- OPM's complexity management approach is *detail-level-based decomposition*, which is in contrast with UML and SysML approach of aspect-based decomposition.

- The *completeness-clarity trade-off* is the tension between the need to specify the system such that all the model facts are represented, while maintaining a clear, comprehensible representation of the system.

- The three refinement-abstraction mechanisms are unfolding–folding, in-zooming–out-zooming, and state-expressing–state-suppressing. A fourth is view-creating–view-deleting.

- *State-expressing* is showing one or more of an object's states; state-suppression is hiding one or more of the object's states.

- Each of the four fundamental structural relation links may undergo unfolding and folding, so there are four kinds of unfolding-folding pairs.

- *In-diagram unfolding* is unfolding in which the refineable and its refinees appear unfolded in the same OPD in which the refinee was originally.

- *New-diagram unfolding* is unfolding in which the refineable and its refinees appear unfolded in a new OPD.

- ***Unfolding*** is a mechanism for refinement, elaboration, or decomposition, which reveals a set of refineables—things that relate to the unfolded thing—the refineable.

- A ***synchronous process*** is a process whose subprocesses have a predefined, fixed order.

- An ***asynchronous process*** is a process whose subprocesses do not have a predefined, fixed order.

- ***New-diagram in-zooming*** is in-zooming in which the refineable and its refinees appear in-zoomed in a new OPD.

- ***In-diagram in-zooming*** is in-zooming in which no new OPD is created, and the refineable appear in-zoomed along with its refinees in the same OPD.

- In-zooming has the semantics of *aggregation-participation* plus positive orderability.

- Process in-zooming determines the (possibly partial) *temporal order* of its subprocess execution.

- Object in-zooming determines the (possibly 2-dimansional) *spatial order* of its parts.

- An ***OPD tree*** is a directed nod- and edge-labeled tree graph whose nodes are OPDs obtained by recursive in-zooming or unfolding of processes in the system, starting with the function—the process in SD.

- *An **OPD set*** is the set of all the nodes in the OPD tree.

- ***Detail level*** of an OPD is the number of nodes in the OPD tree that need to be traversed from that OPD to the root, SD, including SD itself.

- The ***system map*** is an elaborate OPD tree, in which each node in the tree is a miniaturized icon of the OPD, with thick grey arrows pointing from each process in one OPD to its refined (in-zoomed or unfolded) version in the child OPD.

- The ***ultimate OPD*** is single flat representation of the OPM system model.

Table 21.2 OPM model specification of **Dish Washing System**

Dish Washing System OPM model specification	
Graphical specification (OPD set)	*Textual specification (OPL paragraph set)*
SD: **Dish Washing System**	
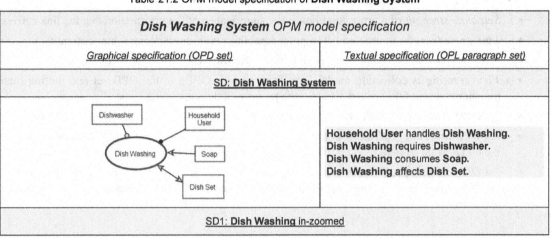	**Household User** handles **Dish Washing**. **Dish Washing** requires **Dishwasher**. **Dish Washing** consumes **Soap**. **Dish Washing** affects **Dish Set**.
SD1: **Dish Washing** in-zoomed	

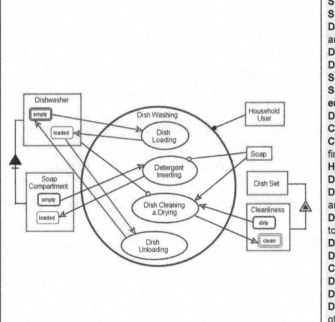	SD is refined by in-zooming **Dish Washing** in SD1. **Dish Washer** consists of **Soap Compartment** and at least one other part. **Dishwasher** can be **empty** or **loaded**. **Dishwasher** is initially **empty** and finally **empty**. **Soap Compartment** can be **empty** or **loaded**. **Soap Compartment** is initially **empty** and finally **empty**. **Dish Set** exhibits **Cleanliness**. **Cleanliness** of **Dish Set** can be **dirty** or **clean**. **Cleanliness** of **Dish Set** is initially **dirty** and finally **clean**. **Household User** handles **Dish Washing**. **Dish Washing** zooms into **Dish Loading**, **Detergent Inserting**, **Dish Cleaning & Drying**, and **Dish Unloading**, in that sequence. **Dish Loading** changes **Dishwasher** from **empty** to **loaded**. **Detergent Inserting** requires **Soap**. **Detergent Inserting** changes **Soap Compartment** from **empty** to **loaded**. **Dish Cleaning & Drying** requires **Dishwasher**. **Dish Cleaning & Drying** consumes **Soap**. **Dish Cleaning & Drying** changes **Cleanliness** of **Dish Set** from **dirty** to **clean**. **Dish Unloading** changes **Dishwasher** from **loaded** to **empty**.
End of **Dish Washing System** OPM model specification	

- Out-zooming provides for incorporating the *middle-out* approach to conceptual modeling by simplifying a complicated OPD while adding an interim level of detail.
- *Semantic strength* of a procedural link is the significance of the information that the link carries.
- *Link precedence* is an ordered list of procedural links with diminishing sematic strength.
- The *primary link precedence* is Consumption = Result > Effect > Agent > Instrument.
- *View creating* is collecting model facts from various OPDs in the OPD set and putting them together in a new OPD called *View* for the purpose of demonstrating a specific aspect.
- An *OPD model specification* is the collection of successive OPDs in the system's OPD tree.
- An *OPL model specification* is the collection of successive OPL paragraphs corresponding to the OPDs in the system's OPD tree, from which duplicate OPL sentences were removed.
- An *OPM model specification* is a side-by-side presentation of the OPD model specification and the OPL model specification, where to the right of each OPD the corresponding OPL paragraph is presented.

21.22 Problems

1. Based on Fig. 21.1, create an OPM model that explains the two specializations of decomposition, what they mean, and which kind is used by what language.
2. Present on object with four states and a process that affects it.
3. Suppress the states that are not relevant to the model in the previous question and add the incomplete state symbol.
4. Model a complex object with three levels of unfolding, including aggregation unfolding and exhibition unfolding.
5. Select two subprocesses from Fig. 21.6. For each, apply new-diagram in-zooming and add model elements as you see fit.
6. Perform out-zooming from the in-zoomed processes in the two OPDs created in the previous problem.
7. What is the ultimate OPD of the system in Fig. 21.6?
8. Is the process in Fig. 21.6 synchronous or asynchronous? Explain.
9. Is the process in Fig. 21.17 synchronous or asynchronous? Explain.

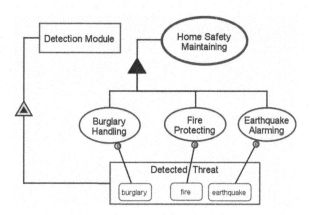

Fig. 21.17 **Home Safety Maintaining** system—a partial model

10. Draw an in-zoomed map of part of the Mid-West of the USA with at least six states, where each state is an object, while maintaining approximate spatial relations among the states.

11. In Fig. 21.13, change the OPDs inside **SDn** and **SDn+1** such that a need to invoke the procedural link precedence shall arise.

12. For the model in the previous problem, create the **Semi Zoomed OPD** analogous to that in Fig. 21.13.

13. In Fig. 21.14, define TO as {**P3**, **P4**, **P5**, **BK**}, perform the out-zooming, and show the resulting **SD**[new], **SD1**[new], **SD1.1**[new], and **SD1.1.1**[new].

OPM Operational Semantics and Control Links

> *Control Flow Semantics presents a unified, formal treatment of the semantics of a wide spectrum of control flow notions as found in sequential, concurrent, logic, object-oriented, and functional programming languages.*
>
> de Bakker and de Vink (1996)

To control the flow of system execution, OPM has precise operational semantics, based on the event-condition-action paradigm and expressed by modifying the procedural links with control modifiers—event and condition symbols. This is the focus of this chapter.

22.1 The Event-Condition-Action Control Mechanism

The OPM process activation mechanism is the way OPM deploys the *event-condition-action* (ECA) paradigm, mentioned in Dittrich et al. (1995) to structure active rules in event driven architecture and active database systems. ECA follows the rule "*On event if condition then action,*" namely, if an event occurs, and an associated condition is fulfilled at the time of the event occurrence, then the associated action is triggered. In OPM terminology, *action* is an OPM process. Such a rule traditionally consisted of three parts, which are listed below along with their OPM interpretations.

- The *event* part specifies the object—the *trigger*, or the object's state or value that triggers the process.

- The *condition* part is a logical test that, if satisfied or evaluates to true, enables the action to be carried out; in OPM the condition is evaluated on the preprocess object set.

- The *action* part consists of updates or invocations on the local data; in OPM this amounts to activating the process, which, upon completion, transforms one or more objects.

The ECA paradigm provide the basis for OPM operational semantics and flow of execution control. At the point in time of object creation, or appearance of the object from the system's perspective, or entrance of an object to a particular state, an event occurs.

> *An **event** is a point in time at which something significant to the system execution happens.*

The object or object state involved in the event can be the source of a procedural link. At runtime, i.e., at the instance level during the system's execution, the occurrence of that event initiates evaluation of the

D. Dori, *Model-Based Systems Engineering with OPM and SysML*, DOI 10.1007/978-1-4939-3295-5_22

precondition for every process to which the object is a source of the link, and the event ceases to exist. If and only if the evaluation reveals satisfaction of the precondition, then the process starts executing. Events can occur also through the end of a subprocess inside an in-zoomed process, as well as through invocation link and exception link, which occur between processes. Thus, according to the event-condition-action paradigm, starting the performance of a process (the "action") has two prerequisites: (1) an initiating event (the "event"), and (2) satisfaction of a precondition (the "condition"). Events and preconditions in concert specify OPM flow of execution control for process performance. The flow of execution control is the consequence of successive event-condition-action sequences that begin with initiation of the system function by an external event and end when the system function either completes executing successfully or terminates abnormally.

22.2 Precondition, Preprocess and Postprocess Object Sets

Every process has a preprocess object set with at least one object, possibly in a specified state. The preprocess object set of a process determines the precondition that must be satisfied before performance of that process starts. The preprocess object set may simply include the existence of one or more objects, possibly in specified states, but it can also be complex and include compound logical expressions using logical AND, OR, and XOR operators. Typical objects in a preprocess object set are transformees—consumees and/or affectees, and enablers. Some of these objects may have a further stipulation regarding flow of execution control, expressed as a condition link, which, as explained below, provides for skipping the process if its precondition is not satisfied.

The postprocess object set determines the process postcondition that the process completion satisfies. Typical objects in a postprocess object set are resultees and affectees.

The intersection of the preprocess object set and the postprocess object set of the same process includes the process enablers and affectees. Consumees are only members of the preprocess object set, while resultees are only members of the postprocess object set.

The involved object set is the union of the preprocess and postprocess object sets. If the involved object set has only one object, it must be a transformee, otherwise it does not conform to the OPM definition of process as a thing that transforms at least one object. Therefore, in a complete OPM model, each process must be linked with at least one transformee, and an OPM modeling tool should check this as a basic part of its model validation.

22.3 Kinds of Control Links

As part of the event-condition-action paradigm underlying OPM's operational semantics, an event link, a condition link, and an exception link express an event, a condition, and a time exception, respectively. These three link kinds are OPM's control links. Control links occur either between an object and a process or between two processes.

Event and condition links do not exist independently. Rather, they are modified versions of the various procedural links. Each procedural link from an object or a state to a process (i.e., object or state in the preprocess object state) has a corresponding event link and a corresponding condition link.

> A **control modifier** is one of the two letter symbols **e** and **c**, added to a procedural link, which add to the semantics of that link the event and condition semantics, respectively.
>
> A **control link** is a procedural link with the addition of a control modifier.

There is no result event link or result condition link, since these are outgoing procedural links, relating to the postprocess object set. When a process completes, it creates the postprocess object set without further condition. Hence, assuming that the process terminates successfully, creation of resultees and change of affectees are automatic and unconditional.

22.4 **Event Links**

> A process **event semantics** is the initiation of that process, which triggers evaluation of that process' precondition.
>
> An **event link** is a procedural link with the control modifier **e**, indicating the addition of event semantics to the link's destination process.

An event link specifies a source event and a destination process—the process that is initiated upon the event occurrence. The event occurrence triggers evaluation of the process' precondition. Satisfying the precondition allows process performance (execution) to proceed, rendering the process active. If the process precondition is not satisfied, then process performance shall not occur. Regardless of whether the evaluation is successful or not, being a point in time, the event is lost. If the process precondition is not satisfied, process initiation shall not occur until another event activates the process.

22.4.1 Initiating a Non-first Subprocess via an Event Link

If an event link is attached to a process P, and P is in-zoomed, like all the other procedural links attached to P, the event link migrates automatically to the first (top-most) subprocess—the one that executes first. The modeler must be very cautious when modeling an event link that is attached to any subprocess other than the first one, because this is akin to interfering with the inner operation of a black box! While trying to trigger a non-first subprocess, one or more of that subprocess' preconditions may not be met because previous subprocesses were skipped. For example, if in Fig. 6.2 the event link is attached to **Message Creating** rather than to **Crash Severity Measuring**, the latter process is skipped, so **Crash Severity** remains none, and therefore **Message Creating** will be skipped too. Moreover, since there is no **Message**, **Help Sending** is also skipped, leaving **Vehicle Occupants Group** at their initial **possibly injured** state, rather than **being helped**.

22.4.2 Enabling and Transforming Event Links

There are two kinds of transforming event links (Table 22.1) and two enabling event links (Table 22.2).

Table 22.1. Enabling event link summary

Name	Semantics	Sample OPD & OPL	Source	Destination
Agent event link	The agent—a human—both initiates and enables the process. The agent must be present throughout the process duration.	 **Miner** initiates and handles **Copper Mining.**	initiating agent	initiated process
Instrument event link	The object initiates the process as an instrument, so it does not change, but it must exist throughout the process duration.	 **Drill** initiates **Copper Mining,** which requires **Drill.**	initiating instrument	initiated process

Table 22.2. Transforming event link summary

Name	Semantics	Sample OPD & OPL	Source	Destination
Consumption event link	The object initiates the process, which, if performed, consumes the object.	 **Food** initiates **Eating,** which consumes **Food.**	initiating consumee	initiated process, which consumes the initiating consumee
Effect event link	The object initiates the process, which, if performed, affects the object. The event link is the link from the object to the process; the link from the process to the object is not an event link.	 is abstracted as: **Copper** initiates **Purifying,** which affects **Copper.**	initiating affectee	initiated process, which affects the initiating affectee

22.4.3 State-Specified Enabling and Transforming Event Links

Table 22.3 describes the two state-specified enabling event links—one for agent, the other for instrument. There are four kinds of state-specified transforming event links. These are summarized in Table 22.4.

Table 22.3 State-specified enabling event link summary

Name	Semantics	Sample OPD & OPL	Source	Destination
State-specified agent event link	The human agent in the specified state both initiates the process and acts as its agent. The agent must be at the specified state throughout the process duration.	 **Healthy Miner** initiates and handles **Copper Mining.**	agent state	initiated process
State-specified instrument event link	The object at the specified state both initiates the process and is instrument for its performance. The instrument must be at the specified state throughout the process duration.	 **Operational Drill** initiates **Copper Mining**, which requires **operational Drill.**	instrument state	initiated process

22.4.4 Invocation Links

Process invocation is an event by which a process initiates a process. An invocation link connects a source process to the destination process that it initiates, signifying that when the source process completes successfully, it immediately initiates the destination process—the process at the destination end of the invocation link. In a normal or expected flow of execution control, the source process does not initiate the new process if the former does not complete successfully. It is up to the modeler to take care of modeling what should happen with any process that aborts, e.g., due to a time exception.

Since by definition an OPM process transforms an object, the invocation link semantically implies the creation of an interim object by the invoking source process that the subsequent invoked destination process immediately consumes. As discussed in Sect. 10.10.3 in an OPM model, an invocation link may replace a transient, short-lived physical or informatical object that a source process creates to initiate the destination process, which immediately consumes the transient object. The physical object **Spark** in Fig. 10.11 is one example; **Record ID** in a query is another.

Graphically, a lightening symbol jagged (and possibly curved) line from the invoking source process to the invoked destination process ending with a closed arrowhead at the invoked process denotes an invocation link. This is the symbol of the common invocation link.

Table 22.4 State-specified transforming event link summary

Name	Semantics	Sample OPD & OPL	Source	Destination
State-specified consumption event link	The source state triggers the process, and if the precondition is satisfied, the process consumes the object.	**Food** — non edible, edible → e Eating **Edible Food** initiates **Eating**, which consumes **Food.**	consumee state	consuming process
Input-output-specified effect event link pair (consisting of one state-specified *event input link* and one state-specified *output link*)	The source state triggers the process, and if the precondition is satisfied, the process changes the object from the source state to the output state.	**Copper** — raw, pure — e Purifying **Raw Copper** initiates **Purifying**, which changes **Copper** from **raw** to **pure.**	affectee input (source) state	affecting process
			affecting process	affectee output (destination) state
Input-specified effect event link pair (consisting of one state-specified *event input link* and one state-unspecified *output link*)	The source state triggers the process, and if the precondition is satisfied, the process changes the object from the source state to some state of the source object.	**Sample** — awaiting test, passed test, failed test — e Testing **Awaiting test Sample** initiates **Testing**, which changes **Sample** from **awaiting test.**	affectee input (source) state	affecting process
			affecting process	affectee
Output-specified effect event link pair (consisting of one state-unspecified *event input link* and one state-specified *output link*)	The source object triggers the process, and if the precondition is satisfied, the process changes the object from some state to the destination (output) state of the object.	**Engine Hood** — rusty, oily, painted — e Cleaning & Painting **Engine Hood** initiates **Cleaning & Painting**, which changes **Engine Hood** to **painted.**	affectee	affecting process
			affecting process	affectee output (destination) state

Table 22.5 Invocation link summary

Name	Semantics	Sample OPD & OPL	Source	Destination
Invocation link	As soon as the invoking process ends, it invokes the process pointed to by the invocation link.	*Product Finishing* → *Product Shipping* **Product Finishing** invokes **Product Shipping**.	Initiating process	Another initiated process
Self-invocation link	Upon completion, the process immediately invokes itself.	*Recurrent Processing* **Recurrent Processing** invokes itself.	Initiating process	The same process

There is a second kind of invocation link—self-invocation link, which enables modeling invocation of a process by itself: Upon process completion, the process immediately invokes itself. A self-invocation link is symbolized by a pair of invocation links, originating at the process and joining head to tail before ending back at the original process shall denote the self-invocation link. Invocation links are summarized in Table 22.5. If a waiting period is needed between two consecutive invocations, a **Waiting** process with specified time constraints (see below) can be inserted as a destination from the invoking process and as a target back to the same process. An invocation link from the last subprocess to its parent in-zoomed process can be used to create loops.

22.5 Condition Links

*A process **condition semantics** is skipping the execution of that process if its precondition is not met.*

*A **condition link** is a procedural link with the control modifier c, indicating the addition of condition semantics to the link's destination process.*

A condition link provides a bypass mechanism, which enables system execution control to skip, or bypass, the destination process if its precondition satisfaction evaluation fails. Without the condition link bypass mechanism, failure to satisfy the precondition causes the process to wait for another event.

Upon the arrival of the new event, that process precondition is evaluated again, and if it is satisfied, the process starts executing, otherwise it is again waiting for the next event. This can cause the control to get stuck indefinitely in that process in an infinite loop. Using the condition link prevents such situations.

As discussed in Sect. 21.17, as is the case with all control links, if a condition link is attached to a process P, and P is in-zoomed, the condition link migrates automatically to the first subprocess (or two or more first concurrent subprocesses) of P. The modeler may move the link from that first subprocess to another subprocess or add another link from the same source to one or more subprocesses other than the first one.

22.5.1 Skipping Takes Precedence Over Waiting

A preprocess object set may include both condition links and non-condition links, i.e. procedural links without the condition control modifier. The distinguishing aspect of condition links is their skip semantics—skipping or bypassing a process if the source object operational instance of the condition link does not exist or is not a the required state. Without the condition control modifier, the non-existence of an operational instance of the procedural link source object causes the process to wait for another event and operational instances of all source objects to exist, possibly in a specified state, thus satisfying the precondition.

Meeting all the conditions associated with all the objects or states in the preprocess object set connected with condition links is necessary to satisfy the precondition and start the process. If the preprocess object set has one or more objects or states connected with non-condition links and one or more objects or states connected with condition links, a conflict may arise between the wait semantics induced by the non-condition link(s) and the skip semantics induced by the condition link(s). To resolve the conflict, the skip semantics is defined to be stronger than wait semantics, as stated by the following *skip semantics precedence OPM principle*.

The Skip Semantics Precedence OPM Principle

Skip semantics takes precedence over wait semantics.

Even if just one of the conditions associated with the condition links connecting with the process does not exist, the precondition satisfaction evaluation shall fail, execution control skips the process, and an event occurs that initiates the next sequential process (or the next two or more parallel processes).

Conditions associated with condition links *are the first to be considered* during precondition evaluation, because if they are not met, the process being considered for execution is skipped, regardless of the evaluation result of the remaining part of its precondition. If the skipped process is within an in-zoom context and there is a subsequent process in this context, execution control initiates that next process, otherwise execution control transfers back to the in-zoomed process.

There are two kinds of basic condition links: condition transforming links and condition enabling links.

22.5.2 Condition Transforming Links

A *condition consumption link* connects a consumee to a process with the addition of the control modifier **c**. Table 22.6 summarizes the basic condition transforming links.

Table 22.6 Condition transforming link summary

Name	Semantics	Sample OPD & OPL	Source	Destination
Condition consumption link	If an object instance exists and the rest of the process precondition is satisfied, then the process performs and consumes the object instance, otherwise execution control advances to initiate the next process.	 **Process** occurs if **Object** exists, in which case **Process** consumes **Object**, otherwise **Process** is skipped.	Conditioning object	Conditioned process
Condition effect link	If an object instance exists and the rest of the process precondition is satisfied, then the process performs and affects the object instance, otherwise execution control advances to initiate the next process.	 **Process** occurs if **Object** exists, in which case **Process** affects **Object**, otherwise **Process** is skipped.	Conditioning object	Conditioned process

If at runtime (i.e., during execution of the system model) a consumee instance exists when an event initiates the process, then the presence of that consumee instance satisfies the process precondition with respect to that object. If evaluation of the entire precondition, which accounts for the entire preprocess object set (of which the consumee is a part) is satisfied, the process starts and consumes that consumee instance. However, if a consumee instance does not exist when an event initiates the process, then, regardless of the rest of the preprocess object set, the process precondition evaluation fails, and the flow of execution control bypasses (skips) the process without executing that process.

A *condition effect link* like its regular, non-condition effect link counterpart, connects an affectee to a process, with the addition of the control modifier **c**. If at runtime an affectee instance exists when an event initiates the process, then the presence of that affectee instance satisfies the process precondition with respect to that object. As with the condition consumption link, if evaluation of the entire precondition, which accounts for the entire preprocess object set (of which the affectee is a part) is satisfied, the process starts and affects that affectee instance, but if not, then the process precondition evaluation fails, and the flow of execution control bypasses the process without executing that process.

22.5.3 Condition Enabling Links

There are two kinds of basic (non-state-specified) condition enabling links: condition agent link and condition instrument link. A *condition agent link* is an agent link from an agent to a process with the addition of the control modifier **c**. If at runtime an agent instance exists when an event initiates the process, then the presence of that agent instance satisfies the process precondition with respect to that object. If evaluation of the remaining precondition is satisfied as well, the process starts and that agent handles its performance. However, if an agent instance does not exist when an event initiates the process, then the process precondition evaluation fails and the flow of execution control bypasses, or 'skips' the process without process performance.

A *condition instrument link* is an instrument link from an instrument to a process, annotated with the control modifier **c**. If at runtime an instrument instance exists when an event initiates the process, then the presence of that instrument instance satisfies the process precondition with respect to that object. If evaluation of the entire preprocess object set satisfies the precondition, the process starts. However, if an instrument instance does not exist when an event initiates the process, then the process precondition evaluation fails and the flow of execution control bypasses, or 'skips' the process without process performance (Table 22.7).

Table 22.7 Condition enabling link summary

Name	Semantics	Sample OPD & OPL	Source	Destination
Agent condition link	The agent enables the process if the agent is present, otherwise the process is skipped.	 **Engineer** handles **Part Designing** if **Engineer** is present, otherwise **Part Designing** is skipped.	conditioning agent	conditioned process
Instrument condition link	The instrument enables the process if it exists, otherwise the process is skipped.	 **Precise Measuring** occurs if **LASER Meter** exists, otherwise **Precise Measuring** is skipped.	conditioning instrument	conditioned process

Figure 22.1 is an OPD with a condition instrument link from **Nearby Mobile Device** to **Cellular Network Signal Amplifying**, which occurs only if an environmental object **Nearby Mobile Device** exists and is otherwise skipped, as there is no point in amplifying if no device is nearby. Table 22.6 summarizes the basic condition transforming links.

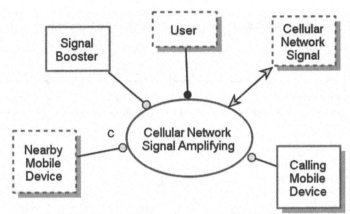

Cellular Network Signal Amplifying occurs if **Nearby Mobile Device** exists, otherwise
Cellular Network Signal Amplifying is skipped.

Fig. 22.1 Condition instrument link (with partial OPL)

22.5.4 Condition State-Specified Transforming Links

Like their event state-specified transforming link counterparts, there are four kinds of condition state-specified transforming links. These are summarized in Table 22.8.

22.5.5 Condition State-Specified Enabling Links

Like their regular, non-state-specified counterparts, there are two state-specified enabling links: state-specified agent link and state-specified instrument link.

A *condition state-specified agent link* is a state-specified agent link, annotated with the control modifier **c**, from a specified state of an agent to a process. If at runtime an instance of the agent exists, or is present, at the specified state when an event initiates the process, then this satisfies the process precondition with respect to that object. If evaluation of the entire preprocess object set satisfies the precondition, the process starts and that agent has to be present to handle it until it ends. Otherwise, the process precondition evaluation fails and the flow of execution control bypasses, or 'skips', performing the process.

> A *condition state-specified instrument link* is a state-specified instrument link, annotated with the control modifier **c**, from a specified state of an instrument to a process.

Table 22.8 Condition state-specified transforming link summary

Name	Semantics	Sample OPD & PL	Source	Destination
Condition state-specified consumption link	The process performs if the object is in the state from which the link originates, otherwise the process is skipped.	Raw Material Sample pre-approved approved c Testing **Testing** occurs if **Raw Material Sample** is **pre-approved**, in which case **Raw Material Sample** is consumed, otherwise **Testing** is skipped.	conditioning specified state of the object	conditioned process
Condition input-output-specified effect link	The process performs if the object is in the input state (from which the link originates) and changes the object from its input state to its output state, otherwise the process is skipped.	Raw Material pre-tested tested c Testing **Testing** occurs if **Raw Material** is **pre-tested**, in which case **Testing** changes **Raw Material** from **pre-tested** to **tested**, otherwise **Testing** is skipped.	conditioning specified input state of the object	conditioned process
Condition input-specified effect link	The process performs if the object is in the input state (from which the link originates) and changes the object from its input state to any one of its states, otherwise the process is skipped.	Message created delivered c Delivery Attempting **Delivery Attempting** occurs if **Message** is **created**, in which case **Delivery Attempting** changes **Message** from **created**, otherwise **Delivery Attempting** is skipped.	conditioning specified input state of the object	conditioned process

Condition output-specified effect link	The process performs if the object is in the input state (from which the link originates) and changes the object from its input state to any one of its states, otherwise the process is skipped.	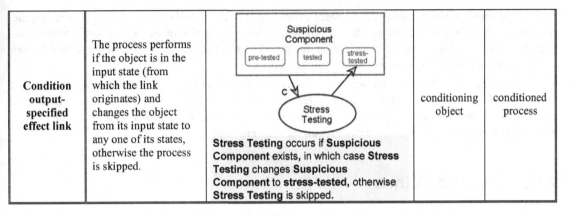 **Stress Testing** occurs if **Suspicious Component** exists, in which case **Stress Testing** changes **Suspicious Component** to **stress-tested**, otherwise **Stress Testing** is skipped.	conditioning object	conditioned process

Table 22.9 Condition state-specified enabling link summary

Name	Semantics	Sample OPD & OPL	Source	Destination
State-specified agent condition link	The agent enables the process if the agent is in the specified state, otherwise the process is skipped.	**Engineer** handles **Critical Part Designing** if **Engineer** is **safety design authorized**, otherwise **Critical Part Designing** is skipped.	conditioning specified state of agent	conditioned process
State-specified instrument condition link	The instrument enables the process if it is in the specified state, otherwise the process is skipped.	**Ultra-Precision Measuring** occurs if **LASER Meter** is **periodically calibrated**, otherwise **Precise Measuring** is skipped.	conditioning specified state of instrument	conditioned process

If at runtime an instance of the instrument exists and is at the specified state when an event initiates the process, then the process precondition is satisfied with respect to that object. If evaluation of the entire preprocess object set satisfies the precondition, the process starts and that instrument must remain existent and at the same state throughout the duration of the process

If at runtime an instance of the instrument does not exist or exists at a different state than the one attached to the link source, then the process precondition with respect to that object is not satisfied, the process precondition evaluation fails, and the flow of execution control bypasses performing the process. Table 22.9 summarizes the condition state-specified enabling links.

22.6 Exception Links

Exception links enable modeling what to do in case of exception in the time execution of a process below a minimal threshold or above a maximal one.

22.6.1 Process Time Duration and Its Distribution

Process may have a **Duration** property (metamodel attribute) with a value expressed in time units, which shall be compatible with ISO 80000-3:2006—*Quantities and units—Part 3: Space and time*, which is part of the group of ISO/IEC 80000 standards that form the *International System of Quantities*. Units of time can be milliseconds [ms], seconds [sec], minutes [min], hours [hr], days [dy], weeks [wk], months [mo], or years [yr]. **Duration** may specialize into **Minimal Duration**, **Expected Duration**, and **Maximal Duration**. **Minimal Duration** and **Maximal Duration** designate the minimum and maximum allowable time for process completion. Time duration is an optional, and, as Fig. 22.2 shows, the modeler can choose to indicate only the expected (nominal) time, minimal and maximal, or all three durations.

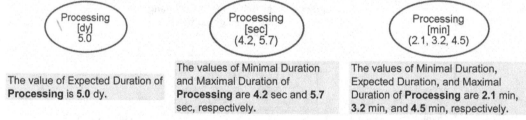

The value of Expected Duration of **Processing** is 5.0 dy.	The values of Minimal Duration and Maximal Duration of **Processing** are **4.2** sec and **5.7** sec, respectively.	The values of Minimal Duration, Expected Duration, and Maximal Duration of **Processing** are **2.1** min, **3.2** min, and **4.5** min, respectively.

Fig. 22.2 Three ways to indicate process duration: Left—expected (nominal) time only, middle—minimal and maximal, right—minimal, expected, and maximal time durations

The value of the process' **Expected Duration** is the statistical mean of the duration of that process. **Duration** optionally exhibits the **Duration Distribution** attribute with a value identifying the name and parameters for a probability distribution function associated with the process duration or a non-analytical distribution. At run-time, the value of **Duration** is determined separately for each process instance (i.e., for each individual process occurrence) by sampling from the process **Duration Distribution**. The **Duration** property provides for defining exception links. There are two kinds of exception link: overtime exception link and undertime exception link.

22.6.2 Overtime Exception Link

The overtime exception link connects the source process with a destination overtime handling process to specify that if at runtime, the performance time of the source process instance exceeds its **Maximal Duration** value, then an event initiates the destination process, which is an overtime handling process.

> *A **maximal-timed process** is a process for which the modeler determines a maximal duration.*
>
> *An **overtime handling process** is a time exception process that determines what to do in case the time performance of a maximal-timed process exceeds its maximal allowable time.*
>
> *An **overtime exception link** is a procedural link from a maximal-timed process to an overtime handling process, indicating that if the duration of a maximal-timed process exceeds its maximal duration, then the overtime exception process is initiated.*

The control modifier for the overtime exception link is a single slanted short bar crossing the link near the overtime exception process (see Fig. 22.3 for the control modifier of the undertime exception link, which is a pair of such bars).

22.6.3 Undertime Exception Link

The undertime exception link connects the source process with a destination undertime handling process to specify that if at runtime the performance time of the source process instance is below its **Minimal Duration** value, then an event initiates the destination process, which is an undertime handling process.

> *A **minimal-timed process** is a process for which the modeler determines a minimal duration.*
>
> *An **undertime handling process** is a time exception process that determines what to do in case the time performance of a minimal timed process falls short of its minimal duration.*
>
> *An **undertime exception link** is a procedural link from a minimal-timed process to an undertime exception process, indicating that if the time performance of a timed process falls short of its minimal allowable time, the undertime exception process is initiated.*

The control modifier for the undertime exception link is a pair of parallel slanted close short bars crossing the link near the overtime exception process. Figure 22.3 is an example of **Undertime Exception Handling**. Here, {instance id=2} is a particular instance (occurrence) of **Processing**, whose **Duration** is **3.4** min. Since this value is less than **30.0** min—the minimal time duration defined for the process class **Processing**, **Undertime Exception Handling** takes place.

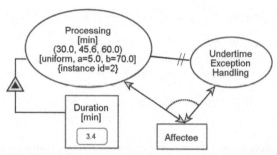

The values of Minimal Duration, Expected Duration, and Maximal Duration of **Processing** are **30.0** min, **45.6** min, and **60.0** min, respectively.
The Duration Distribution of **Processing** is **uniform** with parameters **a=5.0** and **b=70.0**.
Either **Processing** or **Undertime Exception Handling** affects **Affectee**.
Undertime Exception Handling occurs if duration of **Processing** falls short of **30.0** min.
Duration of **Processing** instance id=2 is **3.4** min.

Fig. 22.3 Undertime exception example

A source process may have both overtime and undertime links, each connected to a different destination time exception handling process. Suppose in the example in Fig. 22.3 we add an **Overtime Exception Handling** process, then the additional OPL sentence would be:

Overtime Exception Handling occurs if duration of **Processing** exceeds **60.0** min.

Unlike most procedural links, which connect an object and a process, but similar to the invocation link, the two time exception links are procedural links that connect two processes directly. An implicit interim object **Overtime Exception Message** or **Undertime Exception Message** is created by the OPM's process execution mechanism upon realizing that the process failed to terminate by the maximal allotted time or ended prematurely, falling short of the minimal allotted time, respectively. Since the OPM operational mechanism creates and immediately consumes these objects, their depiction is not explicit in the model. This is similar to the invocation link, which suppresses the creation of an interim object by the source process and its immediate consumption by the destination process. Table 22.10 summarizes the two time exception links.

The exceptions these links handle relate only to time, but they can also be used for modeling execution exceptions. For instance, if a process with minimal time duration attached to an undertime exception link is skipped, which means its duration was 0, then the exception handling process is initiated.

22.7 Transformation Rate

Often the need arises to model consumption of a consumee or effect on an affectee or creation of a resultee not as a one-time event but rather as a continuous process or a discrete process with a quantity larger than 1, transformed over time. We have defined *property* as an attribute of an OPM element. For example, **Perseverance** is a property of OPM **Thing**. If the value of that property is **persistent**, the **Thing** is an **Object**; if it is **transient**—it is a **Process**. In other words, we can say that a property is an attribute at the metamodel level, where **Thing** and **Link** are **OPM Elements**. **Perseverance** is an example of a property of a **Thing**. **Transformation Rate** is a property of a (transforming) **Link**.

Table 22.10 Time exception links summary

Name	Semantics	Sample OPD & OPL	Source	Destination
Overtime exception link	If in runtime the process instance takes more than the maximal process class duration, the overtime exception handling process is invoked	Processing [min] (30.0, 45.6, 60.0) [normal, 45.6, 7.3 — Overtime Exception Handling. **Engineer** handles **Critical Part Designing** if **Engineer** is **safety design authorized,** otherwise **Critical Part Designing** is skipped.	process with maximal time specification	overtime exception handling process
Undertime exception link	If in runtime the process instance takes less than the minimal process class duration, the undertime exception handling process is invoked	Processing [min] (30.0, 45.6, 60.0) [uniform, a=5.0, b=70.0] — Undertime Exception Handling. **Ultra-Precision Measuring** occurs if **LASER Meter** is **periodically calibrated,** otherwise **Precise Measuring** is skipped.	process with minimal time specification	undertime exception handling process

> ***Transformation rate*** *is a property of a procedural link connecting a transformee B and a process P whose value is the rate of transformation of B by P.*

Just as transformation specializes into consumption, effect, and result, so does transformation rate.

> ***Consumption rate*** *is the transformation rate of a consumption link connecting a consumee B and a process P whose value is the rate of consumption of B by P.*
>
> ***Yield rate*** *is the transformation rate of a result link connecting a resultee B and a process P whose value is the rate of creation of B by P.*
>
> ***Effect rate*** *is the transformation rate of an effect link connecting an affectee B and a process P whose value is the rate of affecting B by P.*

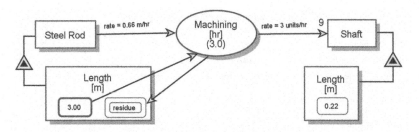

Steel Rod exhibits Length.
The value of Length of Steel Rod is initially 3.00 m and finally residue.
Shaft exhibits Length.
The value of Length of Shaft is 0.22 m.
The value of Expected Duration of Machining is 3.0 hr.
Machining consumes Steel Rod at a rate of 0.66 m/hr.
Machining yields 9 Shafts at a rate of 3 units/hr.

Fig. 22.4 Consumption rate and yield rate example

Effect rate can be expressed more specifically as state change rate.

> ***State change rate*** *is the transformation rate of an in-out link pair whose input and output links connect the input state b_i and output state b_o of an affectee B to a process P, whose value is the rate of changing the state of B by P from b_i to b_o.*

Figure 22.4 provides an example of consumption rate and yield rate. The modeler may create an exception if the quantity of the resultee or the consumee is less than the rate times the expected process duration.

22.8 Computing with OPM

OPM models can be used to carry out numeric calculations. The atomic processes for calculations are the four basic arithmetic operations **Adding**, **Subtracting**, **Multiplying**, and **Dividing**. These are used to devise more involved calculations such as **Averaging**, **Geometric Mean Computing**, etc. Care must be exercised with operations that are not commutative, like **Dividing**, where the roles of the **Dividend** and the **Divisor** must be explicit in order to get the correct **Quotient**. Since the mathematical expressions are much more compact and understood, once a sufficiently low level of computing is reached, the actual formulae can be recorded as parts of the calculating process names.

As an industrial example, suppose for the system in Fig. 22.4 we wish to compute the value of **residue**—the final value of **Length** of **Steel Rod** in meters after it has been cut. This is modeled in Fig. 22.5 by the process **Residue Length Computing** and Fig. 22.6, where **Residue Length Computing** is in-zoomed. The initial **Length** of the **Steel Rod**, **il**, is **3.00 m**. The **Machining** process, which lasts **3 hr**, consumes the **Steel Rod** at a consumption rate of **0.66 m/hr.**

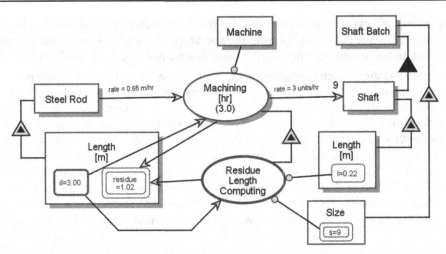

Residue Length Computing requires the value l=0.22 m of **Length** of **Shaft** and the value of **Size** s=9 of **Shaft Batch**. **Residue Length Computing** changes the value of **Length** of **Steel Rod** from il=3.00 m to **residue=1.02**.

Fig. 22.5 SD of the **Machining** system with **Residue Length Computing** as an operation of **Machining**

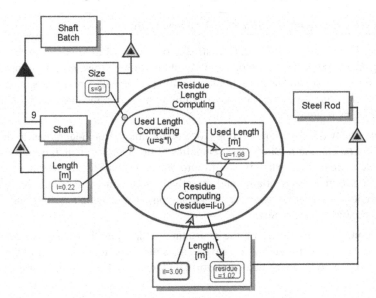

Residue Length Computing from SD zooms in SD1 into **Used Length Computing (u=s*l)** and **Residue Computing (residue=il-u)** in that sequence, as well as **Used Length** of **Steel Rod** in m.
Used Length Computing requires the value l=0.22 of **Length** of **Shaft** in m and the value s=9 of **Size** of **Shaft Set**.
Used Length Computing yields **Used Length** of **Steel Rod** in m with value u=1.98.
Residue Computing changes the value of **Length** of **Steel Rod** in m from il=3.00 to **residue=1.02**.

Fig. 22.6 SD1 of the **Machining** system from Fig. 22.5, in which **Residue Length Computing** is in-zoomed

The **Machining** process generates **Shaft** at a yield rate of **3 units/hr**, therefore in **3** hours we get **9 Shafts**, as indicated by the participation constraint near **Shaft**. The length of each **Shaft** is **0.22 m** and the **Size** of the **Shaft Batch** (cut during 3 hr) is **9**. All these data are provided in the model in Fig. 22.5.

Zooming into **Residue Length Computing** in Fig. 22.6, we see that it has two subprocesses. The first is **Used Length Computing (u=s*l)** and the second—**Residue Computing (residue=il−u)**. The names of the processes contain in parentheses the arithmetic expressions to be carried out by each process. The expression on the first subprocess computes **u**, the value of **Used Length** of **Rod**, as **u=s*l**. It takes **s=9** as the value of the **Size** of the **Shaft Batch** and **l=0.22 m** as the **Length** of each **Shaft**. The product, **u=s*l =9*0.22 =1.98 m**, is the input for the next subprocess, in which the model computes **residue=il-u**, since the length of the residue is the difference between **il**, the value of the initial **Length** of the **Rod**, **3.00 m**, and **u**, the value of **Used Length** of **Rod**, so **residue=il−u=3.00−0.22=1.02 m**. Different parameter values will, of course, yield different results. This example demonstrates how OPM enables mixing conceptual modeling with quantitative modeling which provides reasoning for the various mathematical steps involved in the computation.

22.9 Sets and Iterations

> *A **set** is a collection of object instances of the same class.*

An example of set is provided in Fig. 22.7. **Shaft Batch** is a set of nine object instances from the class **Shaft**, so creating **Shaft Batch** implies iteration of **Machining** nine times, each time producing one **Shaft**. This is a short formal way in OPM to model iteration: Whenever a process is attached with two procedural links of the same kind such that one is a link to a set of n members and the other to a member of the set, the semantics is iteration.

In our example, the two links are result links: one result link is from **Machining** to the set **Shaft Batch**, and the other—from **Machining** to **Shaft**. The semantics of this template is iteration nine times of creating **Shaft**. This is made more explicit when we zoom into **Machining** in SD1, expressing the fact that **Cutting** and **Lathing** are performed sequentially and iteratively nine times to yield the nine **Shafts**. Each **Machining** occurrence is a process instance of **Machining**, within which **Cutting** and **Lathing** occur to create each of the nine instances of **Shaft**.

Iteration can combine any subset of the procedural links. Iteration can, of course, be applied to informatical objects as well, providing a convenient, short way to model iterations, for example, in algorithms, and serve, among many other control constructs (such as Boolean objects), for automated code generation.

22.10 Operational Semantics in In-Zoomed Process Contexts

In-zooming of a process specifies transfer of execution control to subprocesses at the next detail level. Executing a process with an in-zoomed context recursively transfers execution control to the top-most subprocess(es) within the context of the deepest process. Control returns to the in-zoomed process after its last subprocess completes its execution (Fig. 22.8).

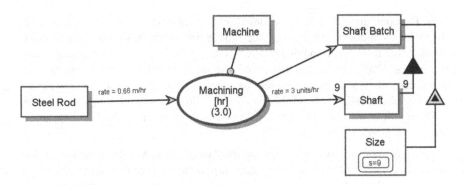

Fig. 22.7 SD of **Machining**, where **Shaft Batch** is a set of 9 object instances from the class **Shaft**, so creating **Shaft Batch** implies iteration of **Machining** nine times, each time producing one **Shaft**

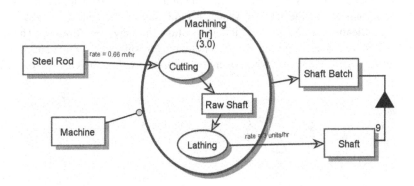

Fig. 22.8 SD1 of **Machining**, in which **Machining** is in-zoomed, expressing the fact that **Cutting** and **Lathing** are performed sequentially and iteratively 9 times to yield the nine **Shafts**

22.10.1 Implicit Invocation Link

> An ***implicit invocation link*** *is a link that is not visible graphically but is implied from the vertical layout of processes within the context of an in-zoomed process.*

Similar to its explicit counterpart, the implicit invocation link signifies initiation of a subsequent process or concurrently beginning processes. Since invocation is an event, satisfaction of the precondition for each subprocess is necessary to allow that subprocess to start executing.

An implicit invocation link can be (1) from a process to its first (or several) subprocess(es), (2) from a subprocess to one or more subprocesses just below it along the time line inside the context of an in-zoomed process, or (3) from the last in-zoomed subprocess(es) to their enclosing, context defining process.

Specifically, (1) upon arriving at an in-zoomed process context, control immediately transfers to the subprocess (es) with the highest ellipse (oval) top-most point within this in-zoomed process context. The implicit invocation link from an in-zoomed process to its top-most subprocess transfers execution control. (2) Along the process timeline, the completion of a source subprocess (or the last subprocess to finish executing in the case of two or more subprocesses that started concurrently) immediately initiates the subsequent subprocess(es) using the implicit invocation link. (3) Upon completion of performing the subprocess with an ellipse top-most point that is lowest within this in-zoomed process context, execution control returns to the in-zoomed process.

When two or more subprocesses have their top-most ellipse points at the same height, then an implicit invocation link initiates each process and they start in parallel upon individual precondition satisfaction. The process that completes last initiates the next subprocess or set of parallel subprocesses.

In the OPD on the left hand side of Fig. 22.9, **Cleaning** invokes **Coating**, so **Cleaning** affects **Product** first and then **Coating** affects **Product**. The invocation link dictates this process sequence. In the equivalent OPD on the right hand side of Fig. 22.9, **Finishing** zooms into **Cleaning** and **Coating**, with the former's ellipse top point above the latter's, so when **Finishing** starts, control immediately transfers to **Cleaning**, and when **Cleaning** ends, the implicit invocation link invokes **Coating**. The two OPDs are semantically equivalent, but the one on the left does not have **Finishing** as an enclosing context, making it less expressive from a system viewpoint while using two links more than the OPD on the left.

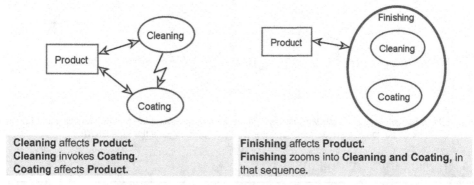

Fig. 22.9 Invocation link (left) and implicit invocation link (right)

22.10.2 Implicit Parallel Invocation Link Set

Graphically, when the ellipse top points of two or more subprocesses within the scope of an in-zoomed process are at the same height (with possible allowable tolerance), these subprocesses are initiated and begin in parallel, and each starts executing subject to the satisfaction of its precondition. In this situation, there is a set of implicit invocation links from the source in-zoomed process to each one of the parallel subprocesses. Process synchronization is such that when the last one of these subprocesses ends, execution control initiates the next subprocess(es). If there are two or more subprocesses with a lower ellipse–top point at the same height, the control initiates them in parallel. If there are no more subprocesses to invoke, control returns to the in-zoomed refineable process.

Figure 22.10 shows subprocesses of **Processing** with the following partial order: **A**, (**B**, **C**), **D**, (**E**, **F**, **G**). **B** and **C** start upon completion of **A**. **D** starts upon completion of the longer process from among **B** and **C**. **E**, **F**, and **G** start upon completion of **D**. Execution control returns to **Processing** upon completion of the longest process from among **E**, **F**, and **G**.

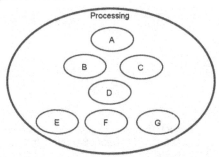

Processing zooms into **A**, parallel **B** and **C**, **D**, and parallel **E**, **F**, **G**, in that sequence.

Fig. 22.10 Partial subprocesses order and implicit parallel invocation link set

Table 22.11 summarizes the implicit invocation link kinds.

22.10.3 Link Distribution Across Context

Graphically, a procedural link attached to the contour of an in-zoomed process has distributive semantics. Leaving a link attached to the contour of the in-zoomed process means that the link is distributed and attached to each one of the subprocesses. The contour of the in-zoomed process has semantics analogous to that of algebraic parentheses following a multiplication symbol, which distribute the multiplication operator to the expressions inside the parentheses.

In Fig. 22.11, the OPDs on the left and right are equivalent, but the one on the left is clearer and less cluttered. An agent link from **A** to **P** means that **A** handles the subprocesses **P1**, **P2**, and **P3**. An instrument link from **B** to **P** means that the subprocesses **P1**, **P2**, and **P3** require **B**. Analogously in algebra, suppose the agent (or instrument) link was a multiplication operator, **A** was a multiplier and in-zooming was addition, such that **P** = **P1** + **P2** + **P3**, and **P** was a multiplicand, then **A*****P** = **A***(**P1** + **P2** + **P3**) = **A*****P1** + **A*****P2** + **A*****P3**.

If an enabler connects to the outer contour of an in-zoomed contour it must connect to at least one of its subprocesses. Consumption and result links must not be attached to the outer contour of an in-zoomed process because this violates temporal logical conditions. With a distributed consumption link, an attempt would be made to consume an already-consumed object by a subprocesses that is not the first to perform. Similarly, a distributed result link would attempt to create an already existing object instance. The modeler needs to be careful when more than one process creates the same object, i.e. more than one instance of the object exists, or two or more processes affect or consume the same object. OPM modeling tools need to track the number of instances of an object.

Table 22.11 Implicit invocation link summary

Name	Semantics	Sample OPD & OPL	Source	Destination
Implicit invocation link	Upon subprocess completion within the context of an in-zoomed process, the subprocess immediately invokes the one(s) below it.	 **Product Terminating** zooms into **Product Finishing** and **Product Shipping**, in that sequence.	Initiating process, whose ellipse top point is above the initiated process	Initiated process, whose ellipse top point is below the ellipse top point of the initiating process
Parallel implicit invocation link set	Top: Subprocesses A and B initiate in parallel as soon as Processing starts. Bottom: Subprocesses B and C initiate in parallel as soon as subprocess A ends.	 **Processing** zooms into parallel **A** and **B**. **Processing** zooms into **A** and parallel **B** and **C**, in that sequence.	Initiating process, whose ellipse top point is above the set of initiated processes, whose ellipse top points are at the same height (within a pre-determined tolerance).	A set of initiated processes, whose ellipse top points are at the same height (within tolerance) and below the initiating process ellipse top point

In Fig. 22.12, the OPD on the left contains invalid consumption and result links, as annotated in the OPL. The consumption link gives rise to the OPL sentence "**P** consumes **C**." The reason is that applying link distribution, the consequence is the three OPL sentences "**P1** consumes **C**.", "**P2** consumes **C**.", and "**P3** consumes **C**.". However, since **P1** consumes **C** first according to its temporal order, the same instance of **C** does not exist when **P2** or **P3** performs, and therefore neither **P2** nor **P3** can consume **C** again. Similarly, the same instance of **B** results only once. The OPD on the right depicts valid links since they specify which of the subprocesses of **P** consumes **C** (it is **P1**) and which one yields **B** (**P2**).

Since attaching a consumption or result link to an in-zoomed process is invalid, when a process is in-zoomed, all the consumption and result links that were attached to it shall be attached initially or by default to its first subprocess. It is the modeler's responsibility to move the links to subsequent subprocesses as needed.

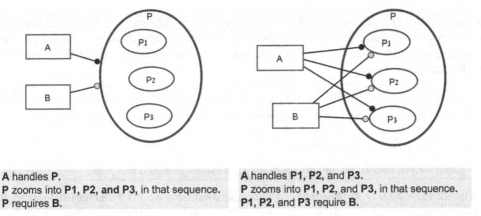

A handles **P**.
P zooms into **P1, P2, and P3**, in that sequence.
P requires **B**.

A handles **P1, P2**, and **P3**.
P zooms into **P1, P2**, and **P3**, in that sequence.
P1, P2, and **P3** require **B**.

Fig. 22.11 Link distribution across in-zooming context. Left: the shorter, correct version. Right: the equivalent loinger version

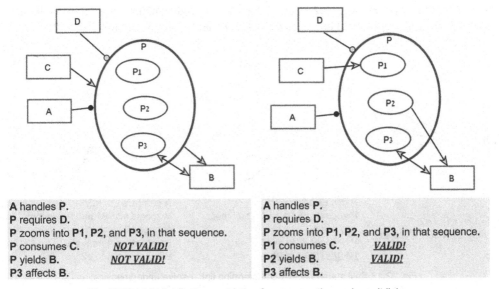

A handles **P**.
P requires **D**.
P zooms into **P1, P2**, and **P3**, in that sequence.
P consumes **C**.   *NOT VALID!*
P yields **B**.   *NOT VALID!*
P3 affects **B**.

A handles **P**.
P requires **D**.
P zooms into **P1, P2**, and **P3**, in that sequence.
P1 consumes **C**.   *VALID!*
P2 yields **B**.   *VALID!*
P3 affects **B**.

Fig. 22.12 Link distribution restriction for consumption and result links

As soon as the modeler in-zooms **P** in Fig. 22.12 and inserts **P1** into its context, the modeling tool should migrate the destination end of the consumption link emanating from **C** from **P** to **P1**. Similarly, the source end of the result link to **B** should also migrate from **P** to **P1**. When the modeler adds **P2**, the modeler may migrate the destination end of the consumption link and/or the source end of the result link from **P1** to **P2**, as Fig. 22.12 shows.

22.10.4 Split State-Specified Link Pairs

When a process that changes an object from an input state to an output state is in-zoomed, the OPD, either in-diagram or new-diagram, becomes underspecified. To restore specification, the modeler must attach both the state-specified input link and the state-specified output link to one of the subprocesses in a temporally-feasible manner.

> *A **split in-out-specified link pair** of process P is an input-output specified link pair whose input and output link constituents connect different subprocesses of P.*
>
> *A **split input link** is the input link of the split in-out-specified link pair.*
>
> *A **split output link** is the output link of the split in-out-specified link pair.*

In Fig. 22.13, the OPD in the middle is underspecified because if **P1** changes **A** from **s1** to **s2**, **P2** cannot do this again, but it can go the other way—change **A** from **s2** back to **s1**, but neither is explicitly specified. **P1** can change **A** from **s1**, i.e., take it out of **s1** and leave it in transition between **s1** and **s2**. In-between **P1** and **P2** there may be one or more other interim subprocesses, during which **A** is still in that transition. **P2** then changes **A** to **s2**. The OPD on the right models this case (without interim subprocesses), creating a split input link from **s1** of **A** to **P1** and a split output link from **P2** to **s2**.

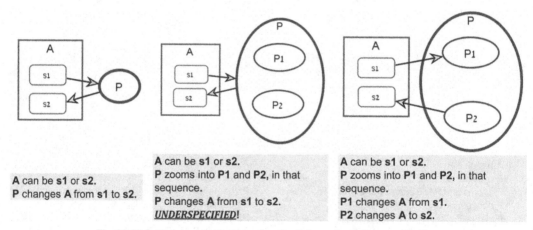

A can be **s1** or **s2**.
P changes **A** from **s1** to **s2**.

A can be **s1** or **s2**.
P zooms into **P1** and **P2**, in that sequence.
P changes **A** from **s1** to **s2**.
UNDERSPECIFIED!

A can be **s1** or **s2**.
P zooms into **P1** and **P2**, in that sequence.
P1 changes **A** from **s1**.
P2 changes **A** to **s2**.

Fig. 22.13 Split state-specified transforming link resolve underspecification

Table 22.12 summarizes the split input-output specified effect link pair. There are no control-modified versions of the split input-specified effect link, because this can cause the of effect link semantics to be distorted. For example, if in Fig. 22.13 **P1** is skipped, **A** stays in **s1**, so if **P2** is not skipped, **A** was not taken out of **s1**, so it cannot change to **s2** according to the semantics of the effect link.

Table 22.12 Split input-output specified effect link pair

Name	Semantics	Sample OPD & OPL	Source	Destination
Split input-output specified effect link pair *The top arrow:* split input link *The bottom arrow:* split output link	An early subprocess of an in-zoomed process takes an object out of its input state. A late subprocess of the same in-zoomed process changes the object to be in its output state.	 **P1 changes A from s1.** **P2 changes A to s2.**	*The top arrow:* Input state of an affected object *The bottom arrow:* Late subprocess of an in-zoomed process	*The top arrow:* Early subprocess of an in-zoomed process *The bottom arrow:* Output state of the affected object

22.11 Involved Object Set Instance Transformations

As a consequence of link distribution, the following constraints apply to operational instances of transformees.

- Each consumee instance in the preprocess object set of a process shall cease to exist at the beginning of the most detailed subprocess of the process that consumes the instance, so that instance is not a member of the postprocess object set of that process.

- Each affectee instance in the preprocess object set of a process that changes that instance as a consequence of the process performance shall exit from its input state at the beginning of the deepest (most detailed) subprocess that changes the affectee.

- Each affectee instance in the postprocess object set of a process that changes that operational instance as a consequence of the process performance shall enter its output state at the completion of the deepest subprocess that changes the affectee.

- Each resultee instance in the postprocess object set of a process shall be created and begin to exist at the completion of the most detailed subprocess that yields the resultee instance.

A stateful object B for which the execution of process P has the effect of changing the state of B, exits from the input state at the beginning of the most detailed subprocess of P that changes B, and enters the output state at the end of the same subprocess of P or some subsequent subprocess of P. Since process P execution takes a positive amount of time, that object B is in transition between states, from its input state to its output state: it has left its input state but has not yet arrived at its output state.

22.12 UML's Object Constraint Language (OCL)

The OPM Parameterized Participation Constraint (PPC) mini-language described in Sect. 17.3 is somewhat reminiscent of Object Constrain Language (OCL), developed by Warmer and Kleppe (1998). OCL is "*a precise text language that provides constraint and object query expressions that cannot be expressed by diagrammatic notation.*" The current OMG OCL version (OMG OCL 2014), explains the motivation for developing OCL by arguing that "*a UML diagram, such as a class diagram, is typically not refined enough to provide all the relevant aspects of a specification. There is, among other things, a need to describe additional constraints about the objects in the model. Such constraints are often described in natural language. Practice has shown that this will always result in ambiguities. ... OCL has been developed to fill this gap. It is a formal language that remains easy to read and write.*"

Comparing OPM's PPC mini-language to OCL, we note that while OCL is a complete language whose current OMG 2014 specification holds 262 pages, the PPC mini-language can be specified in a few pages. It is expressed in the OPD and translated as part of the OPL, and unlike OCL it does not provide for querying. With respect to the claim that OCL "remains easy to read and write" let us consider the constraint example provided in OMG OCL (2014, p. 20):

Married people are of age >= 18. The OCL syntax for this constraint is as follows.

context Person
inv: (self.wife->notEmpty() **implies** self.wife.age >= 18)
and (self.husband->notEmpty() **implies** self.husband.age >= 18)

The corresponding OPM model is provided in Fig. 22.14. The OPL of this model seems to be a bit more humanly comprehensible than the OCL specification above.

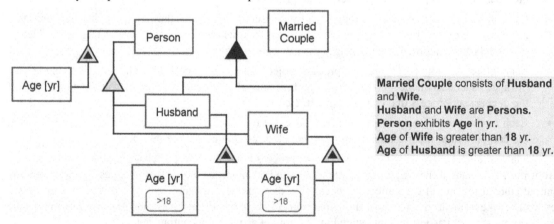

Married Couple consists of **Husband** and **Wife**.
Husband and **Wife** are **Persons**.
Person exhibits **Age** in yr.
Age of **Wife** is greater than **18** yr.
Age of **Husband** is greater than **18** yr.

Fig. 22.14 The OPM model of the constraint "Married people are of age >= 18"

22.13 **Summary**

- An *event* is a point in time at which something significant to the system execution happens.
- Events and preconditions in concert specify OPM flow of execution control for process performance according to the event-condition-action paradigm.
- The *event-condition-action* paradigm stipulates that starting the performance of a process (the "action") has two prerequisites: an initiating event and satisfaction of a precondition derived from the preprocess object set.
- A *control modifier* is one of the two letter symbols **e** and **c**, added to a procedural link, which add to the semantics of that link the event and condition semantics, respectively.
- A *control link* is a procedural link with the addition of a control modifier.
- An *event link* is a procedural link with the control modifier **e**, indicating initiation of the link's destination process, triggering that process' precondition evaluation.
- A *condition link* is a procedural link with the control modifier **c**, indicating that if the precondition of the link's destination process is not met, then that process is skipped.
- The *skip semantics precedence OPM principle* states that skip semantics, induced by a control link, takes precedence over wait semantics, induced by a non-control link.
- A *maximal-timed process* is a process for which the modeler determines a maximal duration.
- An *overtime handling process* is a time exception process that determines what to do in case the time performance of a maximal-timed process exceeds its maximal allowable time.
- An *overtime exception link* is a procedural link from a maximal-timed process to an overtime handling process, indicating that if the duration of a maximal-timed process exceeds its maximal duration, then the overtime exception process is initiated.
- A *minimal-timed process* is a process for which the modeler determines a minimal duration.
- An *undertime handling process* is a time exception process that determines what to do in case the time performance of a minimal timed process falls short of its minimal duration.
- An *undertime exception link* is a procedural link from a minimal-timed process to an undertime exception process, indicating that if the time performance of a timed process falls short of its minimal allowable time, the undertime exception process is initiated.

22.14 Problems

1. Why is the event link in Fig. 3.5 needed?
2. What is the role of the condition link in in Fig. 6.1?
3. Explain why in Fig. 7.1 two condition links are needed.
4. Use Fig. 21.15 as a template and replace **B**, **P**, **P1** and **P2** in it with meaningful things.
5. Explain why each one of the five entries in Table 21.1 marked "invalid" is indeed invalid.
6. Explain why in Fig. 21.13 **P123** (the set TO of thing to out-zoom) cannot contain **P4** and **BK** only.
7. What thing must be added to P4 and BK such that TO becomes valid?
8. Assuming TO is the set as you suggested in the previous question, draw the resulting **SD1.1[new]**.
9. Create the OPM model of uninterrupted irrigating by water as a consumee for the process irrigating. The consumee has an attribute quantity [liter] with value 1000 and the consumption link has a consumption rate [liter/sec] with value 50.
10. Create the OPM model of the following system. **Gasoline** and **Diesel Oil** are resultees of the process **Refining**, which consumes **Crude Oil**. The resultees **Gasoline** and **Diesel Oil** each have an attribute **Volume [m3]**. The **Refining** to **Gasoline** result link has yield rate **[m3/hour]** with value **1000** and the **Refining** to **Diesel Oil** result link has yield rate **[m3/hour]** with value **800**. Assuming there is enough **Crude Oil**, if **Refining** activates and performs for **10 hours**, it will yield **10,000 [m3]** of **Gasoline** and **8,000 [m3]** of **Crude Oil**.

Chapter 23
Logical Operators and Probabilities

Logic and probability theory are two of the main tools in the formal study of reasoning, and have been fruitfully applied in areas as diverse as philosophy, artificial intelligence, cognitive science and mathematics.

Stanford Encyclopedia of Philosophy (2013)

Logical operators, including AND, NOT, OR, and XOR (exclusive OR) enable modeling complex conditions on performance of processes. Using XOR, OPM can also assign probabilities to such outcomes as creating one of several possible objects, or an object in a specific state. We discuss these in this chapter.

23.1 Logical AND Procedural Links

Two or more procedural links of the same kind that originate from, or arrive at, different points along the process ellipse circumference (the process context), have the semantics of the logical AND operator. Graphically, the links with AND semantics do not touch each other on the process contour. We have been using this operator all along as the default without explicitly stating this, as it seems natural. Indeed, textually, the OPL reserved phrase "and" is used to express the logical AND.

The next three examples show the use of AND in various procedural links. In the OPD in Fig. 23.1 (right), the **Safe Opening** process requires both **Safe Owner A** *and* **Safe Owner B**. In Fig. 23.1 (left), opening the **Safe** requires all three keys.

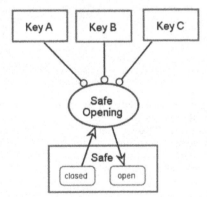

Safe can be **closed** or **open**.
Safe Opening requires **Key A, Key B, and Key C.**
Safe Opening changes Safe from **closed** to **open**.

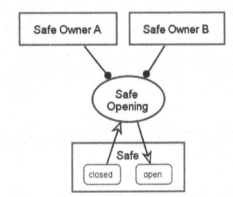

Safe can be **closed** or **open**.
Safe Owner A and Safe Owner B handle **Safe Opening.**
Safe Opening changes Safe from **closed** to **open**.

Fig. 23.1 Logical AND used with agent and instrument links

In Fig. 23.2 (left), **Meal Preparing** yields all three of the dishes. In Fig. 23.2 (right), **Meal Eating** consumes all three dishes.

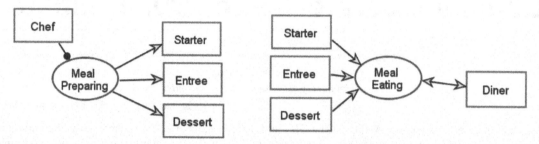

Chef handles **Meal Preparing**.   **Meal Eating** affects **Diner**.
Meal Preparing yields **Starter**, **Entree**, and **Dessert**.   **Meal Eating** consumes **Dessert**, **Entree**, and **Starter**.

Fig. 23.2 Logical AND used with result and consumption links

In the OPD on the left of Fig. 23.3, **Interest Rate Changing** affects the three objects **Exchange Rate**, **Price Index**, and **Interest Rate**. In the OPD on the right, all three effects of **Interest Rate Raising** on **Exchange Rate**, **Price Index**, and **Interest Rate** are made explicit via three pairs of in-out-specified effect links.

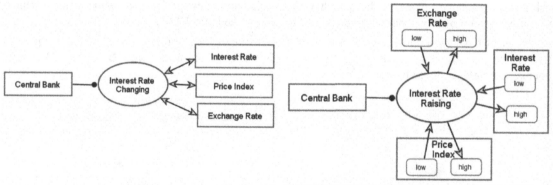

Central Bank handles **Interest Rate Changing**.   Central Bank handles **Interest Rate Changing**.
Interest Rate Changing affects Exchange Rate, Price Index,   Interest Rate can be **low** or **high**.
and **Interest Rate**.   Price Index can be **low** or **high**.
                                                            Exchange Rate can be **high** or **low**.
                                                            Interest Rate Raising changes Exchange Rate from **low** to **high**, Price Index from **low** to **high**, and Interest Rate from **low** to **high**.

Fig. 23.3 Logical AND used with effect link and with in-out specified link pairs

23.2 **Logical NOT**

"NOT" is a unary logical operator which simply reverses the state of any Boolean object (see Sect. 7.1): A binary input of "yes" (positive, 1…) is converted to "no" (negative, 0…), and vice versa. There are several ways to implement NOT in OPM. One is with the flip-flop mechanism, described in Sect. 19.5. Another way is to use states as constraints or conditions for process execution. If, for example, we want to model that a process **P** executes if and only if substance **S** is NOT present, we model the object **S** with two implicit states: **existent** and **non-existent**. We link the **non-existent** state to **P** with an instrument link or an instrument condition link, so **P** can execute only if **S** is in its **non-e**, i.e., when it does not exist.

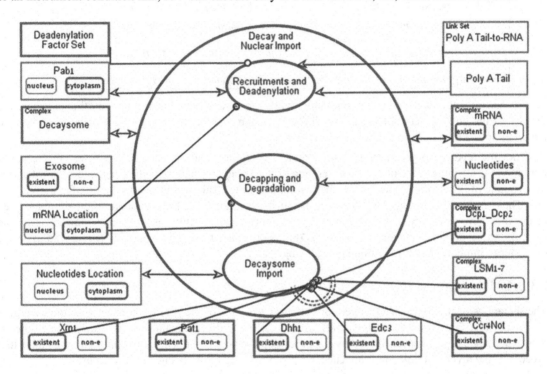

Fig. 23.4 The mRNA Decay and Nuclear Import Process (Somekh et al. 2014) showing the use of NOT via existent and non-existent states of molecules

The **mRNA Decay and Nuclear Import Process** is the in-zoomed process in Fig. 23.4 (Somekh et al. 2014). This OPD shows how the **existent** and **non-existent** states of molecules are used to implement "NOT". For example, the existent state of the complex **CCR4Not** (no pun intended), depicted at the bottom right corner, is linked to **Decaysome Import**—the third subprocess from the top, so only if **CCR4Not** exists can this subprocess take place. However, in this case there are six other substances (such as **Edc3**) that can each enable the process, and they are linked with an OR logical operator (discussed below), so only lack of all the seven substances would prevent **CCR4Not** occurring. If the **non-e** (short for non-existent) state of **CCR4Not** would be linked with a condition link to **Decaysome Import**, that would mean (disregarding other links) that the *absence* of **CCR4Not** is the condition for the occurrence of **Decaysome Import**.

23.3 Logical XOR and OR Link Fans

In order to express OR and XOR graphically, we use link fans.

> *A **link fan** is a set of f ($f \geq 2$) procedural links of the same kind that originate from a common point, or arrive at a common point, on the same object or process.*
>
> *The **convergent end** of a link fan is the end that is common to the f fan links.*
>
> *The **divergent end** of a link fan is the end that is not common to the f fan links.*

The convergent end is attached to one thing, while the divergent end is attached to f things, where f is the size of the link fan set—the number of links in the fan. A link can be a member of both a divergent fan on its source and a convergent fan on its target.

Since the links are procedural, one end is attached to object and the other to processes or vice versa. Formally, the attribute value of the **Perseverance** of the **Thing** attached to the link fan's convergent end is the opposite of the attribute value of the **Perseverance** of the f **Things** attached to the link fan's divergent end. Thus, as the OPD in Fig. 23.5 shows, if the attribute value of the **Perseverance** of the thing attached to the link fan's convergent end is **dynamic** (transient), then the thing is a **Process**. In this case, the attribute value of the Perseverance of the f **Things** attached to the link fan's divergent end is **static** (persistent), implying that these f things are all **Objects**.

23.3.1 The Logical XOR Operator

The semantics of the logical XOR operator is that *exactly* one of the f things connected to the divergent end of the link fan is transformed, enables, or occurs. If the divergent link end is attached to f objects, then *exactly* one object is transformed by the process at the convergent end of the link fan, or enables that process. If the divergent link end is attached to f processes, then exactly one process occurs.

This use of the XOR operator in OPM is in line with the definition of XOR in digital systems, but it may be different from some interpretations of the binary XOR operator with multiple inputs, where the output is 1 for an odd number of inputs and 0 for an even number of inputs. Graphically, a single dashed arc across the f links of the link fan whose focal point is at the convergent end of contact denotes the XOR operator (see Fig. 23.5 left).

The syntax of a link fan of f things with XOR semantics is different for $f = 2$ and for $f > 2$. For $f = 2$, the reserved idiom (split reserved phrase) "either ... or" is used. Since this idiom in natural English is reserved for expressing selection of exactly one of two (but not many) items, for $f > 2$, the reserved phrase "exactly one of" is used. For example, since in Fig. 23.5 (left) the link fan comprises 2 agent links, $f = 2$, so the OPL sentence is:

Either **Safe Owner A** or **Safe Owner B** handle **Safe Opening**.

Suppose an agent link to a third safe owner, **Safe Owner C**, is added to the fan, making f = 3. The OPL sentence then becomes:

Exactly one of **Safe Owner A**, **Safe Owner B**, or **Safe Owner C** handle **Safe Opening**.

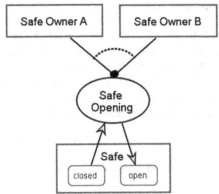 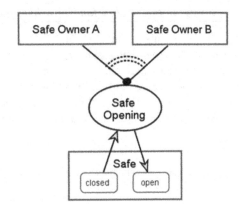

Safe can be **closed** or **open**.
Either **Safe Owner A** or **Safe Owner B** handle **Safe Opening**.
Safe Opening changes **Safe** from **closed** to **open**.

Safe can be **closed** or **open**.
At least one of **Safe Owner A** and **Safe Owner B** handle **Safe Opening**.
Safe Opening changes **Safe** from **closed** to **open**.

Fig. 23.5 Agent link fan examples expressing logical XOR (left) and logical OR (right)

23.3.2 The Logical OR Operator

The semantics of the logical OR operator is that at least one of the f things connected to the divergent end of the link fan is transformed, enables, or occurs. If the divergent link end is attached to f objects, then at least one object is transformed by the process at the convergent end of the link fan, or enables that process. If the divergent link end is attached to f processes, then at least one process occurs. This use of the OR operator in OPM is in line with the binary OR operator with two or more inputs.

Graphically, a double dashed arc across the f links of the link fan whose focal point is at the convergent end of contact denotes the OR operator (see Fig. 23.5 right).

The syntax of a link fan of f things with OR semantics is similar for f = 2 and f > 2. For both, the reserved phrase "At least one of" is used. For example, in Fig. 23.5 (right), where the link fan comprises 2 agent links, the OPL sentence is:

At least one of **Safe Owner A** or **Safe Owner B** handles **Safe Opening**.

Suppose an agent link to a third safe owner, **Safe Owner C**, is added to the fan, making f=3. The OPL sentence then becomes:

At least one of **Safe Owner A**, **Safe Owner B**, or **Safe Owner C** handles **Safe Opening**

23.4 Diverging and Converging XOR and OR Links

> *A converging fan* is a link fan whose links point to its convergent end.
>
> *A diverging fan* is a link fan whose links point to its divergent end.

Table 23.1 presents a summary of XOR and OR converging consumption and result links for $f>2$, showing in the top row that a *converging consumption link fan* is formed when the source things are objects and the destination thing is a process. In a *converging result link fan*, the source things are processes and the destination thing is an object. Conversely, as Table 23.2 shows, when the source thing is an object and the destination things are processes, we get a *diverging consumption link fan*, while when the source thing is a process and the destination things are objects, a *diverging result link fan* is formed.

Table 23.1 Summary of XOR and OR converging fans for consumption and result links

Table 23.2 Summary of XOR and OR diverging fans for consumption and result links

	XOR	OR
Diverging consumption link fan	Exactly one of **P, Q**, or **R** consumes **B**.	At least one of **P, Q**, or **R** consumes **B**.
Diverging result link fan	P yields exactly one of **A, B**, or **C**.	P yields at least one of **A, B**, or **C**.

An effect link is bidirectional, so the things linked by an effect link fan are both source and destination at the same time, voiding the definitions of convergent and divergent link fans. Instead, as Table 23.3 shows, the distinction occurs with respect to multiple objects or multiple processes that a link fan connects.

Table 23.3 Summary of XOR and OR joint effect link fans

	XOR	OR
Multiple objects effect link fan	P affects exactly one of **A, B**, or **C**.	P affects at least one of **A, B**, or **C**.
Multiple processes effect link fan	Exactly one of **P, Q**, or **R** affects P.	At least one of **P, Q**, or **R** affects P.

Since an enabler is an object, both agent and instrument link fans can be diverging, with multiple processes as targets, as shown in Table 23.4, or converging, with multiple enablers as sources, as shown in Table 23.5.

Table 23.4 Diverging agent and instrument link fans

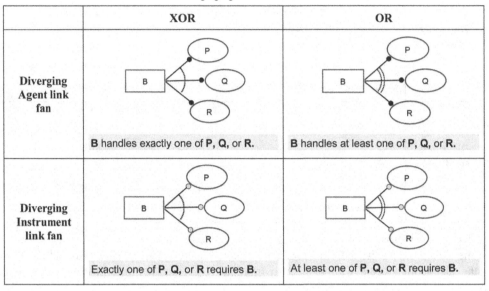

	XOR	OR
Diverging Agent link fan	B handles exactly one of **P, Q,** or **R.**	B handles at least one of **P, Q,** or **R.**
Diverging Instrument link fan	Exactly one of **P, Q,** or **R** requires **B.**	At least one of **P, Q,** or **R** requires **B.**

Table 23.5 Converging agent and instrument link fans

	XOR	OR
Converging Agent link fan	Exactly one of **A, B,** or **C** handles **P.**	At least one of **A, B,** or **C** handles **P.**
Converging Instrument link fan	**P** requires exactly one of **A, B,** or **C.**	**P** requires at least one of **A, B,** or **C.**

Invocation link fans can also be diverging or converging for both XOR and OR, as shown in Table 23.6, where the semantics of questionable combinations is specified.

Table 23.6 Invocation link fans

	XOR	OR
Diverging invocation link fan	P invokes either **Q** or **R**. Semantics: **P** invokes **Q** or **R** with probability 0.5 each. It is possible to assign specific probabilities along the links (see Section 23.7).	P invokes at least one of **Q** or **R**.
Converging invocation link fan	Either **P** or **Q** invokes **R**. Semantics: If both **P** and **Q** terminate at the same time, **R** is not invoked.	At least one of **P** or **Q** invokes **R**. Semantics: This is the same as the OPD without the OR, because invocation is an event link, so its semantics is OR anyway (see Section 23.6).

23.5 Combinatorial XOR and Combinatorial OR

The XOR and OR logic presented so far implies the selection of exactly *one* (for XOR) or at least *one* (for OR). In cases where the fan size $f > 2$, we can generalize the XOR and OR logic to combinatorial XOR and combinatorial OR logic. We extend the logic from 1 to any number *m* links (up to one less than *f*) by replacing "one" in the OPL sentence by *m*, where $m < f$.

23.5.1 Combinatorial XOR

Consider the following OPL sentence, which extends the model in Fig. 23.5.

Exactly one of **Safe Owner A**, **Safe Owner B**, or **Safe Owner C** handle **Safe Opening**.

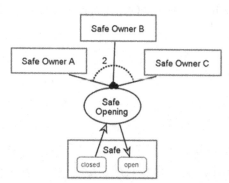

Safe can be **closed** or **open**.
Exactly 2 of **Safe Owner A, Safe Owner B**, or **Safe Owner C** handle **Safe Opening**.
Safe Opening changes **Safe** from **closed** to **open**.

Safe can be **closed** or **open**.
At least 2 of **Safe Owner A, Safe Owner B**, or **Safe Owner C** handle **Safe Opening**.
Safe Opening changes **Safe** from **closed** to **open**.

Fig. 23.6 Example of combinatorial XOR (left) and combinatorial OR (right)

The link fan size here is $f = 3$. If we want to model that exactly two safe owners are needed to open the safe, instead of "one" we write $m = 2$, effectively introducing a combinatorial number of possibilities, in this case "3 choose 2", $\binom{3}{2} = 3$:

Exactly 2 of **Safe Owner A, Safe Owner B**, or **Safe Owner C** handle **Safe Opening**.

In the OPD, we add the number m outside and next to the XOR arc, as demonstrated by the number **2** recorded in the OPD on the left of Fig. 23.6.

In general, in combinatorial XOR we constrain the model to select exactly m of f links, we use the reserved phrase "exactly m of" where $m < f$, and the number of possibilities is $\binom{f}{m}$.

23.5.2 Combinatorial OR

Similar to the combinatorial XOR, we generalize the OR logic to combinatorial OR. We do so by extending the logic from 1 to any number m (up to one less than f) links by replacing "at least one of" in an OPL sentence by "   at least m of", where $m < f$. Using again the OPL sentence above, which extends the model in Fig. 23.5, where the link fan size is $f = 3$, instead of "one" we can write $m = 2$, effectively introducing a sum combinatorial number of possibilities.

At least 2 of **Safe Owner A, Safe Owner B**, or **Safe Owner C** handle **Safe Opening**.

In this case, the number of possibilities is $\binom{3}{2} + \binom{3}{3} = 3 + 1 = 4$. In the OPD, we add the number m outside and next to the OR arc, as demonstrated by the number **2** recorded in the OPD on the right of Fig. 23.6.

In general, for constraining the model to select at least m of f links, we use the reserved phrase "at least m of" where $m < f$, and the number of possibilities is $\binom{f}{m} + \binom{f+1}{m} + \cdots \binom{m}{m}$.

23.6 State-Specified XOR and OR Link Fans

Each one of the link fans described above has a corresponding state-specified version, where the source and destination may be specific object states or objects without a state specification. Combinations of state-specified and stateless links as destinations of a link fan may occur. Figure 23.7 shows on the left a XOR state-specified instrument link fan and on the right an OR mixed result link fan where the links are state-specified for objects **A** and **C** but not for **B**.

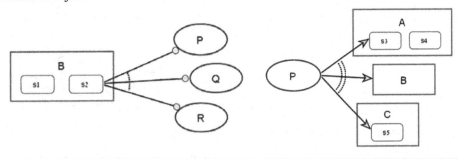

Exactly one of **P**, **Q**, or **R** requires **s2 B**.   **P** yields at least one of **s3 A, B**, or **s5 C**.

Fig. 23.7 State-specified XOR (left) and OR (right) link examples

Two or more processes can have the same state as their source. For example, as the OPD on the right hand side of Fig. 23.8 shows, either **P1** or **P2** (but not both) can consume **B** when it is at state **s1**: Either **P1** or **P2** consumes **s1 B**. If there are more than two processes, the OPL sentence becomes: Exactly one of **P1, P2,** or **P3 consumes s1 B**. A similar situation occurs with state change in the OPD on the right of Fig. 23.8: Either **P1** or **P2** changes **B** from **s1** to **s2**. And for more than two processes: Exactly one of **P1, P2,** or **P3** changes **B** from **s1** to **s2**.

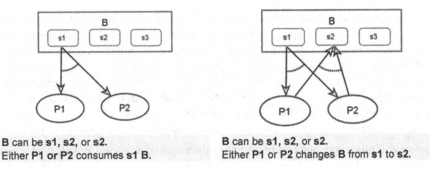

B can be s1, s2, or s2.   B can be s1, s2, or s2.
Either P1 or P2 consumes s1 B.   Either P1 or P2 changes B from s1 to s2.

Fig. 23.8 Left: P1 XOR P2 can consume B when it is at state s1. Right: P1 XOR P2 can change B from s1 to s2

23.6.1 Control-Modified Link Fans

Each one of the XOR link fans for consumption, result, effect, and enabling links and their state-specified versions has a corresponding control-modified link fan: an event link fan and a condition link fan. Table

23.7 presents the event and condition effect link fans, as representatives of the basic (non-state-specified) links version of the modified link fans.

Table 23.7 Event and condition XOR effect link fans

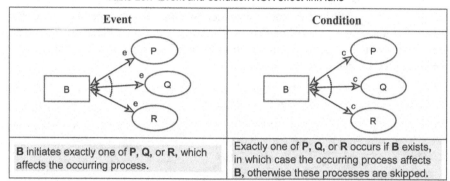

Event	Condition
B initiates exactly one of **P**, **Q**, or **R**, which affects the occurring process.	Exactly one of **P**, **Q**, or **R** occurs if **B** exists, in which case the occurring process affects **B**, otherwise these processes are skipped.

23.6.2 State-Specified Control-Modified Link Fans

Each one of the control-modified link fans, except the control-modified effect link fan, has a corresponding state-specified control-modified link fan. Since these state-specified versions are more complicated than their non-state-specified version, Table 23.8 presents the OPD and OPL of the state-specified cases, and below each such case—the OPL sentence for the corresponding stateless case.

Each XOR link fan in Table 23.7 and in Table 23.8 has its OR counterpart (designated by a double dashed arc) with a corresponding OPL sentence in which the reserved phrase "at least" replaces "exactly".

23.7 Multiple Control Links Have OR Semantics

Event triggers a process independently of any other event link that might be linked to the same process. Therefore, two or more event links attached to a process have the logical OR semantics. **Cancelling** in Fig. 23.9 can be initiated (triggered) by **Bad Weather Forecast** or by **Artist Sickness**. There is no need for both to coexist. In fact, the likelihood that these two objects will be created in the system at the same point in time is practically zero. Therefore, the OPD on the right of Fig. 23.9 is correct. The one on the left is a case when the event that initiates the **Cancelling** is **Bad Weather Forecast**, but if that is the case, **Artist Sickness** is also required. The OPD in the middle is the complementary case: the event that initiates the **Cancelling** is **Artist Sickness**, but if that is the case, **Bad Weather Forecast** is also required.

In a similar way, if more than one condition link is the target of a process P with AND semantics, then all of the conditions must be true in order for P not to be skipped. Suppose the conditions are C1, C2, and C3. Suffice it that one condition is not fulfilled to cause P to be skipped: C1 or C2 or C3. Hence, while the AND semantics holds from the viewpoint of the requirement for process performance, from the skip semantics viewpoint, we are looking at OR semantics. If we want to model that any non-empty subset of the conditions is sufficient, we need to use the OR link fan, as was done in the model in Fig. 23.5.

Table 23.8 State-specified and stateless XOR control-modified link fans

Link fan kind	Event control modifier	Condition control modifier
State-specified consumption link fan	**S2 B** initiates exactly one of **P, Q,** or **R**, which consumes the initiated process. *The stateless case:* **B** initiates exactly one of **P, Q,** or **R**, which consumes the initiated process.	Exactly one of **P, Q,** or **R** occurs if **B** is **s2**, in which case the occurring process consumes **B**, otherwise these processes are skipped. *The stateless case:* Exactly one of **P, Q,** or **R** occurs if **B** exists, in which case the occurring process consumes **B**, otherwise these processes are skipped.
State-specified agent link fan	**S2 B** initiates and handles exactly one of **P, Q,** or **R**. *The stateless case:* **B** initiates and handles exactly one of **P, Q,** or **R**.	**B** handles exactly one of **P, Q,** or **R** if **B** is **s2**, otherwise these processes are skipped. *The stateless case:* **B** handles **exactly one** of **P, Q,** or **R** if **B** exists, otherwise these processes are skipped.
State-specified instrument link fan	**S2 B** initiates exactly one of **P, Q,** or **R**, which requires **s2 B**. *The stateless case:* **S2 B** initiates exactly one of **P, Q,** or **R**, which requires **B**.	Exactly one of **P, Q,** or **R** requires that **B** is **s2**, otherwise these processes are skipped. *The stateless case:* Exactly one of **P, Q,** or **R** requires that **B** is **s2**, otherwise these processes are skipped.

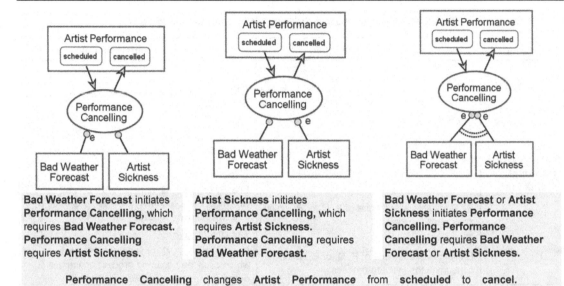

Bad Weather Forecast initiates **Performance Cancelling,** which requires **Bad Weather Forecast. Performance Cancelling** requires **Artist Sickness.**

Artist Sickness initiates **Performance Cancelling,** which requires **Artist Sickness. Performance Cancelling** requires **Bad Weather Forecast.**

Bad Weather Forecast or **Artist Sickness** initiates **Performance Cancelling. Performance Cancelling** requires **Bad Weather Forecast** or **Artist Sickness.**

Performance   Cancelling   changes   **Artist   Performance**   from   **scheduled**   to   **cancel.**

Fig. 23.9 Event link has OR semantics (right) since they are unlikely to happen at the same moment

23.8 **Link Probabilities and Probabilistic Link Fans**

A process **P** with a result link that yields a stateful object **B** with *n* states, **s1** through **s***n*, without specifying a particular state, as in the OPD on the left of Fig. 23.9, mean that the probability of generating **B** at any one particular state shall be $1/n$. In this case, the single result link to the object replaces the result link fan to each of its states, so the OPD on the left of Fig. 23.9 is equivalent to and, being simpler than the one on the right, is the preferred version.

In the left OPD of Fig. 23.10, the result link from **P** to **B**, which has 3 states, means that **P** will create **B** with equal probability, Pr = 1/3, for being created at each one of the three states.

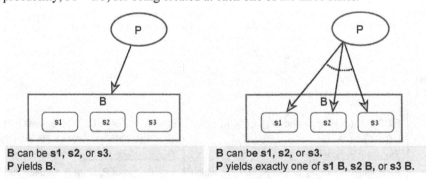

B can be **s1, s2,** or **s3.**
P yields B.

B can be **s1, s2,** or **s3.**
P yields exactly one of **s1 B, s2 B,** or **s3 B.**

Fig. 23.10 Equivalence between result link and a set of XOR state-specified result links

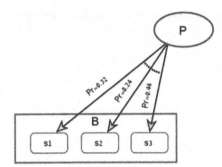

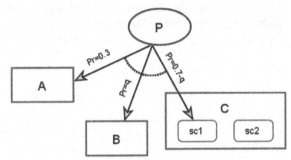

P yields **s1** B with probability **0.32**, **s2** B with probability **0.24**, or **s3** B with probability **0.44**.

The analogous deterministic case:

P yields exactly one of **s1** B, **s2** B, or **s3** B.

P yields **A** with probability **0.3**, **B** with probability **q**, or **sc1** C with probability **0.7–q**.

The analogous deterministic case:

P yields exactly one of **A**, **B**, or **sc1** C.

Fig. 23.11 Probabilistic state-specified object creation examples

Generally, probabilities of following a specific link in a link fan are not equal.

> **Link probability** is an optional attribute value assigned to a procedural link in a XOR diverging link fan that specifies the probability of following that particular link among the possible links in the fan link.
>
> A **probabilistic link fan** is a link fan with a probability value assigned to each of its links, such that the sum of the probability values of all the links is exactly 1.

Graphically, in a probabilistic link fan, a probability value in the form $\mathbf{Pr} = p_i$, where p_i is the link probability numeric value or a parameter, such that $\sum_{i-1}^{f} p_i = 1$. This $\mathbf{Pr} = p_i$ symbol, which appears along each one of the f links in the probabilistic link fan, denotes the probability that the system execution control mechanism will select that particular link and follow that path.

The corresponding OPL sentence is the XOR diverging link fan OPL sentence without link probabilities omitting the phrase "exactly one of..." and adding instead the phrase "...with probability p_i" following each participating thing name with a probability annotation $\mathbf{Pr} = p_i$.

Figure 23.11 shows two probabilistic state-specified object creation examples and their deterministic OPL analogues. In the OPD on the left, process **P** can create object **B** in three possible states, **s1**, **s2**, or **s3**, with corresponding probabilities **0.32**, **0.24**, and **0.44** (totaling 1), as indicated along each result link of the result link fan. In the OPD on the right, **P** can create one of the objects **A**, **B**, or **sc1** C, i.e., **C** at state **sc1**, with the probabilities **0.3**, **q**, and **0.7–q** (totaling 1), respectively.

For a process **P** with a result link that yields a stateful object **B** with states **s1** through **sn**, and with initial state **si**, **P** creates **B** at state **si** with probability 1. If **B** has $m <$ **n** initial states, **P** shall create **B** at one of the initial states with probability $1/m$.

For a probabilistic result link fan, any one of the resultees may be an object without or with a specified state. For all the link fans comprising other procedural link kinds (including those with the event and condition control modifiers), where the targets of the links in the link fan are processes, the source may be an object or a specified state of an object.

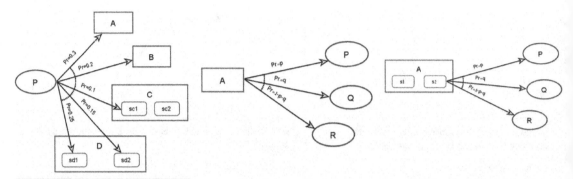

P yields **A** with probability **0.3**, **B** with probability **0.2**, **sc1 C** with probability **0.1**, **sd1 D** with probability **0.25**, or **sd2 D** with probability **0.15**.

P with probability **p**, **Q** with probability **q**, or **R with** probability **1–p–q** consumes **A**.

P with probability **p**, **Q** with probability **q**, or **R** with probability **1–p–q** consumes **s2 A**.

Fig. 23.12 Objects with and without specified states as resultees and consumees of a probabilistic link fan

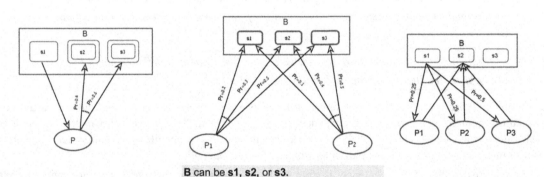

B can be **s1**, **s2**, or **s3**.
State **s2** and State **s3** are final.
P changes **B** from **s1** to either **s2** with probability **0.4** or **s3** with probability **0.6**.

B can be **s1**, **s2**, or **s3**.
States **s1**, **s2**, and **s3** are initial.
P1 yields one of **s1 B** with probability **0.2**, **s2 B** with probability **0.3**, or **s3 B** with probability **0.5**.
P2 yields one of **s1 B** with probability **0.1**, **s2 B** with probability **0.4**, or **s3 B** with probability **0.5**.

Exactly one of **P1** with probability **0.25**, **P2** with probability **0.25**, or **P1** with probability **0.5** changes **B** from **s1** to **s2**.

Fig. 23.13 Examples of various probabilistic state-specified change: from a state to one of two final states (left), probabilistic result to one of three final states (middle), and probabilistic change from one state to another (right)

The OPD on the left hand side of Fig. 23.12 shows a probabilistic result link fan in which **P** yields one of the objects **A** or **B**, or **C** at state **sc1**, or **D** at state **sd1** or **sd2**, each with its specified probabilities. The OPD in the middle of Fig. 23.12 shows a probabilistic consumption link fan in which **A** is consumed, with specified probabilities, by one of the processes **P** or **Q** or **R**. The OPD in the bottom expresses the same, with the additional fact that **A** must be at state **s2**.

Figure 23.13 presents examples of various probabilistic state-specified transformations. On the left is a state change from a state to one of two final states. In the middle—probabilistic creation (result), and on the right—probabilistic change from one state to another.

23.9 **Summary**

- *Logical operators*, including AND, OR, and XOR (exclusive OR) enable modeling complex conditions on performance of processes.
- Two or more procedural links of the same kind that originate from, or arrive at, different points along the process ellipse circumference (the process context), have the semantics of the *logical AND* operator.
- A *link fan* is a set of $f \geq 2$ procedural links of the same kind that originate from a common point, or arrive at a common point, on the same object or process.
- The *convergent end* of a link fan is the end that is common to the f fan links.
- The *divergent end* of a link fan is the end that is not common to the f fan links.
- A link fan with a single dashed arc denotes the *logical XOR* operator.
- A link fan with a double dashed arc denotes the *logical OR* operator.
- A *converging fan* is a link fan whose links point to its convergent end.
- A *diverging fan* is a link fan whose links point to its divergent end.
- Each one of the XOR link fans for consumption, result, effect, and enabling links and their state-specified versions has a corresponding *control-modified link fan*: an event link fan and a condition link fan.
- *Link probability* is an optional attribute value assigned to a procedural link in a XOR diverging link fan that specifies the probability of following that particular link among the possible links in the fan link.
- A *probabilistic link fan* is a link fan with a probability value assigned to each of its links, such that the sum of the probability values of all the links is exactly 1.

23.10 **Problems**

1. Combine the two OPD in Fig. 23.1 to express that each one of the two safe owners must have all the three keys to open the safe.
2. Combine the two OPD in Fig. 23.2 to express that the chef prepares either entrée or starter and dessert, and the diner eats whatever is prepared.

3. In the top-left and bottom-right OPDs in Table 23.1 replace the thing manes with content that will yield sense-making OPL sentences.

4. Repeat the previous question for Table 23.2.

5. Do the same for one OPD in each one of Tables 23.3, 23.4, and 23.5.

6. Chose any three OPDs from the last three questions and add probabilities to them. If needed, modify them.

Chapter 24
Overview of ISO 19450

This book contains a comprehensive coverage of OPM that is compatible with ISO 19450 Publically Available Specification (PAS) titled "**Automation systems and integration—Object-Process Methodology**", and in French: "*Systèmes d'automatisation et intégration—Méthodologie du processus-objet*". The ISO 19450 PAS has been adopted by the International Organization for Standardization (ISO) in December 2015 through the work of ISO Technical Committee 184/ Sub-committee 5 (TC184/SC5) after a six-year effort, mainly by Richard Martin, David Shorter, Alex Blekhman, and this author. This book was prepared in parallel with the ISO 19450 PAS standard, so the two are almost completely aligned with each other. Since the standard (formally PAS) must conform to the rules of ISO for standard authoring, it is structured differently and is not as elaborate as the book. Rather, it is an orderly exposition of OPM that enables tool developers to use it, along with this book, as a solid basis for developing an ISO 19450-complaint software tool to support OPM-based conceptual modeling. ISO standards like ISO 19450 PAS contain normative parts and often also one or more informative parts. To be compliant with the standard, a normative part must be strictly followed, while an informative part is not mandatory. This book is a superset of ISO 19450 PAS. About 90% of the material in this book is aligned with ISO 19450. The rest can be considered as the equivalent of an addition to the informative part of the standard—it should be followed, but ISO 19450 in its current initial form does not mandate it. This closing chapter describes briefly the content of the ISO 19450 PAS, where each section is devoted to a summary of one or more sections of ISO 19450.

24.1 The ISO 19450 Introduction

The first paragraph of the ISO 19450 document's introduction (p.v) is the following.

> Object-Process Methodology (OPM) is a compact conceptual approach, language, and methodology for modelling and knowledge representation of automation systems. The application of OPM ranges from simple assemblies of elemental components to complex, multidisciplinary, dynamic systems. OPM is suitable for implementation and support by tools using information and computer technology. This document specifies both the language and methodology aspects of OPM in order to establish a common basis for system architects, designers, and OPM-compliant tool developers to model all kinds of systems.

The introduction goes on to discuss the generality and industry- and business-wide applicability of OPM as a basis for model-based systems engineering:

D. Dori, *Model-Based Systems Engineering with OPM and SysML*, DOI 10.1007/978-1-4939-3295-5_24

OPM notation supports the conceptual modelling of systems with formal syntax and semantics. This formality serves as the basis for model-based systems engineering in general, including systems architecting, engineering, development, life cycle support, communication, and evolution. Furthermore, the domain-independent nature of OPM opens system modelling to the entire scientific, commercial and industrial community for developing, investigating and analysing manufacturing and other industrial and business systems inside their specific application domains; thereby enabling companies to merge and provide for interoperability of different skills and competencies into a common intuitive yet formal framework.

OPM facilitates a common view of the system under construction, test, integration, and daily maintenance, providing for working in a multidisciplinary environment. Moreover, using OPM, companies can improve their overall, big-picture view of the system's functionality, flexibility in assignment of personnel to tasks, and managing exceptions and error recovery. System specification is extensible for any necessary detail, encompassing the functional, structural and behavioural aspects of a system.

Toward the end of the Introduction section, there is reference to the drafting and authoring of technical documents in general and international standards in particular:

One particular application of OPM is in the drafting and authoring of technical standards. OPM helps sketch the implementation of a standard and identify weaknesses in the standard to reduce, thereby significantly improving the quality of successive drafts. With OPM, even as the model-based text of a system expands to include more details, the underlying model keeps maintaining its high degree of formality and consistency.

The initial motivation for making OPM an ISO standard is to use it as a basis for model-based standards—the contemplated new generation of ISO standards. Indeed, in Dori et al. (2010) we proposed a combined, model-based structured graphical and textual meta-standard approach for specification, verification and validation of complex systems in general and ISO enterprise standards in particular. This methodology, developed under the auspices of the ISO TC 184/SC 5 OPM Study Group, is designed to cope with current inconsistencies and incompleteness of technical documents (Blekhman et al., 2011). To support authors of technical specifications while creating and editing model-based technical documents, we developed Model-Based Authoring of Specifications Environment (MBASE).

In order to overcome the problem of the difficulty humans have with reading long OPL texts due to its mechanistic, repetitive nature, the MBASE framework includes *Tesperanto* (short for *Technical Esperanto*)—an evolution of OPL that is still automatically generated from the OPD but is much more amenable to being read by humans than OPL, even if the text is long (Blekhman and Dori 2013).This framework has been successfully applied in modeling communication in an operation room (Blekhman et al. 2015).

Tesperanto can be considered as a textual version of *The Imitation Game*, better known as *Turing Test*—a test proposed in 1951 by Alan Turing, which was designed to settle the issue of machine intelligence. While in the original Turing Test a human judge has to decide whether she or he is interacting with a human or a computer, in the textual version of Turing Test, the judge has to decide whether a given text was written by a computer or by a human. Quite clearly, OPL text, while being comprised of syntactically correct English sentences will quickly be identified as written by a computer, it will be more difficult for a human to reveal this when presented with a Tesperanto text.

24.2 ISO 19450 Terms, Definitions, and Symbol Sections

Clause 3 of the 19450 PAS includes over 80 definitions of concepts that are used in the standard. These are ordered alphabetically, with *Italicized* words in the definitions being themselves terms defined in this clause. Figure 24.1 is a sample of the ISO 19450 Terms and Definitions Clause, containing some of the terms starting with the letter p. For example, **procedural link** is defined at the top of Fig. 24.1 as a "graphical notation of *procedural relation* in OPM". The term *procedural relation* is in *Italics* because it is also a term in its own right, which indeed happens to appear next alphabetically:

3.57
procedural relation
connection or association between an *object* or *object state* and a *process*

According to ISO directives, the definitions must be phrased such that if we can substitute an Italicized term with its definition and still get a legible, sense-making definition. For example, when we perform the term substitution of **procedural relation** in the definition of **procedural link**, we get:

3.56
procedural link
graphical notation of connection or association between an *object* or *object state* and a *process* in *OPM*

This explains why none of the term definitions neither starts with a capital letter nor end with a period. We can continue with this substitution process twice, first for **process**:

3.56
procedural link
graphical notation of connection or association between an *object* or *object state* and a *transformation* of one or more *objects* in the system in *OPM*

Looking at the definition of transformation, we find:

3.77
transformation
creation (generation, construction) or consumption (elimination, destruction) of an *object* or a change in the *state* of an *object*

So now we get as a definition of procedural link:

3.56
procedural link
graphical notation of connection or association between an *object* or object *state* and a creation (generation, construction) or consumption (elimination, destruction) of an *object* or a change in the *state* of an *object* of one or more *objects* in the system in *OPM*

3.56
procedural link
graphical notation of *procedural relation* in *OPM*

3.57
procedural relation
connection or association between an *object* or *object state* and a *process*

NOTE 1   Procedural relations specify how the system operates to attain its function, designating time-dependent or conditional initiating of processes that transform objects.

NOTE 2   An invocation or exception link signifies a transient object in the flow of execution control between two processes.

3.58
process
transformation of one or more *objects* in the *system*

3.59
process class
pattern for *processes* that perform the same *object transformation* pattern

Fig. 24.1 Sample of ISO 19450 Terms and Definitions Clause

As we see, this is still working, although, unavoidably, the definition gets longer and longer. This can go on until all substitution have been made, and the validity check is done by verifying that no cycle has been created, i.e., the term being defined must not appear anywhere in the definition.

The list of term definitions is followed by Clause 4—**Symbols** and Clause 5—**Conformance**. Then comes Clause 6—**Object-Process Methodology principles and concepts**, discussed next.

24.3   Object-Process Methodology Principles and Concepts

Clause 6 is an overview of OPM. It starts with OPM modeling principles, initially "Modelling as a purpose-serving activity", which discusses how to determine the scope of the model:

> System function and modelling purpose shall guide the scope and extent of detail of an OPM model. ... The function or benefit expectations of stakeholders in general and beneficiaries in particular shall identify and prescribe the modelling purpose. This, in turn, shall determine the scope of the system model.

The use of "shall" is mandatory and prevalent in standards, as the first line in the quote above demonstrates; it implies a mandatory, conformance issue. Next, unification of function, structure, and behaviour is discussed:

> ... The combination of system structure and behaviour enables the system to perform a function, which shall deliver the (functional) value of the system to at least one stakeholder, who is the system's beneficiary. An OPM model integrates the functional (utilitarian), structural (static), and behavioural (dynamic) aspects of a system into a single, unified model. Maintaining focus from the viewpoint of overall system function, this structure-behaviour unification provides a coherent single frame of reference for understanding the system of interest, enhancing its intuitive comprehension while adhering to formal syntax.

The Clause then goes on to elaborate on the difference between function and behavior, the former being a subjective, utilitarian aspect, while the latter is the objective dynamic system aspect. With respect to setting the boundary of the system, 19450 states:

> The system's environment shall be a collection of things, which are outside of the system but which may interact with the system, possibly changing the system and its environment. The modeller shall distinguish these environmental things, which are not part of the system, from systemic things, which are part of the system. The modeller is not able to architect, design or manipulate the structure and behaviour of environmental things even though those environmental things may influence or be influenced by the system.

The last subject in the first subclause of Clause 6 is the clarity-completeness trade-off:

> Overwhelming detail and complicatedness are inherent in real-life systems. Making such systems understandable entails a trade-off that should balance between two conflicting criteria: clarity and completeness. Clarity shall be the extent of unambiguous comprehension that the system's structure and behaviour models convey. Completeness shall be the extent of specification for all the system's details. These two model attributes conflict with each other. On the one hand, completeness requires the full stipulation of system details. On the other hand, the need for clarity imposes an upper limit on the extent of detail within an individual model diagram, after which comprehension deteriorates because of clutter and overloading.

The next subclause in Clause 6—OPM Fundamental Concepts—presents first the bimodal representation of OPM—its graphics text equivalence:

> An OPM model shall be bimodal with expression in semantically equivalent graphics and text representations. Each OPM model graphical diagram, i.e. an Object-Process Diagram (OPD), shall have an equivalent OPM textual paragraph comprised of one or more OPM language sentences using the Object-Process Language (OPL).

Then OPM elements are defined as things and links. This is the first step in defining the OPM metamodel, described in ISO 19450, as shown in Fig. 24.2.

In the sequel, the critical difference between a conceptual models and a runtime model is explained, emphasizing that when constructing OPM models, modelers need to understand the distinction between the conceptual model they are creating and an operational occurrence of that model that they may use to assess system behavior. The modeler may simulate system behavior by creating object and process operational instance occurrences, and then follow the flow of execution control embodied in the connections and OPM semantic rules.

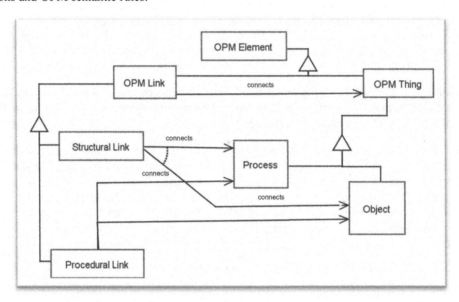

Fig. 24.2 OPM metamodel overview (Figure 1 in ISO 19450)[1]

24.4 The Four Annexes of ISO 19450

The main ISO 19450 document is 100 pages long. It provides an orderly exposition of OPM that is coherent with the specifications in this book, although it is less elaborate and does not contain some details, which can be considered "informative" (see below). The reaming 76 pages of this document contain four annexes, which together complete the definition of OPM from various angles.

Annex A presents the formal syntax for OPL, in EBNF form. Annex B presents conventions and patterns commonly used in OPM applications. Annex C presents aspects of OPM as OPM models. Finally, Annex D summarizes the dynamic and simulation capabilities of OPM.

---

[1]The shading like the one in this figure indicates OPDs and excerpts copied from ISO 19450.

Each annex has an attribute whose values are "normative" and "informative". The term *normative* in ISO standards means that this is an abiding operational part of the standard and shall be followed by whoever claims to conform to the standard.

Conversely "informative" means that this is a non-abiding part of the standard that may be followed but is not mandatory to claim conformance to the standard. In this sense, all the material in this book that is not included in the normative parts of ISO 19450 can be aggregated into another informative annex.

Based on Bibliowicz and Dori (2012), a fifth (informative) annex, in which OPDs are defined with a graph grammar, was planned to be included in ISO 19450. It was finally removed because of technical problems with the multiple graphical elements that were too difficult to handle with the new ISO publication system.

24.4.1 Annex A: Normative: OPL Formal Syntax in EBNF

A *formal grammar* is a set of production rules of the form $V = w$ that describe how to form valid strings from the set of terminals—symbols that comprise the language's alphabet. The alphabet of OPL is the set of all the reserved phrases and punctuation marks. In a *context-free grammar*, every production rule can be applied regardless of the context of a nonterminal. As discussed in Sect. 11.5, while OPL is a subset of English, it is formal. The grammar of OPL is context free. The syntax, exemplified in Fig. 24.3, uses the notation of *Extended Backus–Naur Form (EBNF)*, a notation for expressing the syntax context free grammar languages. The ISO version of EBNF used in ISO 19450 is specified in ISO 14977:1996.[2] The EBNF OPL specification comprises about 400 production rules occupying 12 pages. Here is how OPL is described in the foreword to the Annex.

---

[2]ISO 14977 is a freely available standard that can be downloaded free of charge from http://isotc.iso.org/livelink/livelink/fetch/2000/2489/Ittf_Home/PubliclyAvailableStandards.htm

---

A.4.2 OPL Identifiers

(* Region: Identifiers – This region defines all identifiers used throughout the grammar *)

object identifier = singular object name, [" in ", measurement unit], [range clause]
                    | singular object name, " object", [" in ", measurement unit], [range clause]
                    | plural object name, [" in ", measurement unit], [range clause]
                    | plural object name, " objects", [" in ", measurement unit], [range clause] ;
process identifier = singular process name
                    | Singular process name, " process"
                    | plural process name
                    | plural process name, " processes" ;
thing identifier = object identifier
                    | process identifier ;   (* see 7.1 and 7.2 *)
state identifier = non capitalized word ;
tag expression = non capitalized phrase ;

(* EndRegion: Identifiers *)

Fig. 24.3 A sample of the EBNF notation expressing the context-free grammar of OPL

OPL is a dual-purpose language. First, it serves domain experts and system architects engaged in analyzing and designing a system, such as an electronic commerce system or a Web-based enterprise resource planning system. Second, it provides a firm basis for automatically generating the designed application.

OPL is the textual counterpart of the graphic OPM system specification, corresponding to the diagrammatic description in the OPD set. OPL shall be an automatically generated textual description of the system in a subset of natural English. Devoid of the idiosyncrasies and excessive cryptic details that characterize programming languages, OPL sentences shall be understandable to people without technical or programming experience.

24.4.2 Annex B – Informative: Guidance for OPM

This annex describes several OPM principles that appear in this book, as well as the *multiple thing copies convention*, designed to reduce clutter when a link needs to be drawn between two things in an OPD that are "geographically" remote by allowing duplication of the same thing. To facilitate recognition of the repetition, the modeler may replace thing symbol by a corresponding duplicate thing symbol—a small object or process slightly showing behind the repeated thing, as illustrated in Fig. 24.4.

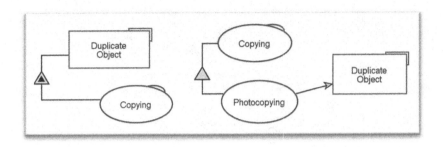

Fig. 24.4 Duplicate object and duplicate process symbols

24.4.3 Annex C – Informative: Modeling OPM Using OPM

Annex C is a rather comprehensive, albeit not complete, model of the important concepts of OPM expressed in OPM. This as a *reflexive metamodel*—a model of OPM that uses OPM to specify itself (Reinhartz-Berger and Dori 2005). A key test of a "good" conceptual modeling language is its reflexive metamodeling capability. As Annex C shows, OPM does it well. The SD in Fig. 24.5 is elaborated in Annex C with about 20 OPDs.

Annex C also provides a metamodel of **Process Performance Controlling**—the process of executing a process that specifies all the details involved in implementing the event-condition-action paradigm using about 10 OPDs at four levels of detail. Figure 24.6 is SD1 of this system model. A complete and executable specification of this system, integrated into the reflexive OPM model, can serve as a reliable and flexible source of an advanced OPM modeling tool implementation.

24.4.4 Annex D – Informative: OPM Dynamics and Simulation

Annex D describes the animated execution of an OPM model and ways to specify and denote the **Duration** attribute of a **Process**. The events presented so far were object or state events: they happened when a specific object became existent or entered a specific state. Among other things, this Annex specifies timed event, which depends on the arrival of a specific time in the system, as shown in Fig. 22.7.

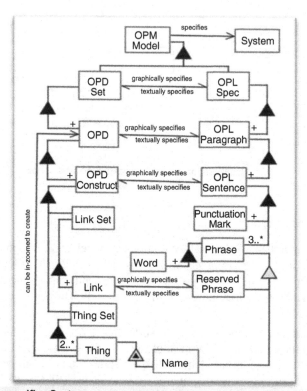

OPM Model specifies System.

OPM Model consists of OPD Set and OPL Spec.

OPL Spec consists of at least one OPL Paragraph.

OPD Set consists of at least one OPD.

OPD Set graphically specifies OPL Spec.

OPL Spec textually specifies OPD Set.

OPD consists of at least one OPD Construct.

OPL Paragraph consists of at least one OPL Sentence.

OPD graphically specifies OPL Paragraph.

OPL Paragraph textually specifies OPD.

OPD Construct graphically specifies OPL Sentence.

OPL Sentence textually specifies OPD Construct.

OPD Construct consists of Thing Set and Link Set.

Thing Set consists of two to many Things.

Link Set consists of at least one Link.

Thing exhibits Name.

OPL Sentence consists of three to many Phrases and at least one Punctuation Mark.

Phrase consists of at least one Word.

OPL Reserved Phrase and Name of Thing are Phrases.

Link graphically specifies Reserved Phrase.

Reserved Phrase textually specifies Link.

Thing can be in-zoomed to create OPD

Fig. 24.5 Top-level OPD (SD) of a reflective OPM meta model (an OPM model of an OPM model)

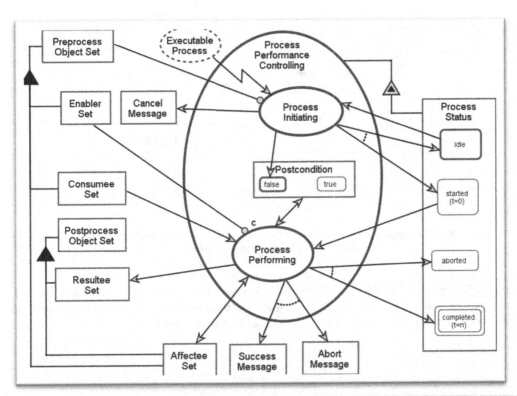

Process Performance Controlling zooms into **Process Initiating** and **Process Performing** in that sequence, as well as **Postcondition**.

Preprocess Object Set consists of **Consumee Set, Affectee Set**, and **Enabler Set**.

Postprocess Object Set consists of **Resultee Set** and **Affectee Set**.

Executable Process is environmental.

Executable Process invokes **Process Initiating**.

Process Performance Controlling exhibits **Process Status**.

Process Status can be **idle, started (t=0), aborted**, or **completed (t=n)**.

Process Status is initially **idle** and finally **completed (t=n)** or **aborted**.

Postcondition can be **false** or **true**.

Postcondition is initially **false**.

Process Initiating requires **Preprocess Object Set**.

Process Initiating changes **Process Status** from **idle** to one of **idle** or **started (t=0)**.

Process Initiating yields **false Postcondition** and **Cancel Message**.

Process Performing occurs if **Enabler Set** exists, otherwise **Process Performing** is skipped.

Process Performing affects **Postcondition** and **Affectee Set**.

Process Performing changes **Process Status** from **started (t=0)** to one of **aborted** or **completed (t=n)**.

Process Performing yields **Resultee Set** and either **Success Message** or **Abortion Message**.

Fig. 24.6 Process Performance Controlling from SD in-zoomed in SD1

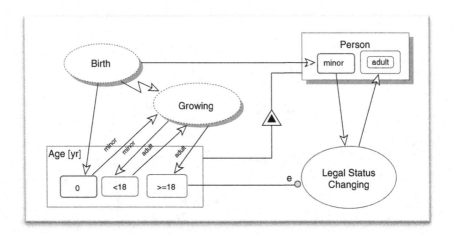

Fig. 24.7 **Legal Status Changing** changes **Person** from **minor** to **adult** when **Growing** changes **Age** of **Person** from **<18** to **>=18.** (Figure D.1 in ISO 19450)

Alternatively, Fig. 24.8 uses the object **System Clock**, which any system may have, either explicitly as in this example, or implicitly, to trigger an event when the **System Clock**, which starts upon **Birth**, and when it reaches **18** yr it creates an event that triggers **Legal Status Changing**.

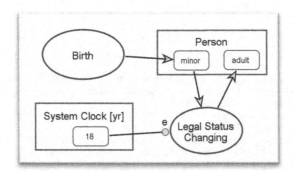

Fig. 24.8 The System Clock event initiating Legal Status Changing (Figure D.2 in ISO 19450)

References

Agile Modeling http://agilemodeling.com/style/activityDiagram.htm#Swimlanes, accessed July 3, 2015.

Ashby, W.R. Concepts of Operand, Operator, Transform. George Washington University, St. Louis, 2001. http://www.gwu.edu/~asc/biographies/ashby/MATRIX/SG/sg_1.html Accessed March 16, 2015.

Arnheim, R. *Visual thinking*. University of California Press, Berkeley, CA, 1969.

Baddeley, A. Working Memory. *Science* 31 Vol. 255 no. 5044 pp. 556–559, January 1992.

Bak, P., Tang, C., and Wiesenfeld, K., Self-Organizing Criticality. Physics Review Letters, 59(4), pp. 381–384, 1987.

de Bakker, J.W. and de Vink, E.P. *Control Flow Semantics*. MIT Press, Cambridge, MA, 1996.

Bar-Yam, Y. Dynamics of Complex Systems. Perseus Books, Reading, MA, 1997.

Berkeley, G. *A Treatise Concerning the Principles of Human Knowledge*. Trinity College, Dublin, 1710.

Bibliowicz, A. and Dori, D. A Graph Grammar-Based Formal Validation of Object-Process Diagrams. Software and Systems Modeling, 11(2), pp. 287–302, 2012.

Blair, C. D., Boardman, J. T. & Sauser, B. J. Communicating strategic intent with systemigrams: Application to the network-enabled challenge. Systems Engineering, 10(4), pp. 309–322, 2007.

Blekhman, A. and Dori, D., Tesperanto – A Model-Based System Specification Methodology and Language. Proc. 23rd Annual INCOSE International Symposium, Philadelphia, PA, USA, June 24–27, 2013.

Blekhman, A., Dori, D., and Martin, R. Model-Based Standards Authoring. Proc. 21st INCOSE International Symposium, Denver, CO, USA, pp. 650–659, June 19–23, 2011.

Blekhman, A., Wachs, J. P., and Dori, D. Model-Based System Specification with Tesperanto: Readable Text from Formal Graphics. To appear in IEEE SMC, 2015. Systems engineering in the product lifecycle

Bock, C. Systems engineering in the product lifecycle. International Journal of Product Development, 2(1–2), pp. 123–140, 2005.

Bock, C. SysML and UML 2 support for activity modeling, Systems Engineering 9(2) pp. 160–186, 2006.

Bolshchikov, S., Somekh, J., Mazor, S., Wengrowicz, N. and Dori, D.Visualizing the Dynamics of Conceptual Behavior Models: The Vivid OPM Scene Player. *Systems Engineering*. To appear, 2015.

Box, G. E. P. and Draper, N. R. *Empirical Model Building and Response Surfaces*, John Wiley & Sons, New York, NY, 1987.

© Springer Science+Business Media New York 2016

D. Dori, *Model-Based Systems Engineering with OPM and SysML*, DOI 10.1007/978-1-4939-3295-5

Bunge, M. *Treatise on Basic Philosophy, Vol. 3, Ontology I, The Furniture of the World*. Reidel, Boston, MA, 1977.

Bunge, M. *Treatise on Basic Philosophy, Vol. 4, Ontology II, A World of Systems*. Reidel, Boston, MA, 1979.

Chein, M. & Mugnier, M.L. Conceptual graphs: fundamental notions.Rev. Intell. Artif. 6(4), pp. 365–406, 1992.

Chen, P.P. The Entity Relationship Model – Toward a Unifying View of Data. ACM Trans. on Data Base Systems 1(1), pp. 9–36, 1976.

Clark, J. M. & Paivio, A. Dual coding theory and education. *Educational Psychology Review*, 3(3), 149–210, 1991.

Coad, R. and Yourdon, E. Object-Oriented Analysis. Prentice-Hall, Englewood Cliffs, NJ, 1991.

Cook, S. In the Foreword to Warmer and Kleppe (1999).

Descartes, R. *Principles of Philosophy* (1647). Trans. Valentine Rodger Miller and Reese P. Miller. D. Reidel Publishing Company, p. 282, 1984.

Dittrich, K.R., Gatziu, S., and Geppert, A. The Active Database Management System Manifesto: A Rulebase of ADBMS Features. Lecture Notes in Computer Science 985, Springer, pp. 3–20, 1995.

Dirks, T. The Greatest Films, 2001. http://www.filmsite.org/gone.html. Accessed March 16, 2015.

DoDAF – DoD Architecture Framework Version 1.5, 2007.

DoDAF – DoD Architecture Framework Version 2.02, Change 1, 2015. http://dodcio.defense.gov/TodayinCIO/DoDArchitectureFramework.aspx. Accessed March 16, 2015.

Dori, D., Object-Process Methodology – A Holistic Systems Paradigm, Springer Verlag, Berlin, Heidelberg, New York, 2002 (ISBN 3-540-65471-2; Foreword by Edward Crawley. Hard cover, 453 pages, with CD-ROM). eBook version: http://link.springer.com/book/10.1007/978-3-642-56209-9/page/1

Dori, D., ViSWeb – The Visual Semantic Web: Unifying Human and Machine Knowledge Representations with Object-Process Methodology. *The International Journal on Very Large Data Bases (VLDB)*, 13, 2, pp. 120–147, 2004.

Dori, D. Words from Pictures for Dual Channel Processing: A Bimodal Graphics-Text Representation of Complex Systems. *Communications of the ACM*, 51(5), pp. 47–52, 2008.

Dori, D., Martin, R., and Blekhman, A. Model-Based Meta-Standardization: Modeling Enterprise Standards with OPM. 2010 IEEE International Systems Conference, San Diego, CA, USA, April 5–8, 2010.

Dori, D. Reinhartz-Berger, I., and Sturm, A. Developing Complex Systems with Object-Process Methodology using OPCAT. LNCS 2813, pp. 570–572, 2003.

Downton, C. In Smolan, R. and Erwitt, J. *One Digital Day*. Time Book/Random House in association with Against All Odds Production, 1998.

Firlej, M. and Helens, D. *Knowledge Elicitation: A Practical Handbook*. Prentice-Hall, New York, 1991.

Fowler, M. *UML Distilled, Second Edition*. Addison-Wesley, Reading, MA, 1999.

Friedenthal, S., Moore A., and Steiner, R. *A Practical Guide to SysML (Second Edition), The Systems Modeling Language*, Morgan Kaufmann, 2014.

Galileo, G. The Assayer, 1623, as reprinted in (Drake, 1957, p. 274)

Grobshtein, Y. and Dori, D. Generating SysML Views from an OPM Model: Design and Evaluation. *Systems Engineering*, 14 (3), pp. 327–340, 2011.

Harel, D. Statecharts: A Visual Formalism for Complex Systems. *Science of Computer Programming* 8, pp. 231–274, 1987.

Harel, D. On Visual Formalisms. *Communications of the ACM* 31(5), pp. 514–530, 1988.

Helighen, F. Principia Cybernetica Web (1997). http://pespmc1.vub.ac.be/occamraz.html   Accessed May 27, 2015.

Holt, J. *UML for Systems Engineering: Watching the Wheels*. IEE Professional Applications of Computing, 2004.

IATA http://www.iata.org/about/Pages/index.aspx Accessed May 31, 2015.

Kant, I. *Prolegomena to Any Future Metaphysics That Will Be Able to Present Itself as a Science* (in German). Riga, 1783.

Kilov, H. and Simmonds, I. D. Business Patterns: Reusable Abstract Constructs for Business Specification. In Humphreys, P., Bannon, K., McCosh, A., Migliarese, P. and Pomerol, J.S. (Eds.), *Implementing Systems for Supporting Management Decisions*. Chapman and Hall, London, 1996.

Klyne G., Carroll, J.J., and McBride, B. *RDF 1.1 Concepts and Abstract Syntax*, 2004 http://www.w3.org/TR/rdf-concepts Accessed March 16, 2015.

Koffka, K. Principles of Gestalt Psychology: New York: Harcourt-Brace, 1935.

Kostovic, I. and Rakic, P. Developmental history of the transient subplate zone in the visual and somatosensory cortex of the macaque monkey and human brain. J. Comp. Neurol., 297: 441–470, 1990. doi: 10.1002/cne.902970309

Latimer, C. and Stevens, C. Some remarks on Wholes, Parts and Their Perception. *Psycoloquy* 8(13), Part Whole Perception (1), 1997.

Lehman, F. (ed.) *Semantic networks in artificial intelligence*. Pergamon, Oxford, UK, 1999.

MacIntyre, J. What's wrong with the noun/adjective/verb object oriented design strategy (2010). https://whileicompile.wordpress.com/2010/08/01/the-noun-adjective-verb-object-oriented-design-strategy-sucks/ Accessed June 9, 2015.

Manola F. and Miller E. *RDF 1.1 Primer*, 2014. http://www.w3.org/TR/2014/NOTE-rdf11-primer-20140624/. Accessed March 16, 2015.

Mayer, R.E. The promise of multimedia learning: using the same instructional design methods across different media. *Learning and Instruction* 13, pp.125–139, 2003.

Mayer, R.E. and Moreno, R. Nine Ways to Reduce Cognitive Load in Multimedia Learning. *Educational Psychologist* 38(1), pp. 43–52, 2003.

Mazanec, M. and Macek O. On General-purpose Textual Modeling Languages. Proc. 12th Annual International Workshop on Databases, Texts, Specifications, and Objects, Zernov, Rovensko pod Troskami, Czech Republic, pp. 1–12, 2012.

Meinhardt, H. *The Algorithmic Beauty of Sea Shells*. Springer-Verlag, Berlin, 1995.

MIT ESD. Massachusetts Institute of Technology Engineering Systems Division Vision. http://esd.mit.edu/about/vmv.html Accessed May 28, 2015.

Mordecai, Y. and Dori, D. I^5: A Model-Based Framework for Architecting System-of-Systems Interoperability, Interconnectivity, Interfacing, Integration, and Interaction, 23rd International Symposium of the International Council on Systems Engineering INCOSE IS-2013, Philadelphia, PA, USA, June-2013.

Ockham, W., *Quaestiones et decisiones in quattuor libros Sententiarum*, Petri Lombardi ed., Lugd., 1495.

OMG OCL Object Constraint Languge, Version 2.4, 2014. http://www.omg.org/spec/OCL/2.4/PDF/ Accessed June 20, 2015.

OMG SysML System Modeling Language, Version 1.3, 2012. http://www.omg.org/spec/SysML/1.3/ PDF/ Accessed March 16, 2015.

OMG UML Unified Modeling Language, Infrastructure, Version 2.4.1, 2011I. http://www.omg.org/spec/UML/2.4.1/Infrastructure/PDF/ Accessed March 16, 2015.

OMG UML Unified Modeling Language, Superstructure, Version 2.4.1, 2011S. http://www.omg.org/spec/UML/2.4.1/Superstructure/PDF Accessed March 16, 2015.

OMG UML for Systems Engineering RFP, 2003. http://syseng.omg.org/UML_for_SE_RFP.htm Accessed March 16, 2015.

Ouellette, J. A Fundamental Theory to Model the Mind. *Quanta Magazine*, 2014. https://www.quantamagazine.org/20140403-a-fundamental-theory-to-model-the-mind/. Accessed March 18, 2015.

Peleg, M. and Dori, D. The Model Multiplicity Problem: Experimenting with Real-Time Specification Methods. IEEE Transactions on Software Engineering 26(8), pp. 742–759, 2000.

Reinhartz-Berger, I, and Dori, D. A Reflective Metamodel of Object-Process Methodology: The System Modeling Building Blocks. In *Business Systems Analysis with Ontologies*, P. Green and M. Rosemann (Eds.), Idea Group, Hershey, PA, USA, pp. 130–173, 2005.

Rescher, N. and Oppenheim, P. Logical Analysis of Gestalt Concepts. *British Journal for the Philosophy of Science* 6, pp. 89–106, 1955.

Rissanen, J. Modeling by shortest data description. *Automatica* 14 (5): 465–658, 1978.

Rumbaugh, J., Blaha, M., Premerlani, W., Eddy, F. and Lorenson, W. *Object-Oriented Modeling and Design*. Prentice-Hall, Englewood Cliffs, NJ, 1991.

Schapiro, M. *Words, Script, and Pictures – Semiotics of Visual Language*. The New Republic, 1996.

Shannon, C.E. and Weaver, J. *The Mathematical Theory of Communication*, University of Illinois Press, 1949.

Smithsonian Institute http://humanorigins.si.edu/evidence/behavior/tools Accessed May 31, 2015.

Somekh, J., Haimovich, G., Guterman, A., Dori, D. and Choder, M. Conceptual Modeling of mRNA Decay Provokes New Hypotheses, 2014. PLoS ONE 9(9): e107085. doi:10.1371/journal.pone.0107085.

Stanford Encyclopedia of Philosophy, 2013. http://plato.stanford.edu/entries/logic-probability/ Accessed July 8, 2015.

TOGAF Version 9.1, The Open Group Architecture Framework, https://www.opengroup.org/togaf/ Slide Decks Management Overview ; 2011. Accessed June 8, 2015.

USPTO 7,099,809 Modeling System, US Patent and Trademark Office, number 7,099,809, Filed: March 15, 2001. Granted: August 29, 2006. http://www.google.com/patents/US20070050180

W3C Consortium, Resource Description Framework (RDF), 2014. http://www.w3.org/RDF/ Accessed March 16, 2015.

Wand, Y. and Weber, R. An Ontological Evaluation of Systems Analysis and Design Methods. In Falkenberg, E.D. and Lindgreen, P. (Eds.) *Information System Concepts: An In-Depth Analysis*. Elsevier Science Publishers B.V. (North Holland), IFIP, pp. 145–172, 1989.

Wand, Y. and Weber, R. On the Ontological Expressiveness of Information Systems Analysis and Design Grammars. *Journal of Information Systems* 3, pp. 217–237, 1993.

Warmer, J. and Kleppe, A. *The Object-Constraint Language: Precise Modeling with UML*. Addison-Wesley, Reading, MA, 1999.

Weber, R. H. and Weber, R. *Internet of Things, Legal Perspectives*. Springer, 2010.

Wertheimer, M. and Reizler, K. Gestalt Theory. *Social Research* 11(1), pp. 78–99. 1944.

Winograd, T. and Flores, F. *Understanding Computers and Cognition*. Addison-Wesley, Reading, MA, 1987.

OPM Principles at a Glance

The OPM principles are listed below in the order they appear in the book.

1. ***The Function-as-a-Seed OPM Principle***—Modeling a system starts by defining, naming, and depicting the function of the system, which is also its top-level process.

2. ***The Model Fact Representation OPM Principle***—An OPM model fact needs to appear in at least one OPD in order for it to be represented in the model.

3. ***The Timeline OPM Principle***—The timeline within an in-zoomed process is directed by default from the top of the in-zoomed process ellipse to its bottom.

4. ***The Minimal Conceptual Modeling Language OPM Principle***—A symbol system—a language—that can conceptually model a given system using ontology with fewer diagram kinds and fewer symbols and relations among them is preferable over a larger ontology with more diagram kinds and more symbols and relations among them.

5. ***The Thing Importance OPM Principle***—The importance of a thing T in an OPM model is directly related to the highest OPD in the OPD hierarchy where T appears.

6. ***The Object Transformation by Process OPM principle***—In a complete OPM model, each process must be connected to at least one object that the process transforms or one state of the object that the process transforms.

7. ***The Procedural Link Uniqueness OPM Principle***—At any level of detail, an object and a process can be connected with at most one procedural link, which uniquely determines the role of the object with respect to the process.

8. ***The Singular Name OPM Principle***—A name of an OPM thing must be singular. Plural has to be converted to singular by adding the word "Set" for inanimate things or "Group" for humans.

9. ***The Graphics-Text Equivalence OPM Principle***—Any model fact expressed graphically in an OPD is also expressed textually in the corresponding OPL paragraph.

10. ***The Thing Name Uniqueness OPM Principle***—Different things in an OPM model which are not features must have different names. Features are distinguishable by appending to them the reserved word "of" and the name of their exhibitor.

11. ***The Detail Hierarchy OPM Principle***—Whenever an OPD becomes hard to comprehend due to an excessive amount of details, a new, descendant OPD shall be created.

12. ***The Timeline OPM Principle***—The timeline within an in-zoomed process is directed by default from the top of the in-zoomed process ellipse to its bottom.

13. ***The Skip Semantics Precedence OPM Principle***—Skip semantics takes precedence over wait semantics.

© Springer Science+Business Media New York 2016

D. Dori, *Model-Based Systems Engineering with OPM and SysML*, DOI 10.1007/978-1-4939-3295-5

Index

Printed in the United States
By Bookmasters